Capita
Women's Labour in Asian Economies

Capital Accumulation and Women's Labour in Asian Economies

New Edition

Peter Custers

CAPITAL ACCUMULATION AND WOMEN'S LABOUR IN ASIAN ECONOMIES
Peter Custers

© 2014 Peter Custers

First Published in India 2014

ISBN 978-93-5002-264-1

This edition is licensed for sale in the Indian Subcontinent (India, Pakistan, Bangladesh, Nepal, Maldives, Bhutan and Sri Lanka)

All rights reserved. No part of this book may be reproduced or transmitted, in any form or by any means, without prior permission of the publisher.

Published by
AAKAR BOOKS
28 E Pocket IV, Mayur Vihar Phase I, Delhi 110 091
Phone : 011 2279 5505 Telefax : 011 2279 5641
info@aakarbooks.com; www.aakarbooks.com

Printed at
Mudrak, 30 A, Patparganj, Delhi 110 091

CONTENTS

PART 3
Women's Role as Agricultural Producers

PART 4
Japanization and Women's Labour

LIST OF ILLUSTRATIONS

Tables

Figures

Maps

INTRODUCTION TO THE NEW EDITION

Women, Labor, and Capital Accumulation in Asia

Jayati Ghosh

One of the enduring myths about capitalism that continues to be perpetuated in mainstream economic textbooks and other pedagogic strategies is that labor supply is somehow exogenous to the economic system. The supply of labor is typically assumed, especially in standard growth theories, to be determined by the rate of population growth, which in turn is also seen as "outside" the economic system rather than in interplay with it.

The reality is, of course, very different: the supply of labor has been very much a result of economic processes, not something extraneous to it. Throughout its history, capitalism has proved adept at causing patterns of labor supply to change in accordance with demand. Migration—whether of slaves, indentured labor, or free workers—has been instrumental in this regard. The use of child labor similarly has been sanctioned and encouraged or disapproved and suppressed in varying economic conditions. But nowhere has this particular capacity of capitalism to generate its own labor been more evident than in the case of female labor.

Women have been part of the working class since the beginning of capitalism, even when they have not been widely acknowledged as workers in their own right. Even when they are not paid workers, their often unacknowledged and unpaid contribution to social reproduction, as well as to many economic activities, has always been absolutely essential for the functioning of the system. All women are usually workers, whether or not they are defined or recognized as such. In all societies, and particularly in developing countries, there remain essential but usually unpaid activities (such as cooking, cleaning, and other housework, provisioning of basic household needs, child care, care of the sick and the elderly, as well as community-based activities), which are largely seen as the responsibility of women. This pattern of unpaid work tends to exist even when women are engaged in outside work for an income, whether as wage workers or self-employed workers. Women from poor families who are engaged in outside work usually cannot afford to hire others to perform these tasks, so most often these are passed on to young girls and elderly women within the household, or become a "double burden" of work for such women. These processes are also integral to capitalism: the production of both use values and exchange values by women is essential for the accumulation process, and, if anything, this reliance has become more marked in recent years.

Despite this, it took a long time for women's struggles to be accepted as an integral part of working-class struggles for a better society. For more than a century, trade unions and other worker organizations tended to be male preserves, based on the "male breadwinner" model of the household, in which the husband/father worked outside to earn money, and the wife/mother did not earn outside income and handled the domestic work. It has taken prolonged struggle and determined mobilization to generate greater social recognition of the role of women as wage workers in different forms, and to bring out the crucial economic significance of unpaid household and community-based work. In the early struggles of workers in Europe after the Industrial Revolution, shorter working hours was a major demand. The shift to factory work (in which large numbers of women and children also participated, at much lower wages than men) was generally unregulated and involved very long working hours, which ranged from ten to as much as sixteen hours per day. Women and children in England were granted the ten-hour day in 1847. In France, workers won the twelve-hour day after the February revolution of 1848. It took until the early or middle part of the twentieth century for workers in most industrial countries to be granted the legal right for a limitation of the working day to eight hours with the provision of overtime for additional hours of work. Of course, this still left out the significant time spent by women in unpaid work, usually within their households.

However, in most developing countries, where a large part of the workforce is not covered by labor protection and regulation, even the condition of regulating the time spent in paid work is still far from being achieved for most workers. The problem of long hours of work is also usually associated with relatively low pay, which affects the health of workers and the possibility of living a minimally satisfying life. For women workers, the problem of long working hours is compounded by the significant amount of unpaid labor they are required to perform.

This means that the issues relating to women's work are qualitatively different from those of male workers. Just increasing paid employment does not always mean an improvement in the conditions for women workers, since it can lead to a double burden upon women whose household obligations still have to be fulfilled. So there has to be a focus on the quality, the recognition, and the remuneration of women's work in developing countries, as well as the conditions facilitating it, such as alternative arrangements for household work and child care. All of these are critically affected by social relationships as well as by economic policies and processes, which determine whether increased labor market activity by women is associated with genuine improvements in their economic circumstances.

There is some historical evidence that with material progress in a society, the socioeconomic conditions of women tend to improve. But this is not automatic; it also reflects the outcome of women's struggles for equality and justice. The growing significance of paid work by women is one aspect of that. In recent times, the ability of women's movements to fight for greater rights and empowerment has been conditioned by the broader economic processes that have determined the explicit participation of women in the labor market. There has been progress as well as reversal, and it is evident that early gains in some societies cannot be taken for granted.

Global Processes Affecting Women

While imperialism remains a defining feature of the world economy, its contours have been changing. The dominance of finance capital, the emergence of new trade links, and the expansion of global production chains based on splitting up the production process across different locations, have all dramatically changed productive structures and labor markets across the world. Both financial and productive sectors have become more concentrated, causing a relative decline in small enterprises that are typically more employment-intensive. Except for a brief spurt in public spending immediately after the global financial crisis in 2008, governments have been less willing or able to use macroeconomic policies to maintain or expand employment. Trade openness has destroyed some livelihoods while creating some new opportunities for income generation and employment, albeit to a lesser extent. These changes have been reflected in transformations in labor markets in different countries. Thus open unemployment rates have increased, and formal or organized sector employment has declined as a proportion of the work force across the world. At the same time, reduced public spending on "social sectors" has tended to burden the unpaid labor of women within households with more of the tasks of social reproduction.

Because of the decline in formal employment, workers have crowded into informal sector activities, perpetuating a vicious circle of poverty leading to low employment generation leading to poverty. Global production chains are growing in significance as a result of technological changes, making production and workforces in different countries more interdependent. There has also been a global increase in unpaid labor within households—predominantly (but not exclusively) performed by women, as governments renege on basic social responsibilities for the provision of public goods and services, and more of the care economy is located in the unpaid sector.

These changes have been particularly marked in developing Asia, which has become both the most "globalized" and the most economically dynamic region of the world. And women in Asia have taken the brunt of the changes, with rapid shifts into (and out of) paid work, greater roles in providing outside income for households, increased rates of migration for work, and greater involvement in unpaid labor. Women have moved—voluntarily or forcibly—in search of work within and across countries and regions, more than ever before. Their livelihoods in rural areas, predominantly in agriculture, have been affected by the agrarian crisis that is now widespread in most developing countries. Across societies in the region, massive increases in the availability of different consumer goods, due to trade liberalization, have accompanied declines in access to basic public goods and services. The expansion of global production chains that rely on the labor of women, especially at the bottom end, has transformed patterns of paid work. In addition, there is a significant globalization of services, which involves both local shifts in workforces and migration of women in the "care" sectors of economies. At the same time, technological changes have made communication and the transmission of cultural forms more extensive and rapid than could have even been imagined in the past. All these changes have had very substantial and complex effects upon the position of women and their ability to control their own lives.

In addition, these economic changes have other adverse social consequences for women. The increasing emphasis on markets and profitability requires luring more consumers into the web of purchase through advertising and attempts to manipulate peoples' tastes and choices. In this effort, advertising companies have notoriously used women as objects to purvey their products. The dual relationship with women, as objects to be used in selling goods and as a huge potential market for goods, creates a peculiar process whereby women are encouraged and persuaded to participate actively in their own objectification. The huge media attention given to beauty contests, "successful" models, and the like, has fed into the rapidly expanding beauty industry in developing Asia, which includes not only cosmetics and beauty aids, but slimming agents, beauty parlours, weight loss clinics, and so on. Many of these trends contribute to the most undesirable and retrograde attitudes toward both women and their appearance, which can push women into newer forms of social oppression that are no less demeaning than earlier explicitly patriarchal forms.

The Contribution of Peter Custers

This is the broader political economy context in which Peter Custers's impressive and comprehensive work on capital accumulation and women's labor in Asian economies should be located. The book was originally published in 1997, but it has a freshness and contemporary relevance that are remarkable. This is because Custers combines a broadly Marxist theoretical perspective with the insights and innovations of feminist scholars, from the German feminist school to other strands such as ecofeminism and developmental feminism, thereby providing a rich analytical and empirical description of how closely intertwined the labor of women in various forms has been with the evolution and current practices of capitalist accumulation, not just globally but at national and local levels.

Custers provides a wide range of insights, which cannot all be summarized here. But some of the more significant of these deserve to be highlighted and noted, especially because they have been more than confirmed by recent feminist scholarship and current actual experience, and because they are likely to become even more important for those concerned with working women's emancipatory struggles in the future. Four issues in particular are noteworthy: the significance of female labor in the extraction of absolute and relative surplus value; the role of unpaid labor; the ways in which women workers have affected capitalist practices of the management of labor and in turn been affected by it; and the part played by women in forming the reserve army of labor. These are all shown through detailed case studies of women workers in different Asian countries (India, Bangladesh, Japan) as well as in broader discussions tracing the history of capitalism. The theoretical strands that contribute to an understanding of these processes are also identified, though in each of these Custers also makes his own valuable contributions.

Women Workers and the Extraction of Absolute and Relative Surplus Value

One of the important insights emerging from Custers's work is how the gender division of work—what he calls the "sectoral sexual division of labor"—is flexible, changing over time according to the need to preserve male power over women and to ensure the greater economic exploitation of women to suit the needs of capital. In a striking example from Bangladesh, he shows how the traditional division of labor between women and men in agriculture has changed because of modernization, while two contrasting cases of women involved in textile and garment production in West Bengal show how the social construction of the sexual division of labor can alter the location, the returns, and the mobility involved in women's work. The use of the male monopoly over instruments of production to relegate women to lower productivity tasks is exemplified in his discussion (based on the famous work of Maria Mies) of crop production in rural Andhra Pradesh in India.

The point is that these segmented labor markets then have major effects in depressing women's wages and allowing for even greater extraction of surplus value from their work. Custers identifies many strategies for increasing the working hours and reducing the wages of women, which contribute to increases in both absolute and relative surplus value. Piece-rate work is a particularly significant weapon in this regard, particularly because it also combines other advantages such as reducing the need for supervision. This use of patriarchal social relations becomes fundamental to the accumulation process itself, which actually requires the continuing impoverishment of certain sections for its success.

This discussion is particularly significant given recent macro processes in Asia that have affected women's involvement in paid work. There have been very rapid shifts in the labor market in the space of less than one generation, as Asian women have been first drawn into paid employment, especially in export sectors, and then ejected from it. The phase of the disproportionately high use of women in export-oriented manufacturing in several rapidly growing Asian economies in the 1980s and early part of the '90s was followed by a period of subsequent ejection of older women and some younger counterparts into more fragile and insecure forms of employment, or self-employment, or even back to unpaid housework. Ghosh and Seguino have shown how gender wage inequality has stimulated growth in developing Asia, with Asian economies that disadvantaged women the fastest growing from 1975 to 1990.[1] Low female wages have spurred investment and exports by lowering unit labor costs, providing the foreign exchange to purchase capital and intermediate goods that raise productivity and growth rates.

This trend towards feminization of employment in Asian countries resulted from employers' needs for cheaper and more "flexible" sources of labor, which meant more casualization of labor, a shift to part-time work or piece-rate contracts, and insistence on greater freedom of hiring and firing. All these aspects of what is now described as "labor market flexibility" became necessary once external competitiveness became the significant goal of domestic policy makers and defined the contours within which domestic and foreign employers in these economies operated. Women workers were preferred by employers in export activities primarily because of the inferior conditions of work and pay that they were usually willing to accept.[2] They had lower reservation wages than their male counterparts, were more willing to accept longer hours and unpleasant and often unhealthy or hazardous factory conditions, typically did not unionize or engage in other forms of collective bargaining to improve conditions, and did not ask for permanent contracts. They were thus easier to hire and fire at will, or according to external demand conditions. Life-cycle changes such as marriage and childbirth could be used as proximate causes to terminate their employment and engage a younger and fresher set of female workers. Greater flexibility was thus afforded to employers to offer less-secure contracts. Further, in certain sectors of the newer "sunrise" industries of the late twentieth century such as computer hardware and consumer electronics, the nature of the assembly line work—repetitive and detailed, with an emphasis on manual dexterity and fineness of elaboration—was felt to be especially suited to women. The high "burnout" associated with some of these activities meant that employers preferred to hire workers who could be periodically replaced, which was easier when the employed group consisted of young, mostly unmarried, women who could move on to other phases of their life cycle.

That the feminization of labor in export-oriented industries was dependent upon the relative inferiority of remuneration and working conditions was evident also because it turned out to be a rather short-lived phenomenon. Already by the mid-1990s—the height of the export boom—women's share of manufacturing employment had peaked in most economies of the region, and in some countries it subsequently declined in absolute numbers.[3] Some of this reflected the fact that such export-oriented employment through relocative foreign investment simply moved to cheaper locations: from Malaysia to Indonesia and Vietnam; from Thailand to Cambodia and Myanmar and so on. But even in the newer locations, the recent problems of various export sectors such as the garments industry worldwide have meant that jobs (especially for women workers) were created and then lost within the space of a few years.

As women became an established part of the paid workforce, and even the dominant part in certain sectors (as indeed they did become in the textiles, readymade garments, and consumer electronics sectors of East Asia), it became more difficult to exercise the traditional type of gender discrimination at work. Besides an upward pressure on their wages, which caused gender wage gaps to come down to some extent, there were other pressures for legislation to improve their overall conditions of work. But these strategies designed to improve the conditions of women workers tended to reduce their relative attractiveness for those employers who had earlier relied precisely on the inferior conditions of women's work and their greater flexibility in terms of hiring and firing to keep their costs low and enhance their export profitability. The rise in wages also had the same effect. As their relative effective remuneration improved (in terms of the total package of wages and work and contract conditions), their attractiveness to employers decreased.

Subsequently, manufacturing in Asia tended to occupy a much less-significant position in the total employment of women, and it also relied less on female employment at the margin. It is increasingly evident that export-oriented production does not always result in formal feminization of the workforce, which is essentially dependent upon the relative inferiority of female wages and work conditions and the use of patriarchal relations to establish control over women workers and keep wages down. If mechanization and newer techniques require the use of more skilled labor, or if the gap between male and female wages is not sufficiently large, export activities do not need to rely more on women's labor. In conditions in which both male and female workers have been forced by adverse conditions in the labor market to accept adverse low-paid and insecure work contracts, as occurred not only in post-crisis East Asia but in other countries of the region, there has been less overt preference for young women workers than was previously observed.

The nature of such work has also changed in recent years. It was already based mostly on short-term contracts rather than permanent employment for women; now there is much greater reliance on them as workers in very small units or home-based production, at the bottom of a complex subcontracting chain. This shift became even more marked in the post-crisis adjustment phase. In Southeast Asia, women have made up a significant proportion of the informal manufacturing industry workforce, in garment workshops, shoe factories, and craft industries. Many women also carry out informal, temporary activities in farming or in the building industry. Home-based workers, working for themselves or on subcontracts, make products ranging from clothing and footwear to artificial flowers, carpets, electronics, and teleservices.

The increasing use of outsourcing is not confined to export firms. However, because of the flexibility offered by subcontracting, it is clearly of even greater advantage in the intensely competitive export sectors and therefore tends to be even more widely used there. Much of this cross-border outsourcing activity is based in Asia, though as Custers notes, the movement can be across geographical locations, even returning to the North when collapses in employment (as in Europe recently) force women to take up such home-based informal work once again. Such subcontracted producers vary in size and manufacturing capacity, from medium-sized factories to pure middlemen collecting the output of home-based workers. The crucial role of women workers in such international production activity based in Asia is now increasingly recognized, whether as wage labor in small factories and workshops run by subcontracting firms, or as homeworkers dealing with middlemen in a complex production chain. A substantial proportion of such subcontracting extends down to home-based work, which provides substantial opportunity for self-exploitation, especially when payment is on a piece-rate basis; also such work is typically left unprotected by labor laws and social welfare programmes. However, even such home-based work may be in crisis, as the textile and garment exports from developing countries face increasing difficulties in world markets and the pressure of competition forces exporters to seek further methods of cost-cutting. The extreme volatility of demand for labor that characterizes factory-based, export-oriented production has also become a feature of home-based work for export production.

The Role of Unpaid Labor

Custers's work is significant because he emphasizes that theory has to be concerned with both the paid and the unpaid forms of exploitation used to gather profits under modern capitalism. As Elson has noted, the unpaid and repetitive services that women perform regularly within households often render it invisible in economic terms, despite its critical nature for both social and economic reproduction.[4] Obviously, this has been a significant feature of capitalist accumulation throughout history. But it also has particularly strong contemporary resonance because of changing macroeconomic policies that have affected the relative allocation of paid and unpaid work.

Thus a crucial feature of work processes across the globe has been the increase in unpaid labor within households—predominantly (but not exclusively) performed by women, as governments renege on basic social responsibilities for the provision of public goods and services, and more of the care economy becomes the province of the unpaid sector. The peculiar combination of increased unemployment and increased requirement of unpaid labor is thus an attribute of labor markets globally. Macroeconomic policies of national governments that have systematically reduced employment opportunities for both men and women, and allowed agriculture in the South to become a precarious and unviable occupation, have also reduced the quality of and access to public goods and services and thrown open many parts of everyday life to market processes that increase inequality. In general, these economic policies have been in the interests of large corporate capital. The rich, and especially large corporations, have benefited from competitive offers of substantial and growing tax benefits, while the common people have been told that there is no money in the state coffers for basic public goods and services. Food security has been threatened in poor countries; other economic rights have been denied; social sectors such as health and education have been underfunded; and workers' protection has been reduced. The increasing emphasis on markets has implied the commoditization of many aspects of life that were earlier seen as either naturally provided by states and communities, or simply not subject to market transaction and property relations. For example, the inability or refusal of several governments to provide safe drinking water has led to the explosive growth of a bottled water industry. A whole range of previously publicly provided services and utilities like power distribution and telecommunications have been privatized. Even the growing recognition accorded to intellectual property rights marks the entry of markets into ever-newer spheres.

All of this affects women and girls most directly. When incomes from work in the family go down, women are forced to seek any form of employment that will keep the household going. When there is less access to food, women and girl children tend to eat less. When the health services are inadequate, women (especially mothers) not only suffer the most, but they also have to bear the responsibility of looking after the sick and the old. When schools lack basic facilities or charge higher fees, girl students find it difficult to attend and are relegated to household tasks. When cooking fuel and clean drinking water are hard to come by, women have to somehow provide them for the family. So, such government policies have led to large increases in the unpaid labor of women, and thereby contributed to a worsening quality of life for them. A consideration of the extent of unpaid work by women indicates that a substantial amount of women's time is devoted to unpaid labor, often at the cost of leisure and rest. Such unpaid labor is likely to have been increasing over time, especially in the past decade. Public policies have played a role in causing unpaid labor time of women to rise because of reduced social expenditures that place a larger burden of care on women, privatized or degraded common property resources, inadequate infrastructure facilities that increase time spent on provisioning essential goods for the household, or simply because even well-meaning policies (such as for afforestation) are often gender-blind.

Women Workers and Labor Management Techniques

While some of these previous features of the interplay between women's work and capitalism are now more widely known and discussed, especially in recent socialist-feminist work, a major contribution of Custers's book is found in the insights he provides into how this has affected systems of labor management. In a particularly important chapter, Custers draws a distinction between Fordist (or Taylorist) systems of mass production and what he describes as the Japanese system, or "Toyotism." He notes that the latter possesses two distinctive characteristics: "the quality control circles of male and female laborers intended to mentally subject them to the corporation's rule, and the structure of subcontracting which entails the transfer of production risk to the manufacturers of components and to the workforce employed by them" (317). He illuminates how the involvement of women workers at the bottom of the production system's hierarchy in Japanese mass production generated this tendency that subsequently was used to created segmented categories of workers with differential rights and bargaining power.

Globally, capitalism is increasingly moving towards this system of production because it enables employers to "solve" some of the constraints to smooth production. While the serial production of mass commodities is not abolished in the Japanese-style production system, the internal hierarchical relations within enterprises and the external relations are both profoundly restructured. Custers describes this as the result of the process whereby multinational companies have continued searching for ways to obtain maximum control over factory workers' thinking processes.

The distinctive feature of Toyotism is the combination of internal decentralization with external centralization. Internal decentralization is reflected in the formation of "labor groups" that are rewarded with common incentives for higher production to enable the disciplining device of peer pressure. This reduces the need for detailed supervision or monitoring and ensures much greater "self-discipline." Far from humanizing labor relations, Custers notes that this has the effect of reducing solidarity among workers and further weakening their collective power. It is interesting to note that this method of managerial control has been increasingly copied by companies across the world, and has even spread beyond the sphere of production into finance. Micro-credit, for example, which was actively promoted as a "development panacea" by multilateral organizations and many governments, has relied on creating groups of women who benefit in common from loans (in what are euphemistically called "self-help groups") so that peer pressure for repayment substitutes for the absence of collateral in lending.

Combined with this is external centralization, which also affects workers negatively. A large corporation's relations with small supplier firms are increasingly regulated by the principles of "just-in-time delivery" (*kanban* in Japanese). These supplier firms, in turn, employ workers with clearly secondary status in terms of workers' rights who are driven by the instability and insecurity of their employers' earning. Methods of transferring risks to workers are firmly entrenched by the informal nature of most work contracts, the reliance on part-time workers, and the use of piece-rate wages.

Once again, this description is remarkably prescient of current processes, as such methods have gone global in nature. The vertical "disintegration" of the production process into complex geographically disparate but controlled chains is its current expression, as evident from much recent research.[5] Two major sets of changes have dramatically increased the relocation possibilities in international production. Technological changes have allowed for different parts of the production process to be vertically split and locationally separated, and these created different types of requirements for labor involving a few highly skilled professional workers and a vast bulk of semi-skilled workers for whom burnout over time is more widely prevalent than learning by doing. They have also enabled geographical relocation in service activities that were previously locationally rigid. Organizational changes have been associated with concentration of ownership and control, as well as with greater dispersion and more layers of outsourcing and subcontracting of particular activities and parts of the production process. Therefore we now have the emergence of international suppliers of goods and services that rely less on direct production within a specific location and more on subcontracting a greater part of their production and distribution activities. This has led to the emergence and market domination of "manufacturers without factories," as multinational firms such as Nike and Adidas effectively rely on a complex system of outsourced and subcontracted production based on centrally determined design and quality control. More recent outsourcing in services, ranging from publishing to back-office work, also combines some amount of flexibility (which implies greater control over workers) with centralized control. In all of these activities, women workers are both essential and dominate the lower end of work processes in terms of pay and lack of control.

Women and the Reserve Army of Labor

Custers correctly identifies the significance of women as a labor reserve for capitalism. In a consideration of Japanese women, he notes that they have always borne the characteristics that Marx described for the major categories of the industrial reserve army: the latent, the stagnant, and the floating. He also notes how the availability of such women workers is conditioned by the broader economic conditions, so that the greater poverty or misery of families sends out greater numbers of women (often younger women) in search of paid work. This is also affected by life-cycle social pressures. He notes that married, middle-aged women employed as part-time workers often most clearly fulfil the general criteria for being part of the labor reserve. They are available as a cheap labor reserve precisely because of their forced absence from the labor market for childbearing and child rearing, but the patriarchal relations underlying this cement their role as insecure, subordinate, and low-paid workers who can be brought into or expelled from jobs whenever employers require it.

One notable tendency in global labor markets is the increase in open unemployment rates across the world. By the beginning of the current century, unemployment rates in most industrial countries were higher than they had been at any time since the Great Depression of the 1930s. But even more significant, and in a break from the past, open unemployment was very high in developing countries. It has continued to grow thereafter, even though the general absence of social security provision or unemployment benefits in the developing world usually means that people undertake some activity, however low paying, and usually in the form of self-employment. It is notable that open unemployment has been growing in the developing countries that are currently seen as the most dynamic in the world economy, such as China, East and Southeast Asian countries, and India, and in many of these economies it has combined with persistently high rates of underemployment.

The decline in formal sector employment, especially in developing countries, has been associated with the proliferation of workers crowded into the informal sector, especially in the low-wage, low-productivity occupations that are characteristic of "refuge sectors" in labor markets. While there are some high-value-added jobs to be found as "informal" self-employment (including, for example, software and some high-end IT-enabled services that allow home-based professional work), these are relatively small in number and certainly too few to make much of a dent in the overall trend, especially in countries where the vast bulk of the labor force is unskilled or relatively less skilled. In turn, this has meant that the cycle of poverty-low employment generation-poverty has been perpetuated and even accentuated because of the diminished willingness or ability of governments to intervene positively in expanding employment generation.

It is worth noting that one important response by Asian women to these changes has been economic migration. Asia has become one of the most significant regions in the world both for the cross-border movement of capital and goods and for the movement of people. The picture of women's migration in Asia today is complex, reflecting the apparent advantages to women of higher incomes and recognition of work, but also the dangers and difficulties of migrating to new and unknown situations with the potential for various kinds of exploitation. It has also been associated with a newer form of production chain: the globalization of the care economy, with women migrating to other (richer) locations where the per capita incomes of households and demographic patterns combine to increase the outsourcing of home-based care work that was previously the unpaid work of women members of those households.[6]

The great value in Custers's book is his succinct description of how so many aspects of gender relations, and the particular forms patriarchy takes, are closely intertwined with processes of capitalist accumulation. His analysis has clear and sharp relevance today for understanding not only the position of women and the possibilities for social emancipation generally, but especially for unravelling the complex nature of contemporary capitalism.

NOTES

1. Jayati Ghosh, *Never Done and Poorly Paid: Women's Work in Globalizing India* (New Delhi: Women Unlimited Press, 2009); Stephanie Seguino, "Accounting for Gender in Asian Economic Growth," Feminist Economics 6, no.3 (2000): 27–58.
2. Lean Lin Lim, "Women at Work in Asia and the Pacific: Recent Trends and Future Challenges," International Forum on Equality for Women in the World of Work (Geneva: ILS, 1994).
3. Ghosh, Ibid.
4. Diane Elson, *Male Bias in the Development Process*, second edition (Manchester: Manchester University Press, 1995).
5. Marilyn Carr, Martha Alter Chen, and Jane Tate, "Globalization and Home-Based Workers," Feminist Economics 6, no. 3 (2000): 123–42.
6. Ghosh, Ibid.

LIST OF ILLUSTRATIONS

Tables

Figures

Maps

Foreword

There is no 'end of history', and while the representatives of the neo-liberalist narrative may view socialism as a phenomenon of the past, class contradiction and class struggle are increasing worldwide. This is made clear from the evidence given in this book, particularly for female workers, strengthening and enhancing Marx and Marxist interpretations of class struggle and capital accumulation in a feminist perspective.

Debates on these topics emerged strongly in the 1970s, when I became acquainted with Peter Custers as a grassroots worker. Both of us were located in different contexts supporting Third World peasant struggles for a just redistribution of assets, and were trying to show that in spite of Marx's proletarianist bias, peasants in Third World countries had a revolutionary potential. In most of the world the situation of peasants and women has remained bleak or has worsened over the past few decades. The main problems that concerned us in the 1970s are still on the agenda, though they were ignored in Western scholarly circles when they became enchanted by the post-Cold War neo-liberalist or globalist rhetoric. Custers' book is, therefore, highly relevant and timely.

Marxist practice and Marxist theory have from the outset—Marx's own life and work(s)—been closely interlinked. Sometimes practice may have been the more outstanding aspect of Marxism; often however, theoretical reflection, debate, disagreement, theses, antitheses and syntheses have been predominant: Marx-*ism*, indeed. Marxism has been portrayed as a science, ideology, millenarian movement or religion. Whatever it is, 'the definitive failure of Marxism' is as obviously impossible as the definitive failure of, say, Christianity, Islam, quantum physics or liberalism. Its influence has changed the face of the earth and the history of mankind and it may well continue to do so in the next millennium. As Custers shows, the same is true for feminism in the past and present.

Social/political/religious movements come and go, but the collective experience of large groups of men and women who participate in them will forever continue to have an influence on behaviour in the processes of evolution and revolution.

Custers' analysis of capital accumulation and the role of women's labour over the past decades in different Asian contexts confirms that the contradiction between the rich and poor, haves and have nots, owners of capital and non-owners has not disappeared but, in fact, has been enhanced over the past decades on a worldwide scale as well as locally in rich and poor countries. These growing contradictions are most easily discernible from the fact that 10 per cent of the world's population that lives in the West (North America and Western Europe) utilizes 24 times as much per capita as 80 per cent of mankind living in the South. This trend was clearly visible in Gerald O. Barney (ed.), *The Global Report to the President of the US*; *Entering the 21st Century* (Washington: Council on Environment Quality and the Department of State, 1980), commissioned by former president Carter, conspicuously ignored by scholars as well as policy-makers. This fact has been confirmed by more recent data presented in the yearly United Nations *Human Development Reports* which, moreover, show that these rich–poor discrepancies have doubled since 1960.

Does this trend not indicate that class contradictions and class struggle are more clearly on the agenda than ever before? This seems particularly so as the 'revolution of rising expectations' promoted worldwide by the media conglomerates is producing, in most cases, a potential 'revolution of rising frustrations'. Such frustrations may, as often happened in the past, find expression temporarily in inter-religious, inter-ethnic, or inter-party strife—the poor against other poor—but how long will it take until 'the common enemy' is more clearly identified by these poor? The Zapatistas in Chiapas, Mexico, are the most recent example where the rising frustrations of peasants and women led to strong protest—and a revolutionary movement—as a direct reaction to effects of 'free market' globalization and the petroleum and mining extravaganza in that area.

The most fundamental of the various growing contradictions appears to remain, probably for several decades to come and deep into the next millennium, that between the global 'bourgeoisie' and the others. In this context the classical statement by Marx about the role of the 'bourgeoisie' may be recapitulated. Marshall Berman, in his *All that is Solid Melts into Air: The Experience of Modernity* (London: Verso, 1983), gives Marx's and Engels' *Communist Manifesto* a prominent place, together with Goethe's *Faust*, as one of the first outstanding reflections on modernity. Berman points out that Marx, like Goethe, was deeply impressed by the 'genius for activity' of the bourgeoisie and 'in a stirring, evocative paragraph, transmits the rhythm and drama of bourgeois activism'. Berman (ibid., p. 95) then quotes Marx's well-known statement in the *Manifesto*:

> Constant revolutionizing of production, uninterrupted disturbance of all social relations, everlasting uncertainty and agitation, distinguish the bourgeois epoch from all earlier times. All fixed, fast-frozen relationships, with their train of venerable ideas and opinions, are swept away, all new-formed ones become obsolete before they can ossify. All that is solid melts into air, all that is holy is profaned, and men at last are forced to face with sober senses the real conditions of their lives and their relations with their fellow men.

This statement appears today more true than ever. In fact, as Berman also noted, the process has accelerated, and the forementioned observations of *Global 2000* and the United Nations show what the main global effects are. Custers' data also confirm this.

Class struggles reacting to accumulation are being waged locally, but the context is determined globally. The bourgeoisie has made advances which Marx in 1848 already, more or less, foresaw. As Custers shows, aspects that Marx ignored, like the exploitation of women, are now coming dramatically into the foreground.

During the next few decades the various kinds of contradictions outlined here will continue and probably become more acute. It is crucial that Marxist men and women of all continents and civilizations get together to assess the influence of these contradictions on the local situations where they are active, as well as on the long-term global trends that form the context of local developments. In reaction to the way the Western bourgeoisie (particularly of the US) is trying to manage the globalization processes to its advantage, one can say that class contradictions have also been globalized and thus become more complicated. People's (such as workers', women's, peasants', religious, environmental and civic) movements, which try and face the manipulations of the global power elite(s), should be able to find common ground rather than be tempted to fight each other on civilizational, religious, cultural, national or ethnic fault lines. This poses a challenge to global Marxist thinking and practice to which Custers has contributed an insightful response.

One wonders about the possibility of having a combined Marxist and feminist initiative—a creative worldwide effort of *globalization from below*. Global Marxist theorizing should emerge from, or at least be closely related to, local efforts and learning experiences, such as those described in this book.

Third World Centre
Catholic University Nijmegen
The Netherlands

Gerrit Huizer

Acknowledgements

The concrete starting point for this research and book project was somewhere in 1992, when I got Professor Gerrit Huizer's support to carry out an investigation into the labour of women involved in the production of clothing in India's West Bengal state. Having observed the severity of exploitation in Calcutta's informal sector through regular visits to the city, I was keen to gather a systematic understanding of the production relations, as experienced by women involved in the manufacture of *punjabis*, frocks and other wear. Since I had kept aloof from the academic world for almost 20 years, I was initially lukewarm to the idea of writing a Ph.D. dissertation. I am, therefore, deeply indebted to Gerrit Huizer, of the Third World Centre in Nijmegen, for having provided me with so much encouragement, inspiration and guidance that, ultimately, I came to embrace the idea of drafting a dissertation as a valid project, and as a suitable framework for the summing up of many years of practical and theoretical research.

The central theme of this book is women's labour (i.e., the variety of productive tasks undertaken by women in Asian economies). The choice of this theme derives, I do not hesitate admitting, primarily from an intellectual conviction. From the middle of the 1980s onwards, I have been convinced that the neglect of women's labour, which has been so characteristic of the economic theories built by male intellectuals, needs to be fundamentally questioned. I thus embarked on an extensive study of feminist writings regarding women's labour, which has ultimately culminated in the project of this book. On the other hand, an emotional element has certainly been involved in the choice of countries on which my dissertation is focused, for the plight of people living in the countries of South Asia—Bangladesh in particular—has occupied my mind for the last 24 years. Over such a long period of time, my views have, naturally, evolved. Nevertheless, it is only because of my prolonged stay in Bangladesh, India and other countries of Asia, that I feel, it has been possible for me to draft a book with such a broad theme as 'capital accumulation' in Asian economies.

There are many people who have helped me to gather my knowledge about women's contribution to agricultural and industrial production in Bangladesh, India and Japan, the three countries discussed in this book. I would like to express my gratitude in the first place to the male and female garment producers in West Bengal who were willing to talk while carrying on their sewing and other tasks; the industrial workers and the peasant men and women in Bangladesh who have been my teachers for many years; and the women workers in Japan who too have willingly shared their experiences with me. I am equally grateful to all the trade union activists who have provided me with the necessary overview of the exploitation their union members are subjected to. As to researchers, I am primarily indebted to Basudev Ganguly and Krishna Bandopadhyay, who have systematically interviewed hundreds of men and women producing readymade garments in Dumdum/Paikpara and Moheshtola/Santoshpur, two areas located respectively in and near the capital city of West Bengal, Calcutta, where the field investigation for this book project was primarily concentrated. As for interpreters, I am grateful to Hiroko Seki and other Japanese friends whose energetic translation work was crucial to the success of my visit to Japan.

The writing of a book can be a very lonely task. Still, I have benefited from the critical comments provided by various friends while I was engaged in drafting the manuscript. Thus, Basudev Ganguly reviewed the contents of Chapter 5 on garment production in West Bengal; Johan van Rixtel has critically reflected on Chapter 9 about ecofeminism; Tineke Jansen similarly has given her comments on Chapter 6 which analyses the garments sector in Bangladesh; and Maithreyi Krishnaraj has critically read and given her encouraging reaction to two of the chapters on women's work in India (Chapter 7 on housewifization and Chapter 9 on ecofeminism). Among other friends and relatives who have been supportive, I wish to mention by name: Hermien van der Weiden who has typed several draft chapters; and my brother, Thom Custers, to whom I owe it that the final part of the work was not too cumbersome, since he volunteered to do the lay-out.

Sumati Nair, my companion, has gone through the whole draft manuscript to correct language errors. She has given me unfailing moral encouragement from the time I started my research on women's labour onwards, and all through the writing of this book. Partly through her research, I am aware that my analytical work remains incomplete since it does not cover biological reproduction. For all the translation work from different languages into English I myself am responsible. I know, of course, that I am responsible also for whatever errors or weaknesses this study still contains.

1

Feminism and the Conceptualization of Women's Labour in Asian Economies

Asia—A Growth Pole of the World Economy

'For the first time in its long history there is the possibility today that the centre of accumulation would shift to the east'.[1] These are the concluding words in an elaborate essay on the history of the international financial system, authored by the Indian economist, Krishnendu Ray. The article, amongst others, details the growing influence of Japanese financial markets and banks on the flow and control of international capital. By 1988, Japanese banks had come to control 35 per cent of all international bank assets, and around the same time Tokyo's bond, foreign exchange and equities market 'had begun to challenge their New York counterparts in size.'[2] Ray sees the present phase in the international financial system as one of transition, and raises the possibility that East Asia, with Japan at the centre, in the future will emerge as the pole of hegemony in the world economy.

Another author who, like Ray, believes that the world balance of industrial and financial power is rapidly shifting, is Frederic Clairmonte. In a recent article on Malaysia's explosive growth, Clairmonte draws a contrast between the negative rate of production growth of 'advanced' capitalist countries for 1993, and an output growth for Asia that has amounted to 7.5 per cent over the last decade. According to Clairmonte, 'in 1950 the anaemic Asia–Pacific region had an exiguous 3.5 per cent of world GDP; in 1994, this share will rise to 22; by the century's end, it will have rocketed to about one-third.'[3] Thus, Asia's growing clout within the world economy is unmistakable.

Moreover, both Ray's and Clairmonte's comments underscore how relevant it has become to scrutinize the 'laws' of capitalist accumulation of countries situated in the Asian continent.

This book puts the spotlight on the experience of three Asian countries—India, Bangladesh and Japan. Whereas the choice of the latter is largely dictated by the country's powerful position in the world economy, the choice of the two former countries has been guided primarily by my prolonged experience of residence, research and academic discussions in countries of South Asia. Based on this experience, and on my reading of the economic evolution in other parts of Asia, I have selected themes which I believe to be crucial for understanding the overall process of capital accumulation in the southern and eastern regions of Asia. The production of readymade garments, for instance, for which I have carried out field research in India and Bangladesh, has been or does constitute a dynamic growth element in most of the economies of these two Asian regions.

Further, I have undertaken this study from a specific angle. When Japan embarked on its modernization programme in the last part of the 19th century, its initial capitalists preferred to recruit young women to toil in their silk-reeling and cotton textile mills. More recently, the country's successful electronic companies have similarly shown a marked preference for women as production workers on assembly lines. Elsewhere in Asia women are likewise considered to be a convenient target for exploitation, in particular in the initial processes of industrialization. Yet, until feminist researchers started taking an interest in women's roles, the analysis of the existing recruitment and employment policies was severely neglected by economists. This study highlights the crucial place of women in the process of capital accumulation in Asian countries. In this introductory chapter I will briefly outline the main theoretical sources from which I have drawn my conceptual framework for fieldwork and comparative analysis.

The Legacy of Marxism and the Contents of this Study

This book explicitly re-asserts the relevance of Marxist concepts for the analysis of contemporary production processes. My experience of discussions at Indian universities, and my acquaintance with the literature which is published in the South Asian region, have taught me that a significantly large section of academicians and writers in the subcontinent continue to insist on the relevance of Marxist tools of economic analysis. They do so alongside Marxist-oriented political parties which continue to constitute a viable force in Indian politics. To mention just two authors whose work I have found useful in the course of my fieldwork: the Bangladeshi academician Atiur Rahman has fruitfully applied Lenin's analysis of peasant differentiation in pre-revolutionary Russia to explain the ongoing process of pauperization in the Bangladeshi countryside; and the Indian author, Manjit Singh, has advocated the supremacy of Marx's theoretical framework for understanding the huge 'informal sector' of the Indian economy.[4]

An Indian magazine which continues to provide scope for Marxist analytical approaches, along with non-Marxist ones, is the Bombay-based *Economic and Political Weekly*. In an article published last year, for example, the noted economist Paresh Chattopadhyay commemorated the writing of Marx's first critique of political economy, the so-called *Parish Manuscripts* (of 1844). Chattopadhyay recapitulated Marx's theory regarding the alienation of labour under capitalism and resumed the discussion as to how such alienation can be abolished.[5] In this study I intend to show how a number of concepts which Marx used to explain the methods of economic exploitation in 19th century Great Britain have become increasingly valid for the analysis of Asian economies.

My acceptance of Marxist economic concepts is, however, not an uncritical one. The cornerstone of Marx's economic thinking was his labour theory of value which, as will be shown in Chapters 2 and 4, formed a further refinement of ideas which had been posed by classical political economists, such as Adam Smith and David Ricardo. Through the formula he proposed on the creation of the value of commodities, Marx sought to explain how a part of this value is appropriated by the owners of capital (surplus value), whereas the labourers are only paid a minimal amount to enable them to maintain their labouring strength. Followers of Marx have insisted over and again that his labour theory of value was not the construct of an isolated individual, for the thesis that labour is the source of all wealth was shared by the classical economists who preceded Marx.[6]

However, Marx's followers have, for over a century, failed to see that his theory of value also shared some of the weaknesses underlying the theories of his precursors, more particularly a deep bias against women. This has only become apparent with the feminist debates of the 1960s and 1970s. For instance, like Ricardo, with whom he agreed that labour time is the measure of value, Marx ignored women's domestic labour when measuring the value of the workers' labouring strength. Like his precursors, Marx overlooked the sexual division of labour between women and men. And like other male economists of his time, Marx's attention was almost entirely focused on what the British feminist author Glucksmann has termed the 'public economy'. The domestic economy, its transformation along with the growth of capitalist relations, and the mutual influence of changes in the public and domestic economy did not constitute an intrinsic part of Marx's economic analysis.[7]

Nevertheless, key aspects of the analysis which Marx presented in *Capital* have been applied in this study to interprete recent developments in Asian economies. Thus, in Chapter 6 on Bangladesh's garments' sector, I will recapitulate and apply Marx's theory of the working day, more specifically his thesis on the creation of 'absolute' surplus value; in Chapter 8, dealing with the loss of land and common property resources by peasants in Bangladesh, I will refer to Marx's views on original or 'primitive' accumulation; in Chapter 11 which describes the management style of the Japanese automobile company Toyota, I will argue, in conformity with Marx's analysis of capital's turnover time, that the company's methods of operation are centrally guided by the urge to abbreviate the turnover time of capital. And in Chapter 12 I will use Marx's view on the reserve army of labour to explain the employment of middle-aged women as part-time labourers.

Historical Waves of Feminism and the Debate on Women's Labour

Before reviewing the labouring experiences of women in three Asian economies, I will highlight key aspects of the debate on women's labour that has accompanied successive movements for women's emancipation in European countries. Thus, after Chapter 2 on the patriarchal bias of 19th-century working class theoreticians, I will explain in Chapter 3 the significance of the German proletarian women's movement which developed exceptional organizational strength during the first 'wave' of feminism (between 1890 and the beginning of the First World War). It is true, of course, that the real history of working class women's struggles extends further back into the past, and was geographically broader than this particular experience.[8] Yet the review of the German movement brings out well that the first 'wave' of feminism did not give rise to a breakthrough at the level of economic theory.

Like my review of the first wave of feminism, that of the second wave presented in Chapter 4 is also selective. Whereas numerous issues were put on the agenda that were/are important to women's lives, I have primarily tried to assess the significance of the discussion on household labour under industrial capitalism. In the late 1960s and early 1970s, women's reproductive labour became the focal point for both action and intense theoretical debate. In Italy and many other Western countries, as also in the United States, housewives and their allies started demanding that their isolated and invisible work be socially recognized, and that they be paid a wage or salary. Concomitantly, feminists effectively started challenging the biased views of male economists, including Marxist ones. They insisted that the domestic labour performed by modern housewives is productive, socially necessary, and indirectly helps the owners of industrial entrepreneurs reap their profits.

I will argue in Chapter 4 that while participants of the household labour debate raised valid criticisms, the process of rethinking economic theory and of building a more comprehensive conceptual framework was incomplete, since leading authors tended to 'delink' domestic labour from the public sphere of the capitalist economy. A fruitful line of thought has more recently been provided by the British feminist author Miriam Glucksmann, whose analysis of domestic labour is both historically specific and class differentiated. Distancing herself from the 'dualistic' assumptions underlying various analytical writings of the second feminist wave, Glucksmann proposes a more 'dialectical' theoretical framework. She vigorously argues that the domestic and public sphere of the capitalist economy should be understood as two poles which are inextricably interlinked.

Still, in my chapters on women's labour in Asian economies I have found the essential teaching of the second feminist wave (that through their reproductive work women create both use and exchange values) relevant for the interpretation of reality. Thus, when discussing the waged work of women 'part-timers' in Japan, I will simultaneously look at the time they spend daily doing the cooking, cleaning and other domestic chores. When analyzing the exploitation of women homeworkers in the Indian states of West Bengal and Andhra Pradesh, the values homeworkers create in the time they do non-waged work will be taken stock of. And again, when describing the productive activities of village women in South Asia, I will try to systematically enumerate what use and exchange values they create. In short, the broad overview of women's labour in Asian economies will demonstrate that the initial lessons of the debate on household labour can be applied in a non-European context.

The Concept of Patriarchy and the Critique of Marxism

Apart from the issue of domestic labour, there are other topics which have been hotly debated in the course of the second feminist wave. Another debate which again has led to a critical appraisal of Marxist theory is that on the history and meaning of patriarchy. When Marx and Engels referred to the patriarchal family, they had in mind the family of the feudal era which was an economic unit (i.e., a unit of agricultural production). The male peasant head directly controlled the family's land, cattle and instruments, and divided the labouring tasks among its members. This patriarchal family was being destroyed, Marx and Engels argued, as production was being relegated to the factory, and as women became independent wage earners under industrial entrepreneurs. Capitalism, they held, would equalize the position of men and women as exploited workers in the (public) economy.[9]

This view has been challenged and criticized by various currents of feminism ever since the heyday of the international women's movement in the 1960s and 1970s. It may be recalled that the impetus to the agitation against women's subordination was provided by radical feminists in the United States—feminists who see patriarchy as *the* determinant social relationship under all modes of production. For radical feminists, all existing social systems are characterized first and foremost by men's domination over women, by the fact that 'every avenue of power in society, including the coercive force of the police, is entirely in male hands.'[10] Class relations (that is, the differentiated position various social groups hold to the means of production) were/are seen as a secondary issue by the radical current of feminists.

The socialist feminist current, which later became more prominent, differed on the meaning of patriarchy and its relation to class. It has justly questioned the proposition that women's energies should be channelled into a common battle against all men. While acknowledging the contribution of radical feminism to the debate on the concept of patriarchy, socialist feminists moved beyond both their view and that of classical Marxism. They admitted that male dominance takes many forms, and that psychological aspects of women's oppression (which are stressed by radical feminists) should not be neglected, but felt a keen need to define the material roots of the structures of patriarchy. Thus, Heidi Hartmann, in her essay on the 'Unhappy Marriage of Marxism and Feminism', argued that 'the material base upon which patriarchy rests lies most fundamentally in men's control over women's labour power.'[11] Socialist feminists hold that women's relations to the means of production are generally different from men's.

In this book, I have followed the socialist current within feminism and agree that, given patriarchy, women's relations to the means of production are different from men's. However, I agree with Miriam Glucksmann's critical comment that one cannot mechanically draw a parallel between, on the one hand, class relations in the public economy (capitalists versus wage labourers, landlords versus tenants, etc.) and, on the other, the relations of men and women in the domestic economy.[12] I have also sought to locate, in this book, men's patriarchal dominance in both spheres of the economy, and at both the economic and social levels of human interaction. As Chapter 6 on the garments' sector in Bangladesh well illustrates, mechanisms of patriarchal control can be situated in both spheres, and the methods of dominance used in one tend to influence what happens to patriarchy in the other sphere of economic life.

The Sexual Division of Labour: An Enduring Element in Factory Production

A theme which has been brought to the fore by feminists along with the growing debate on patriarchy is that of the sexual division of labour, for it is through this division of tasks that men's economic and social dominance in all class societies is given its configuration. Here again feminists have taken both Marxist and non-Marxist economic theories to task, for having failed to draw attention to the gendered work processes that have characterized capitalist production from the industrial revolution to date. As mentioned in my chapter on Fordism and Toyotism (the two main management styles that have been devised in the 20th century), even in the era of mass production sex-typing of industrial tasks has invariably been used to structure the workforce in corporations, their subsidiaries and supplier firms.

While it is undeniable that, as commodity production spreads, the production of daily necessities and the manufacture of tools and equipment is increasingly shifted from the domestic to the public domain and brought under the direct sway of capital, Marx's view, that women's position as (exploited) wage labourers becomes equal to men's, cannot be upheld. Under the capitalist mode of production, the control of women's labour power is differently structured than it was under feudalism. Although male workers employed in Britain's early spinning mills tried to exercise their authority over their wives on the workfloor, they ultimately had to surrender part of that authority to the owners of capital.[13] Yet, as many feminist investigators have pointed out, the sexual division of labour is consciously maintained by modern corporations, remains unequal and oppressive to women, and is often shaped or reinforced by state policies.

This book does not provide an exhaustive analysis of the theme of patriarchy. A consistent theme in almost all subsequent chapters, though, is the division of labour between women and men, and its changing pattern under the impact of modernization. While investigating the labour of women in three Asian economies, I have looked at two aspects of the sexual division of labour, namely the 'social' and the 'sectoral' division of tasks. On the one hand, I have reviewed how, throughout society, tasks in the domestic sphere (i.e., relating to reproduction) are allocated. On the other hand, I have assessed how, in the specific sectors studied, such as in the readymade garments' sector, a hierarchal structure of work tasks is maintained. Through the comparative evidence gathered I have tried to understand what is 'fixed' and what is not in the sexual division of labour.

The Labour of Women in Asia and Currents within Feminism

In writing this book I have benefited from the research and analyses undertaken by women belonging to different currents of international feminism. In spite of the long evolution of feminist thought, and the fierce debates which have been and continue to be waged by feminist authors, many Marxists, in particular in the Third World, continue to think that feminism represents one clearcut trend of thought. There is still little recognition of the fact that feminism comprises a great diversity of thought, and this is unfortunate. While it is not easy to disentangle the philosophical differences that underlie the investigative work of different feminist writers, it is important to realize that feminist attempts to reconstruct economic theory have not yet culminated in a single, new framework, enjoying wide acceptance.

In this book, the reader will not find a comprehensive listing of the schools of feminism. Even if that was possible, it would not serve the specific aim of this publication, namely to highlight women's productive and reproductive roles in contemporary Asian economies. For this purpose, it suffices to refer to four basic currents, each of which have contributed importantly to laying bare a part of women's productive labour: developmental feminism, ecofeminism, the German feminist school and socialist feminism. Except for the German feminist school which has done investigative work into both women's agricultural and industrial work, the research of the other three schools has covered a more selected portion of women's productive activities. I will briefly describe all four schools, in the order in which their views will subsequently be discussed.

Developmental feminism, as the name suggests, is primarily concerned with the position of women in the so-called 'developing countries' (i.e., in countries of the third world). Presuming that existing strategies for achieving economic growth can lead to women's emancipation, and that the central problem is that these growth strategies previously neglected the interests of women, researchers belonging to this current aim at 'integrating women in development'. Chapter 8 records how developmental feminists have documented the processing activities of village women in Bangladeshi agriculture, in particular their tasks in rice-processing. Developmental feminists, however, refrain from making a critical assessment of the dominant mode for the appropriation of economic surplus, which in the case of Bangladeshi agriculture is original or 'primitive' accumulation.

Ecofeminism has made its own limited but crucial contribution to the understanding of women's labour in the rural economy. In Chapter 9 I look closely at the writings of the Indian scientist, Vandana Shiva, who is painfully aware of the negative consequences for women of the ecological destruction wrought by the 'seeds revolution' (i.e., the introduction of high-response varieties of seeds in the name of agricultural modernization). Much more consciously than other schools, ecofeminism moreover poses the social issue of the loss of common property resources. The spread of commercial farming is inevitably accompanied by the enclosure of the commons and by the erosion of the independent subsistence base of peasant women and men in the Third World. However, Vandana Shiva has ignored several aspects of reality which are analyzed by developmental feminists, such as the sexual division of labour and class differentiation among peasant women.

The German feminist school consists of three scholars, Maria Mies, Veronika Bennholdt-Thomsen and Claudia von Werlhof, who have all carried out research into women's work in the Third World. In trying to conceptualize the contribution of women to agricultural and industrial production, they have put forward two theses which will be discussed here separately, namely the thesis on 'housewifization' (the social definition of women as 'housewives' which leads to heightened exploitation), and the thesis that women's work worldwide can be equated with the production of use values for immediate consumption. While recognizing that the analytical work of the members of the German school represents an important stage in feminist theorizing, I have challenged, in Chapter 10, the validity of their thesis of subsistence labour, because I believe that it results in an underestimation of women's role in the creation of an economic surplus.

Finally, socialist feminism will figure in Chapter 12 on women's labour in the Japanese economy. When the debate on household labour in their eyes had become 'deadlocked' in the second half of the 1970s, a number of socialist feminist authors re-oriented their research towards women's waged work in the formal and informal sector of industrialized economies. Like the ecofeminist author, Vandana Shiva, and members of the German school, socialist feminists believe that the dominant processes which women in different parts of the world are subjected to are processes of capital accumulation. Authors belonging to this school, amongst others, theorize about the secondary position of married women in the labour market, and how it relates to patriarchy. My investigation into the position of women wage workers in the Japanese economy confirms that the feminist interpretation of Marx's concept of the labour reserve is appropriate indeed.

A Study Focused on Three Economies

Finally, I wish to briefly describe the major factual themes that have been covered by my investigation. In seeking to visualize the ongoing process of capital accumulation in Asia, I have opted to focus on three major themes, namely, the nature of production relations in the ready-made garments' sector which plays such a vital role in the majority of South and South East Asian countries; agricultural modernization and its socio-economic and environmental effects; and the labour management strategies applied by Japanese corporations to achieve maximum control of their workforce. Although this study does not pretend to give an all-inclusive assessment of the process of capital accumulation in Asia, I believe that these themes comprise decisive parts of that process.

First, in Chapters 5 and 6 I will primarily concentrate on production relations in the garments' sectors of two adjacent territories, the Indian state of West Bengal, and Bangladesh respectively. While they toil in areas which are geographically close, the workers of the production units in these two territories are faced with structures of exploitation which are quite diverse. In West Bengal, the stitchers, finishers and ironers are scattered over many small workshops or toil at home, under a piece-rate regime. Operators of sewing machines and other labourers in Bangladesh's garments' sector, on the other hand, are factory-based and subject to a system of time-wages. Based on fieldwork carried out together with the Indian researcher/writer Basudev Ganguly, these two chapters provide initial confirmation that both Marxist and feminist concepts are required to understand women's labour in contemporary Asia. In Chapter 7 I will review Maria Mies' investigation into lace-making by women homeworkers in India's state of Andhra Pradesh. Her fieldwork can fruitfully be compared with ours on garment production in West Bengal.

In Chapters 8, 9 and 10 I will review various aspects of agricultural modernization in South Asia. Thus, Chapter 8 highlights the economic crisis and social disruption caused by the combined domination of indigenous, commercial capital and of foreign, financial institutions over the Bangladeshi economy. Chapter 9 takes the analysis of the impact of agricultural modernization on women further by focusing, in particular, on the ecological consequences of the change-over from traditional paddy seeds to high-response seed varieties. In

Chapter 10 an economic analysis is offered of subsistence-oriented production activities of village women in India, and of the waged work women increasingly perform in agriculture. The factual material for the analysis of agricultural modernization is drawn both from my own research, and from investigations carried out by these three schools of feminism.

The third theme, covered in Chapters 11 and 12, is that of 'Japanization' (i.e., the typically Japanese methods of capital accumulation). In a period which is just one and a quarter century in length, Japanese entrepreneurs have devised management techniques which are so profitable that they today are being emulated by industrial corporations worldwide. In Chapter 11 I will offer my own theoretical interpretation of the Japanese emphasis on decentralized production, and of the 'quality control circles' used to discipline workers. Chapter 12 brings into focus the importance of middle-aged, married women as a labour reserve for the contemporary Japanese economy. Although I certainly do not pretend to give a comprehensive assessment of the economic policies pursued in Japan, these chapters, to an extent, help to explain why Japan has emerged as a hegemonic power in the world economy. Finally, in Chapter 13 I endeavour to draw basic conclusions on the process of capital accumulation in Asia. While reaffirming the decisive relevance of key Marxist concepts, the chapter advocates the need for an extension of Marxist economic theory with concepts proposed by feminist theoreticians.

Notes and References

1. Ray (1994), p. PE-101.
2. Ibid., p. PE-100.
3. Clairmonte (1994), p. 2403.
4. Rahman (1986); Singh (1991).
5. Chattopadhyay (1994).
6. Lenin, for instance, held that Marx 'with genius consumated' classical English political economy. See Lenin (1976), p. 8 and (1977b), p. 4.
7. For Miriam Glucksmann's critique of Marx, see Glucksmann (1990), pp. 20–22.
8. The experience of French women workers who challenged the 'bourgeois' monogamous marriage as early as the 1830s is described in Mies and Jayawardene (1981); for women workers' struggles in the US which were contemporaneous with the German proletarian women's movement, see Tax (1980); for the movement of the British suffragettes for women's voting rights, see, for instance, Liddington and Norris (1978).

9. Hartmann (1981), p. 1, refers in this context specifically to Engels (1975).
10. Hartmann (1983), p. 14. For a more elaborate discussion regarding the contribution of radical feminists to the debate on patriarchy, see Eisenstein (1979), p. 16. McDonough and Harrison, in Kuhn and Wolpe (1978), p. 11, credit the radical feminist Kate Millet with having made 'one of the first major attempts to provide a thorough theoretical examination of the oppression of women using the concept of patriarchy'. See also Barrett's review of the discussion on patriarchy in Barrett (1980), p. 10.
11. Hartmann (1981), pp. 14–15. See also McDonough and Harrison, in Kuhn and Wolpe (1978), p. 11.
12. Glucksmann (1990), p. 271.
13. Hall (1987), pp. 21–22 records that male spinners in factories often employed their own wives, children and close relatives as their underlings so that it was the authority carried over from his position in the family which suited the adult male to the job of mule spinning.

PART 1

The Discourse on Women's Labour in Historical Perspective

2

The Patriarchal Bias of Working-class Theoreticians: Marx and Proudhon

In 1856, a French feminist, Jenny d'Héricourt, published an article in the magazine *Revue Philosophique et Religieuse*, in which she criticized the anarchist philosopher Pierre-Joseph Proudhon for holding views which were counter to women's equality. d'Héricourt quoted extensively from Proudhon's renowned book *Qu'est-ce que la Propriété?*, in which he argued that any property obtained through exploitation is theft.[1] Yet, in the same book, Proudhon also stated that the sexual differences between women and men raised among them 'a separation of the same kind as the difference of races among animals'. He was 'inclined to the seclusion of women', he said. Completely at variance with his stance that 'liberty is an absolute right without which no society is thinkable', he favoured the enslavement of the female sex.[2]

In criticizing Proudhon for his anti-emancipatory views, d'Héricourt's method of exposure was to confront Proudhon with inconsistencies in his own arguments. It was Proudhon himself who had reasoned that differences in intelligence cannot be used to defend differences in rights between human beings. Yet when it came to women, he held that, since women's intellectual capacities are inferior to men's, women are not entitled to the same rights as citizens as men. These views of the great philosopher are self-contradictory, d'Héricourt stated, unless it is proven that women do not form part of the human species. 'Since the value of the individual is no basis for the allocation of rights between human beings', it cannot be used to argue for inequality in rights between the sexes.[3] And Proudhon himself has expressed the view that 'social balance is obtained through equalization of the strong and the weak'.[4]

The 19th-century epoch in European history was both a period of sharp social conflict and of intense intellectual debates. These debates—

on philosophy, economics and politics—were dominated overwhelmingly by male theoreticians. Whether they tended towards utopian ideas on the creation of socialism, whether they championed an anarchist solution to the prevailing human misery, or held beliefs which subsequently came to be known as Marxist science, most participants in the debates were male intellectuals. As mentioned earlier, there were notable exceptions, such as in France, where feminist ideas flourished briefly in the middle of the 19th century. Yet overall, debates about society's problems and prospects, carried out among intellectuals who sympathized with the growing industrial proletariat, were a male monopoly.

Among these male theoreticians were some (such as the French utopian socialist Fourier, and Marx in his footsteps) who held that the degree of female emancipation forms the 'natural measure' of the general emancipation achieved in a given society. Thus, Marx and his followers tried to develop a theory of women's emancipation. They advocated women's participation in wage labour employment as the basis of their social liberation. Marx's theory remained incomplete; it contained its own patriarchal prejudice, since he overlooked women's domestic labour. Yet he did not consciously or willingly oppose women's freedom or sexual equality. Both he and Fourier admitted that women's demand to be granted equal rights was a just demand.

The opinions voiced by Marx's contemporary, Proudhon, are altogether different. Proudhon is renowned for being the father of anarchism, for being the author of ideas which presumably were much more 'democratic' than those of the 'authoritarian' socialist Karl Marx. His followers have projected Proudhon as a 'libertarian' who refused to compromise on the demand for absolute human equality. Yet Proudhon's views on women stand out as thoroughly male chauvinistic, as illustrated by his words quoted at the beginning of this chapter. It is Proudhon who, in spite of his egalitarian credentials, advocated the complete subjugation of women. In this chapter I will review the patriarchal prejudices held by 19th-century working class theoreticians, foremost among them Proudhon.

Pierre-Joseph Proudhon as an Early Advocate of the Emancipation of the Male Working Class

Who was Pierre-Joseph Proudhon, and how much influence did he wield in the working class movement of his time? First, Proudhon is considered to be the founding father of anarchism as a distinct trend in the workers' movement. In an authoritative historical account of anarchism written by George Woodcock, he is described as the man who, through his intellectual labour, prepared the grounds for this stream of socialism.

> The breadth of his thought, the vigour of his writing, and the penetrative influence he wielded out of his solitude combine to make Proudhon one of the great nineteenth century Europeans whose importance has rarely been fully appreciated in English-speaking countries. In sheer greatness of texture only Tolstoy among the anarchists exceeds him.[5]

Born from peasant stock—his father reportedly became a small craftsman, his mother a cook—Proudhon gathered all his knowledge through independent effort, through self-study. But though he was a self-educated man, he was remarkably successful in developing his writing skills. In the course of his political carreer, he drafted a substantial number of theoretical books, of which the best known is the fore-mentioned *Qu'est-ce que la Propriété?*. In this book he decried property as 'the last of the false gods' and posed the rebellious slogan 'property is theft!'. Proudhon's ideas on decentralism were developed, amongst others, in *Du Principe Fédératif* and in *De la Capacité Politique des Classes Ouvrières en France*.[6] *Système des Contradictions Economiques ou Philosophie de la Misère* is better remembered for the book by Marx, *The Poverty of Philosophy*, in which it was critically reviewed.

Proudhon's political 'baptism' took place in 1848, when discontented workers raised barricades in the streets of the French capital, Paris. He was quick to realize the historic significance of the event—the fact that it constituted the first, distinct uprising of the modern working class—and he openly took the side of the insurrectionaries. In columns of the first newspaper he launched (*Le Représentant du Peuple*), Proudhon expressed his sympathy with the victims of the firing squads, used by the French government to quell the uprising. He also used his position as member of the National Assembly to voice his sympathies for the proletariat. Through the founding of a 'People's Bank' he made a shortlived effort to foster the direct exchange of products among workers. When he challenged the new president-dictator, Louis Bonaparte, in writing, charges of sedition were brought against him, and he was sentenced to three years' imprisonment.[7]

In the 1850s and the first half of the 1860s, Proudhon endeavoured to develop a theory of workers' self-government, based partly on the embryonic experience of workers' councils of 1848. Consequently, his ideas played a prominent role in the insurrection of March 1871, the 'Paris Commune'. When the first experiment was launched to construct a society ruled by industrial workers themselves, followers of Proudhon formed one of the main, if not the majority section, of the insurgent workers. There were those who championed the French philosopher's guidelines on workers' self-government, the so-called 'mutualists'. Another group, the 'collectivists', of which an important section belonged to the First International, also claimed to follow Proudhon's ideas. One contemporary writer who sympathizes with the 'father' of anarchism, argues that the policies of the commune, such as those on its political structure and on the organization of labour, were derived from Proudhon's theory.[8]

Yet while Proudhon did have a decisive influence on the consciousness of French industrial workers in the second half of the 19th century, he was not the only early advocate of workers' freedom from exploitation. Here I wish to draw attention to the initiatives and ideas developed by two French women, Flora Tristan and Jeanne Deroin. Both women, to an extent, were inspired by the 'utopian socialists', whose attitude to women, as stated earlier was radically different from Proudhon's. Although Tristan and Deroin have not left us with an equally impressive volume of writings, their role is noteworthy. It shows that feminist women from very early onwards have concerned themselves with the emancipation of the modern, industrial working class.

Flora Tristan (1803–44) actively supported the self-organization of industrial workers in 1843–44, (before the 1848 Paris uprising which saw Proudhon's rise to prominence). After visiting Peru to claim her share in her family's wealth, and after years of struggle to free herself from her oppressive husband, Flora Tristan made a first-hand investigation into the living conditions in London prisons, factories and slums. Now 'irrevocably committed to the cause of working class emancipation'[9] Tristan drafted a book entitled *Union Ouvrière*, in which she called upon France's 7 million workers—women as well as men—'to proclaim their identity as one separate and distinctive social class', by forming themselves into a single union. The book contained detailed suggestions for the structure of the workers' union, the collection of funds, the election of a central committee, and so on. In a separate chapter she argued that (male) workers should sympathize with the plight of, and should demand equal rights for, women. Subsequently, Tristan undertook a tour of 17 French manufacturing towns to promote her ideas on workers' unity. Although she is believed to have been up against workers' apathy and against male intellectuals who resented her presence, in at least four towns, branches of the workers' organization are said to have been formed. In the course of her tour, however, her health deteriorated, and she soon died from typhoid fever.[10]

Jeanne Deroin's ideas were developed about a decade later, and in direct defiance of Proudhon's. Being self-taught like Proudhon, Deroin argued in opposition to him that the freedom of women did not lie in their motherhood, but in women's right to remunerative work outside the home. While Proudhon thought women had only two possible vocations—housewife or courtesan—Deroin defended a woman's right to engage in industrial work: 'You wish to remove her from the workshop, but we should rather change the workshop, that source of activity and independence.'[11] Deroin reportedly became the first proponent in France of a broad federation of workers' associations. An elaborate plan for such a federation was published in the paper she edited, named the *L'Opinion des Femmes*. According to the French sociologist Evelyn Sullerot, Deroin succeeded in unifying 104 associations of male and female workers. While conducting a workers' meeting in her own home, she was arrested by the police, detained in prison and charged with 'conspiracy'. In the files of the French police she was credited with a 'fateful organizational talent'.[12] In short, not only did feminist women polemize against Proudhon's male chauvinist views, they also exerted a distinct influence on the process of trade union organization in France in the middle of the 19th century.

Proudhon's political philosophy may be summarized against the background of his life and influence. There is, within the context of this study, no scope to describe the entire gamut of his political and economic propositions on working class emancipation. Two central concepts which Proudhon developed should be briefly reviewed though, because they had a constitutive influence on the international anarchist movement, and also affected the debates in the International Working Men's Association (i.e., the First International which was founded in London shortly before Proudhon's death in 1865). These are the concept of workers' self-government, (i.e., the economic organization of a new society) and the concept of federalism, which refers to the political structure advocated by Proudhon for a future, socialist society.

The concept of workers' self-government was suggested in opposition to the idea that the economy should be run by workers' associations under the leadership of, and financed by, the state. The latter was the proposition of a countryman of Proudhon's, Louis Blanc, and it formed the precursor of state socialism. According to Proudhon, enterprises should be controlled by the 'associated producers' (i.e., by industrial workers themselves via councils of elected representatives). Each worker should perform some of the unattractive and heavy tasks, and each should be capable of, and perform, a variety of production tasks. While Proudhon realized that the associated workers did not avail of all specialized knowledge, he reportedly argued that they should themselves appoint their engineers and administrators to receive training. As for the juridical form of ownership in a new, non-exploitative society, Proudhon's views appear to have undergone an evolution in the course of his career. He initially believed that the workers' associations should be the direct owners of the means of production, but he subsequently distinguished between ownership and usufruct. While juridical ownership was to reside in large, agricultural and industrial federations, the associated producers should be granted the status of hereditary tenants, with usufructury right to the means of production.[13]

The concept of federalism was elaborated in the later part of Proudhon's life. It was designed as an alternative to political nationalism and the modern nation-state. Local communities, Proudhon argued, cannot renounce their natural right to sovereignty, but should organize their whole life collectively. Thus, people should locally form 'natural groups', which again are to form larger, political units from below through a process of voluntary association and the building of contractual relations. Foreshadowing the principle that would guide the functioning of the Paris Commune in 1871, Proudhon argued that the coordinating bodies of the local communities should be composed of delegates who are immediately revocable. In this manner, the nation-state would be replaced by a geographical confederation of regions, and Europe would become a confederation of confederations, in which the interest of the smallest province would find as much expression as that of the largest, and in which all affairs would be settled by mutual agreement, contract and arbitration.[14] Proudhon's ideas on both workers' self-government and federalism, in the last part of the 19th century, were propagated and further elaborated by the exiled Russian revolutionary, Michael Bakunin.[15]

Proudhon as an Advocate of Slavery for Women

Let us now consider Proudhon's views on women in some more detail. I have already mentioned how the French feminist Jenny d'Héricourt polemized against Proudhon's male chauvinism. However, Jenny d'Héricourt was not the only French feminist who felt compelled to crusade against his views. Another woman author, Juliette Lamber, for instance, published a booklet in 1861 entitled 'Anti-Proudhonist Ideas', which gained considerable popularity and which saw many re-editions.[16] Thus, Proudhon was a common target of French women who fought for gender equality in the 19th century.

The history of the polemics between Proudhon and his female opponents brings out further, that Proudhon at no time in his life wavered in his anti-feminism. Thus, in 1858, Proudhon published a book entitled *De la Justice dans la Révolution et dans l'Eglise* which has been termed 'his most massive and greatest work'.[17] This book, and more specifically the chapters dealing with the social position of women, triggered a flow of angry reactions from women like d'Héricourt and Lamber. Consequently, Proudhon felt the need to defend his stance. He did so in a book bearing the provocative title *La Pornocracie or les Femmes dans les Temps Modernes*. Although it appeared only after his death, the pre-history of this book shows that the ideas he expressed in it cannot be written off as deplorable, but the excusable product of a senile brain.

First, Proudhon gave the following definition of his term 'pornocracy':

> One can term the pornocracy the second world power of these days; in importance it immediately follows the power of money. It is a secret power, which has manifested itself since long and which is operated by women. It has made itself felt in writings and pamphlets for over the last thirty years.[18]

Women like Jenny d'Héricourt, Proudhon argued, who advocate freedom for women, exert a pernicious influence. Through duplicity and subtle corruption, they create decadence. Women who question the system of the monogamous marriage are a danger to established ethics, and they are as condemnable as prostitutes and harem women.[19] Using insinuative language, Proudhon voiced violent opposition to any extra- or non-marital sexual relations, and he saw it as women's duty to uphold the morals of the modern, bourgeois marriage.

Furthermore, the status of men and women in marriage, Proudhon felt, should not be equal. On the contrary, the husband holds proprietary rights over his legal wife, and he can disown her whenever he sees fit. 'The man should be free to reject his wife *ad libitum*', Proudhon states in *La Pornocracie*, 'for it would be abhorrent to expect that he live with her any day longer than he desires'.[20] Thus, the monogamous marriage is not an institution that places equal obligations on men and women. For Proudhon, the marriage is a legal institution which establishes a man's authority over his wife, in conformity with woman's 'natural subordination': 'the man should be able to freely avail of his wife, but not the wife over him'.[21] Whereas other advocates of the modern monogamous marriage have denied that it is oppressive to women, Proudhon approvingly confirmed that, indeed, the function of the marriage is to regulate women's status as slaves.

Proudhon formulated his views in unequivocal terms. Just as the master has the right to decide over his slaves' life and death in the system of slavery, men should rule over women in the system of marriage, Proudhon unhesitatingly argues. In *La Pornocracie*, he lists six forms of 'misbehaviour' by women which entitle a husband to kill his wife. Amongst the reasons mentioned, some refer to a woman's violation of the morality of the monogamous marriage, such as 'lack of chastity' and 'betrayal'. But being precise about a man's status as the master, he includes 'stubborn insubordination' amongst the crimes justifying murder.[22] In short, Proudhon both admits that the monogamous marriage entails enslavement of women, and further gives a very literal interpretation of men's power as the slave masters in marriage.

A logical next step in analyzing Proudhon's viewpoint is to examine his reasons for propagating the idea that women be kept as slaves. In the chapter on ecofeminism, I will discuss the social prejudices which have accompanied the scientific endeavours of modern, Western intellectuals since the 17th century. As the German feminist author Maria Mies has argued, in the course of the 19th century, sexist and racist ideology acquired a 'materialistic "scientific" foundation'.[23]

When reading Proudhon's *La Pornocracie*, one is, at first glance, surprised at the blatantly unscientific manner in which he defends his anti-feminist views. At one point he argues that women are inferior because, contrary to men, they remain close to animal life. Thus, the female gender is weaker because 'in her freedom and intelligence struggle with less force against the tendency towards bestiality' (*l'animalité*).[24] Elsewhere in the book, he gives a mathematical calculation of women's intellectual inferiority:

> With the best of my knowledge, I have been able to determine the truth of the following proposition: if the man, as expression of power (*puissance*), in proportion to women represents a value of 27 to 8—then the woman, as expression of the idealistic (*l'idéal*), is worth no more than 8 in comparison with a figure of 27 for the man.[25]

Yet, though his views were unscientific, Proudhon did not stand alone. He was not the only prominent 19th-century intellectual who used mathematical calculations to legitimize social inequality. The same was done, for instance, by Francis Galton, a cousin of Darwin. As an advocate of 'selective breeding', Galton became the father of eugenic science (the science which was constructed to prevent the deterioration of the race). As Maria Mies reminds us, Galton introduced the grading system to measure people's genetic quality. 'By applying mathematical methods to eugenics he gave 'scientific' legitimacy to his theories, because mathematical procedures and statistics were considered proof of scientific objectivity.'[26] Thus, Proudhon's method was in tune with a broader trend that existed amongst 19th-century European intellectuals.

Moreover, scientists not only made strenuous efforts to prove the inferiority of the non-white races, they also conducted anatomical research specifically to prove that gender inequality was biologically determined. As the ecofeminist author Carolyn Merchant has pointed out:

> Scientists compared male and female cranial sizes and brain parts in the effort to demonstrate the existence of sexual differences that

> would explain female intellectual inferiority and emotional temperament. Women's reproductive function required that more energy be directed towards pregnancy and maternity, hence less was available for the higher functions associated with learning and reason.[27]

In short, it appears that Proudhon, in asserting women's intellectual inferiority, echoed contemporary endeavours of European scientists intended to 'prove' the need for women's imprisonment in the home.

Further, the view that endured most of Proudhon's ideas on women was his opposition against women's employment outside the home. Proudhon's advocacy of women's subordination to their husbands in marriage was accompanied by an equally strong advocacy of women's exclusive responsibility for domestic work. He opposed any factory work by women, and instead urged women to devote themselves entirely to household tasks. As a safeguard against any potential inconvenience for males, he advised that a man should never marry a woman who is an artist or who engaged in literary activities. This type of woman, he argued, cannot be a proper mother and housewife, since she participates in public life and is economically independent. 'A woman can no longer give birth to children, if her mind, imagination and heart are busily concerned with things like politics, the society and literature.'[28]

In propagating the ideology of the 'housewife', Proudhon voiced within the workers' movement ideas warmly cherished by the class of capitalist entrepreneurs. They indeed favoured relegating their own wives to the home, and were also eager to play off the male against the female section of the proletariat by constructing the ideology of the male 'breadwinner' and the female 'housewife'. As scholars like the German feminist Bennholdt-Thomsen have argued, the housewife emerged in the 'First World' during the 19th century, as the product of a particular history, created by the Church, through such means as legislation or organization of the workforce. For instance, the institution of the monogamous, nuclear family was put forward as a model for working class couples by a law introduced in northern Germany in 1868.[29]

While European states, representing entrepreneurial interests, through legislation and the police force imposed the housewife ideal upon the working class from the outside, the anarchist philosopher Proudhon promoted the same ideal from within. In the First International, followers of Proudhon, along with followers of the German leader, Lassalle, propagated the complete exclusion of women from factory employment, arguing that competition for jobs could not be tolerated. At the General Council of the International held in 1866, French delegates pressed the meeting into accepting the proposition that women's natural place is in the home. Again, at the meeting held in the subsequent year, it was reportedly argued, under Proudhon's influence, that waged work by women should be prohibited: 'in the name of the freedom of the mother, let us withdraw the woman ... from the workshop which demoralises her (i.e., makes her immoral) and kills her'.[30] In short, Proudhon's objective function was to introduce within the workers' movement the ideal of the housewife as nurtured by the bourgeoisie.

Marx's Evaluation of Proudhon's Ideas: 'The Philosophy of Poverty'

Having elaborated Proudhon's social significance, we may now turn to Marx's evaluation of Proudhon's intellectual contribution. How thorough was his critique of the anarchist philosopher? Marx's attitude towards his French colleague underwent, it may be recalled, a sharp evolution. In one of his early writings, *The Holy Family* (written with Frederick Engels), Marx praised Proudhon for his penetrating insights into the subject of property. The anarchist philosopher is presented as a true champion of the working man: 'not only does Proudhon write in the interests of the proletarians, he himself is a proletarian, *un ouvrier*. His work is a scientific manifesto of the French proletariat'.[31] Thus, Marx hailed Proudhon both for his social background (the man was a printer by profession) and for his class stand. Proudhon does not write 'in the interest of self-sufficient criticism', said Marx, but 'in the interests of the proletarians'.[32]

From the publication of the polemical book *The Poverty of Philosophy* onwards, however, Marx clearly distanced himself from his former friend. This book was published in July, 1847, shortly before the uprising in Paris in which Proudhon took the workers' side. Whereas earlier, Marx had hoped that the two men would be allies in the struggle for the liberation of humanity, he changed his mind after reading Proudhon's book *The Philosophy of Poverty*. In the judgement written on the occasion of Proudhon's death, the latter is called a 'living contradiction'. Proudhon, Marx stated, 'wants to soar as the man of science above the bourgeoisie and the proletarians; he is nothing but the petty-bourgeoisie perpetually tossed about between capital and labour, between political economy and communism'. One of Marx's main criticisms was that Proudhon—like the German philosopher, Hegel—presented history as a succession of ideas; that he was not a materialist, but an idealist philosopher.[33]

It is striking, however, that Proudhon's advocacy of the strictest sexual division of labour between women and men—though it had already been tabled when Marx polemized so energetically against his 'petty-bourgeois' opponent—never formed a point in Marx's critique. Like the historian of anarchist movements and ideas, George Woodcock, long after him, Marx saw Proudhon as a transitional figure, whose philosophy was partly shaped by the pre-industrial past.[34] Yet he never distanced himself specifically from Proudhon's ideas on women, nor did he expose the Frenchman as a representative of male chauvinism within the working class movement. Thus, in spite of the severity of Marx's polemical language, he does not appear to have realized that in terms of his views on women's status, Proudhon represented dominant, entrepreneurial interests. I will illustrate the limits of Marx's critique through a review of both Proudhon's *Philosophy of Poverty*, and Marx's counter-publication.

In his polemically written, sharp-edged book, *The Poverty of Philosophy*, Marx aimed both at refuting Proudhon's ideas, and at clarifying his own standpoint with regard to 'political economy' (i.e., in relation to the classical economic theorists, Adam Smith and David Ricardo). Marx covered some of the themes which Proudhon had brought up, such as the theory of value, competition, and the division of labour. A re-reading and comparison of *The Philosophy of Poverty* and *The Poverty of Philosophy* shows that Marx's critique of the anarchist philosopher was not exaggerated by any means: indeed, in his own writing, Proudhon demonstrated his incapacity to grasp the basic contradictions of capitalist society. And given the man's influence within the workers' movement of the 19th century, a refutation of his views was far from being a luxury.

First, wholly in agreement with capitalist ideology, Proudhon defends the need for competition. He argues that competition is, for 'individual forces', the true 'guarantee of their liberty'. Proudhon connects the logic of competition with the inevitable development of the division of labour under capitalism: 'Competition is as essential to labour as division, since it is division itself returning in another form, or rather raised to its second power'.[35] He argues that the division of labour gives birth to liberty and human sovereignty, and that this proves the need for competition: 'Competition, in a word, is liberty in division and in all the divided parts'.[36] In his first equation, then, Proudhon fails to distinguish between the work and production processes which change under capitalism, and the specific 'law' of accumulation, by which the owners of capital are guided, and which leads to murderous competition among them.

Further, in his praise of competition, Proudhon follows the defendants of the capitalist system by claiming that market competition and political democracy are naturally interconnected. In a confusing statement, he suggests that the competition between entrepreneurs and the collective work processes of the industrial workers are identical. Competition is 'the mode by which collective activity manifests and exercises itself, the expression of social spontaneity, the emblem of democracy and equality, the most energetic instrument for the constitution of value, the support of association'.[37] The ideologues of capitalist relations defend the sanctity and permanency of these relations by decreeing that they confirm with a human nature which is presumedly fixed. Similarly, Proudhon proclaims that competition is 'a necessity of the human soul'! In short, Proudhon does not distinguish between competition as the motor of the accumulation process, of capital's growth, and the concrete impact of the operation of this 'law' on the life of the wage labourers.

Moreover, he openly voices very conventional status quo ideas. This is particularly evident when he decries workers' strikes that are staged to obtain wage increments. For Proudhon, wage is a reflection of the true value of products, it is 'the integrant price of all things'.[38] He fails to see that a part of the value created by the labourers is withheld by the entrepreneurs. Consequently, he ends up fighting a losing battle against the tendency of the working class to seek an improvement in its living conditions by using the strike as a weapon.

> In spite of my desire for the amelioration of the lot of the working class, I declare that it is impossible for strikes followed by an increase of wages to end otherwise than in a general rise in prices. That is as certain as that two and two make four. It is not by such methods that the working men will attain to wealth and—what is a thousand times more precious than wealth—liberty.[39]

If the foregoing forms an indictment of Proudhon as an economic thinker, a re-reading of *The Philosophy of Poverty* shows that his credentials as a philosopher are equally weak. For this book of his proves that his understanding of the central law of dialectics (i.e., the 'unity of opposites') was defective. In *The Philosophy of Poverty*, Proudhon discusses, among other things, the relation between use value, which he also terms 'intrinsic value', and exchange value. 'In what consists the correlation between use value and value in exchange?'[40] The author believes that he has exceeded the classical political economists in his understanding of the relationship between the two forms of value. 'The economists have clearly shown the double character of value, but what they have not made equally plain is its contradictory nature.' Proudhon proceeds to argue that the two forms of value are closely interconnected. 'Utility is the necessary condition of exchange, but take away exchange, and utility vanishes.' Since the two are indissolubly interconnected, he concludes without further discussion or debate, 'Where then is the contradiction?'[41]

From this it is obvious that for Proudhon two things are either indissolubly connected or they form two opposites (i.e., stand in contradiction to each other). Such an idea is at variance with the very law of dialectics as formulated by Marx and Engels, following their philosophical precursor Hegel. The law of the unity of opposites states that nature, society and human thought—the whole universe—consist of poles of opposites which, at one and the same time, are interconnected and engaged in mutual struggle. No activity or development is possible without the existence of two contradictory and interconnected parts, and to present reality otherwise, as Proudhon does, goes counter to the very kernel of dialectical thought.[42]

To underline the point, let us take the relationship between the individual and the universal. Should this relationship be understood as one of contradiction or unity? At first, the universal and the individual may seem like disconnected opposites, but in reality there is also identity or unity between the two. 'The individual only exists in the connection that leads to the universal. The universal exists only in the individual and through the individual', Lenin wrote in his short essay on dialectics.[43] To presume that there cannot be, simultaneously, both unity and contradiction between the individual and the universal would be a denial of reality, of 'objective truth'. Similarly to say that there can be no contradiction between use value and exchange value, as Proudhon does, because the two are indissolubly connected, is an erroneous presentation of reality.

Marx's Limited Critique of Proudhon: The Labour Theory of Value

I shall now discuss some of the criticisms of Proudhon made by Marx in his book *The Poverty of Philosophy*. In the section entitled 'Constituted Value or Synthetic Value', Marx criticized Proudhon's theory of value. The labour theory of value is considered to be the cornerstone of Marx's economic theory. Through a critical review of the ideas put forward by the most prominent 'bourgeois' thinkers in the field of economic theory, foremost among them Adam Smith and David Ricardo, Marx concluded that labour time is the true determinant of the value of commodities which are sold on the market. On the basis of this fundamental understanding, Marx laid bare the structure of exploitation under capitalism and provided industrial workers with a theoretical instrument to understand their own conditions of deprivation.

In challenging Proudhon's credentials as an economic theorist, Marx first derided his claim to have discovered 'constituted value' as the cornerstone of economic contradictions. By this term, Proudhon meant that the value of products which are sold on the market consists of a 'synthesis' of use value and exchange value. Proudhon claimed that, thanks to his own conceptualization, he had risen beyond the intuitive level of understanding of Adam Smith, the father of classical political economy. But according to Marx, Proudhon's claim of far-sightedness was false. David Ricardo had already shown a grasp of reality superior to Adam Smith's, when he had formulated his theory of labour value in the year 1817.[44]

Like other economists, Ricardo distinguished between 'utility' and 'exchangeable value'. Although there are some commodities (such as rare statues and pictures) whose value is determined by their scarcity, 'by far the greatest part of those goods which are the object of desire are procured by labour'. According to Ricardo,

> In speaking then of commodities, of their exchangeable value, and of the laws which regulate their relative prices, we mean always

> such commodities only as can be increased in quantity by the exertion of human industry, and on the production of which competition operates without restraint.[45]

Further, Ricardo devised a more precise standard for the measurement of commodities than Adam Smith had done. Smith had wavered. At times he had admitted that the quantity of labour was the only correct measuring tool, but at other times he followed a different direction of thought. Ricardo, on the contrary, devised an internally consistent theory of value. He fully realized that the quantity of labour embodied in commodities determines their value, and he unequivocally stated that the quantity of labour should be measured by labour time. Thus, Marx approvingly quotes Ricardo's statement that labour time 'is really the foundation of the exchangeable value of all things' and that this doctrine is 'of the utmost importance in political economy'.[46]

A second issue which Marx sought to clear up in criticizing Proudhon is that regarding wages. He argues that Proudhon outdid Adam Smith in confounding the value of commodities with the workers' wages. According to Proudhon, 'a certain quantity of labour embodied in a product is equivalent to the workers' payment, that is to the value of labour'.[47] Yet this interpretation, according to Marx, is contrary to economic facts, and it moreover serves to hide the nature of exploitation under capitalism. Here again, Ricardo was more clear-headed, for he had argued that the value of commodities produced for market sale should be distinguished from the amount workers receive for their labouring activities.

When defining the price of labour, the workers' wages, Marx thus supported Ricardo's view. Although he was later to introduce the concept of 'labour power' in order to be able to distinguish between the workers' use of their muscular power in action, and the buying of their labouring strength by entrepreneurs, he did not fundamentally diverge from Ricardo in measuring the payment for the workers' labouring strength. As Marx was to state more elaborately in *Capital*, the correct measure for the value of labour power is the time needed 'to produce the objects indispensable for the constant maintenance of labour'[48]. As will be explained extensively in Chapter 4, Marx here referred to the value of daily necessities which the workers buy on the market.

This conceptualization, to reiterate was close to that of Marx's precursor David Ricardo, for the latter had stated that 'the natural price of labour' depends on 'the price of the food, necessaries, and conveniences required for the support of the labourer and his family'.[49] Both Ricardo and Marx looked at the workers' basic consumption requirements, that is both ignored the domestic labour which women need to perform in the home—child care, cleaning, cooking, etc.—in order to maintain the workers' labouring capacity before and after they perform waged work in factories. Evidently, Marx, the revolutionary opponent of capitalist exploitation, in this respect inherited the patriarchal bias of the classical political economists.

In other words, Marx only partially superseded Proudhon's theory of value. While there is, as indicated earlier, a qualitative difference between the economic theory propounded by Proudhon and that propounded by Marx, when it comes to analyzing household labour both were prejudiced in their own ways. Proudhon advocated the seclusion of women in the home. He wanted to burden women with all domestic chores. Marx did not propagate such ideas; he agreed that women's involvement in wage labour should be defended. Nevertheless, in his theory of labour value which, like Ricardo's, was based on labour time, Marx did not take stock of domestic labour time, of the long hours that women toil for the family in the home. As I have shown in Chapter 4, this patriarchal bias in his economic theory was to be targeted by participants in the household labour debate of the second feminist wave.

A third point on which Marx severely criticizes Proudhon is his conception of the division of labour. Chiding the classical economists for having emphasized, presumably, the advantages of the division of labour, Proudhon endeavoured to draw a balance-sheet of all the 'good and bad sides' of the division of labour. In the process of doing so, Proudhon presumed that the division of labour—like competition—had the character of an eternal law, that it was a 'simple, abstract category'. This ahistorical approach is exposed by Marx. Using concrete facts and data, Marx sets out to prove that the division of labour is a product of eminently historical developments, and not, as Proudhon thought, a separation which 'dates from the beginning of the world'.[50]

To clarify his own point of view, Marx discusses the transition from the stage of manufacturing to that of the 'automatic workshop' when modern machinery was installed. Whereas Dutch manufacturers at the end of the 16th and in the beginning of the 17th century, for instance, 'scarcely knew any division of labour', the division of tasks was greatly extended from the beginning of the industrial revolution.[51] 'Thanks to the machine, the spinner can live in England, while the weaver resides in the East Indies.' And further, 'Thanks to the application of machinery and of steam, the division of labour was able to assume such dimensions that large-scale industry, detached from the national soil, depends entirely on the world market, on international exchange, on the international division of labour.'[52]

Thus, to Proudhon's belief in an eternal division of labour, Marx counterposed his own view on the historical evolution of the division of labour. Yet here again, as in his critique of Proudhon's theory of value, his critique has weaknesses which would ultimately surface. For how was one to correctly project the historical evolution of the division of labour? In *The Poverty of Philosophy*, the first great social division of labour is identified as having been the contradiction between towns and villages, between urban and rural areas. Thus Marx states that 'it took three whole centuries in Germany to establish the first big division of labour, the separation of towns from the country. In proportion, as this relation of town and country was modified, the whole of society was modified.'[53]

This view by Marx has been subjected to a double critique by feminist authors. The first division of labour in the long social evolution of humanity was not that between urban and rural areas, but between women and men. Long before the first urban centres arose, a certain division was developed in prehistoric foraging bands. For instance, tasks relating to the gathering of vegetables and roots from the forests were mainly entrusted to women, whereas men were in charge of hunting animals with bows and spears. Various female anthropologists in recent decades have stressed the important economic role of women in prehistoric societies, since through their food-gathering activities, they provided their kin groups with the bulk of their food.[54]

In his own discussion regarding the history of the division of labour in *The Poverty of Philosophy* and elsewhere, Marx ignored the gender division of labour because he thought it was 'natural' and 'fixed'. Yet in fact, as women anthropologists have pointed out, the gender division of labour initially was rather flexible. Among tribal communities which follow a prehistoric mode of living, for instance, women do play a role in collective hunting along with men. Thus, Eleanor Leacock has found that women among the Montagnais–Naskapi in Canada occasionally went for short hunting trips, or went on long hunts if they chose to do so.[55] In other words, though a certain gender division of tasks did emerge, it was an informal one, and it was far from fixed.

The theme of the sexual division of labour, its origin and informal character in foraging societies, is strikingly ignored by both the classical political economists and by their radical critics, including Marx. Like his precursors Smith and Ricardo, Marx on the whole failed to elucidate how the gender division of labour evolved historically, and how in his time capitalists made use of it in order to enhance their profits. Most currents of feminism in consequence do question the sufficiency and the comprehensiveness of his analysis regarding the contradiction between capital and labour. Unless a precise understanding is developed regarding the emergence of the sexual division of labour in prehistory, and unless the specific role of the sexual division of labour under capitalism is analyzed, the critique of Proudhon's undialectical theory remains incomplete indeed.

Summary: The Unity and Struggle between Marx and Proudhon

The growth of industrial workers' struggles in 19th-century Europe was accompanied by an intense intellectual debate in which both women and men took part. In France, in particular, there were several courageous women (such as Flora Tristan and Jeanne Deroin) who in word and deed tried to defend the interests of male and female factory workers. Yet, on the whole, the progressive intellectual debate was heavily dominated by male philosophers. Amongst the most prominent working class theoreticians were the Frenchman Pierre-Joseph Proudhon, the father of international anarchism, and Karl Marx, who debunked Proudhon's theory of value in his book *The Philosophy of Poverty*.

There is no doubt that a vast difference separates these two philosophers, both influential in their day. Marx, handling the method of dialectics developed by the philosopher Hegel, succeeded in analyzing many of the essential features of capitalist society, and in revealing (part of) the secret of the exploitation by industrial entrepreneurs. He inherited and further elaborated the thesis of the so-called political economists, that labour is the source of all wealth, of all value. Marx's key thesis, like that of David Ricardo, states that the value of commodities sold on the market should be measured by looking at the amount of time that waged workers spend on producing them. The theoretical sharpness displayed by Marx was lacking in Proudhon. Although Proudhon proposed political concepts like 'workers' self-government' and 'federalism' which have guided subsequent generations of anarchists, his understanding of economic relations lagged behind even that of David Ricardo. Unlike Ricardo, Proudhon did not identify labour time as the measure of the value of commodities.

Yet, having explained these vast differences and contrasts between Marx and Proudhon, we nonetheless note a certain identity and unity between the two philosophers, for a patriarchal bias is present in the writings of both. While Proudhon openly advocated the strictest division of labour between women and men, and the total subjugation of the female sex, Marx believed that women's emancipation is the measurement of a society's progress. Yet a closer look at his economic theory shows that Marx did not give recognition to the labour performed by women as housewives, and that he basically looked upon the sexual division of labour as 'naturally' given. A full understanding of women's labouring activities, therefore, can only be obtained by addressing the patriarchal bias that was shared by both male theoreticians.

Notes and References

1. Woodcock (1979), p. 105.
2. d'Héricourt (1856), p. 5.
3. Ibid., p. 9.
4. Ibid., p. 14.
5. Woodcock (1979), p. 100.
6. Ibid., pp. 130–32.
7. Ibid., pp. 117–20.
8. Langlois (1976), p. 26.
9. Jean Hawkes' introduction to Tristan (1986), p. xxiii.
10. Ibid., pp. xxiii–vii.
11. Sullerot (1979), p. 108.
12. Ibid., p. 111.
13. Guérin (1970), p. 43.
14. Guérin (1970), p. 63; Woodcock (1979), pp. 130–32.
15. Guérin (1970).
16. Albistur and Armogathe (1977), p. 318.

17. Woodcock (1979), p. 129.
18. Proudhon (1970), p. 13;
19. Ibid., p. 43.
20. Ibid., p. 16.
21. Ibid.
22. Ibid.
23. Mies and Shiva (1993), p. 180.
24. Proudhon (1875), p. 41.
25. Ibid., p. 35. See also Sullerot (1979), p. 85.
26. Mies and Shiva (1993), p. 181.
27. Merchant (1980), pp. 162–63.
28. See, for instance, Proudhon's comments (1875), p. 85, on women in the arts and in literature. Further, he argues (p. 59) that women's subordination to men is not at all arbitrary, but based on men's virility.
29. Bennholdt-Thomsen (1988b), p. 159; Mies (1986b), pp. 105–6.
30. Sullerot (1979), p. 105; Thönnessen (1976), p. 22.
31. Easton and Guddat (1967), p. 361. See also Lenin's conspectus of *The Holy Family*, in Lenin (1973), p. 23.
32. Ibid.
33. Karl Marx's letter to J. B. Schweitzer, 24 January 1865, in Marx and Engels (1973), p. 24.
34. Woodcock (1979), p. 133.
35. Proudhon (1888), p. 223.
36. Ibid.
37. Ibid., p. 270.
38. Ibid., p. 149.
39. Ibid.
40. Ibid., p. 73.
41. Ibid., p. 77.
42. Lenin (1973), p. 357.
43. Ibid., p. 359.
44. Marx (1975), p. 43.
45. Ibid., p. 45.
46. Ibid.
47. Ibid., p. 53.
48. Ibid., p. 49.
49. Ricardo (1817), pp. 90–91.
50. Marx (1975), p. 124.
51. Ibid., pp. 127–28.
52. Ibid., p. 129.
53. Ibid., p. 119.
54. See, for instance, Draper (1975), p. 77 and Slocum (1975), p. 36.
55. Leacock (1981), pp. 40, 149. See also Kelkar and Nathan (1991), p. 2.

3

The Proletarian Women's Movement in Germany and Women's Labour

'It is time to revive the memories of our past struggle, a struggle which today can be a rich source of moral reinforcement and political instruction'. 'The history of socialism is the school of life. We always derive new stimulus from it'. 'Historical experience is [the modern proletariat's] only teacher; its *Via Dolorosa* to self-liberation is covered not only with immeasurable suffering, but with countless mistakes'.[1] These quotations from the Polish revolutionary Rosa Luxemburg, who built her political carreer in Germany, are a befitting opening statement for this chapter on the mass movement of working class women in Germany in the last two decades of the 19th and the first decade of the 20th century.

The German movement was, perhaps, the richest and most significant women's movement to emerge in any European country during the first feminist wave. Whereas in England, for instance, women fought pitched battles around the demand for equal voting rights, and whereas in this famous movement of suffragettes female factory workers played an active part[2], it was in Germany that a specific movement of working-class women emerged, which was rather well structured and involved literally hundreds of thousands of persons. In this movement, agitation was not limited to the demand for women's right to vote in elections, as a whole range of other demands (economic and political) were also taken up. Moreover, the instruments of action used, too, were varied. They included the factory workers' favoured weapon, the strike, as well as consumers' boycotts and actions (referred to as 'political boycotts').

Further, and contrary to what is often assumed due to the lack of historical knowledge, a lively debate on women's labour was carried on alongside the proletarian women's movement. Well over a century ago, German activists belonging to both the 'bourgeois' and the 'proletarian' wing of the women's movement started investigating and debating the conditions of exploitation of women labourers. The debate on household labour, it is true, was not carried to such great theoretical lengths as during the second feminist wave. Yet other aspects (which are crucial to our understanding of women's degradation under capitalism) were raised or fiercely debated, such as the fact that women often were the actual breadwinners of their families; the history and nature of the sexual division of labour and the inequality in wages between women and men; and the exploitation of unmarried, young women and married women as part of the so-called 'reserve army of labour' (which I have detailed in Chapter 12). Many of the analytical points made at the time retain their validity today.

This chapter endeavours to assess both the strengths and weaknesses of the earlier debate on women's labour in Germany. It brings into focus attempts by leading Marxist spokespersons, such as August Bebel and Clara Zetkin, to construct a genuine theory of women's emancipation. It also exposes some of the inherent weaknesses in the Marxist position which could not be overcome. Yet, to avoid a one-sided emphasis on failures, I will also describe the remarkable organizational achievements of the movement. For there is no doubt that the organizational strength gathered by the German proletarian women's movement has not been equalled by any other women's movement in any Western country, either during the first or the second feminist wave.

Orientation, Organizational Structure and Tactics of the Proletarian Women's Movement

During the first decade of the present century, from 1900 to 1910, Germany saw the rapid expansion of a mass movement of working-class women. The movement's target was very comprehensive, for it encompassed women who toil in three different sectors of women's labour: women employed in large factory compounds; those in sweatshops and in home industries; and women active in the 'sector' of household labour. The forms of struggle, and the varied forms of organization used, allowed the movement to steadily expand its base, and allowed women from all three sectors to join. What were the factors causing such a tremendous outburst of militancy by women in Germany? Here I wish to give a concise summary of 'objective' circumstances as a preliminary to an evaluative discourse.

In the first place, it is appropriate to recall that women (and children!) were 'the first word of the capitalist application of machinery'. Among the protagonists of women's emancipation in the German working-class movement of the time, the view prevailed widely that women had gradually been drawn into wage labour as industrial development had progressed. 'At the start of capitalist development, the male worker finds only male workers ranged against him in the labour market.'[3] This view tended to heighten fears of women displacing male wage labour in factories, but it was at least partly misconceived. Thus, in textiles, the bedrock of industrialization, women were present from the very start. From their early days, yarn-spinning factories engaged a substantial number of adult women. In the Saxonean spinneries, women around the middle of the 19th century formed the majority of those employed.[4]

It is probably true, as August Bebel claimed, that female participation in wage labour grew proportionally towards the end of the last century. In *Die Frau und der Sozialismus*, he stated that between 1895 and 1907 male employment rose by 10.55 per cent, whereas women's employment rose by the much higher figure of 44.44 per cent.[5] Yet this did not form the main impulsion for the emergence of the proletarian women's movement. More important objective factors appear to have been the fact that women were invariably forced to survive on starvation wages, that their working time knew virtually no bounds, and that their conditions of labour were extremely unhealthy. Thus, the number of seamstresses who lost their lives due to tuberculosis was a record high (48.6 per cent), and the same illness also carried to death many washerwomen who were forced to toil in half-dark cellars and back premises, in an overheated atmosphere.[6]

The extraordinary length of women's labouring time—apart from household chores—was noted too. Thus, the voice of the proletarian women's movement, the fortnightly *Die Gleichheit*, reported that the labouring week of ironers and washerwomen around the turn of the century lasted up to 100 hours. This, consequently, became one of the workers' main grievances when they launched a movement. The textile sector too was notorious for its long working week. As August Bebel noted 'in textiles where women constitute over half the labour force, labour time everywhere is longest'.[7] This sector, in 1903, was to see a tenacious struggle for the 10-hour working day, and in this strike female wage labourers played a leading role.[8]

Further, the phenomenon of low wages also aroused indignation. Women's wages were generally far below those of their male colleagues—in the 19th century they often did not exceed 50 per cent of men's. Even where they performed the very same work, women did not receive equal remuneration. In an investigation which was carried out in the city of Mannheim in 1893 and was cited by Bebel, it turned out that more than 99 per cent of female factory workers belonged to the lowest-paid category.[9] In the cigarette branch, the average weekly wage of women in 1911 is stated to have been DM 6 to 8, whereas bare subsistence required minimally DM 9 to 10. In short, inequal pay at starvation levels was a common feature of all female employment in Germany in the early part of this century, and though inequality in pay did not become an issue in the class struggles of the time,[10] the demand for wage increments frequently did.

Women in Germany—as noted by various authors/participants in the movement—formed a crucial section of the industrial reserve army, described by Marx in *Capital*. They were specifically employed to press down the general level of wages, and to facilitate intensified exploitation of the whole working class.[11] A typical example was that of the women homeworkers who stitched shirts, socks and aprons in the city of Berlin—persons who in Marx's parlance would be called the 'stagnant' section of the labour reserve. The wages of the women stitchers, according to August Bebel's sources, were at most half those required for subsistence needs.[12] Along with female labourers in sweatshops, homeworkers were the first to be mobilized by the proletarian women's movement. They appear to have provided the organized movement with its initial social base.

The foundations of the movement were laid in the 1880s, when a section of female wage labourers got organized. This reportedly happened first in Berlin, where there were a large number of women homeworkers. Thus, in 1885 a Women Workers' Association was founded in this city, with mutual aid as a guiding idea. Apparently, the initiative for forming such an association was taken by Gertrude Guillaume-Sack, who was originally an 'outsider', but who 'joined the camp of the Social Democrats'. According to Maria Mies, Guillaume-Sack used the meetings of the women workers' associations held in various cities to spread socialist ideas and attack the militarism of the German bourgeoisie.[13]

The official Marxist emancipation theory, as also the policy designed by Clara Zetkin (who emerged as the main leader of the proletarian women's movement in the 1890s), proclaimed that female workers should join the same trade unions as their male colleagues. After the repeal of the anti-socialist laws when trade unions could start functioning openly, the Social Democratic Party sought to abolish separate platforms of working women. Yet integration proved far from easy, since many male workers were hostile to women who participated in trade union meetings. 'Many were also against any agitation among women and treated the woman question in a frivolous way.'[14] Thus, the leadership of the proletarian women's movement had to adopt a practical attitude. In some cases women workers formed independent unions, in other cases they joined mixed unions.

In the course of the last decade of the 19th century, and the first decade of the 20th century, membership of women workers in trade unions developed by leaps and bounds. According to Karin Bauer, until the middle of the 1890s women were a minority even in unions representing industries where they formed half the workforce, such as the textile and the tobacco sector. In 1896, substantial growth in membership was registered in the wake of a strike by confectionary workers in Berlin, but by the end of the year many of the new union members had left. A second leap occurred a decade later, in 1905–6. This time, the decisive factor reportedly was the enthusiastic implementation of a resolution by the proletarian women's movement's key body, the Women's Conference, to institute Complaint Commissions for female labourers. Overall, the membership of women in trade unions increased from less than 5,000 in 1892 to well over 200,000 on the eve of the First World War.[15]

Yet trade union organizing, though promoted by the proletarian women's movement, was not its main form of organizing. The movement's structure was strongly influenced by the prevailing state repression, and by that fact that even after the repeal of the anti-socialist laws there continued to exist a prohibition on women's participation in politics. The state forced women to be very creative, and also ensured that they were tested in struggle. Thus, leading women from 1889 onwards set their mind on building Agitational Commissions which, in view of the mentioned prohibition, lacked regulations and formal membership. Members were elected in open mass gatherings of women workers. The first Commission was set up in Berlin, at the initiative of the German delegation to the Founding Congress of the Second International. It was subsequently assigned a national coordinating role.

As repression intensified around 1894–95, with meetings frequently being called off at the last minute or disturbed by the police, the Agitational Commissions were quickly replaced by an alternative structure—that of Trusted Individuals (German: *Vertrauenspersonen*). These were activists who were responsible for the coordination of local agitational work and who, like members of the Agitational Commissions previously, were elected at mass gatherings. Needless to say, the Trusted Individuals also operated at a semi-legal level or illegally. Both successive structures functioned as channels for the recruitment of women to trade unions, and both were charged with the task of distributing the journal of the proletarian women's movement, *Die Gleichheit* (Equality).[16]

Three more institutions should be mentioned to explain the proletarian movement's phenomenal growth: Women's Conferences, Educational Associations, and the magazine *Die Gleichheit*. Each was to become the target of attack by the (right wing) leadership of the Social Democratic Party to which the proletarian women's movement was organically linked. The first Women's Conference was held in 1900, when the movement began to flourish, entering its phase of mass resistance on a national scale. The conferences, which took place throughout the first decade, were important not only as platforms where internal, organizational questions were debated and decided upon, and as forums where male chauvinist attitudes (such as of trade union leaders) were criticized, but also as a means for women to jointly prepare for the annual Congresses of the Social Democratic Party. The conferences greatly enhanced the movement's democratic functioning.[17]

The movement, from its early days, also availed of its own vehicles for political education—the Educational Associations which were established from 1892 onwards. They were frequently closed through police intervention, but invariably re-appeared under different names. The Educational Associations were 'in embryo, special mass organizations of women'. As a consequence of a decision taken in 1900, they targeted proletarian housewives in particular—a strategy which seems to have been very effective. By 1907, there existed 10,302 Educational Associations throughout Germany, many times more than the elected *Vertrauenspersonen.* When women were officially integrated into the Social Democratic Party in 1908, the closure of the Associations was fiercely opposed by women activists.[18]

But it was the fortnightly paper, *Die Gleichheit*, which was decisive in providing the loosely structured proletarian women's movement with ideological coherence. The paper regularly contained detailed reports about the plight of different categories of women workers, and it also provided a forum for debates on women's rights and organizational tactics. Started in 1891, *Die Gleichheit* never drew a sharp distinction between the political education of the cadres and the masses, but the latter was given a more concrete shape from 1905 onwards. Henceforth, the magazine contained supplementary pages for housewives (about mother and child care), and this helped strengthen its role as a mass organ. The circulation of *Die Gleichheit* expanded from 4,000 in 1901 to 112,000 in 1913. The magazine, moreover, gained international recognition when it was adopted as the official organ of the International Movement of Working Women in 1907.[19]

Let us now look at another factor in the process of growth—the tactics of struggle chosen by the movement. Strikes as a weapon were, as is to be expected, used frequently, and they helped to reach female labourers (i.e., to expand membership of the proletarian women's movement in both the formal and the informal sector of the economy). A major strike initiative in the middle of the 1890s paralyzed the garment's sector in Berlin, and it is said to have aroused many socially isolated homeworkers who were won over during strike meetings. Further, female workers were in the frontline of a well-publicized strike staged in textile factories in Crimmitschau in 1903. For five long months 6,000 labourers refused to resume work, in spite of a state of siege and a prohibition on the holding of gatherings. They reportedly were very successful in winning over scabs who were brought in from afar. In all wage and strike struggles held in Germany in the early part of this century, the author Karin Bauer states, female labourers played a leading part.[20]

Yet one cannot understand the power of the proletarian women's movement, unless the diversity in the forms of action women used are highlighted. There were many instances where housewives were aroused to manifest their solidarity with striking men. Thus, when the miners in Saarland downed their tools in 1893, women held their own rallies in support of their husbands' demands. This was repeated during a strike of port workers and sea men in Hamburg in 1896.[21] In other cases, social solidarity was extended by broader sections than male workers' spouses alone, and took the form of consumer boycotts, such as, for instance, when the bakery workers in the city of Hamburg struck in 1898. Here, many housewives would not buy bread from bakeries where the owners did not acceed to the demands of the bakery-hands, the *bäckergesellen*. The boycott tactic is said to have contributed greatly to the success of the strike.[22]

The significance of the boycott in the strategy of the proletarian women's movement in fact grew steadily as the movement advanced. It was not just employed to demonstrate solidarity with waged workers' economic demands and supplement their strike struggles, but also to pressurize the government to acceed political rights to women. Both in 1894 and in 1897, large agitational campaigns were staged against a law (*Lex Recke*) which envisioned an aggravation of political disenfranchisement of women and youngsters. A decade later, in 1908, both female wage labourers and proletarian housewives were mobilized against the exclusive Three Classes Parliament of Prussia. Elections to parliament were boycotted with the demand that all men and women be given the right to vote. The campaign frightened Social Democratic Party leaders and induced some of them to charge women with 'terrorism'.[23]

Thus, in the course of the first decade of the 20th century, the proletarian women's movement grew from strength to strength, partly due to the fact that the importance of involving working-class housewives was increasingly recognized. The shift is noted, amongst others, by Sabine Richebächer, in her well-documented book on the evolution of the proletarian women's movement. The movement was oriented towards all categories of women workers—female labourers in factories, sweatshops and the home. Clara Zetkin wrote in 1908 in *Die Gleichheit*, 'It is in the interest of the common workers' movement, in particular of trade unions, that all proletarian women are won over to the idea of solidarity, not just female labourers.' Precisely because working-class housewives were drawn in large numbers, the proletarian women's movement, by the end of the decade, numbered over 82,000 members. By now it had become a major factor in German politics.[24]

Impediments: Proletarian Anti-feminism and Revisionism

The achievements of the proletarian women's movement are further illustrated if we consider the major impediments the movement faced.

The movement's expansion occurred in spite of continuous opposition within the worker's movement against women's organizing and against female employment in factories. Proletarian anti-feminism, which argued, in line with the views of the French anarchist Proudhon,[25] that women's rightful place is in the home, and that women should not be allowed to compete with men for jobs in factories, originally held sway over the working-class movement in Germany. Thus, the Workers' Association set up by Lassale in 1867 is said to have adopted a resolution stating that 'the employment of women in the workshops of modern industry is one of the most scandalous abuses of our time'.[26]

At this point it may be noted that the earliest opposition against proletarian anti-feminism was not voiced by Marxists, but by a spokeswoman for liberal feminism, Louise Otto-Peters. In the revolutionary period of 1848, she had already advocated women's right to gainful employment outside the home, and to full participation in political life. Otto-Peters founded the first women's journal in Germany (*Frauen-Zeitung*) in 1849.[27] When the Lassaleans adopted their standpoint against women's employment in industry and excluded women from the demand for voting rights, she condemned it. Thus, although she was a liberal feminist, her views on the exploitation of proletarian women 'were more progressive' than those of 'most of the men who adhered to socialism, and most of the male workers organized in the Working Men's Associations'.

Subsequently, with the direct purpose of countering the views of the Lassaleans, some followers and collaborators of Marx (foremost among them Engels, Bebel and Zetkin) set out to elaborate a theory of women's emancipation. Their basic tenets, which gradually gained ground and were accepted by the German Social Democratic Party as official policy by the time of the Erfurt Congress (1891), were that as a consequence of mechanization and deskilling, the employment of women in modern industry was inevitable. Moreover, since waged work for the first time provided women with economic independence, their participation in 'social production' was the natural base for their future emancipation under socialism. The standpoint was, for example, advocated by Clara Zetkin at the International Workers' Congress held in Paris in 1889, and it formed the initial theoretical foundation for the proletarian women's movement.[28]

Yet, even while the emancipatory view prevailed and the women's movement grew in strength, proletarian anti-feminism continued to be voiced by significant sections within the Party, especially by sections within the party-oriented trade unions. One spokesperson, Edmund Fischer, in an article which sparked off a major debate in 1905, posed the question: Is the unchangeable course of development leading to a situation where women generally will go out to work, and is this to be welcomed? Fischer let no doubt exist as to his own judgement: 'The emancipation of women goes against the nature of women and of mankind as a whole. It is unnatural and hence impossible to achieve'.[29]

Such views remained long dormant in the Social Democratic Party, but after the First World War they became the vehicle for pushing millions of (married) women out of wage labour employment back into the home. During the war, women's employment expanded in the steel, chemical and machine-building industries, and also in munitions factories. Yet shortly after the end of the war, the German government decided to replace female factory workers massively with demobilized soldiers. In implementing this policy it was helped greatly by the anti-feminist views which, along with Bernstein's revisionism (see later), had regained predominant influence within the Social Democratic Party. By now the women's wing had been brought fully under the control of the party's central leadership, and most women leaders who, like Zetkin, had held emancipatory views, were out.[30]

The second related line of attack on the proletarian women's movement was predetermined by the contradiction between the revolutionary and revisionist current within the Social Democratic Party. Germany is reputed to have been the first country where, under the garb of Marxism, the idea of peaceful transformation towards socialism was propagated. The two main proponents in the debate are well-known figures. On the one hand was the revisionist Eduard Bernstein who set forward his thesis in a series of articles entitled *Problems of Socialism*, and a book *Evolutionary Socialism*. Opposed to him stood Rosa Luxemburg, who defended a revolutionary stance in articles entitled *Sozialreform oder Revolution?*, which were first published in pamphlet form in 1899.[31]

It is to be noted that the major controversy, the two-line struggle within the Social Democratic Party, in fact erupted well before the proletarian women's movement ascended, before it grew into a powerful mass movement. This latter happened, as indicated earlier, in the first decade of the present century. Ideological struggle around the threat of revisionism raged at two Party Congresses held in Stuttgart and Hannover, in 1898 and 1899 respectively. The outcome seemed favourable: in Hannover, the resolution condemning revisionism, proposed by Rosa Luxemburg, was carried by 215 against 21 votes. In practice, however, the revisionist influence throughout the following decade continued mounting under the motto 'one does not say things, one simply does them'.[32]

Meanwhile, the proletarian women's movement mushroomed, through strike actions, boycott initiatives and other campaigns. Though some leading women, such as Lily Braun, took a reformist stance, the majority, led by Clara Zetkin, sided with the revolutionary group. When, within the party, it gradually became evident that the Party leadership 'voted' revisionist, while the revolutionary Left was in opposition, it did not immediately affect the relatively autonomous women's movement. Both revisionism and the militant women's movement, at least until 1908, were mounted simultaneously. From 1908 onwards, however, a process was set into motion whereby the revisionist leadership frantically tried, and largely succeeded, in bringing the proletarian women's movement under its control. Here it took advantage of the fact that, in 1908, the government officially granted women the right to participate in politics. At the Party Congress held that year, a resolution was adopted which henceforth forbade women to maintain 'special political organizations'.

For the time being, the Educational Associations, Women's Conferences and other institutions of women's autonomy survived, and the pressure to integrate was warded off. But in the next major conflict over the holding of the Women's Conference in 1910, the proletarian women's movement suffered a major organizational defeat. Highhandedly, and without democratic consultation, the Party leadership decided to postpone the Conference date.[33] In 1911, the national women's conferences were replaced by regional conferences—a step which was consciously intended to counter women's capacity to influence party policy. From then onwards, the limited autonomy which the women's movement had enjoyed was undermined step by step.

Thus, after the Women's Conferences had been abolished, the Women's Bureau of the party was targeted by the party's male leadership. And the point of culmination was reached when, after the outbreak of the First World War, Clara Zetkin had to resign from the editorship of the independent publicity organ, *Die Gleichheit*. The magazine had been one of the few party organs to take a principled stance against militarism and the war, in defiance of the official party line. Therefore, the take-over by the revisionists of *Die Gleichheit* meant a double loss—a loss both for the proletarian women's movement and for the revolutionary stance within the Social Democratic Party. Women's militancy and revolutionary politics in pre-war Germany and during the First World War were intertwined.

Women's Labour: A Common Theme of Bourgeois and Proletarian Feminists

A debate was woven around this powerful movement on the labouring conditions faced by women workers. The significance of the debate lay partly in the fact that it was joined by women belonging to different stands. Some bourgeois women started addressing themes like the sexual division of labour and the need for legal protection of women workers well before the ascendance of the proletarian women's movement. Clearly, the economic realities of women's misery and exploitation were too stark to be ignored. I will summarize later some of the themes discussed by leading authors in the debate and show that the German debate, roughly a century ago, in many ways fore-shadowed the contemporary feminist debate on the nature of women's labour under capitalism. Even the theme of domestic chores—which has been a central one during the more recent, second wave of international feminism—was raised.

First, whereas some participants in the German debate tended to repeat the patriarchal prejudice that women are the weaker sex, and that female wage employment expands because entrepreneurs make increasing use of labour power 'of slight muscular strength', others strongly disagreed with this view. One example is Hedwig Dohm, an essayist belonging to the bourgeois school in the women's movement. In an article she wrote in 1874 entitled 'The Division of Labour Between Man and Woman', she cited numerous concrete instances of heavy work by women. In English brick kilns where women had to lay bricks to dry, they some times had to walk accross hot pipes. In flax spinneries the heat was virtually unbearable, and the toil was so heavy that most women labourers died early, when they were just 28 or 30 years old. In French workshops women were employed, amongst others, to do glass polishing. They had to turn the wheel with their feet all day. There are factories, Dohm wrote, where female labourers are forced to stand in water 12 hours a day throughout the year.[34]

With these and other examples, Hedwig Dohm illustrated that female wage labourers are not by any means exempted from strenuous activities. On the contrary, they are often singled out to do the heaviest toil. 'At no time have women anywhere been exempted from the most tiresome and repulsive labour.' According to her, factors other than differences in muscular power determine the unequal industrial division of labour between women and men. In reality, 'intellectual' and 'profitable' labour is reserved for men, while women are restricted to 'mechanical' and 'poorly paid' work. In all jobs that require extensive training, women's position is a secondary, subordinate one. Clearly, well over a century ago, Hedwig Dohm questioned the 'sectoral' sexual division of labour which exists between male and female wage labourers.

A second recurring theme is that of women as breadwinners of the family. Here the prevailing ideology of bourgeois society was opposed—the ideology which holds that wages earned by women are merely additional to, and unimportant, compared to those earned by the 'chief breadwinner'—the male head of the family. And the opponents belonged to diverse currents. Thus, both Hedwig Dohm and August Bebel wrote that capitalist entrepreneurs often prefer to employ women who are either wholly or partially responsible for feeding a family. According to Hedwig Dohm, 'There are workshops and factories where there is a conscious preference for female labourers who have to maintain children. The rich factory owner knows that they have to feed their children at any cost, and therefore do not shrink away from any work.'[35]

August Bebel elaborated the theme of women as breadwinners in his book *Die Frau und der Sozialismus*. The book gained enormous popularity and was reworked by the author several times over to incorporate new data. Bebel quoted various surveys to show that women frequently sought factory employment out of sheer necessity, because their husband's earnings were insufficient. For instance, labour inspectors in Berlin found that over 50 per cent of women employees whom they interviewed thought their husband's income was too meagre to survive. Inspectors from many other cities and districts in Germany, along with trade union sources, gave similar evidence.

On the whole then, the 'great majority' of female employees 'worked, since they needed to.'[36]

A third point which was hotly debated concerned the cause(s) of women's extremely low wages. The fact that female labourers were generally paid a 'hunger wage', and that they invariably belonged to the worst-paid category of the proletariat, has already been cited as one of the objective factors in the emergence and rapid growth of the proletarian women's movement. Details abound in the book by Bebel, mentioned earlier, to show that even where women spent an amount of labouring time equal to men, their wages were far lower. Bebel, here, referred specifically to the experiences of women wage employees in railways, postal services, and educational establishments. For an author like Bebel acquainted with Marx's analysis of the reserve army of labour, it was evident that women's employment is specifically resorted to in the search for the cheapest labour.[37]

But why was female wage labour so cheap? For a full explanation, the structure of patriarchy needed to be laid bare, and this was done (without the use of that concept!) by women holding a variety of ideological views. Here there was no 'pure demarcation' between proletarian and bourgeois authors. On the Social Democratic side there was, for instance, the view expressed by the author Rita Hort. Commenting on unequal wages in *Die Gleichheit*, she spoke about the 'historically grown injustice against the female sex' as playing a 'decisive role' in the payment of inferior wages. Inferiority in performance was just a pretext. 'Since she was and is oppressed as a member of her sex, since she does unpaid labour as a housewife in the capitalist money economy, the female employee is paid rather worse than the man, even where she performs the same (*gleiches*) as him'.[38] Here Rita Hort, even if vaguely, already referred to the socially-accepted sexual division of labour as a causative factor.

Further, *Die Gleichheit* did not autonomously decide to devote a whole series of articles to the theme of unequal wages. It, in fact, was compelled to do so by the publication of a book written by a leading spokeswoman of the bourgeois feminist movement, Alice Salomon. Salomon gained a reputation as an advocate of women's participation in social welfare professions. She wrote extensively on topics concerning wage labour by women. In *Gleicher Lohn für Gleicher Leistung* (Equal Wages for Equal Performance), written as a doctoral dissertation, she argued that the unequal wages between women and men were a consequence, amongst others, of the sexual division of labour existing in factories. 'Women frequently occupy positions for which very little training is required.'[39]

Salomon also mentioned other factors, such as the fact that women bear the responsibility for all domestic chores. 'For centuries women have predominantly worked in the home, for the family. The labour of the housewife until today is not being paid for, and is therefore valued low.' The poor esteem that the labour of the housewife enjoys inhibits women from demanding proper wages. The misuse by entrepreneurs of women's position in the family, Salomon argued, was facilitated by the fact that social prejudices are internalized, and that female wage labourers see themselves primarily as housewives. 'Girls see their job as a traditional phase in their life.' Since their daughter would ultimately marry and make a home, parents hesitated to spend money on her education. 'Thus, all women's labour gets the seal of being provisional, and the wages are pressed down.'[40] Salomon thus hinted at the effects of patriarchal ideology.

Finally, some women came up against the prejudice—shared by Marxism and by leaders of the proletarian women's movement—that household labour is not productive. The myth was fought with fervour by Käthe Schirmacher who, as early as 1905, described women's domestic labour as anonymous, non-recognized and non-valued, but nevertheless indispensable labour. 'Our present culture rests on domestic servitude', Schirmacher proclaimed. 'The labour of women in the home is the *sine qua non* of men's professional labour outside the home.'[41] According to her, and contrary to patriarchal ideology, the labour which women perform for the family is productive in two ways. For one, women manufacture clothes, bake cakes from flour, eggs and butter, and they produce, for instance, lampshades from silk. These are all goods the character of which, as values, nobody disputes. Moreover, Schirmacher argued, it is mothers alone who produce 'the most valuable of all values', the 'thinking and acting value' which is called a human being. Unfortunately, according to the author, few countries have rewarded women for performing domestic chores by granting women political rights. It is true that Schirmacher did not discuss these views at an abstract theoretical level, as participants in the feminist debate of the 1960s and 1970s were to do. Yet Schirmacher's exposition of the doubly-productive character of women's domestic work is broadly in agreement with the outcome of the more recent household labour debate, which is dealt with in Chapter 4.

In short, the German women's movement of the late 19th century and the first quarter of the 20th century, has not only left us the legacy of a precious, practical experience in organizing and mobilizing working-class women. A review of the debate, conducted by women belonging to both the proletarian and the bourgeois currents of the movement, illustrates that many of the themes, which today are being researched and analyzed by feminists, were already posed in Germany at the beginning of the 20th century. In fact the debate was far richer than is generally assumed. Though the term patriarchy was less in vogue at that time, compared to the second feminist wave, issues like the relationship between the sexual division of labour and patriarchy, and between the structure of wage exploitation and the family were put on the agenda of the movement then.

The Theoretical Views of Zetkin and Luxemburg

What remains is to point out some of the theoretical weaknesses of both the proletarian women's movement and the revolutionary current of the Social Democratic Party. I will do so by looking at the views of two representative women—Clara Zetkin and Rosa Luxemburg. More than any other participant in the debate on women's labour, it was Clara Zetkin who gave the movement of female wage labourers and working-class housewives its ideological and organizational shape. She was the undisputed leader of the proletarian women's movement. From the magazine's very inception in 1890 up to the First World War, Zetkin guided the work of *Die Gleichheit*. She was also a key figure of the Social Democratic Party's left wing which, as a whole, does not seem to have grasped the strategic significance of the proletarian women's movement.

To what extent did Clara Zetkin develop comprehensive ideas on women's exploitation under capitalism? I will review some of the formulations used in *Die Arbeiterinnen und Frauenfrage der Gegenwart*, an important pamphlet which Clara Zetkin drafted in the founding period of the proletarian women's movement. First, Zetkin stated that in prehistoric times the basis was laid for women's economic and social dependence, through the 'original' sexual division of labour in which women's role was to perform 'productive activities of maintenance', while men did '(conquering)–acquiring–defensive' tasks. In pre-capitalist economies men were the family entrepreneurs who exploited the labour power of their wives. Within this narrowly-defined sphere of the communal household, women were 'the main production force'.[42]

Under capitalism, many of the production tasks previously performed by women in the home—like processing food and sewing clothes for the family—are transferred to industries. After all, the industrially organized mode of production is able to provide articles of daily necessity far more cheaply than women as small producers can. Thus, the production of food and other consumption goods is transferred, and 'women's activity is relayed from the home to society'. Clara Zetkin argued that capitalism brought fundamental changes in the division of labour between women and men. She stated that 'the development of the means of production destroys the economic base for women's work within the family'. In the course of the same process, women throw off the yoke of their husbands' economic dominance, which is replaced by that of capitalist entrepreneurs.

Zetkin's line of reasoning was in tune with the Marxist emancipation theory. Like Bebel and other Marxist proponents of women's emancipation, Zetkin championed women's right to wage labour employment. 'To impose restrictions upon women's labour', she stated, 'would be as much as trying to turn back the wheel of history'. Here, in speaking of women's labour, Zetkin evidently referred only to work done by women outside the home as wage labourers in industries. Women's employment in factories was inevitable. 'The production relations know no sentimental or personal considerations, they (are determined by) economic laws which are as inescapable as natural laws.'[43] Whether men liked it or not, women's employment in industries was bound to spread.

Implied in her line of argument, as stated in the pamphlet, is the idea that household labour is bound to disappear, and die a natural death. Much later, Clara Zetkin was to plead in favour of the social recognition of the tasks of motherhood. In a document she drafted after the demise of the proletarian women's movement in 1920, she repeatedly referred to the need to value mothering tasks as 'social performance'.[44] Yet she never made a fundamental theoretical appraisal of household labour under capitalism. Her unilinear mode of thinking left no scope for a theoretical assessment of working-class women's domestic chores. In contrast to Käthe Schirmacher, who, as seen earlier, fought for recognition of household labour, Zetkin (as will be shown in Chapter 7) was mainly concerned with the defense of women's right to participate in wage labour outside the home.

In short, while Clara Zetkin played a tremendously stimulating role, activating many working-class women; while her organizational and agitational skill in building a movement of exploited women is undeniable; while in practice the movement she helped construct took stock of the 'objective' misery of proletarian housewives, theoretically she does not appear to have fully grasped the complex nature of the relationship between capitalism and patriarchy. Although there was a real, and increasing, scope for mobilizing working-class housewives, in the realm of Clara Zetkin's ideas their role remained undervalued, conforming with the tradition of Marxism.

Rosa Luxemburg shared with Clara Zetkin a staunch commitment to anti-militarism. In an appendix to *Sozialreform oder Revolution?* and in her book *Die Akkumulation des Kapitals*, she tried to develop a Marxist analysis of the problem of militarism, which she saw as the inevitable outgrowth of the capitalist mode of production.[45] When the First World War broke out, both Clara Zetkin and Rosa Luxemburg led demonstrations and other struggles against the German government's war mobilization. Both actively supported all efforts to foment mass discontent against the First World War. Both fiercely opposed the Social Democratic Party leadership's reconciliatory attitude towards the imperial government, and both resisted the 4 August betrayal of working class politics in the name of Germany's 'national interests'.

Whereas, initially, both women were shocked and shaken by the failure of the Social Democratic Party leadership to stand firm against the chauvinist war propaganda of the German government, events during the war soon gave them reason for new hope. The first peace demonstration was held on 15 March 1915, in front of the Reichstag, the German parliament, at the initiative of women. The following year some strikes were staged in munitions factories, and again female participation was predominant. The same year, over 60,000 women in the cities of Berlin and Bremen struck work, when Karl Liebknecht, the well-known left-wing leader, was condemned to imprisonment for his anti-militarist speeches. Subsequently, resistance against the war, and against the economic hardships it caused, escalated rapidly. In January 1918, more than a million female and male labourers in the armaments industry went on strike, inspired by the example of the Russian revolution. Clearly, it was women who took the lead in the agitation against the unjust war.[46]

Yet, in spite of the revolutionary determination displayed by working-class women, Rosa Luxemburg did not share Clara Zetkin's strong commitment to the proletarian women's movement. She rarely intervened in the debates of the women's movement described earlier, and she also did not actively participate in the efforts by Clara Zetkin, August Bebel and others to elaborate a Marxist theory of women's emancipation. Her classically Marxist understanding of the specific exploitation of proletarian women—wage labourers and housewives—is clearly reflected in her own writings. This is surprising in view of the very real importance of the women's movement for her own revolutionary ideals, and it had serious consequences.

Whereas women's position within the industrial reserve army of labour was debated and analyzed by both bourgeois and proletarian participants in the women's movement, Rosa Luxemburg strikingly ignored the whole question in her exposition of the laws of modern capitalism. In her works *Einführung in die Nationalökonomie* and *Die Akkumulation des Kapitals*, she basically paraphrased Marx's theory. She referred to the same categories as the master had done and ignored the vast, and most manipulated section of the 'floating reserve'—the millions of young, unmarried girls and married women with children.[47]

Secondly, whereas an attempt was made in her time, though rudimentary, to explain the productive nature of household labour, Luxemburg took the anti-feminist position that the scientific understanding of capitalism precluded defining her labour as productive. When, in her article on women's suffrage and class struggle, she referred to housework and the rearing of children, she stated bluntly:

> This kind of work is not productive in the sense of the present capitalist economy no matter how enormous an achievement the sacrifices and energy spent, the thousand little efforts add up to. This is but the private affair of the worker, his happiness and blessing, and for this reason non-existent for our present society. As long as capitalism and the wage system rule, only that kind of work is considered productive which produces surplus value, which produces capitalist profit.[48]

Against the background of the evolution of the proletarian women's movement described earlier, and of the debates among various feminist authors at the time, the failure of the German revolution appears in a new light. As is known, Rosa Luxemburg was the chief ideologue of the new, revolutionary party nucleus which emerged during the war years as a split-off from the degenerated Social Democratic Party. It has long been emphasized that she and others realized far too late the need for building an alternative organization. As essential, perhaps, is the fact that she did not consciously attempt to give theoretical expression to a mass movement of proletarian women, which could have functioned as the main social base for a revolutionary alternative, for the bold attempt to build proletarian power after the World War.

Rosa Luxemburg's famous essay 'Social Reform or Revolution', which first appeared in 1899, and was republished almost a decade later, set a clear demarcation between the revisionist and revolutionary currents within social democracy. It marked the divide between those who considered the achievement of legal reforms under the old order as a purpose in itself and those who, like herself, considered such reforms to be mere means—vehicles in the proletariat's march towards the overthrow of the old order. But what social forces should be seen as the true base for building an alternative to the reformist, Bernsteinian trend? This question was not faced by her, though objective reality—working women's abject misery and unending toil—as also the subjective experience of the proletarian women's movement, provided at least part of the answer.

'Self-criticism, cruel, unsparing criticism that goes to the very roots of things, is life and light for the proletarian movement'.[49] Ultimately, what badly failed to emerge from practice was a comprehensive, conclusive theoretical understanding of women's labour under capitalism. The official theory of women's emancipation, as elaborated by Bebel, Zetkin and others, was of course far more progressive than, and contrasted sharply with, proletarian anti-feminism, as voiced by people like Lassalle and Edmund Fischer. The Marxist theory of women's emancipation at least did offer working-class women a chance to take part in class struggles. Yet the need for women's leadership, on par with men, was not posed. And although the debates within the women's movement threw up many constructive ideas about the relationships between capitalism and patriarchy, about household labour and the sexual division of labour, and so on, a summing up of practice and theory which a talented revolutionary like Rosa Luxemburg was capable of, unfortunately was never made.

Summary: Contrasting Features

The double contradiction in the developments described here needs to be stated in conclusion. For however extraordinary the experience of the proletarian women's movement, however praiseworthy the attempt by leading Social Democrats to construct a theory of women's emancipation against stiff opposition by male chauvinist leaders on the Party's right, the movement continued to suffer from a double contradiction—that between theory and practice on the one hand, and between the proclaimed and the analytically weak demarcation by the proletarian from the bourgeois women's movement, on the other.

First, there is the contrast between the proclaimed need for a pure demarcation between the proletarian and the bourgeois wing of the women's movement—and the reality that female authors belonging to both wings contributed crucially to the debate on women's toil. In particular, when it came to analyzing the relationship between capitalism and patriarchy, between wage labour exploitation and the structure of the family, women like Hedwig Dohm and Alice Salomon did raise their own, constructive points. When reviewing the whole debate carried on during the historical German movement, the least that could be said is that the dividing line was blurred.

Second, there is the contrast between the proletarian women's movement's own theory and its practice. Whereas creative tactics, such as social and political boycotts, were devised so as to engage proletarian housewives in struggle, at the theoretical level the Marxist prejudice against domestic work continued to be strong. This is evidenced by the views on household labour expressed by such eminent leaders as Rosa Luxemburg, the main theoretician on the Party's left, and Clara Zetkin, the undisputed leader of the women's movement. Organizational advances, particularly large during the first decade of the 20th century, were not matched equally by theoretical progress.

This, then, is perhaps the most crucial point to be made about the experience of those days, that is, that the practice of the proletarian women's movement outgrew its theoretical maturity. In the context of the historical and comparative overview of this book, this point is of overriding importance indeed. For whereas many analytical contributions have recently been made by feminists towards the understanding of household labour and women's wage work, in terms of actually building a movement of female wage labourers and domestic slaves, the experiences that have been gathered by German women in the beginning of the 20th century appear to be unsurpassed. The contemporary women's movement can draw invaluable practical and organizational lessons from the proletarian women's movement in Germany.[50]

Notes and References

1. Luxemburg (1971), pp. 169–70, 280, 324.
2. Liddington and Norris (1978).
3. Bebel (1979), p. 170.
4. Bauer (1978), p. 36, has stated: 'Historically, in the first half of the 19th century, women's labour did not displace men's.... The men who crowded to the factories already found women present'.
5. Bebel (1979), p. 173.
6. For data on tuberculosis deaths, see Bauer (1978), p. 126. On health risks for women workers see also Bebel (1979), pp. 184–85.
7. Bebel (1979), p. 172.
8. For details regarding the labouring conditions of ironers and washerwomen, see Brinker-Gabler (1979), p. 387; on the length of the working week in the textile sector, see Bebel (1979), p. 172; on women textile workers see Richebächer (1982), p. 32.
9. Bebel (1979), p. 181.
10. On the failure of the German working-class movement to raise the issue of equal pay, see Bauer (1978), p. 118.
11. Marx (1977a), p. 589.
12. Bebel (1979), p. 182.
13. Mies and Jayawardena (1981), p. 136. On women workers' associations established in the 1880s, see also Richebächer (1982), p. 171.
14. Mies and Jayawardena (1981), p. 138.
15. Bauer (1978), p. 120.
16. On the Agitational Commissions and the system of Trusted Individuals, see Bauer (1978), pp. 61, 85; Mies and Jayawardena (1981), pp. 138–39; Richebächer (1982), pp. 177, 191.
17. Richebächer (1982), p. 210.
18. On the Educational Associations, see Bauer (1978), p. 85.
19. For details on the magazine *Die Gleichheit*, see Richebächer (1982), pp. 120, 233; see also Bauer (1978), p. 92. For further insights into the organizational methods of the proletarian women's movement, see the yearly reports of the 'Trusted Person' in charge of coördination at the centre, printed in *Die Gleichheit*, for instance, Baader, '*Bericht der Vertrauensperson der Genossinnen Deutschlands*', *Die Gleichheit*, Supplement, 23 August 1905.
20. For the events surrounding the Crimmitschau strike, which was betrayed by the (male) trade union leadership, see Bauer (1978), p. 132; Richebächer (1982), pp. 226–27.

21. Richebächer (1982), p. 208.
22. Ibid.
23. Bauer (1978), p. 78; Richebächer (1982), p. 250.
24. For Zetkin's statement in *Die Gleichheit*, see Richebächer (1982), p. 249. Richebächer (ibid., p. 201) notes a certain division of tasks within the movement: whereas for most wage labourers the priority lay with trade union organizing, the political work within the Educational Associations was largely carried out by working-class housewives.
25. Quoted in Thönnessen (1976), p. 15.
26. Mies and Jayawardena (1981), p. 136.
27. For Otto-Peters' views, see also Brinker-Gabler (1979), p. 111.
28. For a short excerpt from Zetkin's speech at the Paris Conference, see Thönnessen (1973), p. 39. For an elaborate critique of the Marxist emancipation theory, see Mies and Jayawardena (1981), p. 141.
29. Quoted in Thönnessen (1976), p. 98. According to Thönnessen, the mere fact of the publication of Fischer's ideas (in *Sozialistische Monatshefte*) can be taken as a symptom of the approaching revision of the old theory of women's emancipation. In 1971, Fischer was to reinforce his thesis in the context of a discussion on female labour in the war time (ibid., p. 104).
30. Thönnessen (1976), p. 89.
31. Luxemburg (1971), p. 52.
32. See Howard's introduction to Luxemburg (1971), p. 31. See also Walters' introduction to Luxemburg (1974), p. 7.
33. See Richebächer (1982), p. 255. For the conflict over the continued existence of the Educational Associations, see Bauer (1978), p. 87.
34. Brinker-Gabler (1979), p. 124.
35. Ibid.
36. Bebel (1979), p. 180.
37. Ibid.
38. The article by Rita Hort in *Die Gleichheit* is cited by Bauer (1978), p. 117. Bauer also cites an article in the same magazine in which the loss of money for the working class, due to the low level of female wages, is calculated on the basis of 250 labour days per year, and 2.5 million women workers. The amount is stated to be DM 550 million.
39. For the relation between the debate on unequal wages and Salomon's book, see Bauer (1978), p. 116. For Salomon's views, also see Brinker-Gabler (1979), p. 194.
40. Brinker-Gabler (1979), p. 198.
41. For Schirmacher's essay on household labour, see ibid., p. 256.
42. For the pamphlet by Clara Zetkin, see ibid., p. 134. The same point regarding the productive role of women in the pre-capitalist economy was made by Zetkin in her speech at the Party Congress in Gotha in 1896. See Bauer (1978), p. 203.
43. Brinker-Gabler (1979), p. 142.
44. See the document *Richtlinien für die Kommunistische Frauenbewegung* drafted for the Communist International, Bauer (1978), p. 256.
45. See Luxemburg (1971), p. 135; (1981a), p. 398.

46. For details on women's resistance against the German war policy, see Bauer (1978), p. 139 and Richebächer (1982), p. 279. The struggles against the war are also discussed in Graham Locke's introduction to Liebknecht (1973), p. xiii.
47. Luxemburg (1981a), p. 311; (1981b), p. 753.
48. Luxemburg (1971), p. 220. The article is based on a speech given at the second Social Democratic women's rally in Stuttgart, 12 May 1912.
49. Quoted from the pamphlet 'The Crisis in Social Democracy'. See Luxemburg (1971), pp. 324–25.
50. Compare my evaluation with that given in Mies and Jayawardena (1981), p. 111.

4

The Legacy of the Second Feminist Wave: The Debate on Household Labour Revisited

More than half a century after the demise of the German proletarian women's movement, in the late 1960s and the early 1970s a new and powerful feminist movement arose internationally. From the United States through Western Europe to Japan, and in a number of Third World countries, women founded their own autonomous groups and collectives, wrote pamphlets and sought publicity, staged demonstrations, and even national women's strikes, to show their deep discontent with their own conditions of life. In the course of these struggles, feminist activists demanded both control over their own bodies and greater equality in social life. Raising the slogan 'the personal is political', the new generation of feminists made the oppression in their private lives a matter of public concern.

This new period of women's activism, moreover, did not just bring new issues to the fore. As has already been stated here, women also struggled to build a new theoretical framework—a theory that would appropriately express the specific nature of their oppression. First advanced by US-based radical feminists, the concept of 'patriarchy' came to be commonly used by diverse currents of the movement as the term for the system of male dominance. Much energy was spent on tracing the history of patriarchy and defining its material base.[1] Some groups even went so far as to openly challenge the whole Western intellectual tradition. In its Manifesto, published in 1970, the Italian feminist group, Rivolta Femminile, defiantly proclaimed: 'We hold systematic thinkers responsible for the great humiliation imposed on us by the patriarchal world'.[2]

The broad debate staged on the labour of the modern housewife had far-reaching consequences. For years, women in Italy, Great Britain, Germany and elsewhere carried on a lively theoretical discussion on the nature of domestic work under contemporary capitalism.[3] The debate and the campaigns it engendered, as will be shown below, had limited parameters. Thus, women initially did not theorize the character of home-based, non-waged work in the rural areas of Third World countries; they did not dialectically conceive of the relationship between the public and private economy, nor was a conscious effort made to organically link the interests of housewives with those of women employed as waged workers in offices and factories. Nevertheless, the debate on household labour had a lasting, emancipatory significance, for it laid bare a fundamental weakness in economic theory—the failure to give recognition to, and assess, women's unpaid domestic work.

This chapter then reviews a key theoretical debate. After recalling the powerful impact of the protests which women in Italy staged (an example which also helps to point out the contradictions in the second feminist wave), I will briefly describe the points of view on household labour put forward by leading spokeswomen of the second feminist wave (Benston and Dalla Costa), and raise questions regarding the narrow focus of the campaign 'wages for housework'. I shall then draw the consequences of the debate for Marx's labour theory of value by making a critique of Marx's formula on value creation and proposing its extension, essential to incorporating the housewife's economic role. In the last part of the chapter, I shall highlight the historical research of Miriam Glucksmann, who has shown the way forward by conceptualizing the public and the domestic economy as poles of an integrated whole. Unlike the previous chapter, this chapter is specifically devoted to the reconstruction of economic theory.

The Second Feminist Wave in Italy: A Highly Influential Social Movement

To illustrate both the successes and some of the 'defects' of the second feminist wave, I shall first describe the impact of the new movement in Italy. In 1968, student uprisings disrupted the stability of political rule in France and other countries of Western Europe. As in France, student activism in Italy combined with that of factory workers to produce an outpouring of broad mass discontent. Some 5 million workers joined strikes during the 'hot autumn' of 1969, including many female wage workers. Within this environment of social ferment and class struggle, autonomous feminist groups critical of the established left (i.e., the Communist Party) and its Marxist doctrines mushroomed in cities all over Italy. They founded magazines such as *Effe* which boldly raised subjects that previously were taboo.[4]

One of the issues which figured prominently in the rapidly growing agitation was the right of divorce. In 1970, parliamentary political parties passed a divorce bill which granted general permission to dissolve marriages without requiring that a reason be stated. As Lucia Chiavola Birnbaum, who has faithfully recorded the experience of the Italian women's movement, states, after its promulgation the divorce law became the subject of a heated, public controversy. The Italian Roman Catholic church and its parliamentary ally, the Christian Democratic Party, started a campaign to get the divorce law repealed, while women's groups launched a counter-campaign which turned out to be highly effective. In 1974, an anti-divorce referendum was held. Whereas about 90 per cent of the electorate took part, 60 per cent voted to sustain the divorce law.[5]

Another issue which gained prominence was women's right to abortion. From 1970 it was taken up by the Movimiento di Liberazione della Donne (MLD), a network of local, feminist collectives based in Rome. According to Birnbaum, in 1971 between 1 and 3 million abortions were performed in Italy in the face of a law which defined abortion as a crime. The campaign for the repeal of the punitive abortion law was punctuated by several large women's demonstrations. Both in 1975 and in 1977, 50,000 women marched in processions through the streets of Rome. The campaign culminated in the adoption of the abortion law of 1978, which stipulates the right to an abortion paid by the national government for any woman over 18 years of age within the first 90 days of pregnancy.[6]

The second feminist wave thus left a deep imprint on Italian society. Though the women's campaigns were complicated by the powerful presence of the Catholic church, their success was facilitated by the fact that militant feminist groups sought the cooperation of the parliamentary-oriented women's organization linked to the communist party, the Unione Donne Italiane (UDI). Flexibly combining their strengths, women of different political persuasions pushed through a number of legal reforms relating to women's marriage status, women's right to control their own bodies, and women's position in the labour market. The 1977 law for equality of treatment (Legge Di Parita) established women's right to several fringe benefits on par with men.[7]

It is within this context that the Italian debate on, and social struggles around, household labour should be situated. In 1972, Maria Rosa Dalla Costa published an essay entitled '*Potere Femminile e Sovversione Sociale*', in which she put forward her own theoretical analysis of women's domestic work. Dalla Costa stressed the need for housewives to enter the social arena of struggle to break their isolation: 'we should leave the house, and we should refuse domestic work as work that has been imposed upon us and that has never been paid for'.[8] From this perspective, Dalla Costa tactically supported the idea of a campaign around the demand 'wages for housework'.

Dalla Costa was not the first of the new generation of Italian feminists to draw attention to women's unpaid household work, nor was her view seen as the only possible one.[9] Yet the booklet she drafted was influential in bringing the theme into focus, and it provided feminist activists with theoretical 'ammunition'. Several conferences were held (such as in Padua in 1972 and Naples in 1973) where women debated their plight as housewives. By the middle of the 1970s, women in different Italian cities were out in the streets with banners highlighting the demand that housework be remunerated. In Padua a women's collective was formed that advocated the need to develop an international strategy in favour of the wage demand as the single most important issue for women.[10]

The evaluation of this campaign has been varied. According to Lucia Chiavola Birnbaum, the issue of wages for housework 'can produce a broad band of women's solidarity, and it did so in Italy, where it has been a major pivot of discussion on women's condition in groups not otherwise open to other feminist issues'.[11] As evidence, she cites amongst others the fact that the Christian Democratic Party in 1979 presented a bill to the Italian parliament, which suggested that the housewife–mother be given an allowance. The Communist Party, Italy's second major political party at the time, in the early 1980s is said to have acknowledged the importance of the wage campaign, since it presumably helped the country's 12 million housewives understand feminist issues.[12]

Yet, while the campaign contributed to generating public debate, it also appears to have had an 'isolationist' impact. Most striking, perhaps, is that the campaign in support of women without waged work was disconnected from the struggles of the equally isolated 'women workers without factories' (*operaie senza fabbrica*). In the late 1950s, female homeworkers in the garments' sector in several regions of Italy (notably Emilia and Toscana) had staged strikes and demonstrations to obtain wage improvements and other benefits. The campaign resulted in the adoption of a law on homeworking, which was followed by further struggles to guarantee its enforcement and to press for the institution of labour contracts around piece-rate wages. Thousands of homeworkers picketed factories, and also staged highway blockades.[13]

These struggles, moreover, were resumed in the first part of the 1970s (i.e., in exactly the same period when the campaign 'wages for housework' spread). Once again, the adoption of a law to regulate homeworking (1973) gave an impetus to homeworkers' efforts to get organized and defend their rights. In the city of Naples, with its vast cottage industries, for instance, autonomous committees were set up at the neighbourhood level, resulting in the founding of a League of Homeworkers.[14] The struggles were highly significant, given the extreme difficulties isolated homeworkers, like housewives, face in mustering collective strength. Yet the campaign 'wages for housework' did not programmatically address itself to homeworkers' rights, nor did any organic link exist between the struggles on the two fronts. An alliance of these two categories of women—housewives and homeworkers—does not seem to have materialized.

Conceptualizing Housework: Benston and Dalla Costa

After having illustrated, through the Italian example, the richness of the struggles waged by women in the decade of the second feminist wave, I will discuss some of the standpoints formulated on the labour of the modern housewife. Though there were many participants in the debate, I will restrict myself to highlighting the views of two representative writers, namely the American author Margaret Benston and the Italian feminist Maria Rosa Dalla Costa. A comparison of the theses proposed by these two women sufficiently demonstrates, I believe, how in the course of the debate pertinent questions were raised regarding the male bias in Marx's labour theory of value. Well-known Western Marxist journals, such as the *New Left Review*, felt obliged to allocate space to the household labour debate.[15]

When the second feminist wave was on the rise internationally, Margaret Benston wrote an essay, 'The Political Economy of Women's Liberation', which was first published in 1969. At the time, the essay formed a watershed in the discussion within the women's liberation movement of the United States. Benston argued with force that 'the roots of the secondary status of women in fact are economic', for it can be shown that 'women as a group do indeed have a definite relation to the means of production'.[16] Thus, Benston marked her distance from those feminists in the United States who held a 'bourgeois' notion of the family, believing that it is a superstructural, not an economic unit. In rejecting this notion, Benston (re)started the long search for the material base of women's oppression.[17]

Benston looked for a 'structural definition' of women which would correspond to that of the proletarian wage earner. In order to define women's position, she proposed to analyze women's domestic work. How serious is the burden of domestic work in industrial societies? The argument is often advanced, Benston wrote, that the work in the home has been much reduced, but this is only partly true.

> Except for the very rich, who can hire someone to do it, there is for most women an *irreducible minimum* of necessary labour involved in caring for home, husband and children. For a married woman without children, this irreducible minimum of work probably takes fifteen to twenty hours a week; for a woman with small children the minimum is probably seventy to eighty hours.[18]

Then, if contrary to current notions, and contrary also to the expectations of many Marxists, the burden has not been removed, how should the role of domestic labour be analyzed? Here, Benston took her cue from the distinction in economic theory between the production of use values and exchange values, between production for immediate use and the production of commodities for the market—a distinction to which reference has been made earlier. Citing the view of the economist Mandel *in extenso*, Benston argued that women, like peasants, produce use values for consumption in the home. She called this production socially necessary. 'In sheer quantity, household labour, including child care, constitutes a huge amount of socially necessary production.'[19] Yet, according to her, household labour, like peasant production, remains 'pre-capitalist in a very real sense'.[20]

Elsewhere in this book, we will see that the members of the German feminist school, more recently, have likewise stressed the similarities between the work of Western housewives and that of (Third World) peasants. Yet, long before the members of this school defined women's domestic tasks as 'non-capitalist', Benston had essentially made the same point. She too believed that women as a group work outside the money economy. She also argued that domestic labour typically creates useful products and services directly consumed by the family. Like the German feminist school, Benston defined women as subsistence producers: 'We will tentatively define women, then, as a group of people who are responsible for the production of simple use values in those activities associated with the home and the family.'[21]

A crucial leap forward in the household labour debate was taken in 1972 by the Italian feminist Maria Rosa Dalla Costa. In the essay 'Female Power and the Subversion of the Community', she wrote that, in her analysis of the women's question, she wished to concentrate 'on the position of the woman in the working class'.[22] Adopting a standpoint which, a few years later, would be philosophically elaborated by the German feminist, Claudia von Werlhof (to be discussed in Chapter 7), the Italian author argued that an understanding of the exploitation of working-class housewives is central to our understanding of the process of exploitation under the capitalist system in general. Their position is decisive 'for the position of all other women'.[23]

Second, Dalla Costa shared with Benston a critique of superstructural notions of the family. According to her, housewives are not just consumers. Their role is not only to buy capital's commodities and thus contribute to the realization of values, but also to produce. Whereas, under feudalism, men and women as serfs toiled together 'in an equality of unfreedom', capitalism has created separate spheres.[24] While men are recruited to do 'free' wage labour, women are locked up in the home, and their work in the isolated nuclear family remains invisible. This has made it easy to ignore their contribution to the creation of social wealth. Yet the Marxist view that domestic labour is 'unproductive', in Dalla Costa's view, is wrong.

Further, when elaborating on the productivity of the housewife, Dalla Costa took a far bolder departure from Marxist theory than Benston before her had done. She pointed out that the housewife does not just produce simple use values, but commodity labour power, which can then be sold by the husband on the labour market. In her essay, Dalla Costa explicitly criticized the misconceived notion that women are only producers of use values. This is a notion, she said, which places women 'outside the working class'.[25] It needs to be clearly stated, she held, that domestic labour, apart from producing pure use values, 'fulfils an essential function in the production of surplus value'.[26]

Dalla Costa admitted that household labour is qualitatively different from wage labour, and that, contrary to the latter, the former is not directly regulated by capital. Nobody is at all concerned how much labour time is required for women's domestic activities—her labour time knows no end. Housewives remain 'enchained to pre-capitalist labouring conditions'. Yet the housewife does not stand outside the process of what Marx called surplus value production (i.e., the accretion of capital through the hiring of labour power and its use by the entrepreneur). Her labour constitutes the foundation upon which this process can be started. The housewife and her toil are the very basis of the process of capital accumulation.

For Dalla Costa, then, the central characteristic of domestic work is that it produces a special commodity, namely labour power. The productivity of the housewife, through the creation and maintenance of labour power, she proclaimed, is the very precondition for the productivity of the (male) wage labourer. 'Through the wage the exploitation of the non-wage labourers is organized.'[27] Although Dalla Costa's essay, as I will argue below, left the relation between women's domestic labour and their waged labour unclarified, it did form a milestone in the discussion on Marx's value theory. By defining women's domestic labour as productive in a twofold sense, by seeing it squarely as value creation, by insisting that the entrepreneur, in the course of the 'socialized production cycles', relies both on the unpaid labour of the housewife and on the paid labour of the wage employee, Dalla Costa provided, at the theoretical level, a (rudimentary) solution to the question which had been unresolved ever since Marx wrote *Capital*.

Narrow Focus of the Movement: 'Wages for Housework'

Having recorded some of its pathbreaking achievements, we now need to mark several problematic aspects of the household labour debate. I have stressed earlier the fact that the debate, in my view, generated theoretically refreshing ideas. Still, the debate did not result in a feminist version of the theory of value, a full reformulation of Marxist economics. By the second half of the 1970s, the debate ended in something like a blind alley, as several feminist authors, including Veronika Beechey, have admitted.[28] A section of the researcher activists decided to shift their attention and re-focus on women's waged work. The intensity of the debate was not matched by equally strong, shared conclusions. What was the reason for this deadlock in the debate?

One of the controversies that developed centred around the movement's slogan 'wages for housework'. Feminist critics of Dalla Costa and the campaign have admitted that this demand 'has at least taken to women the proposition that housework is indeed work'. Yet the demand has also been criticized for being 'reformist'.[29] By demanding payment for domestic chores, participants in the 'wages for housework' campaign failed to question the sexual division of labour which relegates all domestic chores to women. Nor did the slogan in itself question the isolated position of modern housewives. The demand did not suffice to overhaul the structures of patriarchy.[30]

Further, a major obstacle for building a genuine class-oriented movement was that in trying to solve the riddle in traditional Marxist theory, the target for organizing women was narrowed down. When Dalla Costa supported the 'wages for housework' slogan, she coupled it with the need for housewives to wage 'socialized struggles'. Thus, she pleaded in favour of 'socialization of the fight of isolated workers'. But she did not show why this socialization necessarily required the particular slogan she advanced, nor did she draw upon history to show how proletarian housewives in the past have succeeded in socializing their resistance. As stated in the previous chapter, German housewives in the beginning of this century got united and waged mass struggles by linking up with female wage labourers, such as in their boycott of the Prussian parliament.

Thus, the campaign 'wages for housework' fizzled out partly because of its narrow programmatic basis. Initially, Dalla Costa appeared to grasp that women are also a vast reserve army of labour which entrepreneurs can tap whenever they like. Yet she did not conceptually interlink the role of women in both spheres of production with each other, and her target of attack was mainly the injustice of capitalism (and the traditional left parties) against the isolated housewives.

Nowhere did she draw on the effective example of German women—female wage labourers and proletarian housewives—building a common platform. Neither she nor her colleagues propagated an alliance of women wage labourers and domestic slaves for the joint battle against capitalism and patriarchy. As the example of the struggles of Italian homeworkers discussed earlier illustrates, the campaigns in support of different sections of women workers developed along separate tracts.

This same narrow view can be seen in Margaret Benston's essay, 'The Political Economy of Women's Liberation'. On the one hand, Benston indicated that she was aware of the fact that women, apart from performing domestic chores, participate in wage labour. She was conscious of the fact that women hold a specific place among the various sections of wage labourers. Thus she wrote that 'the history of women in the industrialized sectors of the economy has depended simply on the labour and needs of that sector. Women function as a massive reserve army of labour.'[31] This reference to women as part of the industrial reserve army is, of course, basically in agreement with what was propagated at the time of the German proletarian women's movement, and by socialist feminists more recently. It implies that the sexual division of labour extends to the sphere of wage labour relations also.

Still, Benston did not define wage labour as a basic sphere of women's work. Take, for instance, this statement: '[Notice that] women are not excluded from commodity production. Their participation in wage labour occurs, but as a group they have no structural responsibility in this area and such participation is ordinarily regarded as transient.' And Benston contrasted women's lack of a structural responsibility with men's tasks under capitalism: 'Men, on the other hand, are responsible for commodity production: they are not, in principle, given any role in household labour.'[32] Thus, Benston voiced the view which has long been propagated by industrial entrepreneurs, namely that women's contribution to the production of values in the wage sphere is only of a secondary and temporary kind.

This view can be refuted with statistical data on women's employment in capitalist countries. As Heleieth Saffioti states, 'statistics show that industrialization of a nation's economy has always made use of both the male and female workforce'.[33] For instance, in 1866, women comprised 30 per cent of the total workforce in French industry.[34] The percentage has tended to fluctuate in Western European countries, reaching a peak during periods of war, such as during the First and Second World Wars.[35] According to Saffioti's data, in recent decades the proportion of women among the total force of waged employees has remained above a third in the majority of industrialized countries. Clearly, by seeing women's involvement in wage labour as transient Benston confounded reality and patriarchal ideology. It is the latter which defines women's wage labour as transient.

An apt refutation of the view that women have 'no structural responsibility' in the sphere of waged work is provided by Miriam Glucksmann in her book on women assemblers in the new industries established in Great Britain in the 1930s. According to her, whereas British capital had previously concentrated on producing heavy capital goods (such as trains, ships and engineering machines) for export, it now began to produce domestic consumer goods (such as electric appliances and processed food) for the British home market. The labour force recruited to do the monotonous tasks on the assembly line in these new factories consisted exclusively of women. The traditional craft unions failed to appreciate the changed realities, but women, in Glucksmann's words, became the 'prime workforce' of the new industries. They were incorporated into the 'central circuit of capital' as never before.[36]

In short, by upholding the view that women as a group work outside the money economy, and women in general are basically housewives, Benston provided a narrow theoretical conception of women's labour which was biased against women assemblers and other female wage employees. Both she and Dalla Costa realized that women are exploited as domestic workers, but they failed to grasp that women are exploited in a twofold sense—as those who pave the way for capitalist production and exploitation through the production of labour power, and as those who, along with men, are producers of industrial commodities for the market. We need to incorporate the theoretical analyses of domestic work into a broader conceptualization of women's toil.

Marx's Interpretation of the Labour Theory of Value: Need for a Critique

To carry forward Dalla Costa's critique of Marx's labour theory of value which credited only wage labour with causing the accretion of capital, I propose to review and extend Marx's theory. In order to do justice to the feminist critique, Marx's formula on value creation needs to be transformed. But first I wish to underline the feminist critique—that Marx ignored women's domestic work—by scrutinizing that part of his theory where he discusses the 'value of labour power' (i.e., the value of the human energy that is applied to the production of market commodities). This issue of the value of labour power is addressed by Marx in a specific chapter in the first volume of *Capital*, as also in *Wages, Price and Profit*. I will repeat below what I had briefly stated earlier when referring to David Ricardo's views on the 'price of labour'.

First, both in *Capital* and *Wages, Price and Profit* (which has been termed 'a whole course of political economy pressed into an eighty-page pamphlet')[37] Marx draws a distinction between labour and social labour when discussing the difference between the production of use values and exchange values. Whereas he calls the latter social, he refuses to admit that the former can be termed social:

> To produce a commodity a certain amount of labour must be bestowed on it. And I say not only *labour* but *social labour*. A man who produces an article for his own immediate use, to consume it himself, creates a *product*, but not a *commodity*. As a self-sustaining producer he has nothing to do with society.[38]

By granting the label 'social labour' exclusively to commodity production, Marx implicitly denies that the production of use values, performed by women in the home and which is necessary to sustain the strength of waged workers, has a social character. Yet such labour has much to do with production in society, including capitalist society.

Marx is equally biased when he discusses the value of labour power. In *Wages, Price and Profit* (which is similarly worded as *Capital*),[39] he states that its value should be determined in the following manner:

> Like that of every other commodity, its value is determined by the quantity of labour necessary to produce it. The labouring power of a man exists only in his living individuality. A certain mass of necessaries must be consumed by a man to grow up and maintain his life. But the man, like the machine, will wear out, and must be replaced by another man. Besides the mass of necessaries required

> for his own maintenance, he wants another amount of necessaries to bring up a certain quota of children that are to replace him on the labour market and to perpetuate the race of labourers. Moreover, to develop his labouring power and acquire a given skill, another amount of values must be spent.[40]

This frequently-quoted paragraph is a rare reference which Marx makes to the domestic economy. The reproduction of the labouring strength of waged workers is seen by him as one involving merely the buying of daily necessities, not as a process involving the transformation of raw materials into articles of consumption or other productive work. Moreover, Marx here as elsewhere leaves no room for doubt that he believes that the (male) wage labourer takes full responsibility for his own (and his dependents') maintenance himself. 'The working man reproduces the value of his labouring power', Marx states literally. He nowhere discusses the role of (domestic) labour in restoring human labouring strength, which is universally performed by women, nor does he present the capitalist system as a unity of two separate but interlinked spheres of production—the public and the domestic sphere. He devotes his attention almost entirely to the public, and virtually none to the domestic economy.

Here I wish to discuss the possibility of extending Marx's labour theory of value by reviewing his formula on value creation, and comparing it with the formula of one of his precursors, the political economist, Adam Smith. Rosa Luxemburg, the Polish revolutionary theoretician, has given a clearheaded description of the differences in viewpoint between the two masters, and their schools of thought, in her book *Die Akkumulation des Kapitals* (The Accumulation of Capital).[41] Her account of the historical emergence of Marx's formula helps us understand how it can be overhauled. I will now paraphrase Rosa Luxemburg's views.

First of all (and from a historical point of view this is crucial) both Marx and Adam Smith, the father of the classical school of political economy, held that the value of the goods which are sold on the market is determined by the quantity of the labour embodied in these commodities. Thus Adam Smith too (though he was not altogether consistent, as Marx and Engels pointed out)[42] defended the view that the value of the aggregate social product is composed of the wages which are paid to the workers, and of a surplus of unpaid labour, which in the form of profits and interest accrues to the propertied classes (entrepreneurs and landlords). Where then did Smith, in Marx's eyes, go astray? What precisely was wrong with his theoretical conception?

Rosa Luxemburg, following Marx, referred to that value which is incorporated in new products, but which does not get changed in quantity in the course of the process of production (i.e., the value of raw materials and instruments of labour). In Marxist economic theory, the composite of these values is termed 'constant capital'. According to Marx and Luxemburg, Adam Smith had overlooked the role of this part of capital—constant capital or '*c*'. In Rosa Luxemburg's words: 'What he [Smith] forgot, or rather overlooked, is the fact that, apart from being able to create new value, labour can also *transfer* to the new commodities the old values incorporated in the means of production employed.'[43]

Rosa Luxemburg cites a concrete instance to substantiate the point, namely the baking of bread by the baker. The value of bread is larger than the total amount of paid and unpaid hours spent by the baker in producing it, as the bread also incorporates the value of the flour—which in an earlier phase was the product of the miller's labour, and before that, as grain, had been the outcome, the fruit, of the farmer's toil. 'Since all work on materials [material labour] presupposes means of production of some sort which themselves result from preceding labour, the value of this past labour is of necessity transferred to the new product.'[44] Adam Smith missed this point, and thus could not propose a complete formula on the creation of value.

The difference between the classical theory of value and its Marxist counterpart—as summarized by Rosa Luxemburg—is reflected in two different formulae. Smith's formula for the value of commodities was $v + s$ (the division between paid and unpaid, variable and surplus labour). For Marx, however, value is composed of three elements: $v + s + c$. The element he added thus was c, constant capital, or the value transferred to the new product from the means of production, in the process of the manufacturing of commodities. Rosa Luxemburg has emphasized that it took Marx prolonged and thorough thinking before he discovered the formula.

Yet, however pathbreaking Marx's contribution was in supplementing the classical theory of value, today, more than a century after Marx's death, we should no longer hesitate to admit that his theory of value carried a deep patriarchal prejudice, just as Adam Smith's did. Feminists have explained how Marx's theory contained its own injustice, in particular the part of his theory where the value of labour power is analyzed. Marx overlooked the fact that the maintenance of wage labourers requires, apart from consumption, that women also perform household tasks. Just like the value theory of the classical, political economists which he sought to correct, Marx's theory too was biased. Here I merely wish to lay bare—more extensively than feminists to my knowledge have done—how Marx's theory leads to a radical underestimation of the quantity of labour needed to produce commodities. In a sense, his theory covers up as much as it reveals.

Let us look once again at Rosa Luxemburg's example of the baking of bread. Before the baker can perform his paid and unpaid labour ($v + s$), it is not only necessary that someone cooks for him and does the cleaning and other maintenance jobs in the home. It is not only true that someone performs this work without being paid. It also needs to be brought out that the means of production employed by the baker—flour, oven, fuel, etc.—incorporates household labour undertaken in the past, by the wife or another relative of the miller, farmer, and so on. Thus, the element of c, too, contains twofold, unpaid labour performed in the past—the previous production of raw materials and other means of production by wage labourers, as well as previous household labour needed to produce and reproduce the labour power of these waged employees.

By way of conclusion, the main ideas may be summarized as follows. Both conceptions of the labour theory of value—that of Adam Smith and Karl Marx—concealed part of the unjust reality of exploitation. In order to 'incorporate' the contribution of women in performing domestic/household labour and other reproductive tasks, Marx's formula $v + s + c$—the cornerstone of his economic theory—needs to be extended and refined. If we wish to do justice to all those women in society who are doubly exploited, such an overhauling of Marx's labour theory of value is unavoidable. In short, the critique of Marx's critique of political economy, which was given a powerful impetus by Benston, Dalla Costa, and others, needs to be carried forward.

In what way, then, should Marx's theory of labour value be extended? First, we should be clear that the given proposition—that the process of exploitation consists of twofold unpaid labour—indeed represents an extension of Marx's theory rather than a negation of his formula on value creation. Second, the basic method for extending Marx's theory, it seems to me, is to calculate the labour time of (proletarian) housewives. In conformity with the view of his precursor, David Ricardo, Marx had observed that exchangeable value is determined by the quantity of labour embodied in the commodities. As stated before, in his early work *The Poverty of Philosophy*, Marx had approvingly quoted Ricardo, who had argued that labour time 'is the real foundation of the exchangeable value of all things', and that this doctrine is 'of utmost importance in political economy'.[45] Thus, in order to determine the value of commodities, a quantitative assessment of the (female and male) wage workers' labour, and the time they spend in producing for the entrepreneur, is essential.

Similarly, if Marx's theory is to be extended to bring out the labour contribution of housewives and other women to the reproduction of labour power, a quantification of the time they spend on domestic work will be essential. As mentioned earlier, some initial general data are available for this purpose. Thus, it has been brought out that though in industrialized societies the burden of labour has been reduced, it is in particular the task of child care which continues to weigh heavily. The feminist author Margaret Benston in 1969 recorded that 'a mother with young children must spend at least six or seven days a week working close to 12 hours'.[46]

Yet, to quantify women's domestic work we cannot mechanically extend Marx's theory. For one, when women are employed directly by capitalist entrepreneurs, the labour time they personally spend on domestic work may be affected by the intensity of wage labour exploitation. Often, other female members of the family may be entrusted with domestic chores, but possibly, a contraction of time spent on reproductive labour also tends to take place as a consequence of their prolonged toil as wage employees. How wage labour and domestic labour affect each other quantitatively and qualitatively, therefore, needs to be further investigated. One thing seems clear—that women who have to perform both waged work and domestic chores carry an extremely heavy load.

In short, the extension of Marx's theory on exploitation requires that we quantify women's domestic work—a task which cannot be accomplished without further practice, and detailed investigations. It may be possible to state in general terms, as Benston did, what is the minimum time required for domestic chores. Similarly, it may be stated with confidence that the labour day of most married women who are responsible for raising small children, even in industrialized societies, remains very long. I will cite quantitative evidence later on the burden of domestic work carried by women lace workers and garment producers in two Indian states, and of women workers in Japanese factories. A more thorough re-assessment will be made then, when women workers in countries of the North and the South who are subjected to both wage and non-wage labour exploitation, themselves draw up the full matrix of their toil.

The Domestic Economy and the Public Economy: Glucksmann's Dialectical Understanding

An author who has tried to supersede the limitations of the household labour debate of the 1970s in a different manner, and without negating the debate's results, is Miriam Glucksmann. In her book *Women Assemble*, she is not concerned with Marx's abstract formula on value creation, but with the concrete historical evolution of capitalism in Great Britain during the period between the First and Second World Wars. Focusing on industries where goods were produced for mass consumption, such as electric appliances and processed food, she highlights the changes that occurred both within and between the domestic and the public economy. The theoretical understanding developed thus is highly dialectical, in the sense that the domestic and the public economy are seen as two interconnected poles forming an integrated whole. At the same time, the author is critical of both previous Marxist and feminist theorizing.

Glucksmann forcefully argues that sociological theories, which have taken their lead from Marxism, 'have been guilty of privileging the public world of production to the virtual exclusion of the domestic economy'.[47] She believes that there is something thoroughly wrong with theories which explain the class position of people solely on the basis of the position they hold within the public domain of production as wage labourers. In Marxist-inspired theories, the public domain of commodity production 'is analyzed as if it was completely insulated from that of the reproduction of labour power, although in reality the two form an integrated whole'.[48] Since Marxist and 'conventional academic' theoretical frameworks, the author states, encompass only one aspect of economic reality, they are inevitably one-sided. In contradistinction from Marxism, Glucksmann proposes a theoretical framework which looks at the 'total social organization of labour', encompassing the two domains of the public and the domestic economy.

However, while Glucksmann is keenly aware of the fact the women's movement has brought the recognition of domestic labour, she also questions the approach used in some socialist and feminist writings of the 1970s to treat the domestic economy as a non-capitalist institution, as a separate mode of production which is not intrinsically connected to the public, economic domain. Since it was often presumed that both the domestic and the public economy were characterized by different internal principles, 'the actual ways in which the two were connected with each other at any particular historical juncture was not usually a major focus of analysis'.[49] The most common tendency has been, she argues, to presume that capitalism operates in the sphere of production, and patriarchy in the sphere of reproduction.[50] Thus, Glucksmann believes that 'feminist theory has not pushed nearly far enough' in developing an analytical framework that presents the domestic and the public economy as an interconnected whole.

I have referred earlier to the central law of dialectics, the 'law of contradiction', which states that nature, society and human thought consist of 'poles of opposites'. For Glucksmann, the domestic and the public economy should be seen precisely as opposite poles belonging to one integrated whole. In order to understand economic changes in a particular society, she argues, it is necessary to look separately at the evolutions taking place at any particular point in time in each, (i.e., in the public and the domestic spheres of the economy), but it is equally necessary to understand how changes within the one sphere are related to changes in the other. 'The necessity for analysing each pole in its own right does not detract from the fact that the distinctness of each can be fully understood only in its relation to the overall structure which comprises both.'[51]

The significance of Glucksmann's philosophical statement, can best be understood by briefly reviewing her analysis of the changes in Britain in the period between the two World Wars. To establish a concrete basis for her analysis, Glucksmann interviewed a number of women who were employed in factories turning out new mass consumer goods, such as radios, electric appliances (like irons) and packaged food (like sponge cakes and biscuits). While male workers were employed as indirect workers in such factories, the owners exclusively recruited women as direct assembly-line producers, subject to the strictest control through the conveyor belt.[52] Their work as assemblers not only signified a new form of employment for women and a shift in women's employment pattern in the public economy, but also affected women's employment in the domestic economy as domestic servants. Changes within one pole were interrelated with changes within the other pole of the British economy.

Glucksmann, amongst others, scrutinizes statistical data on the evolution of women's employment to assess the importance of the changes that took place. Whereas women's employment in the textile industry declined (official figures registered a loss of over 120,000 women's jobs between 1923 and 1938),[53] their employment in electrical engineering industries registered an increase. The number of women workers in this sector reportedly rose by 123 per cent between 1921 and 1931.[54] Consequently, the share of electrical engineering in women's overall employment in the public economy, and the percentage of women as a proportion of all workers, increased manifold. Whereas men's employment in electrical engineering between 1921 and 1931 rose by 43 per cent, women's rose almost three times more than this. Consequently, women's share of total employment in the sector rose from 26.6 to 32.4 per cent.[55] All these changes transformed the lives of numerous British women. Yet the given data only covers changes that occurred in the domain of the public economy, that is, within one single pole of the British economy.

Another even more important change in women's employment, noted by Glucksmann, is in the employment of domestic servants. Government Census data for 1931 artificially boosted the numbers of domestic servants, partly as a result, Glucksmann believes, of government policy which encouraged unemployed women to train for and seek domestic work. But by 1951 the number of private, domestic servants had decreased by over three-quarters of a million jobs ('to nearly one-seventh of its 1931 levels').[56] Glucksmann devotes as much attention to this shift in employment pattern, which concerned the domestic economy, as she does analyzing the expansion of women's jobs in electrical engineering. For, in her eyes, the move away from domestic service 'represented one of the most dramatic changes in employment of the first half of the twentieth century'.[57] And Glucksmann relates this change to the one which occurred in the public economy. As the interviews she held confirm, many former domestic servants and their daughters, when offered the opportunity, opted to work on the assembly-line in a factory rather than in a middle-class home.

This is just one illustration of the interconnections which existed between changes in the public and the private economy in the inter-war years. In Glucksmann's view, the shift from domestic service to factory employment had an impact on the overall process of capital accumulation in the British economy. Whereas domestic service constituted a specific form of wage relation 'involving work *inside* of the domestic economy but *outside* of a woman's own home',[58] the money wages that domestic servants received represented only a part of their remuneration, since a large part was paid in kind. Domestic servants were only marginally integrated into the circuit of commodity production and consumption, whereas factory workers were more fully integrated into both circuits. Thus, the movement of a large number of women out of employment in the domestic economy into employment in the public domain had the effect of 'integrating working class women much more fully into the production and consumption circuit of capital'.[59] Here again, the structural transformation can only be understood if the two poles of the economy are visualized as one interconnected whole.

Further, the example of the decline in the employment of domestic servants, illustrates not just the need for a historical and dialectical approach to the issue of household labour, but of a class-differentiated approach as well. In the debate of the 1970s, it was often overlooked that the question of women's domestic work, of the reproduction of labour power, historically did not form a uniform question for women belonging to different social classes. On the contrary. The material basis of the debate of the second feminist wave may be located in the growing 'convergence' in positions. The position of housewives belonging to the middle class and those of women belonging to the working class became increasingly similar during the period after the Second World War. Yet, in the preceding period of capitalism, the position of these two categories of women was far from similar. This is also brought out well by Glucksmann's analysis.

Before the First World War, the position of working-class and middle-class women was relatively sharply differentiated. In middle-class homes, much of the domestic work of cleaning, cooking and the transformation of raw materials into goods for family consumption was performed by working-class women, who, all over Europe, formed a highly exploited section of waged employees. The isolation, in particular of residential domestic servants, was extreme, and their hours of toil knew virtually no bounds. Their organization was therefore seen as a crucial task by members of the German proletarian women's movement in the beginning of this century.[60] On the other hand, and contrary to middle-class women, working-class women had always performed their own domestic labour (i.e., the reproduction of the labour power of their husbands, children and themselves). Prior to the era of mass-produced consumer goods, the participation of both classes in the commodity economy was limited and the number of tasks performed at home relatively large, but the domestic economy in these two classes was organized on entirely different lines.

From the 1920s and 1930s onwards, the rapid expansion in the production of electric household appliances and processed food entirely changed the picture. As working-class women chose to join factory work in the new industries, and middle-class women faced a shortage of domestic labourers, women belonging to the middle class increased their participation in the commodity economy by buying electric vacuum cleaners and irons, readymade garments instead of clothes sewn at home, and factory-produced biscuits and cakes instead of home-baked food. On the other hand, the participation of the former domestic labourers-turned factory workers in the commodity economy also increased, in particular when the combined, 'family income' of working-class women and men enabled them to similarly buy electrical appliances and other mass-produced consumer goods. In Miriam Glucksmann's words, in spite of persisting differences in the size of income, ultimately 'both middle and working classes became integrated into the circuit of capitalist consumption in the same way'.[61]

Thus, the transformations which have occurred both in the public and the domestic economy have ultimately led to a certain convergence in the position which middle-class and working-class women hold in relation to capital. Whereas, formerly, middle-class women as owners stood opposed to many working class women as their servants, in this century both sections of women have been drawn into employment outside the home on an increasing scale. As consumers of mass-produced goods too, middle-class and working-class women in industrialized countries of the North today fulfil the same function for capital's process of the realization of surplus value. The modern housewife has been created through a process that has affected both the public and the domestic economy. This process and its outcome can only be fully understood through a historical and class-differentiated approach, such as Glucksmann presents.

A final, crucial point to be drawn from Glucksmann's analysis concerns the changed relationship between the public and the domestic economy, (i.e., the increased importance of the latter 'in the whole circuit of capital accumulation'). In the 19th century, Marx visualized capitalism as a system of universal commodity production, in which all production takes the form of commodities. He depicted commodities as a unity of the opposites 'use value' and 'exchange value', and basically ignored the continuing production of use values in the domestic economy. He presumed that in the economy that existed in the England of his days, all productive work had been brought under the direct sway of capitalism. In Marx's words, 'The wealth of all those societies in which the capitalist mode of production prevails, presents itself as "an immense accumulation of commodities", its unit being a single commodity.'[62]

The historical tendency of the capitalist mode of production is to integrate ever new quarters of society and areas of the world into the sphere of commodity production. Yet Marx's lack of analysis of the dialectical relation between the domestic and the public economy made it difficult to visualize the gradually increasing penetration of commodity relations into the domestic economy. As indicated earlier, Marx presumed that the participation of workers' families, as purchasers, in the commodity economy was limited to the buying of daily necessities, such as staple food. Glucksmann's historical analysis of the evolution in Britain during the period between the World Wars clearly illustrates the fact that the situation has never remained static. The purchasing of household appliances, radios, televisions and other mass-produced consumer goods by working-class families, which has become a growing reality over the last 50 years, affects both the public and the domestic domain of capitalist economies.

As Glucksmann states, in the phase of capitalist development that preceded the First World War, the role of workers' families in the commodity economy was very limited. On the one hand, male workers were primarily employed in capital goods industries, producing 'traditional staples' such as trains, ships and engineering machinery—goods which they did not themselves buy and consume: 'they produced wealth for their employing class and received a wage sufficient to pay for rent and fuel, and to purchase a minimum of commodities and raw materials for consumption in the household.'[63] On the other hand, much of women's energies went into transforming raw materials into goods for consumption—use values—cloth into shirts and flour into bread.

> The bulk of the labour necessary to turn the raw materials into finished goods was done by women in the domestic economy, either on an unpaid basis as wives or as domestic servants employed by middle- and upper-class households, but in both cases working under relations of production quite different from those of commodity production.[64]

The switch to the mass production of goods for domestic consumption has, since the 1920s and 1930s, led to an enormous expansion of the sphere of commodity production and thoroughly altered the internal structure of, and the relationship between, the public and the domestic economic domain. For instance, the expansion of the food-processing industries meant that many more raw materials, henceforth, were transformed into edibles within factories. At the same time, Glucksmann states, the function of the wage earned by members of the working class altered. As workers shifted from the purchasing of raw materials to that of finished goods, the importance of their wages for the realization process of capital became much more crucial than it had ever been before. 'The form and the function of the wage altered historically as an effect of the qualitative change in the relationship between the two poles or structure of polarity.'[65] Clearly, both changes described have signified an expansion of the commodity economy at the expense of home-based production for immediate use.

Summary: Towards a Transformation of Economic Theory

To sum up the main lines of argument of this chapter, the household labour debate of the late 1960s and early 1970s has signalled a major breakthrough at the level of economic theory. Contrary to the traditional Marxist assumption about the unproductive character of domestic labour, it was shown that such labour involves both the production of simple use values for direct consumption and, more importantly, the production and reproduction of the special commodity labour power. In concrete terms, this means the bearing and rearing of children (future labour power), maintenance/care of the husband who is a waged employee, and restoring the female waged worker's own labouring strength. Thus, domestic labour involves the creation of two forms of value—use values and a special, exchangeable value.

While all these can be considered to be positive results, I have also noted some of the debate's defects. Though the household labour debate, by singling out a part of women's labour, helped to renew economic theory, the simultaneous tendency to overlook the waged aspect of women's work was problematic. From this one-sided assessment the danger arises that feminists in their turn—although very differently from Marx—underestimate the burden of women's toil. Secondly, the movement's slogan 'wages for housework', with its reformist overtones, remained a controversial one. As the central demand of the campaign around domestic work, it weakened the movement's class orientation, and made it difficult for feminist activists to orient themselves solidly towards those burdened with a double workload (i.e., domestic slavery plus waged work).

Further, I have indicated two possible directions for deepening the insights of the household debate. First, if Marx's formula on the creation of value, $v + s + c$ (representing variable, surplus and constant capital), is scrutinized on the basis of the theoretical conclusions formulated by participants of the second feminist wave, we are forced to admit that Marx radically underestimated the amount of labour that goes into the production of commodities. To give weight to women's contribution to value creation, the content of each of these three elements should be reformulated. To reiterate, v, s and c contain, apart from the labour performed directly under the entrepreneur, labour performed indirectly to their benefit (i.e., by women in the home). The production of surplus value involves twofold exploitation—of the domestic slave and the wage labourer.

Finally, another direction for fruitful theoretical thought has been suggested by Miriam Glucksmann in her research on the evolution of the British economy in the period between the two World Wars. Glucksmann uses a historical and dialectical approach to analyze the changed position working-class women occupied, connecting transformations in the public domain (for instance, the employment of women as assemblers in electric engineering firms) with changes in the domestic economy (the decline in the employment of domestic servants). She concludes that the changes in the two spheres—the domestic and the public—are closely intertwined. Differing with feminists who have presumed that the public and domestic economy are separate entities characterized by different internal principles, she argues that the two should be understood as interconnected poles, forming an integrated whole. The way forward, beyond the limited parameters of the household labour debate, seems to lie in a theoretical framework which looks at the total social organization of labour, encompassing the two domains of the public and the domestic economy.

Notes and References

1. See, for instance, Eisenstein (1979); Hartmann (1981); Kuhn and Wolpe (1978); Sargent (1986).
2. See Bono and Kemp (1991), p. 40.
3. See, for instance, Birnbaum (1986), p. 132; Bono and Kemp (1991), p. 260; Coulson et al. (1975); Dalla Costa and James (1972); Malos (1980); Secombe (1974); West (1980).
4. Birnbaum (1986), p. 90.
5. Ibid., p. 103.
6. Ibid., p. 105; Bono and Kemp (1991), p. 211.
7. Birnbaum (1986), p. 110.
8. Dalla Costa and James (1973), p. 47.
9. For references to unpaid domestic work in the Manifesto of Rivolta Femminile, see Bono and Kemp (1991), p. 39.
10. See Birnbaum (1986), p. 135.
11. Ibid., p. 130.
12. Ibid., p. 141.
13. Cutrufelli (1977), p. 96.
14. de Marco and Talamo (1976), p. 136.
15. Coulson et al. (1975); Gardiner (1975); Secombe (1974).
16. Benston (1980), p. 119.
17. For a short review of the standpoint on women's work in the American feminist movement preceding the publication of Benston's essay, see Malos (1980), pp. 8–10.
18. Ibid., p. 124, emphasis added.
19. Ibid., p. 121.
20. Ibid.
21. Ibid.
22. Dalla Costa and James (1973), p. 27.
23. Ibid.
24. Ibid., p. 30.
25. Ibid., p. 42.
26. Ibid., p. 39.
27. Ibid.
28. Beechey (1987), pp. 7–8. Several participants in the debate on household labour re-adopted more orthodox, Marxist notions. For instance, the Conference of Socialist

Economists (1977), p. 10, states: 'The approach we have come to adopt uses a more orthodox interpretation of value theory in that it defines value as socially necessary labour time embodied in commodities. The value of labour power is therefore defined as the value of the commodities necessary for the reproduction and maintenance of the worker and his family.' Vogel, in Sargent (1986, p. 195), also returns to orthodox notions: 'Ten years after the domestic labour debate began, certain questions appear to be settled. As it turns out, it is relatively easy to demonstrate theoretically that domestic labour in capitalist societies does not take the social form of value-producing labour.'

29. Birnbaum (1986), p. 135, argues that the Padua collective constructed 'a reformist version of the theory'.
30. Malos (1980), p. 37, lists a series of alternative demands, including workplace demands for paternity leave and pension rights for women who have spent years of their lives as housewives.
31. Malos (1980), p. 125.
32. Ibid., p. 121.
33. Saffioti (1978), p. 53.
34. Ibid., p. 54.
35. Ibid., p. 53.
36. Glucksmann (1990), pp. 2, 7.
37. Marx (1977a), p. 164. See also Marx (1973c). The quote is from Martin Nicolaus' introduction to Marx (1973b), p. 61.
38. Marx (1973c), p. 34, emphasis in original.
39. In *Capital* (Marx 1977a), p. 167, Marx discussed the value of labour power: 'We must now examine more closely this peculiar commodity, labour power. Like all others it has its value. How is that value determined? The value of labour power is determined, as in the case of every other commodity, by the labour time necessary for the production, and also consequently the reproduction, of this special article. So far as it has value, it represents no more than a definite quantity of the average labour of society incorporated in it. Labour power exists only as a capacity or power of the living individual. Its production consequently presupposes his existence. Given the individual, the production of labour power consists in his reproduction of himself or his maintenance. For his maintenance he requires a given quantity of the means of subsistence. Therefore the labour time required for the production of labour power reduces itself to that necessary for the production of those means of subsistence; in other words, the value of labour power is the value of the means of subsistence necessary for the maintenance of the labourer.'
40. Marx (1973c), p. 45.
41. Luxemburg (1981a).
42. See, for instance, Engels (1977), p. 235: 'the determination of the value of commodities by wages...in Adam Smith still frequently appeared side-by-side with its determination by labour time'. In *Grundrisse*, Marx (1973b), p. 104, mainly credited Adam Smith with having broadened the conception of the so-called 'physiocrats' about wealth-creating activity: 'It was an immense step forward for Adam Smith to throw out every limiting specification of wealth-creating activity—not only in manufacturing, or commercial or agricultural labour, but one as well as the others, labour in general'. In reality, both Smith's and Marx's views

were male-biased, both ignored women's wholly unpaid, domestic work, and both can be criticized for not having addressed 'labour in general'.

43. Luxemburg (1981a), p. 41, emphasis added. See also Lenin (1977), p. 47.
44. Luxemburg (1981a), p. 41.
45. Marx (1975), p. 45.
46. Malos (1980), p. 129.
47. Glucksmann (1990), p. 270.
48. Ibid., p. 269.
49. Ibid., p. 265.
50. Ibid., p. 13. An example of a feminist author who sees capitalism and patriarchy as operating in two separate spheres is Christine Delphy. See Barrett (1980), p. 14.
51. Glucksmann (1990), p. 258.
52. Ibid., pp. 143, 197.
53. Ibid., p. 51.
54. Ibid., p. 58.
55. Ibid.
56. Ibid., p. 50.
57. Ibid., p. 53.
58. Ibid., p. 252, emphasis added.
59. Ibid., p. 253.
60. For an analysis of the position of domestic servants (*dienstboten*) in Germany around the turn of the century, see Braun in Brinker-Gabler (1979), p. 41.
61. Glucksmann (1990), p. 254.
62. Ibid., p. 43.
63. Ibid., p. 266.
64. Ibid.
65. Ibid., p. 267.

PART 2

The Industrial Work of Women in India and Bangladesh

5

Home-based Women Labourers in the Garment Industry in West Bengal

'Industry heavies want to get in on the ground floor of a business that is poised to explode.' Euphoric is, without exaggeration, the right term for the language and style of the *All India Directory of Readymade Garment Dealers*, published in 1990. The report gave a point-by-point description of the rapid growth in the production of readymade garments in India. According to its figures, the total value of the domestic market in such garments stood at Rs. 3,000 crore (roughly $1 billion) in the given year, and the expansion rate was stated to be 30 per cent per year. Moreover, the report predicted a further acceleration in the market growth for the 1990s.

The main, though not the only drive behind this rapid growth is undoubtedly what is called 'the consumer revolution' which has taken place recently, mainly in India's towns and cities. Whereas, until the 1980s, most Indians preferred to wear traditional dresses like *dhotis* and *saris*, urban middle-class men, and increasingly women, are shifting to Western-style trousers, shirts, skirts and frocks. Thus, the forementioned Directory estimates that within a decade, the percentage of fabrics from Indian textile mills that goes into the manufacturing of readymade garments will increase from 8 or 10 per cent to no less than 80 per cent.

One factor facilitating such a rapid shift is the fact that India, more than, for instance, the neighbouring country of Bangladesh, has a powerful, indigenous textile industry. Thus, raw materials for the burgeoning readymade garments' sector do not need to be imported, since cotton clothes and other raw material inputs can be procured from 'local' textile mills. The mill owners' expansion into the new business is facilitated by the fact that they possess a ready infrastructure for the sale of the new products. As the 1990 report explains, 'They want to cash in on their brand names and distribution channels'.

However, it should be noted that the production of readymade garments in India does not generally take place in factories, but in smaller industrial units, in what is now fashionably called the 'informal sector'. Although the small-scale industries sector, in India and elsewhere, has become the focus of much academic investigation only since the 1970s, in fact this sector has consistently provided the lion's share of India's industrial output and employment opportunities.[1] With regard to the sector producing readymade garments, the supply-lines of cloth and the marketing of dresses are dominated by India's powerful business houses, multinationals and members of the traditional merchant communities. Production itself, however, is subcontracted to small-scale units (i.e., to workshops known in West Bengal as *daleej*, or to male and female stitchers, labouring at home).

Garment Production in Calcutta: The Sector's Evolution and Basic Features

The West Bengal readymade garments sector shares common features with the same sector elsewhere in India, but it also has a number of distinct features. First, West Bengal has a very small share of garment exports. While a sizeable number of production units in and around cities like Delhi, Bombay and Madras are geared towards export markets, the production of trousers, shirts, frocks and other dresses in and around the metropolis of Calcutta is almost wholly channelled to markets in India's eastern region. According to the Apparels Export Promotion Council, New Delhi, in 1980 only 2.6 per cent of India's garments exports originated from Calcutta compared to 57.5 per cent from Delhi and 26.2 per cent from Bombay.[2] The situation has not changed significantly since.

Second, our investigation into the sector confirmed that garment production in West Bengal is predominantly subcontracted via a multi-tier structure to tailors running small workshops with a workforce of

20 machine operators at most, or directly to male and female tailors operating a sewing machine in their own homes. Although, in the past, factories used to exist in the sector, today the 'manufacturers' prefer to subcontract almost all production activities, except the cutting of cloth. The result is an extremely complex web of relationships, and the subjection of the workers to a very high rate of exploitation. The predominant form of wages is the system of piece-rates, known locally as the *furan* system.

Third, and this distinguishes the situation in West Bengal from cities elsewhere, the readymade garments sector is completely neglected by the state government. The left-oriented government, which has been in power since the late 1970s, has promoted investments in agriculture and, to an extent, the interests of tenants and farmers as well. It has actively wooed India's large industrialists and provided them with investment facilities. But it has patently ignored the potential of readymade garments production. Credit schemes for manufacturers are non-existent, and the workers, whose interests the government claims to represent, remain seriously underpaid. According to a local activist of the CPI(M) (Communist Party of India, Marxist), the main component of the ruling coalition, when the state minister visited the garment-producing area of Moheshtola–Santoshpur, representatives of the population told him about the numerous complaints but they have not heard from him since.

Fourth, the sector provides employment to a large number of women. The production tasks of these women workers vary, but they are uniformly homeworkers. Precise employment figures do not exist, but reliable sources estimate that the total number of garment workers is at least half a million, and the majority are women. And whereas the workforce in the Moheshtola–Santoshpur area includes many male tailors, in the Dumdum–Paikpara area the stitching tasks are subcontracted to female tailors. In this geographic area, which does not have a long history of garment production, women form almost the entire workforce. Calcutta's readymade garments sector thus confirms the trend indicated by Nirmala Banerjee for the city. Women are increasingly participating in wage-labouring activities, but predominantly in the informal sector of the economy.[3]

Further, in order to understand the character of West Bengal's readymade garment production, we need to focus on the existence of two geographically distinct patterns of production relations. One is found in the southern fringes of the city, in Moheshtola–Santoshpur, where dresses like *punjabis*, shirts, children's wear and trousers are manufactured. The other distinct pattern exists in the Dumdum–Paikpara area, on the northern side of the city and in the surrounding villages. Not only do production relations vary significantly in these two areas but the employment patterns for women, whose labour is the focus of my concern, are clearly at variance as well.

There is, to start with, a difference in the length of time the two areas have been engaged in manufacturing clothes. In Moheshtola–Santoshpur, we can speak of a long tradition, of a tailoring profession which was transmitted by resident families over many generations. The first tailors are said to have settled in the area in pre-British times, as part of the entourage of the nawab. In colonial times, they continued their profession by making dresses for European residents. In the 19th century, some 125 years ago, market-oriented garment production was started. Yet, according to local manufacturers (known as *ostagars*), the real expansion of production occurred around the time of the struggle for the creation of the state of Bangladesh in 1971. Shortly after this country's liberation, huge quantities of garments are said to have been exported to the new-born nation.

The history of garment production in the Dumdum–Paikpara area is much shorter. Here, its emergence is closely related to the immigration of, mainly, Hindu refugees from East Bengal/Bangladesh. During the wave of communal riots that accompanied the partition of the subcontinent in 1947–48, hundreds of thousands of Hindus fled their homes in East Bengal. Many of them settled on the northern outskirts of Calcutta city and, as a source of survival, opted to engage in the production of readymade garments. Both the women stitchers and the owners share the same background of migration. Contrary to those belonging to the tailoring community in Moheshtola–Santoshpur who are mostly Muslims, almost all follow the religion of West Bengal's majority (i.e., Hinduism).

The employment patterns for women are geographically distinct as well. In Moheshtola–Santoshpur, women are entrusted with what are seen as subsidiary tasks. In the division of labour prevailing here, they perform tasks like unstitching and washing (old pants), hand-sewing ornaments (on *punjabi* dresses), piercing buttonholes and removing loose threads. They are not supposed to do 'male' jobs like stitching and embroidery, the two principal tasks involving the use of machinery. In Dumdum–Paikpara, the situation is very different. Here women are not just employed to do subsidiary tasks, like hemming blouses, but form the bulk of the workforce. They are allowed to operate sewing machines. Speaking from an overall sectorwise view, it is only the job of cutting clothes which is consistently monopolized by men.

Another important characteristic of garments production in West Bengal is that the turn-over time of the owners' capital is short. Since the size of capital of most *ostagars* is relatively small, they need to maintain the pace of investment and re-investment of their capital. Speed, a quick turn-over, can compensate for the lack of a sizeable amount of money resources. As Marx explained (both in *Grundrisse* and *Capital*), an owner of a small amount of capital can make a sizeable profit, or even exceed the profit-rate made by a bigger capitalist, provided the turnover time of his capital is short.[4]

In West Bengal's garments sector, the turn-over time of capital is invariably short. This can best be illustrated with information about Moheshtola–Santoshpur, since relatively more data could be collected from *ostagars* who live in this geographic area. The value of the weekly turn-over of *ostagars* in this areas is as follows: the biggest *ostagars* can muster Rs. 2 to 3 crore; the medium-sized *ostagars*' capital ranges between Rs. 50 lakh (5 million) and Rs. 2 crore; the third layer of *ostagars* possesses Rs. 1 to 25 lakh; and the category of small owners owns less than Rs. 1 lakh. Whereas only a few *ostagars* belong to the first group, the last-mentioned category has thousands of members.

Invariably, however, all *ostagars* re-use their capital within a period of just one week. At the beginning of the week, the *ostagars* procure a stock of cloth (cloth reportedly accounts for 75 to 80 per cent of the cost price of most garments)[5] from a merchant at Barrabazar, which is the main centre of cloth-trading in the city. After completing the whole production cycle, a week later the garments are brought to the market for sale. The *ostagars* do their weekly trading at Harisha *haat* and Mongla *haat* near Howrah station. The latter is not just a market where local consumers make their choice. Regular buyers also include scores of traders from neighbouring states. Sales results are immediately re-invested in the production that takes place the following week.

How many steps need to be undertaken within a week's time? The example of *punjabi* production illustrates well that the chain of production tasks can be quite long (see Figure 5.1). While being turned from raw material into *punjabi* dresses, the cloth travels between no

The Production Structure of **Punjabis** *in Moheshtola*

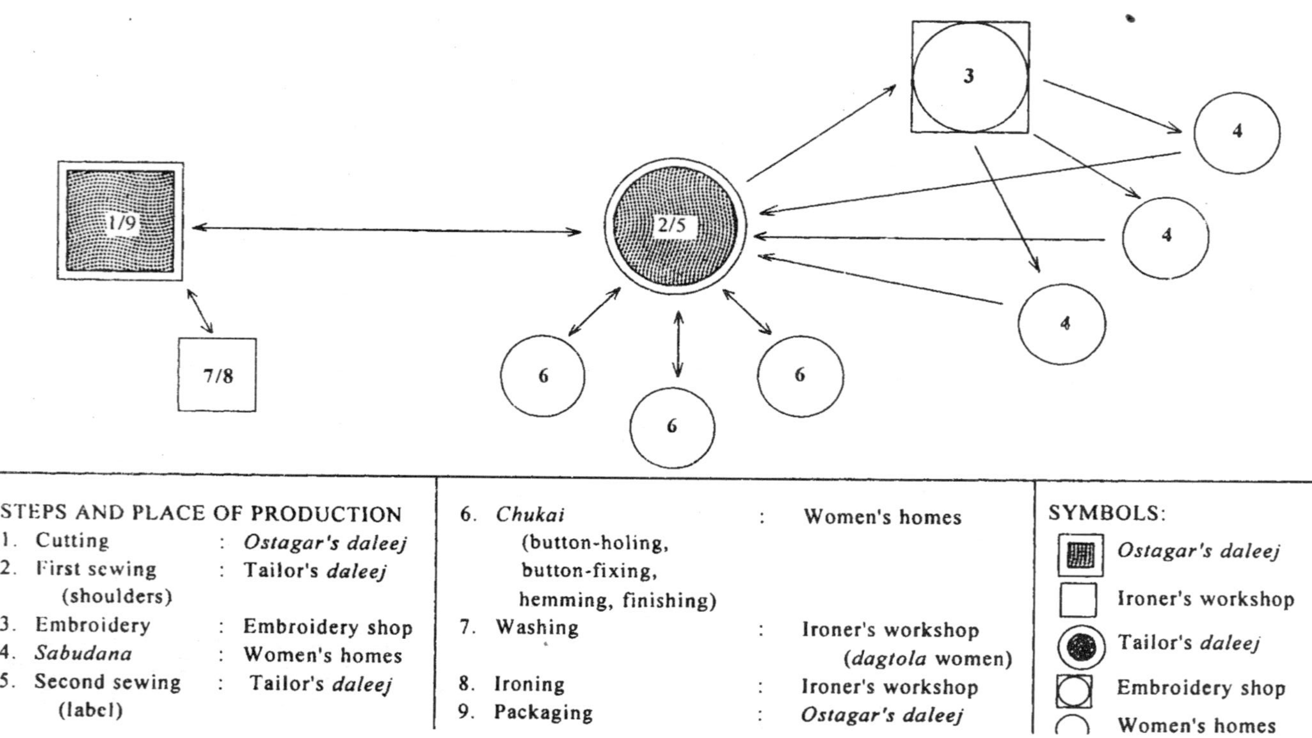

less than five different production places—the *ostagar's* residence and workplace, the tailor's workshop (*daleej*), the embroidery shop, women workers' homes and the ironer's workshop. During this process, nine different production tasks are performed, three of which are women's tasks—ornament-sewing by hand; several tasks defined as 'finishing' (button-fixing, hemming and the removal of loose threads), and the hand-washing of the end product to ensure that the *punjabi* is clean. Given the short turn-over time of the *ostagars'* limited capital, the workers are constantly under pressure to complete their tasks.

Village Women's Production Tasks in the Moheshtola–Santoshpur Area

Kholai–dholai is a term that is peculiar to the process of re-manufacturing old pants, which takes place in a part of Moheshtola called Chatta Kalikapur. In the dark verandas of their village huts, old and young women spend long days preparing second-hand trousers for re-stitching in the workshops. First, they undo the stitching of old pants (*kholai*). Then the pieces of cloth are washed with soap and starched with arrowroot (*dholai*). Before they hand over the clothes to the male stitchers, the women also do a round of ironing.

These tasks are extremely laborious and low paid. Paid on piece-rates, a *kholai–dholai* woman homeworker can earn a maximum of Rs. 20 to 22 per day if she manages to process 100 pairs of trousers (see Table 5.1). However, to get the figure for her net earnings, the cost of charcoal, soap and arrowroot needs to be deducted from this amount. Moreover, to earn this sum a woman is forced to toil for 13 or 14 hours (i.e., neglect her household tasks and her health). Thus, it is only in the period preceding festivals, when the pressure to finish orders is particularly high, that the small groups of women relatives, collectively, unstitch and wash old pants until late at night.

Though a regular feature of cloth production in Chatta Kalikapur, the re-manufacturing of old trousers is considered 'second-rate production'. Its growth appears to date from 1971, when the people of East Bengal waged their Independence war and scores of relief goods found their way to the tailoring community near Calcutta. Since many tailors could not cope with the ever-increasing price of new cloth, they accepted the relief goods as a welcome source of raw materials.

Table 5.1

Working Hours and Wages for Producers of Trousers in Moheshtola–Santoshpur

Division of Labour	*Average Daily Income (Rs.)*	*Daily Average Working Hours*	Daleej*/home rented unit*	*Sex*	*Wage Rate (Rs.)*	*Periodicity of Payment*	*Availability of Work during a Week (Days)*
1	2	3	4	5	6	7	8
Cutter	**50**	12	*Daleej*	Male	0.75–1.20 (dozen)	Weekly	4
Darjee	25	12	*Daleej*/home	Male	4.50–5.50 (dozen)	Weekly	4
Chukai	6	9	Home	Female	0.30 (piece)	Weekly	3
Old pants	12	10	Home	Female	0.25 (piece)	Weekly	3
Kholai-dholai ironing	12	11	Home	Female	0.25 (piece)	Weekly	3
Embroidering	40	12	Rented unit	Male	2.50 (piece)	Weekly	5

Source: Ganguly and Custers (1993).

The procurement of old pants has since been broadened. One portion continues to hail from outside the country, mainly the United States, but many old pants are also collected by hawkers from the city's middle-class and well-to-do families. The *ostagars*, who are in control of the production and marketing of these pants, own less capital than those manufacturing new pants.

Similarly, the involvement of women as labourers is a recent phenomenon. A generation ago, all the production tasks in the tailoring sector of Moheshtola–Santoshpur were performed by men. With the introduction of machines, a transformation has taken place in production tasks like stitching, embroidery and interlocking. Manual tasks are now delegated to women, while men hold on to tasks involving the use of machines. This division of tasks along gender lines itself leaves women in a secondary position. Moreover, it also implies the continued threat of replacement. Women workers in Chatta Kalikapur complain that, after the 'latest invasion' of machines, their opportunities for getting work have been reduced.

The *kholai–dholai* women and other female homeworkers, moreover, suffer from a double discrimination. Besides being excluded from machine operation, they are also restrained in their physical movements. The tailoring population of Chatta Kalikapur (which constitutes 60 per cent of the total population) is entirely Muslim, and feel uneasy as a religious minority. Thus, they tend to be conservative. For women this means that strict values of purdah (seclusion) are maintained, and they are prohibited from participating in work outside the home. In short, women and girls who prepare the old pants for re-stitching are at the lower end of the production hierarchy.

Another production task specifically performed by women is *sabudana*, the hand-sewing of ornaments, which is the fourth step in the process of producing *punjabi* dresses. Scattered over the villages surrounding the main centre where the *punjabis* are stitched, scores of women spend the whole day at home with needle and thread. They do *sabudana*—sewing a coarse thread in looplike fashion along the borderline of the neck and the button-line on the chest. This is a job that takes little training, so many girls join the trade at primary school-age. *Sabudana* is work done by women of all ages. This category of labourers consists of the married and unmarried relatives of male tailors, operating the sewing machines in the *daleej*. The orders are brought home to the women either by the *ostagar* or by a male family member.

Just like the unstitching and washing of old pants, in fact like all homework in the sector, *sabudana* is paid at piece-rates. The rate varies slightly, but is about Rs. 1 per *punjabi* completed. During the busy season (i.e., in the period preceding the Muslim festival of Eid and during the period when most marriages take place), a *sabudana* woman's earnings could amount to Rs. 150 per week. During the off-season, the weekly pay is quite low, about Rs. 40 to 50). Still, *sabudana* women are a bit less deprived economically than, say, the stain-removers or the *dagtola* women to whom I will refer later. Many are wage-earners along with their male relatives. Some of the interviewees admitted that they spend a part of their income on 'luxury' items on things they personally like. The labouring burden of these homeworkers is nonetheless heavy. Apart from spending, on an average, seven to eight hours sewing threads, they almost invariably have to do four or five hours of household chores. The prevailing strict sexual division of labour ordains that males are exempted from all responsibility for domestic tasks, even on days when they are free from wage work.

In contrast, the women say that all the key decisions regarding education, medical expenses, and so on, are taken by the men who consider themselves the rulers at home. Even a widow like Nur Aksam says that it is not she, but her sons, who take the major decisions. Further, the rules of purdah are strictly enforced. In the existing Muslim community, women cannot go out alone, but only under male guidance. Several ornament-sewing young women said they were forced to stop studying in school because their male relatives feared social condemnation for breach of purdah rules.

Do *sabudana* women, who clearly contribute to family maintenance, willingly accept all patriarchal prescriptions? Do they consider males to be superior? How do they feel about the existing sexual division of labour which excludes them from machine operations and confines them to the home? Most women interviewed expressed some form of discontent about gender inequality. Typically, several of them said that men are not by nature superior, but that this view is merely imposed by society. Significantly also, several expressed a desire to be able to operate a sewing machine, as a few of their sisters had started doing. Says Murshida Begum, 'Of course women can run sewing machines, it is just that we are not allowed to!'[6]

A third category of women homeworkers in Moheshtola–Santoshpur are the *chukai* women who are present in the production of both *punjabis* and pants. A *chukai* woman's task varies somewhat, but it generally entails making button-holes, fixing buttons and removing loose threads. *Chukai* is seen as the 'finishing part' of clothes production, as a minor job too demeaning to be allocated to men. In the Moheshtola–Santoshpur area, both illiterate and educated women are involved in *chukai* work. As a production task performed by women at home, *chukai* work is clearly low status and is, again, decidedly low paid.

Many of the *chukai* women are early risers. They get up before dawn, at 4:30 or 5:00 a.m., to perform various household chores, like making tea, sweeping the yard and cleaning utensils, before starting their day as wage labourers. Like their sisters employed in other stages of the garments production chain, they carry a double burden of labour. Yet the rewards for their long hours of toil are low. The piece-rates for *chukai* work range from 0.15 to 0.30 paisa. Lutfan Bibi of Chatta Kalikapur, whose survival depends on the *chukai* of children's pants, completes 30 pieces per day, earning a paltry Rs. 6. Her weekly income of Rs. 24 (for four days work) is close to the average earning for such work.

A comparison between the position of the male cutters and the *chukai* women brings out the degree of inequality in wages existing in the sector. Whereas a cutter (whose work is seen as skilled work) is paid a regular time wage and receives a festival bonus, *chukai* women are paid on the basis of piece-rates and are deprived of any fringe benefits. While a cutter's monthly income could easily be Rs. 1,500, a *chukai* woman's earnings are no more than one-tenth of this. According to Rahima Khatun, another *chukai* woman, in the off season subsequent to the Hindu festival of Kali Puja her income comes down to Rs. 4 or 5 per week.

Moreover, in the production hierarchy, all men, including co-workers, are women's superiors. A *chukai* woman's direct employer could be the owner, the *ostagar*, who farms out the production of *punjabis* or pants; he could be a petty *ostagar* who himself sews pants along with the male machine operators employed in his workshop; or he could be a male relative, a worker dependent on stitching clothes and paid, like her, per piece. Yet, whatever the man's position within the overall hierarchy in the garments' sector, to the *chukai* women and other female workers, the man who delivers and later collects the orders from them is a boss, an *ostagar*.[7]

Finally, women who work at removing stains are undoubtedly the poorest, most deprived, of all the women employed in the production of garments. They are called *dagtolas*, and their job is to remove stains from newly-sewn *punjabis*. *Dagtola* women are almost invariably migrant women. They are not hereditarily involved in the tailoring sector, but mostly hail from distant places in the Sundarban area, Diamond Harbour, and so on, where their husbands used to engage in lowly paid, irregular jobs like roof-making. In South Kankhuli, husbands look for odd jobs while their wives provide the family's main income through back-breaking toil as *dagtola* women.

Dagtola work forms the final stage of *punjabi* production. The women stain-removers are not employed by *ostagars* but by ironers who, like them, are migrant workers. From sunrise till sunset, these women are burdened with the task of washing *punjabis*. They soak the *punjabis* in large earthen pots, then rub the clothes between the backs of their thumbs. Oil stains caused by the sewing machines are removed by scratching with their nails. After a 12-hour work day, they have to use an oily cream and/or the heat of fire to soften their hands. Many *dagtola* women can be recognized by the ulcers on their fingertips.

The income derived from their menial tasks is clearly insufficient for their survival. An ironer pays a *dagtola* woman 10 paisa per *punjabi* washed. On an average, washer-women complete about 100 pieces per day, earning at most Rs. 60 to 70 a week, whereas the rent for their family's mud hut amounts to Rs. 70 a month. And while they are the main providers of the family income, most *dagtola* women lack the means to properly feed their children. There are days, for instance, when Farida Bibi of Santoshpur is unable to cook, and can only give her four hungry children *chira* (puffed rice) or just water. Undernourishment among these washerwomen and their kin is, therefore, not an exception but the rule.

The social status of *dagtola* women, who are invariably Bengali Muslims, is as deplorable as their economic plight. They suffer from patriarchal oppression both at the hands of male *ostagars* and their own husbands. Some are beaten by their men, while others have been abandoned. Rabiya Bibi, for instance, was her husband's third spouse. After she gave birth to their only son, the man disappeared. Rabiya Bibi now lives in constant fear. The *ostagar's* sons harass her, and threaten that if she does not succumb to their desires, she will have to vacate her hut. Due to the *dagtola* women's extreme poverty, they are easy prey. Whenever the work of cleaning *punjabis* is not available, for instance, during the four months of winter, *dagtola* women are found working as maidservants in the houses of the *ostagars*.[8]

Women Machine Operators in Dumdum–Paikpara: Homeworkers with Self-esteem

A review of the position of women machine operators—those women who, like men, stitch clothes with sewing machines—shows how varied the position of women workers is. This category of female labourers is found almost exclusively in the Dumdum–Paikpara area of the metropolis. In fact, here they form the vast majority (over 90 per cent) of the workforce employed. Like their sisters employed elsewhere as ornament-makers, finishers, and so on, these women are also homeworkers. While their male colleagues in Moheshtola–Santoshpur, as already indicated, frequently share a working space with other male tailors, the women machine operators in Dumdum–Paikpara toil individually within the confines of their own home.

Yet, in spite of their individualized, atomized existence, these women enjoy a greater degree of self-esteem than their sisters on the southern fringe of the city. First, unlike the latter, they do control a significant means of production. Each woman stitching blouses, frocks or petticoats is the owner of one or two sewing machines. In terms of the profit calculations of the manufacturers who farm out the stitching work to them, this means, of course, that production costs (for constant capital) are transferred to the exploited workers. Yet the ownership, however limited the amount of capital involved, does provide the women stitchers with some social prestige.

Moreover, and unlike their sisters in Moheshtola–Santoshpur, the female workers in Dumdum–Paikpara are directly employed by the male manufacturers or their intermediaries. True, as workers they do not enjoy any security. The interviews taken with home-based stitchers clearly illustrate that they can be dismissed by their boss any time, for reasons such as illness or in retaliation for 'insubordination'. Yet the crucial difference with their sister homeworkers on the southern edge of the city is that they are never employed via a male wage worker. They do not form a sub-layer in a hierarchy, where the 'true' male tailors and embroiderers stand above them, for they themselves are the principal producers of blouses, frocks and petticoats.

Contrary to other homeworkers, the women stitchers bring their orders home themselves. This would seem to follow logically from the fact that the stitchers are the direct employees of the owners, but also points at a crucial cultural difference between them and the women homeworkers at the other end of Calcutta city—the women machine operators are not subject to the rules of purdah. Thus, they do not need to rely on their husbands or sons to bring their orders home, but go to collect the cloth and threads from the owner or contractor themselves. Finally, and again contrary to the practice in the Muslim communities of Moheshtola–Santoshpur, the women stitchers in Dumdum–Paikpara collect the remuneration for their toil from the owners, the malik, themselves.

The labouring burden of a woman machine operator in the Dumdum–Paikpara area of Calcutta is no doubt heavy. In the course of our investigation some nine female frock-stitchers were interviewed, varying in age from 14 to 43 years. Invariably, all the workers had to perform both household tasks and wage labour. We asked them to indicate the number of hours they spend daily on each type of work. Apart from seasonal differences in work pressure, the average, normal working day of these frock-stitchers turned out to be almost 15 hours, out of which about eight hours are spent on domestic chores. Where the family includes other females, domestic work is shared with mothers, sisters and/or daughters but never with the male members of the family.

Like all other women homeworkers in the sector, the producers of frocks are paid on the basis of the piece-rate system. At first glance, the rate they are paid seems to be higher than that of the *chukai* women and other female wage labourers in the Moheshtola–Santoshpur area—Rs. 10 per dozen frocks stitched. Since it takes roughly an hour and a half for an adult to complete a dozen pieces, these homeworkers claimed they completed at least four dozen frocks every day.[9] Spending six days a week bent over their sewing machines, they earn about Rs. 250. In the months preceding the puja festivals, their working days are longer, and their income rises concomitantly to Rs. 350 or even Rs. 400 per week.

Though this is clearly higher than the income of the *dagtola* and *chukai* women referred to earlier, it is not the net income of a woman stitcher. First, some owners subtract Rs. 1.80 per dozen for the cost of the threads, which they supply to the stitchers. Second, like her male counterparts in Moheshtola–Santoshpur, a frock producer subcontracts a part of the production tasks, namely the finishing task of fixing hooks or buttons to the frocks. According to Ranibala Das of Dakshin Rabindranagar, the rate for this work is 60 paisa per dozen (i.e., 6 per cent). 'Moreover, since the machine is ours, it is we who are responsible for maintenance and repairs. A new machine has to be mended once every year, an old machine three or four times.' And, of course, ownership of the sewing machines also means that the women stitchers have to account for depreciation costs. Another factor negatively influencing her pay is that the owners hold the stitchers responsible for any production failures. In case he disapproves of any product, the pay cut, according to Ranu Kundu, is Rs. 20 to 30. So, ultimately, the earnings of a woman stitcher are still quite meagre, in spite of her lengthy working day (see Table 5.2).

Nevertheless, in all cases the income of the stitchers is essential to the survival of their families. Their fathers or husbands, being painters, rickshaw drivers or masons, do not earn an income that could be termed a steady wage, sufficient for the family's maintenance. The stitchers interviewed contributed at least 50 per cent, and often the major part, of the family's overall earnings. It therefore would be wrong to call their income 'supplementary', as patriarchal ideology dictates. In fact, the earlier description of the frock producers illustrates the double contribution which they and other women home-workers make to their families' survival. Through their domestic work, these women ensure that their own labour power and that of their husbands and children is (re)produced. As stitchers of frocks they, moreover, produce exchange values. Thus, the amount of use value and exchange value they create each day far exceeds that of the male members of their families.[10]

Regarding struggles against exploitation, it is in Dumdum–Paikpara that some women stitchers are known to have taken an autonomous initiative to stand up for their own rights. In the past, militant mass struggles of garment workers have mainly been concentrated in the Moheshtola area. According to Moslim Ali Mandal, a cutter who played a leading role in workers' movements in the area, there have been several waves of struggles. In 1956, 24,000 *darjees* marched in procession to the state Assembly. In 1967, the movement of the tailors reached another peak with a strike lasting for 19 days. In 1975, *darjees* raised their voice in protest once again. They did so in 1983 too, with a 10,000-strong procession led by Moslim Ali personally.[11]

Table 5.2

The Labour Time and Wage Rates of Women Garment Producers in Dumdum-Paikpara

Division of Labour	*Average Daily Net Income (Rs.)*	*Daily Average Working Hours*	*Work Place*	*Wage Rate (Rs./Dozen)*	*Periodicity of Payment*	*Availability of Work during a Week (Days)*
					Blouse (plain cut)	
Darjee	9	6	Home	6.00	Weekly	3
Hemming women	3	4	Home	1.50	Weekly	3
					Blouse (Bombay cut)	
Darjee	12	6	Home	8.00	Weekly	3
Hemming women	5	4	Home	2.50	Weekly	3
					Petticoat (plain cut)	
Darjee	9	6	Home	4.00	Weekly	3
					Petticoat (Chap)	
	10	6	Home	5.00	Weekly	3

Source: Ganguly and Custers (1993).

Notes: Most of the women hire sewing machines for Rs. 30–40 per month.

Cutting is done according to the pattern laid down by the owner, in most of the cases at his home.

Chap literally means pressure. *Chap* petticoats have a second sewing, and the second stitching is called *chap*.

These recurrent struggles resulted in government laws covering labour relations in the sector, and tripartite agreements involving a trade union body called the West Bengal Tailors' Union. But the laws have largely remained unimplemented. Moreover, the struggles have clearly focused on the demands of the male tailors, and not on the specific interests of the subordinate women homeworkers in Moheshtola–Santoshpur. Their plight is conveniently ignored by the Tailors' Union. The only women's initiative we came accross was of women machine operators in Dumdum–Paikpara producing frocks. This was described as follows by one of the participants, Shimarani Das:

> In 1988–89 we formed a Frock *Samiti* without the assistance of any political party. At that time the owners' rate was Taka 6–7 per dozen. We told the owners to increase the rate, and we stopped work for three weeks. Also, we prevented women from outside the locality from taking any orders. All this occurred in the period before the yearly pujas, i.e., when the owners make most profit. The owners understood the danger, and they were willing to sit down with us to discuss our grievances. In the meeting, a minimum rate of Taka 10 per dozen was fixed.[12]

Unfortunately, this successful struggle has not resulted in the formation of a trade union. Many of the women stitchers interviewed felt the need for an organization to defend their interests. They argued that a collective organization would help reduce the level of economic exploitation: 'If we could have a union, the piece rate could be further increased'. However, the basic infrastructure to sustain a broadbased organization is lacking. Thus, the Frock *Samiti* remains an isolated initiative with a limited membership of about 200 persons, and women like Shimarani Das deplore that they cannot engage in organizing and struggles to defend their sisters' and their own rights.

Profile of a Blouse Stitcher: Chabi Mitra of Dakshin Rabindranagar

Chabi is 20 years old and has been sewing blouses for the last five years. She started *darjee* work when she was studying in school. She left school after being promoted to Class V. Of her three sisters, the elder one is married to a worker in a small factory, but the factory has been closed for several months. Chabi is her parents' second child. Her younger sister is studying in Class IX, and she does not do any *darjee* work. Chabi has no brothers.

Chabi starts working at 6:30 a.m. and breaks at 10:30 a.m. to have a bath and eat snacks and lunch. She resumes work an hour and a half later, at 12 o'clock, and continues working till 4:00 or 5:00 p. m. She produces both 'plain-cut' and 'Bombay-cut' blouses. Orders for the first type of blouse are more frequent. The 'Bombay-cut' is a special type and involves double stitching. Chabi produces four or five dozen plain cut blouses during her working day of eight or nine hours, and three dozen when she sews 'Bombay-cut' blouses. She earns about Rs. 300 per month, which she hands over to her father. She is proud that she can contribute to the family's survival.

With regard to the division of labour within the family, Chabi's mother does all the household chores. Moreover, for the last year, her mother has started hemming the blouses Chabi makes. This involves hand-sewing around the neck and upper arms, sewing the front button line, and tacking hooks or buttons on to the blouse. The payment for these tasks is Rs. 1.50 per dozen whenever the work is subcontracted to an outside woman. When the woman doing the hemming is Chabi's mother, the money obviously stays at home.

Chabi's health is poor, yet she toils willingly since she knows it will be a great burden on her father to earn the family income all alone. Her father is a mason. Whenever he finds work, he can earn Rs. 50 to 60 per day. A couple of years back, he fell from a scaffold while working and broke his legs. He spent four months in hospital but never regained his health totally. He can no longer take the risk of 'riding' a scaffold. During the rainy season he is bereft of work, and is idle for at least four months. During this period he gets no pay.

Chabi takes work from a local contractor, Shyamal Das, who brings cloth from a big owner living near Dumdum junction. Shyamal cuts the cloth and, along with the thread required for sewing, distributes the cut pieces to women like Chabi. The owner actually pays him weekly, but subcontractor Shyamal pays the women workers on a monthly basis, giving false excuses (such as the owner has not yet handed over the wages). Moreover, Shyamal temporarily withholds and accumulates part of the wage. For instance, a *darjee* who has worked for a month and a half will receive payment of one month's work only; the rest of the payment is always delayed. With regard to the supply of raw materials, the owner, besides cloth, provides thread, buttons and hooks. A dozen plain cut blouses requires one reel of thread; for the 'Bombay cut' type of blouses, a little more than one reel is required.

Before working with Shyamal, Chabi worked for Bankim Mullick who is a very big owner of a blouse-making unit at Bahiragata Colony near Dumdum junction. At one point she had to undergo an operation because she was suffering from appendicitis. The stitches due to the operation continue to cause pain. After she was operated, she had to abstain from work for a long time. Moreover, given her poor health ever since, she is afraid of travelling long distances to collect her orders. Bankim Mullick still owes her Rs. 100 for previous work. Now she tries to avoid a repetition of the situation faced earlier.

> The owner never pities us. If I fail to deliver my work in time owing to my ailing health, my work will be given to another woman. Then I will remain deprived of work for several days. Therefore, whatever happens to my health, I always try to deliver my work on time.

Chabi does not get any bonus or any kind of extra allowance. She thinks she is underpaid, but cannot say so for fear of losing work. When she was working for Bankim Mullick, around 135 women had been working for him for many years, but had never asked for a pay rise. Chabi is burdened with the thought, 'If my income stops, how can my father manage to bear the whole burden of the family's expenditure—the house rent (Rs. 105 per month), educational expenses for my sister, medical expenses for all of us, including my elder sister's family?'[13]

Garment Production in West Bengal and the Concept of the Informal Sector

After having described the various categories of women labourers, let us now interpret the facts. A concept that in the last two decades has frequently been used to explain conditions such as those that exist in West Bengal's garments sector is the 'informal sector'. Emmanuel Romatet has taken the history of the debate on the concept of the 'informal sector' as his starting point. According to him, the concept originated in research work undertaken under the auspices of United Nations institutions in the 1970s, in particular in economic investigations carried out for the ILO.[14]

The concept of the informal sector is useful, insofar as it exposes the vast differences existing between labouring conditions in large factory complexes in and near major cities and those prevailing in small workshops and home-based industries. Whereas factory workers have access to trade unions, and frequently enjoy the benefits of social legislation, informal sector workers tend to be unorganized, are disregarded by state legislation, and suffer from limitless exploitation. Romatet cited as one of the advantages of the use of the concept of the informal sector, that this made it possible 'to identify one target group always overlooked in planning'—the urban poor—living in slums surrounding the metropolises.[15]

Romatet's short review of the literature on the subject, however, also exposed some of the main weaknesses underlying the concept. The economist, John Keith Hart, in the early 1970s suggested that the distinction between the 'formal' and 'informal' sectors be used in order to renew the dualism theory. This theory, which held that Third World economies suffer from a dichotomy between modern and traditional sectors, had become the subject of much controversy. Hart did not deny that a dichotomy existed; he just proposed to change the terminology. In the course of the debate on the 'informal sector', however, it was pointed out that this sector does not lack linkages to the 'formal sector'.[16] In fact, as the discussion on Japanization in Chapter 11 clarifies, multinational corporations and other capitalist enterprises frequently subcontract work to the informal sector so as to circumvent employment legislation and reduce production costs.[17]

Moreover, many of the characteristics described in the literature on the subject of the informal sector could well be covered by terms commonly used in classical, Marxist economic theory. Thus, the ILO mission report on Kenya, which according to Romatet gave the 'official stamp' on the renewal of the dualism theory, included as typical features of the informal sector that labourers here are very mobile, and that it is the entry point for immigrants from villages in search of an urban job. Marx in *Capital* explained that labouring conditions under capitalism are not homogeneous, and that it is in capitalism's interest that a part of the working class is employed in home industries where exploitation is particularly severe. Thus, while it is true that many of the features listed by Romatet apply to the garments sector in Calcutta, its male and female workers could equally well be covered by Marx's concept of the industrial reserve army.[18]

Significance of the Piece-rate System—Marx versus von Werlhof

Another point for analysis is the specific form of exploitation of women workers in the garments sector in Calcutta. We have seen earlier that, whether they are stitchers (as in Dumdum–Paikpara) or 'subsidiary workers' engaged in unstitching trousers, fixing buttons and removing loose thread, or in soaking and washing newly-produced *punjabis* (as in Moheshtola–Santoshpur), the women employed in the sector are uniformly homeworkers paid on the basis of the *furan* or piece-rate system. How does one evaluate this system? How does one interpret the specific conditions of these women labourers in terms of economic theory?

In *Capital*, Marx noted that both forms of wages, time wages and piece wages, often exist side by side. In England during his time (i.e., in the middle of the 19th century), the same category of workers could be subjected to both kinds of wage regime, depending on where exactly they were employed or what nationality they belonged to. Thus, the compositors in London and the shipwrights of the London port worked by the piece, while their colleagues in the country were paid by the day. Again, in the saddlery shops of London, French workers were paid piece wages, while time wages were paid to the English workers. In the latter case, discrimination was obvious, as the two different forms of wages were often applied 'for the same work'![19]

The owners in the contemporary garments sector of West Bengal, likewise, apply the time and piece wage system side by side. For instance, in South Kankhuli, where *punjabis* are produced, time wages are paid to the male cutters and the tailors employed in the *ostagars'* own workshops, while other male tailors and embroiderers, and all categories of subsidiary, female labourers, are paid according to the number of pieces produced. The dividing line here seems to be between workers toiling under an *ostagar's* immediate supervision and those to whom work is directly or indirectly subcontracted. While in the first case the owner himself regulates their daily working time (up to 14 hours), in the second case the working time is regulated by the product, by the time required to complete a piece.

Marx goes on to explain the specific character of the piece-rate system.

> Since the quality and intensity of the work are here controlled by the form of wage itself, superintendence of labour becomes in great part superfluous. Piece wages therefore lay the foundation of the modern 'domestic labour'. . . as well as of a hierarchically organized system of exploitation and oppression.

On the one hand, piece wages facilitate the interposition of parasites between the capitalist and the wage labourer (i.e., middlemen); on the other hand, the piece-rate system allows the capitalist to subcontract work to a head labourer who then undertakes the enlisting and payment of his assistant workers.[20]

Marx's analysis, written 130 years ago, is exactly the same as what exists today in the garments sector in West Bengal. The *ostagars* in Moheshtola–Santoshpur and the owners in Dumdum–Paikpara have made the supervision of production work superfluous through the extensive application of the piece-rate system. Some of them in northern Calcutta farm out the stitching via intermediaries. Others, for instance in South Kankhuli where *punjabis* are made, delegate work to head labourers and tailors who run small sweatshops where they share the workload with other male workers. Above all, the application of the piece-rate system facilitates the exploitation of domestic labour, of women, on the widest possible scale. Clearly, Marx's explanation is not outdated.

The position of homeworkers is analyzed differently by Claudia von Werlhof, a member of the German feminist school. She analyzes present-day reality in terms of the dichotomy between 'free wage labour' on the one hand, and the 'housewife' on the other. In her view, the ever-increasing expansion of the informal sector leads to the abolition of the first type of worker. The conditions of increasing numbers of workers approximate those of the housewife, the individualized, atomized worker whose labour is not regulated by a wage. How far do the conditions of labour faced by women garment workers of West Bengal 'approximate' the theory propounded by von Werlhof?

Here it is useful to distinguish between the sociological character of these women's work, and the economic nature of their toil. In sociological terms their conditions, to an extent, resemble those of the modern, Western housewife. True, their life in Calcutta's slums and in the villages near the city is not as atomized, and their isolation is less absolute, compared to that of Western women working within the four walls of their own homes. Yet it is true that the garment workers are uniformly homeworkers. As we have seen earlier, unlike the male cutters, tailors and embroiderers, all categories of female labourers employed in the sector, including the women machine operators, perform their production tasks at home. In sociological terms, then, we can speak of the 'housewifization' of their labour.

Yet the data collected on women garment workers' economic position does not support Claudia von Werlhof's argument, for it would be wrong to believe that the category of the free wage labourer is leaving the scene. True, very few workers enjoy any fringe benefits. The only extra allowance is an Eid bonus which is paid to some of the male cutters and tailors, consisting of the paltry sum of Rs. 50 per year. Also, none of the garment workers, whether male or female, enjoy any of the fringe benefits which regular workers in industrialized countries receive, (such as medical insurance, unemployment benefits and a pension for old age). Nevertheless, the entire workforce in the sector consists of free wage labourers, in the sense that they are subjected to a capitalist regime of payment.

Both the time wage system and the piece wage system, (which regulates the production of the vast majority of the workers) are decidedly capitalist systems. Marx said about the piece wage system (i.e., the system which disciplines women homeworkers in and around Calcutta): 'Wages by the piece are nothing else than a converted form of wages by time', and 'the difference of form in the payment of wages alters in no way their essential nature, although the one form may be more favourable to the development of capitalist production than the other.' And after having explained how the piece wage gives a wider scope to individuality than time wages, Marx even concludes that 'piece wage is the form of wages most in harmony with the capitalist mode of production'.[21] In short, while Claudia von Werlhof's thesis on 'housewifization' correctly explains the women garment workers sociological conditions, it fails to correctly define the economic or production relations under which they work.

The Sexual Division of Labour: Different Dividing Lines between Men's and Women's Work

I will now discuss a specifically feminist topic—the character of the sexual division of labour. We have seen earlier that both in Moheshtola–Santoshpur and in Dumdum–Paikpara clear dividing lines exist between male and female tasks. In both geographical areas it is presumed that there is a sphere of men's work which excludes women, and a sphere of women's toil from which males are exempted. To recall just one example: in Dumdum–Paikpara, all the women interviewed, without exception, stated that only female members of their families participate in domestic chores. Equally significant, however, is the fact that the sexual division of labour in the two geographical areas is not structured in the same way.

In the case of Moheshtola–Santoshpur, all machine operations are done by men (i.e., men have a full monopoly over this important means of production). The sexual division of labour, then, is not perennially fixed along the lines of specific production tasks, although at first glance this would appear to be so. How the introduction of machines tends to change the sexual division of labour is exemplified by recent experiences in Battala, where the production of children's dresses is concentrated. In this relatively prosperous area, modern machines (for tasks like button-holing, button-fixing, and hemming) have been introduced by the area's *ostagars*. Though such finishing tasks formerly used to be performed by women, as we have seen earlier when referring to *chukai* women, the operation of these new machines is not entrusted to female but to male workers.

In Dumdum–Paikpara, the dividing line between the spheres of women's and men's work is sharply different. All stitching machines (i.e., the main machinery used for the production of dresses) are operated by women. Here the main dividing line is between women's home-based wage labouring activities and wage labour performed by men outside the home. While some male family members are employed at the owner's residence (for instance, as cutters) or engage in non-garment-related wage labour outside, women do all the home-based production tasks—whether stitching or finishing frocks and blouses, or household chores. This same divide does not exist in Moheshtola–Santoshpur, for a section of the tailors here do their stitching work at home. Nurul Haque of South Kankhuli, for instance, spends his days sewing, while his wife and daughters do finishing tasks or *chukai*. All this toil occurs in the mud shanty which is their home.

From this it follows that the sexual division of labour in production is not fixed. Evidence from Moheshtola–Santoshpur indicates that this division of labour changes over time, according to the need to preserve male power via ownership over machines. The evidence cited furthermore shows that within the same industrial sector differences in the organization of the sexual division of labour can be large, depending on the geographic location of the production of clothes. And although cultural factors seem to have an impact on the way this division of labour is structured, it is striking that the divide between women's work within the home and men's work outside is clearest in Dumdum–Paikpara, where the norms of purdah presumably do not hold sway. The view that the sexual division of labour in production is rooted in natural differences between women and men, in short, is untenable; this view is not based on reality but on patriarchal prejudice, as feminist scholars hold.

Summary: Towards a Marxist–Feminist Transformation of Economic Theory

In this chapter I have reviewed the labouring conditions faced by women workers employed in the garments sector in and around Calcutta city, a sector which has several centuries of history, but which has recently expanded under the influence of the 'consumer revolution'. Though a large number of males and children are also employed in this sector, women form the main workforce. They are exclusively employed as homeworkers combining their wage labouring tasks with their daily household chores, but can be divided into at least six categories performing distinct production tasks. The differences between production relations in the two geographic regions where garments are mainly manufactured, Moheshtola–Santoshpur in the south and Dumdum–Paikpara in the north, provided a fruitful basis for comparison.

The garments sector in West Bengal exemplifies the informal sector labour on which so many slum dwellers and villagers have to rely for their subsistence. Many of the workers are migrants who have fled the eastern part of Bengal (now Bangladesh) as refugees (this is true of the garment workers in Dumdum–Paikpara), or hail from rural areas where they could no longer survive (this applies to the ironers, *dagtola* women and other garment workers in Moheshtola–Santoshpur). All the work is subcontracted to small workshops, *daleej* or the workers' homes. Production jobs in the sector are extremely poorly paid, and whatever protective legislation exists is ignored by the sector's manufacturers with impunity.[22] Yet, although all these features are commonly associated with the 'informal sector', this concept does not suffice to explain the sector's production relations, in particular the conditions under which women toil.

A full explanatory framework is only provided by the economic theories developed by Marxists and feminists. The garments sector is characterized by subcontract relations, running from the big *ostagars*, via the small workshops owned by small *ostagars* and male tailors, to the homes. A very tiny section of workers is paid a time wage, whereas the overwhelming majority of male workers and all the female workers are paid by the piece. As Marx pointed out, the piece-rate system reduces the need for supervision and thus lays the foundation for a 'hierarchically organized system of exploitation'. It is this system that facilitates the intensification of exploitation and the extension of the working day. As the experience of the garments sector in West Bengal shows, the piece-rate system, indeed, imposes workers' 'self-control'.

Yet, to account for the double labouring burden carried by women, we need to refer to the feminist discussion on patriarchy. The comparative evidence of the two geographical areas, Moheshtola–Santoshpur and Dumdum–Paikpara, shows that there is no fixed division of labour between women and men. The sexual division of labour is determined by the need to maintain male dominance, and changes along with the evolution of the given sector over time. What is common to women workers in both geographic areas is that they alone are responsible for the domestic chores. It is the imposition of these tasks on women which, under the system of patriarchy, is fixed. In consequence, even in Dumdum–Paikpara where the female stitchers have a higher status than their sisters elsewhere, women's work, contrary to men's, comprises the double task of waged and domestic work.

This double toil and its value are not accounted for by traditional Marxist economic theory, the scope of which is too narrow since it addresses waged labour only. Women's work can only be accounted for by a Marxist–feminist theory, by a theory which is concerned with both the paid and unpaid forms of exploitation used to gather profits under modern capitalism.

Notes and References

1. Shirokov (1980), p. 165, provides extensive data on the predominance of small-scale and domestic industries. Manjit Singh (1991), pp. 53–54, similarly notes that Indian industrialization since the country's independence from British rule has been heavily weighed in favour of production in small-scale units.
2. Figures cited by Romatet (1983), p. 2118. Manjit Singh (1991), p. 67, gives the following figures on the growth of India's garment exports: 'During 1980, the value of garment exports from India was Rs. 435.5 crore, which increased by almost five times to Rs. 2148.6 crore in 1988. The trend is further reinforced by the share of garment export to the total value of export over the period'.
3. Banerjee (1985). According to her, 'recent trends show that in the urban areas women's employment is increasing at a significant rate in an otherwise stagnant labour market', and 'the overwhelming majority of women work in the unorganized sector—this is in sharp contrast to the experience of the male workers whose numbers are almost evenly divided between the two sectors'.
4. For instance, Marx (1973b), p. 519.
5. Romatet (1983), p. 2119.
6. This summary is based on nine interviews of *sabudana* women by Krishna Bandopadhyay, October 1992.
7. Based on 12 interviews of *chukai* women by Basudev Ganguly and Krishna Bandopadhyay, September–October 1992.
8. Based on interviews of *dagtola* women by Krishna Bandopadhyay and Basudev Ganguly, October–November 1992.
9. The young girls interviewed said that they manage to stitch about two dozen frocks per day.
10. Based on interviews with nine frock producers by Krishna Bandopadhyay, November 1992. For a discussion on women's contribution to value creation in terms of economic theory, see Chapter 4.
11. Interview by Basudev Ganguly, 1992. See also the following paragraph.
12. Interview by Krishna Bandopadhyay, November 1992.
13. Interview by Basudev Ganguly, 1992.
14. Romatet (1983), p. 2115. See also Breman (1976), pp. 7–8.
15. Romatet (1983), p. 2117.
16. Ibid., pp. 2115–16. Breman (1976), p. 22, holds that 'the thesis of an urban dualism is untenable and that, instead of using the concepts formal–informal, we should make a distinction between differently articulated production relations which may appear in varying importance in the economic structure of Third World countries'.
17. Breman (1976), p. 21, refers to the 'dependence and subordination' of the informal on/to the formal sector, but does not discuss the subcontract relations which constitute the structural link between companies of the fore-mentioned and the latter sector in the Japanese model.

18. See Chapter 12. Breman (1976), p. 31, on the basis of his own field research, supports the thesis of labour reserve, according to which the existence of a mass of irregularly employed workers has a negative effect on the wages paid to (fixed) employees in large companies. For another critique of the concept of the informal sector, see Manjit Singh (1991), p. 2. According to Singh, p. 3, the concept has been severely criticized 'for its ahistorical connotations'. The author insists that the informal or unorganized sector needs to be placed in perspective by starting from 'a historical analysis of capital itself'.
19. Marx (1977a), p. 516.
20. Ibid., pp. 518–19.
21. Ibid., p. 521.
22. According to informants interviewed by Basudev Ganguly, a minimum wage for the garment sector has been proclaimed by the West Bengal government, but this legal regulation is commonly ignored by the *ostagars* and other intermediaries.

6

Wage Slavery among Women Garment Workers under the Factory System in Bangladesh

'The readymade garments industry is the success story of the modern manufacturing sector after independence.'[1] Like in neighbouring India, the production of trousers, shirts and other modern wear in Bangladesh is characterized by a phenomenal annual growth rate. From being a sector which, at its inception in the late 1970s, had only a few production units, over a decade and a half it has expanded into an industry comprising at least 1,100 units. Today, garment companies in Bangladesh employ, by far, the largest number of wage labourers in any of the industrial sectors. This sector's position in the urban economy is paramount.

Garment production in Bangladesh shares some similar features with garment production in West Bengal. Like the workforce turning out clothes in Moheshtola–Santoshpur and Dumdum–Paikpara, the workforce of garment manufacturers in the Bangladeshi cities of Dhaka and Chittagong is largely composed of women. This feature is unique to the country's garment sector. In jute mills, the number of women labourers, according to the Census of the Labour Office of 1991, is only a tiny minority—573 women out of a total of 250,000 employees.[2] Evidently, the jute mill owners prefer to employ men. Owners of garment factories, on the contrary, show a marked preference for the recruitment of (young) women. They constitute the bulk of the sector's workforce. In fact, the interior of Bangladeshi garment factories have long lines of women stitchers bent over sewing machines.

Yet, in spite of some similarities, the differences between the production structures in West Bengal and Bangladesh are vast. In Bangladesh, there is no hierarchy of subcontract relations, with women toiling at the bottom end in the confines of their homes. Bangladeshi garment women, by and large, are not home-based but work in factories. Unlike their sisters in West Bengal, they are generally not subject to a regime of piece-rates but to time wages. Nor are their tasks diversified. While a woman garment worker in West Bengal could be a machine operator, a *chukai* or a *dagtola* woman, the identity of women garment workers in Bangladesh is basically one. Their task is uniformly to stitch trousers and shirts at sewing machines.

The specific reason for drawing attention to the Bangladeshi experience in this study, then, is that its garments production is almost wholly concentrated in factories. Due to the emergence of this sector, women, for the first time in Bangladesh's history, have been recruited in large numbers to toil as collective workers in factories. Their number, per unit, ranges from 100 or 150 to 1,500 or more. Moreover, since most production is geared towards exports, Bangladesh's experience exemplifies the fact that throughout the Third World, millions of young women today are employed in 'world market factories'. They are the target for exploitation in export-led growth strategies. This chapter tests the relevance of Marx's theory of the working day, formulated on the basis of conditions in 19th-century British factories.

International Relocation of Garments Production and 'Re-run' within the Third World

The rise of a powerful sector of garments production in Bangladesh needs to be understood in a fast-changing international context. The global economy's textile and garments sectors have been characterized, for several decades now, by a vast process of relocation. First there was a movement from the centres of industrialization in Europe and the United States to the Middle East, and to countries of the Far East. More recently, companies have moved towards other parts of the Third World, as well as to the former socialist countries of the Soviet bloc, like Russia and Eastern Europe. This process, and its particular consequences for countries of the European Union, has been summed up well in a recent article by Laurent Carroué.[3]

According to Carroué, the textiles and garments sector of the European Union have lost 1 million and 400,000 jobs, respectively, within a period of just 15 years. In France, the sector's employees numbered

Table 6.1
The Place of Readymade Garments in the Exports of Bangladesh

Item	*July–December 1993*	*July–December 1992*
Garments	692.5	618.7
Jute goods	145.3	161.5
Frozen food	124.7	89.5
Leather	76.4	77.4
Hosiery/knitwear	83.4	77.1
All exports	1,287.2	1,205.7

Source: *Far Eastern Economic Review*, 1994.
Note: Bangladesh's top five exports are listed. Figures are in US$ million.

765,000 in 1970. By 1980 the number had fallen to 527,000, and 10 years later only 361,000 jobs remained. A certain portion of the readymade garments formerly produced in Northern European countries is now being imported from Southern Europe—from countries like Greece, Spain, Portugal and Italy. Here, a major share of the clothes is stitched by labourers toiling in small workshops. Thus, whereas in Germany production units with less than 20 workers employ only 18 per cent of the sectoral workforce, in Italy such informal sector workers constitute 45 per cent. Out of 58,000 micro-enterprises with less than 10 workers in the European Union, half are located in Spain and Italy alone.

When the process of international restructuring started in the 1950s and 1960s, the first area of relocation was the Middle East. Some countries around the Mediterranean sea have made the textiles and garments sector the centrepiece of their industrialization policy. Consequently, textiles and garments in Morocco, for instance, have emerged as the second largest industrial sector. According to Laurent Carroué, the sector today employs 180,000 persons. Again, in Tunisia, the sector furnishes no less than 50 per cent of all manufacturing jobs, and provides 35 per cent of the country's exports. Turkey, helped by a tripling of its import quota of readymade garments into the United States after the Gulf War, has a reported 2 million textile and garment workers occupying a third of the country's industrial employment. As in Southern Europe, much of the stitching occurs in small units belonging to the so-called 'informal sector'.

The principal stimulus for Western European companies to relocate their textile and garments production is the existence of low wages.

As Figure 6.1 shows, the level of wages paid to textile and garment workers in Morocco and Tunisia is about one-tenth of that paid in France. The literature on international restructuring generally associates this practice with 'social dumping'. The primary aim is to evade high labour costs in countries of the North, and to benefit from the lack of social protection for industrial workers elsewhere. This practice is further facilitated by the structural adjustment programmes which are uniformly imposed by the International Monetary Fund and the World Bank on countries of the South. These countries face pressure to increase the value of their exports in order to earn hard currencies for the repayment of their foreign debts. The motto of the resident representative of the World Bank in Bangladesh says it all: 'Either export or die'.[4]

Figure 6.1
Expansion in Bangladesh's Garment Exports

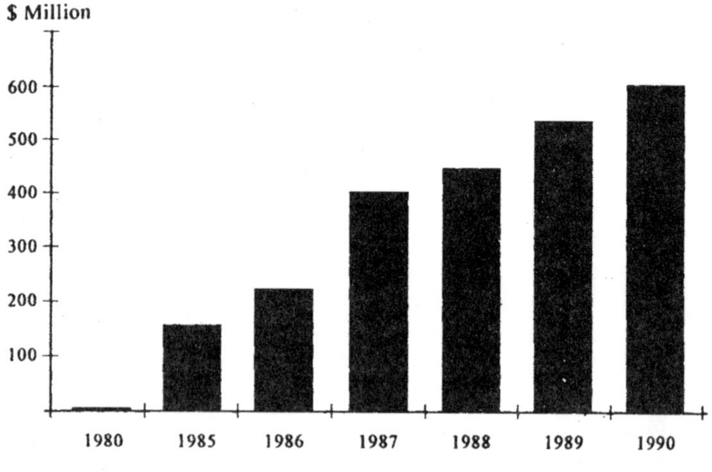

Source: GATT, *International Trade*, 1990–91, in Jackson (1991), p. 21.

Once production has been relocated, however, no Third World country can be sure that orders from Western Europe and the United States will continue to come in. The world market in readymade garments, over the decades, has seen a process of 'run and re-run'—of a second transfer of production from one area in the Third World to another one. The re-run in some cases has also occurred back from the Middle East and Asia to Northern Europe and the United States, as has happened in the production of fashionable dresses requiring short supply-lines. The collapse of socialist governments in Eastern Europe and the former Soviet Union has occasioned the most recent re-run. Production transfers to these countries are facilitated by their

Figure 6.2

Competition in the Textiles/Garments Sector by Countries with Low Wages, 1993 (in US$)

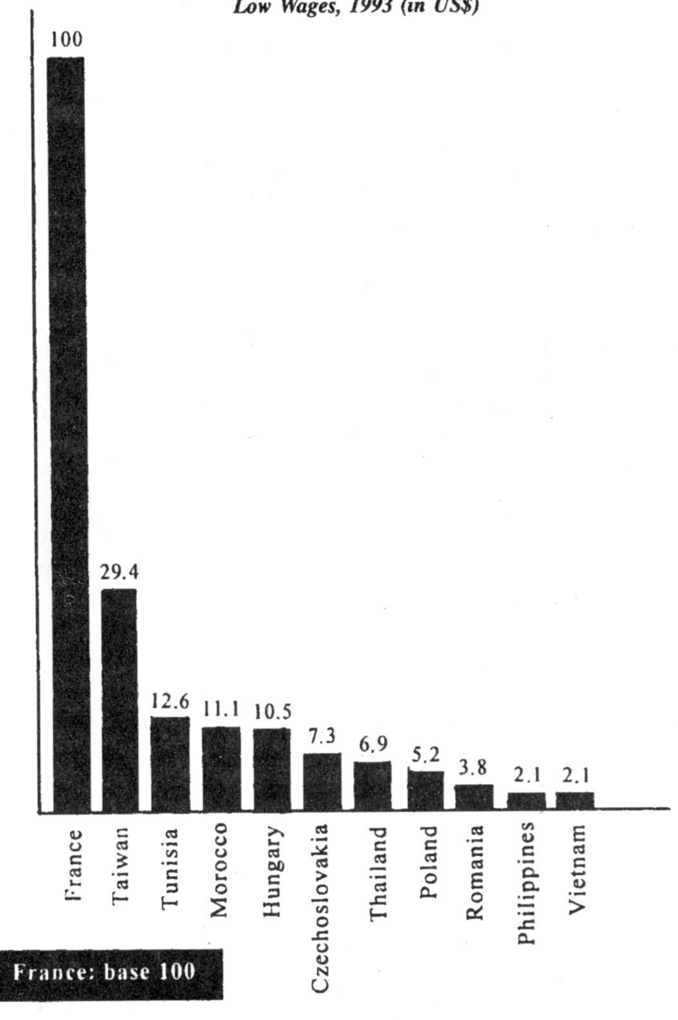

Source: *Le Monde Diplomatique*, December 1993.

relative geographic proximity to Western Europe, the existence of a ready infrastructure and the availability of a skilled workforce.

A typical case of re-run within the Third World is the shift of garment production from the so-called 'tiger' or 'newly industrialized' countries' (NECs) of East Asia (Hongkong, Singapore, Taiwan and South Korea) to other parts of Asia. The city-state of Hongkong, for instance, after the Second World War opted in favour of an export-oriented strategy of industrialization centred around textiles and garments. Faced with increasing wage costs locally, large companies in the late 1970s started transferring orders and production sites to countries of South Asia, where wage levels were and are much lower. According to a report of the Dutch research centre SOMO, some 70,000 women workers lost their jobs in the textiles and garment sectors of Hongkong between 1984 and 1991 alone.[5] Since the mid-1980s, large-scale relocation of production has also taken place to China, which now is said to possess the fastest growing clothing and textile sector in the world.[6]

The impact this second and third re-run has on Asia and the world market in readymade garments is vast. With countries (stretching from Indonesia to Pakistan) pursuing an export-oriented strategy of industrialization comparable to that of the 'tiger' countries in an earlier phase, each now avails of a textiles and garment sector employing hundreds of thousands, if not millions, of women workers. At the same time, East Asian entrepreneurs, using the tested ingredients of stiff exploitation and the suppression of trade union rights, have surfaced as managers of garment factories in other Third World regions, such as Central America and Southern Africa. Companies based in Hongkong and South Korea have shifted production, for instance, to Lesotho, where today 25,000 people are employed in the garments industry.[7] In order to evade the quota system which limits each Third World country's access to the markets of countries of the North, it is, in particular, the final stage of production of clothing (i.e., stitching and ironing) which is time and again shifted to new 'pastures'—countries where an easily exploitable workforce is at hand.

Bangladesh's Garment Exports: Subcontracting in the World Economy

How does one situate Bangladesh's experience within this international context of run and re-run? Since the first factories were founded in 1976, the Bangladeshi garments sector has developed by leaps and bounds. In 1984, the number of factories increased to 177; by 1992 there existed 1,100 factories, according to the figures of the Bangladesh Garment Manufacturers and Exporters Association.[8] While some of the factories were set up as joint ventures, most are owned by Bangladeshi entrepreneurs. Yet, while the emergence of a class of private entrepreneurs is a new phenomenon for Bangladesh, the development of the garments sector does not herald a process of independent industrialization.

First, the garment factories are largely dependent on the import of raw materials. While the local capacity to produce some of the inputs (like threads and cartons) is said to have grown somewhat in recent years, 97 per cent of the principal raw material, the fabric, continues to be imported from the 'tiger countries'. By and large, the cloth, buttons and other inputs are imported from countries like South Korea and Taiwan. East Asian entrepreneurs 'discovered' Bangladesh in the late 1970s, when they were looking for ways to circumvent the export quotas of Western countries.[9] Thus, the production of trousers and shirts is structurally linked to the textiles sector of these countries. It has no links to the indigenous textile sector of Bangladesh, the history of which long predates that of the new, export-oriented garments sector.

Meanwhile, the contribution of garments to Bangladesh's export earnings has grown at an astounding rate. According to GATT figures, the export of clothing earned Bangladesh a mere US$ 2 million in 1980. Ten years later, in 1990, the figure stood at US$ 612 million which signifies a more than 300-fold increase. And in the following year, the US$ 1 billion threshold was crossed, the increment over one year thus being about 40 per cent. However, it should be kept in mind that these figures do not constitute net earnings, since two-thirds of the dollar earnings do leave the country to pay for the massive quantity of fabrics and other inputs imported from newly industrialized East Asian countries.

Nevertheless, the impact of readymade garments on Bangladesh's overall export earnings has been vast. In the mid-1970s, jute products (like hessian sacks) formed 75 per cent of Bangladesh's export income. Today, garment factories are the country's top earner, providing over half of the overall export income.[10] Unfortunately, the change in the composition of Bangladesh's exports has not helped to decrease its external dependence. While the manufacturing of jute products is based on the indigenous cultivation of raw jute, as mentioned earlier, this is not the case with the manufacturing of clothes. The country's previous dependence on jute exports was problematic given falling jute prices in the world market. Yet the relative shift towards garment exports has not made the Bangladesh economy less fragile.

Thus, the case of Bangladeshi garments illustrates the international process of run and re-run, and the meagre advantages which this process bears, in particular for the smaller countries of South Asia. As is true for so many other Third World countries, the drive to set up production units has been wholly provided by external factors—the search by international competitors for the cheapest possible labour. The result has been as questionable as the transformation of agriculture.[11] The garments sector has significantly enhanced Bangladesh's short-term capacity to earn hard currencies, but at an equally significant cost of heightened external dependence.

Further, the production structure of Bangladeshi garments is characterized by subcontract relations, but these differ sharply from those we have observed for West Bengal. Whereas in West Bengal, the sector is dominated by Calcutta's big traders, the Marwaris, who sell fabric for the production of clothes to small manufacturers, the *ostagars*, in Bangladesh the industrial manufacturers themselves occupy centre-stage. Domestically, they are not chained to more powerful economic actors. Nevertheless, externally, in terms of relationships to the world market, we can speak of chains of subcontracting to which Bangladeshi manufacturers are tied. In terms of the international economy, the position of the manufacturers is at the lower end of the sector's production hierarchy.

First, agents based in Hongkong and South Korea supply Bangladeshi entrepreneurs with inputs. They form an intermediate level between the textile factories in their own countries, where the spinning and weaving takes place, and the Bangladeshi units where the cloth is cut, sewn, ironed and packed into cartons for export. Their role does not end here. The same agents have also been instrumental in finding outlets for the finished goods in various countries of the North. As a well-researched essay published by the World Development Movement states, 'Garment owners still often rely on the same South Korea- or Hongkong-based agent to feed them both the order for shirts for a buyer in Britain, and the fabric from which the shirts are to be made.'[12]

Further, most orders for Bangladeshi shirts, trousers and polos are provided by large retail trading firms located in the United States and Western Europe. These retail trading firms form the top of the production pyramid in the international garments sector, both in terms of capital and profit. Companies like Marks and Spencers (United Kingdom) and C&A (the Netherlands) harness capital resources, compared to which the capital of Bangladeshi owners is a pittance. They also earn the lion's share of the profits which are made on the back of the Bangladeshi workforce. According to calculations made by Michael Chossudovsky, shirts produced in Bangladesh are sold in developed countries for five to ten times their imported price.[13]

The prevalence of low wages is the principal reason for the relocation of garments production to Bangladesh, as can easily be demonstrated through comparative figures. Whereas the hourly wage of a worker in an American garment factory in 1984 was calculated to be $7.53 on an average, that of a Bangladeshi worker was no more than $0.25, roughly 3 per cent of the former. Bangladeshi wages are also much less than those in 'tiger' countries like Hongkong and South Korea. In fact, they are at the bottom-end of the wages paid in Asia.[14] And though the productivity of stitchers in Bangladeshi factories is markedly lower than that registered by most other countries with a garments sector, the difference is minor compared to the differences that exist in terms of hourly wages. As will be further illustrated later, Bangladesh has been able to make a dent in the international market in clothing primarily due to the super-exploitation of its labourers.

Initial Profile of the Workforce

Before analyzing in detail the labouring conditions in the garment factories, I will give a short, general profile of the workforce. Precise estimates of the size of the workforce are difficult to give, but recent sources, like trade unions, mention figures ranging from 800,000 to 1 million.[15] A garment factory's workforce is composed of men, young and adult women, and child labourers under 14 years of age. The owners prefer to employ male workers for staff functions and tasks like cutting, defined as 'skilled'. The stitchers (i.e., the bulk of the workforce) are almost exclusively women. Child labourers are recruited as helpers for jobs like cutting threads.

The women workers can broadly be divided into three categories in terms of their social background. According to trade union activists interviewed in 1992,[16] the majority (60 per cent) have entered the factories directly from the rural areas and belong to poor peasant families. Of the remaining 40 per cent, half are members of urban, poor families. Many of these women have found their way to Dhaka and other cities as part of an extensive process of migration from the villages to urban slums, which is closely related to the massive expulsion of peasants from the soil.[17] A third category of women workers are those with a lower-middle-class, urban background. Thus, the garments sector attracts a diversity of women. Interviews with female machine operators confirm that many migrant women prefer stitching jobs to working as domestic servants, which is considered more degrading than a job in a factory.

A survey of 1,000 garment workers carried out in 1985 by the Commission for Justice and Peace, Bangladesh, cited high figures for the educational level of garment workers. According to this report, 55.5 per cent had attended school up to levels varying from Class VI to Class X, and 39.8 per cent had passed the secondary level examination.[18] Trade union sources confirm that many of the garment workers with an urban, lower-middle-class background have received at least a primary education, and the percentage of educated garment workers is on the increase. Consequently, the average level of education of women workers in the garments sector is much higher than that of women in Bangladesh in general.

While this phenomenon has much to do with the country's high level of unemployment, other characteristics of the workforce are linked to the conscious recruitment policy pursued by garment owners. Both trade union representatives and journalistic sources state that about 80 per cent of the women workers are unmarried.[19] As in the case of world market factories in South East Asia, the owners show a marked preference for young women (16 to 20 years old) as labourers. One reason is their desire to be assured of a pliant labour force. Another reason is their desire to evade legal regulations about granting maternity benefits. When the factory management discovers that a young woman worker is pregnant, she risks being dismissed.[20]

Violations of the 1965 Factory Act and Other Methods to Enhance Exploitation

In the following sections I will focus on the working day in the garment factories. The working conditions in garment units of the major cities, Dhaka and Chittagong, in many ways are similar to those Marx referred to when analyzing the conditions existing in British industries in the early 19th century. According to Marx, as soon as people are 'drawn into the whirlpool of an international market dominated by the capitalist mode of production', and the sale of their product for export becomes the entrepreneurs' principal interest, forced overwork becomes the rule. The search for maximum profits is reflected in a ruthless drive to extend the working day.[21] Marx conceptualized the latter by using the term 'absolute' surplus value which he distinguished from 'relative' surplus value.[22]

An increase in relative surplus value is obtained through a proportional change between necessary and surplus labour time, such as through a speed-up in work rhythm. In this case the total length of the working day remains the same. An increase in absolute surplus value is achieved by extending the number of hours industrial workers have to toil. In Marx's words, 'the production of absolute surplus value turns exclusively upon the length of the working day'.[23] Since the extension of the working day was the principal method by which British capitalists in the first half of the 19th century enhanced their profits, Marx gave detailed, numerical accounts of labourers' working time, and compared them with the specifications regarding working hours in British factory laws.

Following Marx's approach, we can best discuss the exploitative practices of contemporary Bangladeshi factory owners and their extraction of absolute surplus value by providing a factual account of the working time labourers are forced to toil, and by comparing these data with the regulations regarding working hours enshrined in the law. A central reference point should be the Factory Act of 1965, a law introduced long before the founding of Bangladesh, which officially remains valid even today. This Act provides, in Clause 2, a definition of a 'factory':

> a building or premise in which a number of 10 or more labourers are set to work or have been on any one day in the last 12 months, and in which a specific process of production is being implemented, with or without the use of electricity.[24]

Given this definition, the owners of garment units are duty-bound to apply the regulations of the Factory Act, since the number of labourers who cut cloth, stitch and do the work of ironing in their premises generally exceeds, by far, the minimum number cited in the Act.

One of the clauses of the Factory Act specifies 'working time'. According to Clause 53, the daily working time of factory employees should last nine hours at most, including an hour of rest. The weekly working time is stated to be maximally 48 hours. The Act further states that a worker may be asked to perform one hour of overwork per day, or several hours more than the regular 48 hours in a week. However, working time may not exceed 10 hours per day. The maximum number of hours per week is 60. Over a year, the average may not exceed 56 hours per week. Moreover, according to Clause 51, workers should be provided with a weekly holiday. They may not be employed for more than 10 consecutive days without a day of rest. In case workers are deprived of their weekly holiday, Clause 52 states, they are entitled to an 'indemnity holiday' within a prescribed period of two months.[25]

We will see later that the hallmark of the Bangladeshi garments sector is that all factories are engaged in numerous violations of the Factory Act. For instance, violations have been recorded of the prescription regarding rest time (i.e., its reduction to 15 minutes only). The clause regarding the weekly holiday is, in spite of trade union protests, not being implemented by the majority of the factory owners. Surveys carried out by both human rights organizations in Bangladesh and trade unions have further exposed the extent to which factory owners violate the stipulations regarding the maximum length of the working day and the working week. To mention just one instance: According to the investigation of the Commission for Justice and Peace, in 52.9 per cent of the garment factories the hours of overwork amounted to 21 or more per week.[26] Clearly, the extension of the working day beyond the legal maximum is highly characteristic of the garments sector. Indeed, it is as characteristic for today's realities in Bangladesh as it was for the British industries described over a century ago by Marx.

In order to measure the degree of exploitation of the women garment workers and the extraction of absolute surplus value, the issue of overwork needs to be discussed in detail. There are, of course, numerous variations in the precise number of hours women are set to stitch. The length of the working day is, in practice, determined by each individual owner. A key variable which operates throughout the sector is, one could say, 'seasonal'. When an owner accepts an export order which has to be delivered at short notice, he demands that his labourers sweat as many hours extra, beyond the legal maximum, as is physically possible. Yet, even if we ignore this variable, the average working day of women garment workers is far longer than what the Factory Act prescribes. For most of the women it lasts from the early morning until late at night. The emergence of the garments sector has created a new scene in Bangladeshi society—that of many thousands of women returning to their homes in city slums after 10 or 11 p. m. at night.

When preparing a publication on the garments sector, which exposes the most common violations of the Factory Act, Philip Gain interviewed a number of factory owners. One of the things two of the owners admitted is that overtime in their factory is obligatory. One of the owners, Mohammed Billah, stated with impunity that in his factory the workers are forced to work 70 hours of overtime per month.[27] The Factory Act of 1965 allows for a maximum of 27 hours of overwork per month. Taken at face value, Billah's statement implies that the women workers in his enterprise are, on an average, obliged to toil 43 hours more per month than what is legally permitted. Presuming that a month comprises 26 working days, this owner extracts from his workers about two hours of extra labour every day.

Further, the extension of overwork into the night, when forced upon women labourers, is a legal violation in itself. Clause 65 of the Factory Act contains a prohibition on nightwork for women: 'No woman can be set to work outside the period lasting from 7 o'clock in the morning till 8 o'clock in the evening.' The government can exempt specific enterprises from this rule, but in such cases the working time cannot last longer than from 5:00 a.m. till 8:30 p. m.[28] Yet numerous garment factories force the women stitchers to toil beyond 8 p. m. Worse, as both independent researchers and trade union sources confirm, some factories force them to operate sewing machines throughout the night. According to Philip Gain, there are instances where women workers have to toil 48, 72, or even more hours at a stretch.[29] In such cases, as will be obvious, more labour is extracted than what is physically possible.

This ruthless extraction of labour provides the garment owners with an illegal source of absolute surplus value. The Factory Act of 1965 attempted to put a brake on the exploitation of industrial workers by making, in Clause 58, the following stipulation: that payment for overtime work should be double the amount paid for regular hours of work.[30] Yet garment owners frequently deprive their workers of overtime pay, as has been illustrated by a number of factory strikes centred around the non-payment of overtime bills.[31] A typical case is the strike in Flint Garments Private Limited, which is one of the oldest export-oriented garment factories in Dhaka, employing 250 persons, of which 230 are women. In December 1993, workers went on strike demanding the payment of three months outstanding salary, and five months overtime.[32]

According to leading members of a progressive trade union, there are many kinds of irregularities in the payment of overtime:

> First, we are not given any scope to keep an account of overtime. The management holds a register, but in practice payment is made for only a third of the extra hours worked. Second, overtime bills are kept in abeyance for 2 or 3 months, the factories delay the payment in contravention of the law. Third, the average pay-rate for overtime work is 40 to 60 per cent, instead of the 200 per cent of the regular, hourly wage which the law prescribes.[33]

By extending the working day and paying an overtime rate well below that stated in the Factory Act, garment owners further increase the rate of exploitation which their workers are subjected to during normal working hours of the day. These practices provide a clear instance of the appropriation of absolute surplus value in the sense in which Marx used the term.

There are two further ways in which factory owners increase their own profits at their workers' expense—by using the punishment system and by employing child labour. The idea of imposing fines on the labourers under various pretexts is not new. In late 19th-century Russia, this method was used to deprive workers of part of their wages. Rose Glickman has given a pointed description of this system in a book about the position of women workers in pre-revolutionary Russia. For instance, workers were penalized for infringements of factory discipline and unauthorized holidays as well as for events in their private lives (such as marriages and deaths). Women workers were specifically punished when they needed to briefly interrupt their working time to nurse their babies. Furthermore, many factories set impossibly high production quotas for the full payment of wages and made deductions for uncompleted work. According to her, the system of fines was 'the most devious and widespread method for bringing down the workers' real earnings'.[34]

Under the factory system in contemporary Bangladesh, fines are imposed on women workers for an equally varied number of reasons. According to trade union activists interviewed in 1992, punishments are meted out, for instance, when a woman stitching clothes makes a production error. 'In case one worker makes an error, 4 to 5 hundred workers are penalized; they are not given their payment for overtime.'[35] Thus, owners misuse small incidents in order to achieve their aim of extending the time when the labour power of their workers is freely available to them. For non-payment of overtime means that the labour value created during the given period is appropriated without any costs. The practice, it hardly needs to be re-stated, goes counter to the rules regarding over time payment set by the Factory Act.

Another example cited by trade unions is that of an owner who cuts a worker's wage for failing to report for duty on a Friday. This is a case of punishment for non-compliance with an illegal practice. As mentioned earlier, the Factory Act dictates that entrepreneurs must grant their workers one day of rest a week, but many owners do not respect this basic right.[36] A woman stitcher risks losing two to three working days of pay if she ignores the owner's instruction to appear on a Friday. Like the other examples mentioned earlier, this is also a case where the owner heightens the exploitation by illegal means. The fact that workers are obliged to toil on a Friday already implies an increase in the surplus labour time. The imposition of a fine makes that extraction of surplus labour, and its appropriation by the entrepreneur, two fold.

A third example may be mentioned—one where the intensification of exploitation is combined with an extension of labouring time. First, the owner of the garment factory decides to speed up production. He exerts pressure in order to achieve an increase in output—more shirts and trousers produced within the same number of working hours. Where previously 50 clothes were stitched in one hour, he demands that 60 pieces are completed within the same period of time. Thus, he obtains a larger output without having to pay anything extra to the workers (i.e., without an increased outlay of variable capital). If the workers fail to meet the new target, he imposes a fine in the form of non-payment of overtime. Thus, the owner 'kills two birds with one stone': in this case he has obtained both an increase in the amount of clothes turned out by the machine operators in the same working time, and an unpaid extension of the working day. Increased extraction of relative surplus value is combined with an extra extraction of absolute surplus value.

The widespread use of child labour in garment factories in Bangladesh was brought to the fore internationally after the American Senator, Harkin, introduced a Bill in August 1992 in the US Congress known as the Child Labour Deterrence Act. The law called for a ban on the import of goods produced in companies where children under 15 years of age are employed. The draft law created near panic in Bangladeshi clothing factories, some 400 of which are reported to be primarily dependent on exports to the United States. Garment owners, the Dhaka press and trade union representatives denounced the Harkin Bill as a protective measure. Yet, within a few months, some 30 factories had been affected by massive lay-offs. One owner admitted that he had dismissed more than 80 per cent of his workforce—300 children out of a total of 350 employees.[37]

The Harkin Bill can be criticized on various grounds. The law appears to be an attempt to protect the American domestic market against being flooded with cheap goods produced with under-aged labour. It lacks any provisions to guard against the negative consequences of the ban for all those families in urban slum areas in the Third World who, for their survival, are dependent on the income contributed by children. The number of people in Bangladesh whose survival is put at stake is large. A quarter of the workers in the garment factories are estimated to be non-adults, and 50,000 have not reached the age fixed by American law. Yet, although the Harkin Bill has been severely criticized in Bangladesh, there is no doubt that the exploitation of children is very severe, and that factory owners engage in practices prohibited by the Factory Act. The Act sets both an age and time limit. Only after reaching 14 years of age can a child be employed, for a maximum of five hours per day.[38]

The illegal exploitation of children in garment factories can be measured, first, in terms of the long hours they are forced to toil. When a young child of 6 or 7 years enters a factory, he or she is generally given the position of a 'helper', entrusted, for instance, with the task of cutting threads after the clothes have been stitched. Further, in spite of the very young age of the helpers, no special provisions are made to limit their working time, or to ensure that they can enjoy the yearly holiday which the Factory Act prescribes for children and adolescents (30 days).[39] Whether a child is 14 years, or older or younger, he or she is expected to sweat the same number of hours in the factory as male and female adults. Thus, cases have been reported where children of 14 years are forced to do overtime work amounting to 100 hours per month.[40] The owners neither respect the legal time limit for child labour, nor limit their hours of toil to the working time the Factory Act has fixed for adults.

Further, the monthly wages paid to child labourers by the factory owners in Bangladesh justify the term super-exploitation. A helper is paid a paltry Taka 200 to 300 per month (US$ 5–7), or a sum equal to the hourly wage of a person employed in the informal sector of the American economy. The money, as indicated earlier, can be crucial for a family of Dhaka slum dwellers, since adult members of such families are frequently unemployed. Yet the amount does not cover the costs of reproduction of the child labourers themselves, not to speak of the costs of reproduction of other family members. The practice of employing child labourers in garment factories increases the amount appropriated as surplus value, but the method enables the owners to even circumvent the need to pay for necessary labour time.[41]

Marx's labour theory of value draws a basic distinction between necessary and surplus labour time. Whereas during both sections of the working day value is created by the workers, the necessary labour time covers the period when they produce only the value of their own labour power—the value of the means of their subsistence. The additional value (i.e., the value created during the remaining part of the working day) is pocketed by the capitalist owners. As mentioned earlier, in the household–labour debate which raged during the second feminist wave, the defect of this theory was pointed out. While Marx's distinction is valid, it does not give recognition to necessary labour which is non-waged, and which is performed by women in the home. The reproduction of labour power requires more toil than the labour of factory workers which Marx terms 'necessary labour'.

Marx's theory can be used to illustrate how the owners in the Bangladeshi garment sector raise the rate of surplus value creation. As stated earlier, Marx expresses the degree of exploitation in the formula $v : s$, in which s represents surplus value and v necessary value. One way in which the rate of exploitation is enhanced is, for instance, by illegally extending the period during which fresh recruits are employed as 'trainees'. According to the regulations of the Factory Act, a woman who is appointed to do stitching should hold the status of a 'probationer' for a maximum period of three months.[42] Yet the report of the Commission for Justice and Peace revealed that 40.2 per cent of the garment workers are made to work as trainees for 4–6 months, while 18.2 per cent remain trainees for 6 months or longer. The average wage of a trainee was calculated to be Taka 300, well below the costs of reproduction of the women workers' labour power. By paying below-subsistence wages to 'trainees', the owners restrict their costs for *v* and expand the amount of value they appropriate as *s*.

The same practice is also used in relation to women who belong to the factory owners' regular workforce. One of the injustices both 'trainees' and 'regular' female employees face is that their wages are lower than those of male workers. As in agriculture and other sectors of the Bangladeshi economy, women workers in the garment sector complain that their wages are much lower than those of their male colleagues. Thus, according to female trade union representatives interviewed, 'for the same post and the same skill a man is paid Taka 1,500, while a woman receives only Taka 900. Similarly, a male helper is given Taka 500 per month, while a female helper gets only Taka 300.'[43] The justification which the owners cite to explain this practice is the existence of gender differentiated wage levels in society at large. The consequences of the policy are that many women workers remain undernourished, and their wages do not cover the reproduction costs of their own labour power.[44] As elsewhere, the factory owners make use of patriarchal ideas to press down women's wages below subsistence level.

Finally let us look at the question of women workers' combined labour time—waged and non-waged. Here we note significant differences in the necessary labour time of the stitchers and other clothing workers employed in the informal sector of West Bengal, India. Contrary to the necessary labour of the latter, the necessary labour performed by women in Bangladeshi factories is predominantly wage labour.[45] Due to the owners' practice of limitless extension of the working day and working week, the women have very little time left to personally do household chores. They often have to depend on the reproductive labour done by other female members of their families. Further, the average wage of female machine operators in Bangladesh (about Taka 1,000 per month) is relatively higher than that of the West Bengal homeworkers. Yet it is well below what is needed to cover their consumption requirements.[46] In short, although women garment workers in Bangladesh are made to toil exceedingly long hours, they too are deprived of part of their consumption fund.

The Influence of Patriarchy on the Position of Women Garment Workers

I shall now go beyond issues of class exploitation to highlight the patriarchal domination over women garment workers. The factory owners, to start with, are engaged in widespread violations of those women's rights which have been enshrined in laws. Some of these have already been mentioned (such as the violation of the prohibition on night work for women workers), but many more can and have been pointed out by trade union activists and researchers. Thus, the Factory Rules issued in 1979 within the framework of the Factory Act contain a specific provision on toilet facilities. According to these rules, separate toilets for men and women should exist in factory premises, with at least one toilet for every 25 workers.[47] To my knowledge there is no quantitative data on the number of toilets in garment factories. Yet it is widely acknowledged that the rule is violated by many factory owners.

Other legal provisions are concerned with women's reproductive tasks, and seek to establish the responsibility of factory owners in employing women with small children. Clause 87 of the 1965 Factory Act stipulates the following regarding child care: wherever more than 50 women are employed in a factory, 'child care facilities should be provided for children less than 6 years of age'. The rooms are to be run by experienced and well-trained women; they should be spacious, clean, have ample light and be ventilated; and they should be well-equipped with the necessary conveniences like beds and toys, and with arrangements for washing children's clothes. Factory owners are also responsible for providing meals during working hours in the child care centres.[48] In the course of his investigation, Philip Gain did not find even one garment factory running a child care centre.[49] The tactic used by the owners to circumvent this and other legal regulations concerning women is to, primarily, recruit unmarried women.

The owners' evasion of payments for reproductive tasks is most apparent in relation to pregnancy and childbirth. A law dating from 1939, which officially is still in force, contains details regarding women workers' maternity benefits. They are entitled to six weeks leave before delivery, and to another six weeks after the delivery of a baby. During her leave the woman is also entitled to her regular wage, if she has been employed in the given factory for at least nine months.[50] Moreover, the law strictly prohibits the dismissal of any woman worker during her maternity leave. The owners' disregard for this law takes various forms. They either dismiss a woman worker when it is discovered that she is pregnant, or do so when she applies for maternity leave.[51] Thus, pregnant women are ever at risk of losing their jobs, and are forced to hide the fact of their pregnancy.

The logic of the garment owners is thus to reject any responsibility for the costs of child-bearing and child-rearing. They prefer to recruit women as the cheapest labourers, but refuse to face the consequences of this policy. They want to exploit children as the cheapest possible labour power, but refuse to take responsibility for their upbringing. As long as children are only future labour power, the responsibility for raising them lies with women, who in this capacity are defined as non-workers. The owners' attitude is in tune with prevailing patriarchal ideology which relegates the responsibility for reproductive tasks to women alone. And although legal regulations, such as the 1939 law on maternity benefits and the Factory Act, do stipulate owners' responsibility, in practice the manufacturers have the Bangladeshi state on their side, for the authorities fail to enforce the legal regulations regarding women workers' rights.

In the previous chapter it has been argued, on the basis of evidence drawn from garments production in the informal sector, that the sexual division of labour is not perennially fixed but is determined by the 'need' to enforce male dominance. In Moheshtola–Santoshpur in West Bengal, male dominance was structured via men's monopoly over machines, while in Dumdum–Paikpara no such male monopoly existed and many women were found to be operators of sewing machines. In the latter area, the division of labour was organized along the lines of work that is performed inside the home, versus work that is performed outside the home. This contrasted again with the situation in Moheshtola–Santoshpur where men, just like women, were found to engage in the production of clothes within the confines of their own homes. Yet a sectorwise sexual division of labour existed in both geographic areas.

The literature on the history of factory work by women brings out the fact that a gendered division of labour has been a feature of factory-based production ever since the industrial revolution.[52] Where both the employment of women outside the home and their involvement in machine work were found to be beneficial to capital accumulation, other mechanisms were devised to ensure women's subordination to men. One way to ensure such subordination is to use skill distinctions against women workers. Thus, various feminist authors, including Anne Phillips and Barbara Taylor, have forcefully argued that the categorization of a specific industrial job is intimately linked to the gender doing the work. Male workers have often struggled to retain their dominance within a factory's sexual hierarchy by insisting that their own work be defined as 'skilled' and women's work as 'semi-' or 'unskilled'.[53]

One instance that has been cited in the literature is precisely that of the clothing industry. Throughout this century, machining in the clothing trade in Britain has been done by people of both sexes. As immigrant males were forced to take on jobs behind machines, usually done by women as semi-skilled workers, 'they fought to preserve their masculinity by re-defining [their] machining as skilled labour'.[54] Moreover, the lack of recognition for the skills involved in factory work performed by young women is related to the fact that these skills have been obtained informally, through training from mothers and other female relatives. This counts, for instance, for the manual dexterity required for the industrial sewing of clothes. As Diana Elson and Ruth Pearson argue, 'since industrial sewing of clothing closely resembles sewing with a domestic sewing machine, girls who have learnt such sewing at home already have the manual dexterity and capacity for spatial assessment required.'[55]

We should briefly view the division of labour in Bangladesh's garment factories against this background. At first sight, a breakdown of male dominance appears to have occurred. The bulk of the workforce of the Bangladeshi factories are young women of 16 to 20 years, the majority of whom are unmarried. They are neither subject to a husband's nor to a father's authority on the workfloor, but to the impersonal authority of the factory owner and his representatives. Where the machine operators are married women, the transfer of authority to the factory owner often leads to violent reactions by disgruntled husbands. Thus, the maltreatment of Sufiya (see the following interview) appears to be related, at least partially, to her husband's inability to enforce his dominance in day-to-day life. Nevertheless, a hierarchy does exist in the garment factories too. Thus, staff functions and jobs defined as 'skilled' are generally occupied by men, whereas the work performed by the female stitchers is defined as 'semi-skilled'.

The example of Bangladeshi garments illustrates well how the patriarchal division of labour is enforced through definitions of skill.

Many of the women stitchers, like the 'skilled' male spinners in 19th-century Britain,[56] hail from rural areas, and they require some on-the-job training in order to do the sewing of shirts and trousers for exports. Nonetheless, factory owners prefer female operatives precisely because of their 'natural' dexterity and patience, which, feminist authors believe, women have not inherited but obtained through their socialization. By defining their work as 'semi-skilled', the owners make sure that the workforce is disciplined, and that their wages remain far below those of the average male employee. Moreover, since most trade union initiatives in the Bangladeshi garments sector are dominated by men, the pay-scales set by the owners and the government have so far gone unchallenged, as has the hierarchical, sexual division of labour in the industry.[57] Trade unions have questioned the wage rates but not the categorization of jobs.

There are two broader issues of women's inequality which need to be specifically addressed, both forms of oppression which garment workers share with many other women in Bangladesh. One is that of physical harassments, of sexual violence. Women workers are regularly insulted and abused while on their way to and from the factory. Although they need to travel late at night because of the long working hours, the owners refuse to make any arrangements for their transport and safety. Thus, women garment workers, like all other women in Bangladesh, face numerous risks of violence in the streets, including beatings, acid throwing and rape. A typical case is that of Rehana, a young worker raped on the night of 30 September 1993 when she was on her way from the factory to her home.[58]

Sexual oppression inside the factory can take the form of sexual harassments by male supervisors and, worse, the attempt by owners to turn women into prostitutes. The latter practice is not unique to the Bangladeshi garments sector, but appears to be organized in a specific manner. A garment owner generally does not use the factory premises for sexual exploitation, but will try to lure a girl he considers beautiful into accompanying him to a hotel. The girl is called to the owner's office and offered sweets and money in exchange for an agreement to be prostituted. In case she refuses, the woman worker, reportedly, will be dismissed from her job.[59] Her refusal to be prostituted is punished, and treated as an act of insubordination and indiscipline.

Another issue affecting women is that of dowry marriages. In the next chapter I will discuss the transformation of the payment system around arranged marriages in Bangladesh. The traditional bride-price, which obliged the family of the bridegroom to provide money and/or goods as a kind of insurance for the bride, in recent decades has increasingly been replaced by the dowry system, which forces a girl's parents to pay exceedingly high sums of money if they wish to marry her off. This system is creating havoc in the rural areas, since it contributes to pauperization and the eviction of peasants from their soil. The system is also causing an escalation of violence against women, including 'dowry deaths'.

Although most trade union publications and reports about labouring conditions in the garments sector ignore this, the dowry system affects the lives of women employed in the factories in many ways. First, the unmarried status of some women workers is related to the fact that their families have not been able to muster the necessary resources to find them a marriage partner. Further, peasants interviewed in Bangladeshi villages state that they send their daughters to work in garment factories in order to earn the dowry money themselves, and the existence of this practice is confirmed by some women unionists.[60] Thus, the key reason why these girls break with a tradition, which for centuries has excluded women from working outside the home, lies in patriarchy—the need to fulfil the demands of a system which leads to their renewed enslavement in the home.

Moreover, while women workers who are married contribute crucially to their family's income, they are not free from the tyranny of the dowry system. After surrendering their wage to their husband, they sometimes continue to be harassed with the demand that they bring additional money as dowry from their parents' home (see the following story of Sufiya). Clearly, garment workers invariably have to face a double structure of oppression: the capitalist exploitation of their labour is interwoven with the patriarchal oppression that pervades the entire fabric of Bangladesh's society. While as workers they face conditions which distinguish them from female peasants and women belonging to the urban middle class, as women they are subject to similar injustices.

Factory Exploitation and Violence in the Home: Agonies of the Garment Worker Sufiya

In the lives of many women garment workers in Bangladesh, stiff exploitation in the factory and patriarchal oppression at home are closely intertwined. This is well exemplified by the story of Sufiya, a worker interviewed by Philip Gain.[61] Sufiya became a factory labourer because of the pressure of her husband's incessant dowry demand for money. She was married to Shahabuddin, a truck driver, when she was only 7 years old. When she was 11 years old, she moved to his home. Five years later, at 16, she gave birth to her first child. From then on, her husband constantly harassed her, insisting she bring money from her father who was not a wealthy person. Since he was never satisfied with what she brought, Sufiya ultimately decided to enlist for a job. In 1983, she entered a factory called Imakulet Garments located in Mirpur.

The owner of the factory used standard methods of exploitation, described earlier, to exploit his workforce. Sufiya's first job was to assist a machine operator, for which she was paid a wage of Taka 260 per month. She had to continue working as a 'trainee' after her three-month probation period was over. The workers of Imakulet Garments did not know that, according to the law, they had the right to be automatically appointed as permanent workers after three months labour in the factory. There were various other violations of the Factory Act. Overtime was forced, lasting up to 10 p.m. at night. The workers had to toil all through the night for eight to ten days a month. Sufiya's payment for overtime work was only symbolic (Taka 1 per hour). Machine operators were paid a wage rate for overtime that was no more than their normal hourly rate. Thus, no one received what was their due according to the law.

Her job in Imakulet Garments neither gave Sufiya economic independence nor freed her from her husband's violent behaviour. She would rise daily at 4:00 a.m. to prepare breakfast and lunch for her husband, her child and herself. She would leave home by 6:00 or 6:30 in the morning, only to return after 10:00 p.m. at night. While she was left no time to nurse her own child, her earnings did not even suffice for sustenance. To augment her income, Sufiya would embroider *punjabis*, sitting under the light of a street lamp. Yet all her hard-earned money was taken by her husband who always kept a watch on her. Whenever she spoke to another man, he would beat her mercilessly. If she did not serve a meal he deemed proper, she would have to face his fists.

Dissatisfied with her low wage which did not increase, Sufiya got a job in Sahela Garments. Here the labouring conditions were so oppressive that she could sustain herself for only a month and a half.

In Sahela Garments, the working time virtually knew no limits. 'You can say that the working time lasted all day and all night. The rest period granted to the workers was from 4 o'clock at night until 10 o'clock in the morning. Meal times were one hour around lunch, and another hour in the evening.' In this case, the owner did not hesitate to stretch the working time beyond the workers' physical capacity. Sufiya fell ill and decided to leave the factory. Since the managing director wanted to withhold her wage, she mobilized some boys from her neighbourhood who threatened the factory accountant. This is how she succeeded in making him pay.

During 1987 and 1988, her husband's ill-treatment became unbearable, and Sufiya barely escaped death. In 1987, he tried to kill her by throwing kerosene over her body while she was asleep. She was saved by her daughter who woke her up by crying loudly. The next year, in August, he almost cut her throat with a blade. This time her neighbours saved her. A month later, her husband, who was joined by her in-laws, beat her up in the house, then dragged her on to the street, only to continue the violence in public. She went to a police station to demand justice, but was told that her case would only be taken up if she paid a bribe—'Without money we won't move'. Even the 'law enforcers' were not willing to help. One day, her husband picked her up from the street, shackled her with ropes and detained her. As her desire to stay with her husband waned, Sufiya started thinking of a divorce.

Sufiya's agonies continued after she began working in a factory called Babylon Garments. The wage she received here, she felt, was reasonable—Taka 1,200 per month. Yet it is evident that Babylon's owner, too, used inhuman methods to increase the rate of exploitation. Thus, the owner would not allow his workers the use of the toilet for more than two minutes. Another method to increase surplus labour time, according to Sufiya, was the imposition of a fine. If a worker arrived five minutes late in the factory, her wage for overtime work was cut. Meanwhile, her husband's behaviour did not improve. He wasted whatever money she brought in by drinking, and he continued beating her. Caught between the factory owner's oppression and her husband's, Sufiya decided to leave her job. Her husband responded by abandoning her.

Sufiya's story demonstrates that the participation of Bangladeshi women in factory production, in itself, does not necessarily lead to greater freedom. While the experience of the women garment workers has led to a 'recomposition' of patriarchy, the road these women have to travel to reach their own liberation remains long. Sufiya once more tried her luck by taking a job in Sparrow Apparels in 1987. She subsequently lost her job after quarrelling over the introduction of the piece-rate system in the factory.[62] Today she is free from her husband's tyranny, but feels unhappy as long as her children remain under her former husband's control. Her only consolation is that she is not alone. 'In the villages of Bangladesh, there are thousands of Sufiyas searching for the road towards their own liberation amidst intolerable oppression.'

Evolution of the Trade Union Movement

Finally, a short note on the evolution of the trade union movement in the garments industry. On 27 December 1990, a fire erupted in Saraka, a factory located on the outskirts of Dhaka. The fire was caused by the non-observance of safety standards as laid down in official regulations. It killed at least 25 women and children, and wounded many more. News of the carnage spread like wildfire to other garment factories. Within days, the city saw the anger of women workers explode, as thousands of garment labourers marched through the streets demanding proper compensation for the victims of the Saraka incident. The spontaneous outburst, moreover, led to the founding of the first broad-based trade union movement. Until 1990, owners' intimidation had been a major impediment to trade union initiatives. Workers were physically threatened if they protested. Where workers were found to have enlisted as members of a union, they would be dismissed *en masse*. Yet, this time, the use of musclemen was ineffective in stemming the resolve of women workers to get organized.[63]

Since early 1991, trade unions have tried several strategies to recruit members and promote the setting up of factory-level workers committees. One has been to build the broadest possible solidarity around one concrete workers' strike. On 19 March 1991, the 800 workers of Comtrade Apparels, a factory owned by a company called Beximco, were locked out by the management. The workers reacted with a 13-day sit-in strike in front of the factory gate, combined with other actions to muster public sympathy. The management was compelled to re-open the factory and reinstate trade union activists who had been dismissed. Yet, within half a year, the offensive against the workers was resumed. On 21 October 1991, the management declared a second lock-out. The workers in turn encircled the offices of the Garment Owners Association. They held torchlight processions, and their representative union, then named the Unity Council, called for a general strike which it claimed was successful in 80 per cent of Dhaka's garment factories.[64]

Nevertheless, the movement subsequently faced a temporary setback, partly because of government-sponsored repression. Armed police guards were stationed at factory gates in order to break the movement. When the lock-out continued and the movement fizzled out, the union, whose leadership mainly hailed from Comtrade Apparels, was forced to rethink its strategy. In the next phase, it tried to relaunch strikes by linking up with mainly male workers in other industrial sectors. Employees in jute and textile mills faced the threat of massive retrenchments, as a consequence of conditions set by the World Bank and the International Monetary Fund for granting structural adjustment loans. The joint action councils set up for the workers in the jute and textile sectors, in 1991 and 1992 launched nationwide protests like road and railway blockades and general strikes, opposing both the proposed retrenchment policy and the privatization of factories. Trade unions in the garments sector tried to 'hook on to' these struggles, by combining the agitation around common demands—like the demand regarding a national minimum wage—with agitation around the garment workers own demands.

More recently, a third approach has been used, in particular by a union named the National Garment Workers Federation (NGWF). In 1993, it combined public campaigns around the elementary demands of all garment workers with support to strikes in individual factories. Thus, it held processions of workers in Dhaka city for the demand that May Day be observed as a holiday in the sector, and has similarly campaigned for the payment of bonus, which workers are entitled to in other industrial sectors of Bangladesh. In addition, the Federation has supported plant-level women workers' struggles, many of which have centred around illegal closures, non-payment of salaries and/or overtime pay. In a number of such instances, the Federation was able to sign an agreement with the factory management in which the workers' demands were conceded, either wholly or partly. In the case of Flint Garments, the management was made to agree to the payment of salaries and overtime dues, after police personnel called in by the management had failed to break a physical blockade of the factory gates by women workers.[65]

The trade union movement in the Bangladeshi garments sector over the last three years has made progress which was unthinkable earlier, and which far exceeds what has been achieved among women garment workers in West Bengal.[66] Whereas, previously, garment owners had succeeded in imposing a virtual ban on organizing activities in the sector, some unions now have struck roots and are, to an extent, able to defend women workers' rights. What is more, an awakening has taken place among a workforce of women who formerly lacked experience with trade union practices. On the other hand, the movement's strength to date does not suffice to put a serious break on the ruthless exploitation prevalent in the sector: membership is limited to a small minority of the workers, and the movement is split into too many small trade union factions to be fully effective. Moreover, since most unions are dominated by men, they tend to see the labourers as part of a homogeneously exploited class. Though some do raise the issue of the responsibility of the owners for payment of women's reproductive role, the different aspects of patriarchal oppression are not systematically addressed.

Women's Factory Work in Bangladesh and the Thesis of the German Feminist School

The experience of women garment workers provides an occasion to, once more, assess the relevance of the thesis put forward by the German feminist school of Mies, Bennholdt-Thomsen and von Werlhof. I have argued earlier that the condition of the homeworkers who produce clothes in and around Calcutta can only be equated with the labour of the Western housewife in a sociological sense. The thesis on housewifization as presented by von Werlhof fails to capture the economic mechanism of these homeworkers' exploitation. With regard to factory work in the garments sector in Bangladesh, it can similarly be stated that the thesis of the German feminist school brings out no more than a part of the conditions prevailing here.

The German feminist school's essential critique of Marxist economic theory is that its scope is too restricted, in that it limits its analysis to the contradiction between wage labour and capital, while ignoring work which is non-waged.[67] Here the thesis of the German feminist school helps to lay bare the non-waged, necessary labour which is performed by women garment workers in addition to their prolonged hours of factory work. Thus, married women (who form a minority of the workforce), before leaving their huts at dawn, have to prepare meals for their husbands, children and themselves, and again are faced with household chores after returning home late at night. Moreover, the creation and maintenance of the labouring strength of unmarried, young women also involves necessary labour which is non-waged.

Nevertheless, the exploitation of women garment workers can only be fully grasped if we consider both the 'original' accumulation and the capitalist accumulation they are subjected to. Thus, as many young girls are forced to seek factory employment in order to earn a dowry which will be transferred to the bridegroom's family, they are subjected to a process of original accumulation by men.[68] Yet it is true, at the same time, that the factory regime, which takes advantage of the patriarchal relations existing in the society at large, imposes upon women work rules which are devised to maximize surplus labour. To analyze the violations of the Factory Act about the working day and the working week, it was crucial to refer to Marx's central thesis on the appropriation of surplus labour time.

Since the 1970s, world market factories (factories which are part of a global division of labour and produce commodities exported to the developed countries of the North) have sprung up in various parts of the Third World. Whether the companies produce the most 'advanced' electronic goods, such as chips, or dresses for mass consumption, their managers invariably prefer to employ young, migrant women whom they expect to be docile and 'naturally fit' for the painstaking tasks said to require 'nimble fingers'.[69] An effective analysis of this significant trend in the world economy needs to draw on both feminist concepts like patriarchy and the sexual division of labour, and on an extended version of Marx's labour theory of value. The thesis of the German feminist school, which takes no cognizance of surplus labour time, fails to address the conditions of women's exploitation in world market factories.

Summary: Marx's Theory of the Working Day Remains Valid

I have explained here the contemporary validity of Marx's theory of the working day, based on a concrete analysis of readymade garments production in Bangladesh. Devised to lay bare the economic exploitation in factories in 19th-century Britain, Marx's theory states that capital accumulation is made possible by the appropriation of surplus value—value which waged workers produce in addition to what is needed for their own sustenance. As Marx illustrated with ample facts drawn from official sources, British entrepreneurs achieved this through the almost limitless prolongation of the working day (i.e., through the appropriation of what he called absolute surplus value).

The owners of garment factories that have mushroomed since the 1970s in the main cities of Bangladesh—Dhaka and Chittagong—use methods that are strikingly similar to those of their 19th-century British counterparts. They enhance their profits by imposing fines for non-attendance on weekly holidays, thus appropriating the fruits of several days of their labourers' toil. They force their employees to do lengthy hours of extra work, without observing the legal regulations concerning overtime. And, above all, they uniformly violate the rules in the country's Factory Act regarding working time. Ruthless extension of the working day is, once again, the favourite method of extracting surplus value. This is far more characteristic of the garments sector than any other sector in the Bangladeshi economy.

Yet, while Marx's theory of the working day is clearly applicable, it is necessary, also, to be aware of structural differences between 19th-century British industries and those in contemporary Bangladesh. For, unlike owners of the former, Bangladeshi garment owners are at the lower end of an international chain of subcontract relations, extending from production units in Bangladesh, via intermediaries, to retail trading companies in countries of the North. As stated here, garment production has been relocated to, and re-relocated within, the Third World, in order to tap cheap sources of wage labour. While local entrepreneurs obtain a part of the surplus value created, they do not get the major share. Thus, whereas the extraction of surplus value is organized by Bangladeshi owners, its fruits are overwhelmingly reaped by companies in the North.

Finally, whereas Marx's theory of the working day helps us understand the mechanism of economic exploitation, it does not conclusively explain why more than four-fifths of the garment workers are women. Nor does it lay bare the various ways in which women's subordination, in the factory and in the family, is organized. To grasp, for instance, the hierarchical structure of labour relations in the factory, with women restricted to doing semi- and unskilled work, we need to refer to feminist analyses regarding the sexual division of labour. And as I have shown in the discussion on the dowry system, women workers are not just subjected to capitalist exploitation (i.e., the extraction of the surplus value which they create) but also to a process of original accumulation by men. In short, as in the case of the garments sector in West Bengal, only a combination of Marxist and feminist concepts can explain women workers' daily realities.

Notes and References

1. *Bangladesh: Country Study and Norwegian Aid Review* (1986), p. 36.
2. For data on the number of women workers in various industrial sectors of Bangladesh, see Akhtar (1992).
3. Carroué (1993), pp. 18–19.
4. See the interview with Christopher Willoughby, resident representative of the World Bank in Dhaka, Bangladesh, in *SüdAsien* (Dortmund, Germany), 15 October 1992, p. 70.
5. Rosier (1993), p. 16.
6. According to Neil Kearney, General Secretary of the International Textile, Garment and Leather Workers Federation (ITGLWF), 'China is going to be the dominant producer in the textile, leather and clothing sector. Billions of dollars have been invested here, especially by the more industrialized countries of Asia, like Hongkong and South Korea'. See *Clean Clothes*, Vol. 2, February 1994, p. 4.
7. Ibid., p. 3.
8. See Jackson (1992), p. 21.
9. Ibid., p. 22.
10. According to figures of the Metropolitan Chamber of Commerce and Industry (Dhaka), in *Far Eastern Economic Review*, 14 April 1994, total exports for the period July to December 1993 stood at US$ 1.2872 billion, of which the export of garments was US$ 692.5 million (see Table 6.1).
11. See Chapter 8 of this book for details.
12. See Jackson (1992), p. 24.
13. Interview with Michael Chossudovsky, 'World Bank Playing the Role of a Parallel Government?' *Holiday* (Dhaka), 13 March 1992: 'Take the garment industry in Bangladesh which sells a dozen shirts for about US$ 35 to the developed countries. Out of that $35, some $26 are spent for imported materials. From the rest you have some $5 labour costs, and then the remainder is for capital expenditure and a small amount of profit. But those shirts are sold in the developed countries for 5 to 10 times their imported price.... For each shirt which is produced in Bangladesh and sold in the world market for $3, the GNP of the importing OECD countries is going up by about $32.'
14. See Philip Gain (1990), p. 9, for comparative figures on wages in countries producing garments for exports (1981–82). Comparing the wage level in India's garments sector with that in Germany, Manjit Singh (1991), p. 68, states that in

1980 'a male worker from West Germany earned 22 times the wage of an Indian male worker'.

15. '*Bekleidungsindustrie in Bangladesh: Wirtschaftserfolg durch Kinderarbeit?*' *SüdAsien*, 11 February 1993, cites a figure of about 600,000 employees. Recent figures cited by trade union sources in the Bangladeshi garments sector are higher.
16. Personal communication by representatives of the Bangladesh Garment Workers and Employees Federation, October 1992.
17. See Chapter 8. The extent of migration is indicated by Rahman's article (1994), which refers to a total of 22 million urban slum dwellers in Bangladesh. The majority of the slum dwellers are stated to be landless peasants hailing from villages where employment opportunities are lacking.
18. Gain (1990), p. 6. See also Banu (1985), p. 45.
19. Gain (1990), p. 13.
20. According to representatives of the Bangladesh Garment Workers and Employees Federation interviewed in October 1992, a woman worker who takes maternity leave is dismissed from her job.
21. Marx (1977a), p. 226.
22. Ibid., p. 476.
23. Ibid., p. 477.
24. These and other clauses of the Factory Act are listed in 'The Current Labour Law and the Garment Industry' (in Bengali), in *Garments*, the organ of the Bangladesh Workers and Employees Federation, May 1993, p. 2. A full discussion on workers' legal rights is also contained in the booklet written by Gain (1990).
25. See Gain (1990); *Garments* (1993).
26. Gain (1990), p. 7.
27. Ibid., p. 105.
28. See *Garments* (1993), p. 2. See also Gain (1990), p. 29.
29. Gain (1990), p. 7. See also Sultana (1989).
30. See *Garments* (1993), p. 2. See also Gain (1990), p. 24.
31. See, for instance, reports on the conflicts in Baron Garments and Ducks Garments Ltd, published in *Clean Clothes*, No. 1, November 1993, p. 12. The National Garment Workers Federation, in press releases brought out in July and August 1993, reported that the struggle for outstanding salaries and overtime pay by employees of Baron Garments and Ducks Garments were victorious. See also the report on the sit-in-strikes for payment of outstanding salaries by workers belonging to three other factories (Susan, Denim and Ahmed), published in *Rupali*, Dhaka, 9 September 1993.
32. See the report on the struggle of women workers in Flint Garments, published in *Clean Clothes*, Vol. 2, February 1994, pp. 13–14.
33. Interview with representatives of the Bangladesh Garment Workers and Employees Federation, October 1992. According to Sultana (1989), p. 3, '80 per cent of the owners record only half of the overtime which the workers toil'.
34. Glickman (1984), p. 6.
35. Statement by representatives of the Bangladesh Garment Workers and Employees Federation.
36. Ibid. Other examples of the punishment system are cited in the personal interviews of women garment workers by Philip Gain (1990). In one of the factories, a day's wage was cut in case a worker appeared late at work for three consecutive

days (ibid.), p. 36. According to Selina Asma (ibid.), p. 38, in Baron Garments a worker was deprived of a day's wage if he or she appeared five minutes late on the job.

37. See Khondker (1993).
38. Gain (1990), p. 37. See also *Garments* (1993).
39. Gain (1990); *Garments* (1993).
40. See Jackson (1992), p. 4.
41. For a discussion on the distinction between necessary and surplus labour time, see Marx (1977a), p. 204.
42. Gain (1990), p. 18. See also Sultana (1989).
43. Statement by representatives of the Bangladesh Garment Workers and Employees Federation in October 1992.
44. According to Sultana (1989), p. 3: 'It is amazing that people manage to survive at the [given wage] levels, and it is not that the cost of living is equally low. The wages do not suffice for the workers to be able to eat protein even one day per month and many workers are undernourished. We believe that the wages are so low that they do not allow the workers to live as human beings.'
45. See Chapter 5.
46. The underpayment of women workers is, for instance, reflected in the calculations Gain (1990, p. 8) has made of the monthly rice requirements of a family of five members, which amounts to Taka 2,700 per month. The common demand of the trade union movement in Bangladesh, including that of the trade unions in the garments sector, is that the national minimum wage should be fixed at Taka 1,400 per month.
47. See for instance Gain (1990), p. 12.
48. See *Garments* (1993). See also Sobhan (1992).
49. Gain (1990), p. 13.
50. Gain (1990), p. 25; Sobhan (1992).
51. According to representatives of the Bangladesh Workers and Employees Federation, interviewed in October 1992.
52. Hall (1987), pp. 19–20, for instance, notes that the mechanization of spinning was accompanied by the carry-over of the family economy into the factory; in particular, after the invention of the mule, the task of spinning was taken over by male machine operators who often employed their own wives and children as their assistants in the factory.
53. Phillips and Taylor (1976).
54. Ibid., p. 82.
55. Elson and Pearson (1986), p. 74. On the ideological dimensions of skill definitions, see Barrett (1980), p. 167.
56. Hall (1987), p. 22: 'Men had gone into mule spinning in the factory because it was an important job. Those men who became spinners had not for the most part been weavers previously; rather, they tended to be immigrants from the countryside or from Ireland who were coming into the towns seeking work.'
57. See, for instance, the pay scale proposed by the Bangladesh Garment Workers Federation, in Gain (1990), p. 7, which maintains the same distinctions between skilled, semi-skilled and unskilled work as defined by the Bangladesh government.
58. Protest against the incident was voiced by the National Garment Workers Federation, led by General Secretary, Amirul Haque Amin. See *Rupali*, 6 October 1993.

59. Reported by representatives of the Bangladesh Workers and Employees Federation, interviewed in October 1992.
60. According to interviews with peasants in Faridpur district, Bangladesh, October 1992, and representatives of the Bangladesh Workers and Employees Federation, October 1992.
61. This is an abridged and translated interview in Gain (1990), pp. 57–60.
62. This application of the piece-rate system appears to be an exception in Bangladeshi garment factories.
63. See the report published in *Samachar*, March–April 1991.
64. See the reports published in *Samachar*, June–July 1991 and March–April 1992.
65. See the report published in *Clean Clothes*, February 1994, pp. 13–14.
66. Compare these developments with those recorded in Chapter 5.
67. Mies et al. (1986).
68. See Chapter 8 for details.
69. See, for instance, Elson and Pearson (1986).

7

The German Feminist School and the Thesis of Housewifization

> Political economy as the science of the conditions and forms under which different human societies produce and exchange, and under which products are accordingly distributed each time—political economy in this expanded sense is yet to be created. The scientific knowledge we possess of economy so far is almost totally restricted to the evolution and development of the capitalist mode of production.[1]

This quotation from Frederick Engels forms the 'opening shot' in a now celebrated article by the German feminist, Claudia von Werlhof, in which she proposes a novel conceptualization of women's labour, which she appropriately calls 'the blind spot in the critique of political economy'.

In her attempt at theorizing women's labour, and indeed at re-analyzing the whole capitalist system, von Werlhof joined two other German feminists, Maria Mies and Veronika Bennholdt-Thomsen, who like her have spent considerable time investigating the labouring conditions of rural women in Third World countries. Whereas von Werlhof and Bennholdt-Thomsen have done their main research in Latin American countries, Mies has spent a considerable period of time as a field researcher in Andhra Pradesh, India. All three women share the same critical attitude towards 'bourgeois' and Marxist economics, as was manifested by leading participants of the household labour debate described earlier. Von Werlhof, Mies and Bennholdt-Thomsen, however, have used their concrete, Third World experiences to formulate theses on women's labour which, they believe, are more universal in scope than the thesis brought forward by the household labour debate.

Moreover, unlike the development feminists (to be discussed later), who silently adopt categories of, but never directly confront, Marxist economic analysis, these three German feminists have devised their theory as an open critique of Marxism. Thus, in the introduction to a joint book which summarizes the three authors' views, both women and colonies are identified as 'neglected spheres': 'The inclusion of these neglected spheres transforms previous social theories root and branch by placing new contradictions and relations centre-stage.'[2] Criticizing Marxism for seeing propertyless waged workers as the sole source of surplus value, of economic growth, the authors suggest instead viewing the relation between wage labour and capital as 'one part of a much more comprehensive contradiction between *human labour in general* (including non-wage labour) *and capital*, with an additional contradiction between waged and non-waged labour'.[3] In this book, von Werlhof, Mies and Bennholdt-Thomsen have presented themselves as members of the same school of thought, as theoreticians sharing common themes and common theses.

I will review two theses of the German feminists here. First, I will discuss their thesis on '*housewifization*', a term which has been variously interpreted, but basically refers to the social definition of women as non-producing housewives. Next, I will review their thesis on the identification of women's labour with 'subsistence labour' (i.e., with women's responsibility for the upkeep of their families). Whatever one's ultimate judgement on the theoretical position these German authors take, their work, in my view, constitutes a crucial stage in feminist theorizing. It is one of the most serious attempts so far to overcome the patriarchal bias in Marxist economic theory.

Domestication of Women: Common Theme in Feminist Literature

First, a general note on the theme of housewifization, or the domestication of working-class women. This theme has been popularized and elaborated by Maria Mies and others of the German feminist school. In her book *Patriarchy and Accumulation on a World Scale*, Maria Mies links the creation of the housewife ideology with the development of European capitalism.[4] Quoting extensively from historical sources, she illustrates how the ideal of the domesticated, privatized woman, 'concerned with "love" and consumption and dependent on a male breadwinner',[5] first spread among the bourgeoisie, then among small property owners (i.e., the petty-bourgeoisie), and finally among the working class. Even the concept of the nuclear family originally had 'clear class connotations', and was imposed on the class of industrial labourers—the modern proletariat.

Before discussing Mies' specific interpretation of the theme of domestication and its application to the lace sector in Andhra Pradesh, I would like to point out that this has been a common theme in feminist literature since the 1970s. Thus, several feminist authors have analyzed the 'domestic science movement', which gathered strength in the United States in the 19th century and reached its zenith in the first part of the 20th century. Led by prominent, well-to-do women and backed by vested male interests, the movement, according to Barbara Rogers, 'sought to provide a "scientific" rationale for confining women to unpaid, domestic work'.[6] The idea put forward was that women should see their task of domestic work as a vocation, and should turn their responsibility into a professional activity. In one of the essays quoted by the American historian Matthaei, it was argued that 'housekeeping is a many-sided business calling for theory and practice in scientific management'.[7]

Not coincidentally, Matthaei notes, the language employed resembled that of Frederick Taylor, the father of scientific management in industry.[8] In some articles published in conjunction with the campaign on scientific homemaking, it was suggested that housewives should emulate the rationalization being achieved in factory work. Time and motion studies should be made so as to 'revolutionize' housework! Meanwhile, the scientific basis of 'domestic science', as Ehrenreich and English have pointed out, was weak. According to them, the frenzy of cleaning and dusting, for instance, rested on an extremely dubious 'germ theory'—the failure to keep everything free of dust and germs was suggested as being 'akin to murder'.[9] Another tenet of the domestic science movement was the idea of 'maternal deprivation'—if mothers were not constantly available to take care of their children, the effect would be to increase juvenile delinquency. This theory, as feminists have pointed out, helped men to evade their paternal responsibility. Here again, facts were twisted to suit the ideology of the domesticated wife, free from wage work outside the home.

Furthermore, as Matthaei states, 'the scientific homemaking movement was logically followed by the glorification of consumption as the distinct vocation of women'.[10] In the pre-capitalist economy, women were involved in a variety of productive activities in and around the home, like weaving clothes, making cheese and churning butter. Articles on 'scientific homemaking' urged the replacement of homemade with store-bought goods, arguing, amongst others, that machine-made goods were superior in quality. When factory-based commodity production began gradually replacing women's subsistence labour, the 'scientific homemaking' movement provided ideological support to this economic development by suggesting a new vocation for women: 'on account of the change in economic conditions of production, . . . women have gained a whole new field of economic activity, that of consumption'.[11] Thus, feminist research has amply illustrated that the ideology of the housewife, whose tasks are limited to house-keeping and consumption, has been consciously advanced by upper- and middle-class women, along with the industrialization of Western societies, through the 19th and 20th centuries.

The Lacemakers of Narsapur: History and Evolution of the Production Sector

To clarify the strength of the thesis on 'housewifization' put forward by the German feminist school, as well as certain risks of over- and misinterpretation it harbours, I have chosen to structure my discussion around Maria Mies' book on the labour of women lacemakers in Andhra Pradesh. This work is based on field research carried out in the late 1970s in and around a small town, Narsapur, located near the coast. Here, impoverished women produce lace goods for the world market, relying merely on their hands and needles. Some were widows with children, others were married women with unemployed or wage-earning husbands. Mies and her colleagues arranged for group discussions, took numerous interviews, and gathered data through a household survey. The survey brought out that in a significant percentage of the families, women were the principal income-earners.[12] A large majority of the laceworkers belonged to a rural caste called Kapu, whose status had recently risen with the transformation of the agrarian economy. Mies' book systematically analyzes both the nature of the production process in the sector and the dynamics of the sexual division of labour.

In order to understand the theoretical arguments Mies draws from her findings, it is necessary to first briefly summarize the historical emergence and evolution of the sector. The origins of the lace industry, Mies states, are 'closely connected with the history of the missions in the Godavari Delta'.[13] In the 19th century, missionaries connected with a Baptist Congregation mission, looking for potential converts, taught lace-making patterns to converted members of two Untouchable castes, the Malas and the Madigas, in order to help them survive in the face of famine. The missionaries provided the thread, and collected the finished goods which they sent as gift parcels to friends and dignitaries in Scotland, England and Ireland. Thus, in its first phase, the production of lace in Narsapur was not organized along commercial lines, but was a non-profit activity aimed at soliciting donations for missionary work.

This changed around the turn of the century. Two former teachers at the mission school, Jonah and Josef, stepped in to organize and expand lace production for export. According to Mies, they introduced the classical putting-out system into lace-making, which was already known to Indian businessmen in the 16th and 17th centuries.[14] Orders and designs were obtained from foreign sources, initially for collars, cuffs and attached lace. They distributed the work through a selected group of female agents who would visit the women artisans to give them threads and designs, and would subsequently come to collect the crocheted pieces. Some of them were also employed to stretch and sort out lace in the houses of the exporters. In any case, women were not only involved as producers, but held other positions in the production hierarchy as well. The method of payment employed by Jonah and Josef was the piece-rate system, previously discussed.

Along with the commercialization and expansion of production, the composition of the workforce also changed. Thus, Jonah and Josef brought in Agnikulakshatriya women who belonged to the fishermen's caste. Mies notes how these newly-recruited lacemakers, and the converted Untouchable women, were turned into housewives. Both apparently gave up work outside the home when they started lacemaking—the Agnikulakshatriya women had sold fish, and the Mala and Madigas had worked in the field. One of the factors which, she hypothesizes, was responsible for this transformation was the ideology spread by the missionaries. The image of womenhood taught in the girls' schools opened by the missionaries 'was basically that of the housewife and mother'.[15] But confinement in the home, Mies states, is also a traditional status symbol in India. Thus, Christian converts may also have wanted to emulate the example of well-to-do castes in Hindu society.

Finally, in the course of time a third category of women were drawn into the lace industry—those from the more 'respectable' castes, living not in the town of Narsapur itself but in the surrounding villages. This, as will be further explained later, has increasingly occurred since the 1960s, and is closely connected with class changes that have taken place in villages in this part of Andhra Pradesh. Women were recruited in large numbers, in particular, from a caste of agricultural producers called Kapus. The example of the Kapu women illustrates the existence of secluded work spheres among more well-to-do castes. Kapu women interviewed as a part of Mies' research stated that they had always been *goshami* (they had always led secluded lives and been exempted from fieldwork).[16] Thus we note, at the outset, that the concept of the domesticated wife is not a purely Western concept, but has a long tradition among affluent sections of the rural population in South Asia itself.

The evolution of the lace-making industry in this century is rather uneven, at least till the 1960s. During the period between the two World Wars, and again immediately after the Second World War, the export of lace expanded considerably. The list of countries which became customers of the Narsapur merchants grew steadily, and by 1953 the market value of lace goods produced reached a record Rs. 6 million.[17] Yet, after this peak, the industry faced a setback which, according to Mies, was mainly due to the imposition of quotas by importing countries, and to the rise of machine-made lace in foreign markets. Shortly after the Second World War the lace merchants formed two associations to press for the removal of export restrictions and for the supply of a sufficient quota of thread, but these failed to curb the cut-throat competition in the sector and the situation remained anarchic. The lace merchants also failed to arouse the government's interest in the sector, at least until 1960.

An important moment in the history of the sector was the founding, in this year, of a Handicraft Advisory Board in Andhra Pradesh. A subcommittee of the Board made an on-the-spot investigation into lace-making in Narsapur. Its report mentioned that 100,000 women were engaged in the industry, earning less than Rs. 15 per month on an average, and that about Rs. 1 million worth of lace was being exported every year from the town. In spite of the difficulties faced in the 1950s, the lace industry had emerged as, by far, the biggest handicrafts industry in the state in terms of production, export, workers and commercial establishments. The subcommittee's report suggested various measures to the government for promotion of the industry, such as credit aid and sales promotion. But whatever practical steps the government took primarily 'had the effect of changing the class and caste composition of the exporters'. The appointment of a Quality Marking Officer, for instance, according to Mies, was purposely intended to 'introduce a new group of exporters into the lucrative lace business and break the monopolistic tendencies of the older firms'.[18]

The new group of lace exporters who entered the lace business during the 1960s were mainly wealthy farmers—kulaks—who had benefited from the introduction of Green Revolution technology in agriculture. They looked outside agriculture for investment, and found the lace industry a suitable arena for earning quick and easy money. These kulaks were further attracted by the export incentives provided by the government, and by the bank loans available to those interested in investments in lace.[19] Of the various caste communities represented among the class of capitalist farmers, the Kapus were numerically the strongest. They were also the most successful in expanding into the lace industry. The entrance of the Kapus changed not only the caste composition of the merchants (formerly they were Christians, Brahmins and Vaishyas), but also that of the workforce. As noted earlier, the majority of lace producers today consists of Kapu women. They were obviously recruited by new merchants belonging to their own caste.

A third round of dynamic growth was achieved in the 1970s. Due to the extremely low production costs, lace goods and other Indian handicrafts became mass consumer goods available in big supermarkets in Europe, Australia and the US. Arab countries with their petro-dollars also became important customers of the Narsapur merchants. In 1976, two years before Maria Mies made her field investigation, the total lace production of the Narsapur area was estimated to be Rs. 8–9 million, and there was potential for further growth.[20] Whereas a small percentage of lace was marketed in Indian cities, the bulk was either directly or indirectly exported. In 1978, lace exports constituted no less than 90 per cent of the foreign exchange earned through the export of handicrafts from Andhra Pradesh. Yet, as Mies noted, 'if one looks at those who are actually gaining from this boom, one realizes that they are all men'.[21]

Narsapur's Lace Industry and the Garment Industry in West Bengal: A Comparison

Before describing Mies' analysis of the work of lacemakers, it will be useful to review the production structure in the sector in comparative terms, by comparing, and where necessary contrasting, this with the structure in West Bengal's garments sector. This will serve, to a certain extent, to underline the broader relevance of Mies' analysis. To start with, the process of capital accumulation taking place in the two sectors—the lace sector in Andhra Pradesh and the garments sector in West Bengal—cannot be equated. The former is intimately tied to the world market. Thus, part of the accumulation of profits does not take place in Andhra Pradesh but in the importing countries where the lace goods are sold. In contrast, capital accumulation through the production of clothes in and around Calcutta is concentrated in West Bengal and in other states in the eastern part of India, as this production is almost entirely domestically oriented. Yet, leaving aside, for the moment, this important distinction, several points of similarity can be marked.

First, in both cases, production is organized on the lines of the putting-out system. This means that both the production tasks relating to lace-making and those relating to the production of *punjabis*, trousers, frocks and other dresses are delegated via a complex web of subcontracting. The main mechanism that regulates production is basically the same in both cases—*ostagars* in one, and agents in the other, distribute key raw materials (such as threads and/or cotton cloth) to the actual producers. After they complete their tasks, the finished products are collected by the *ostagars* or agents who pay the workers by the piece. Mies quotes R.K. Mukherjee to show that this system already existed in India in the 16th and 17th centuries, when 'rising entrepreneurs were at the earliest stage of development'. In eastern India *dadni* merchants were paid advances by European companies, so that they, in turn, could advance money to the weavers 'in conformity with the "putting-out" system which had come into vogue'.[22] Thus, it appears that the present practice of delegation of production can be traced to this historical experience.

Another feature is that the production structure, in both cases, is dominated by a numerically small number of merchants. As I have noted earlier, the most powerful actors in the garments sector of West Bengal are big merchants of Calcutta's Barrabazar, who distribute the principal raw material, cloth, to numerous *ostagars* whose command over capital resources varies greatly. In the lace industry under review, the only raw material required for the production of lace is cotton thread, the distribution of which is virtually monopolized. According to Mies, in 1978 all the thread used in lace-making around Narsapur came from two firms—Alexander and Finlays and J and P Coats, based in Kerala. They supplied their threads to just three stockists, who had themselves become big exporters of lace goods.[23] But whereas the orientation towards the domestic market provides *ostagars* significant outlets for the independent sale of their readymade dresses, the export orientation of lace-making operates like a funnel. Reportedly, there were, in the late 1970s, merely 30 to 40 active exporters, 'of whom 15 to 20 are big exporters who do their business through commercial banks'.[24]

What complicates the analysis of production relations in both cases is the fact that the position of *ostagars* and agents often overlaps with that of skilled workers. In Moheshtola–Santoshpur in West Bengal, many tailors who are skilled in stitching *punjabis*, trousers and other dresses, themselves act as small *ostagars*. They not only spend time behind a sewing machine, but also subdivide production tasks and collect finished goods. Thus, they perform a double role, of both labourers and agents in the putting-out system of production. A similar phenomenon is observed by Mies for the lace industry of Narsapur. Here, considerable skills are required for *athukupani* (joining of 'flowers' or patterns together). According to Mies, many *athukupani* workers, in the course of time, have emerged as small agents themselves.

> These were women who were both craftswomen and knew something of the business. They learned about the prices in the local markets, they had to deal directly with the exporters, and some of them, or their husbands, later tried to start a business of their own.[25]

However, whereas this double role in Moheshtola–Santoshpur is exclusively performed by male workers, in Narsapur there are also women who hold the status of producer-cum-intermediary.

The fact that some women have emerged as intermediaries is partly a consequence of the differential nature of the division of labour in the lace industry. We have seen that in Moheshtola–Santoshpur, the manufacturing of *punjabis*, for instance, is divided into nine distinct production tasks, three of which are women's tasks (ornament sewing, hemming/button-fixing and handwashing). In the case of lace-making, the number of subtasks is less. Mies mentions three different types of lace work—*chetipani* or handwork, which is the elementary task of making a pattern or 'flower'; *athukupani* or attachment work, which means the joining together of the various patterns; and *kazakattu* which consists of fixing lace borders to pieces of cloth or joining several cloth pieces into a whole piece, like a tablecloth or a pillow case.[26] These tasks are all female tasks (i.e., women's production role is paramount). Male labourers are only employed in the very last stage of lace production, when lace is stretched and made flat, a task which is performed by older women or men in the houses of the exporters. In the horizontal division of labour in lace-making, which according to Mies has been organized to 'wrest control from the actual producers over their products',[27] there is hardly any place for labourers who are males.

A specific method of keeping control, which invites comparison with that used in the production of dresses in the Dumdum–Paikpara area of Calcutta, is the system of paying advances. As Mies notes, 'middlemen and exporters give money advances towards their wages to the artisans who then have to work for them to pay back the advanced wages'.[28] The advances may be 30 to 50 per cent of the wages, and the rest is paid when the lace is collected. In investigating the payment practices of the owners employing women as stitchers of frocks and blouses in Dumdum–Paikpara, we discovered a reverse kind of practice—payment of the wage is done only partly, when the women stitchers deliver the completed orders. Many owners keep the remaining part of the wage (up to 50 per cent) suspended, and pay an accumulated sum after about half a year. This method both serves to keep control over the dispersed workforce, and allows the owners to appropriate the interest on these 'savings'. The difference in the two methods referred to can probably be explained by the differential degree of poverty faced by the Andhra laceworkers and the Bengali stitchers. The system of giving advances on wages, Mies observes, is partially an outcome of the extreme poverty among the lacemakers. 'Their consumption fund is too meagre to last them through till they have finished the work.'[29] Moreover, piece-rates in the lace industry being exceptionally low, the exporters can afford to pay the workers an advance as a kind of loan.

Pauperization of Lace Workers versus the Enrichment of Exporters

I will review Mies' theoretical analysis, which takes us beyond the initial analysis of informal sector labour presented earlier. First, however, we should note the process of pauperization which has deeply affected the laceworkers. Mies has recorded some of the personal interviews taken in the course of her field investigation in her book. Those with rural women were carried out in a village called Serepalem where, Mies states, land alienation has occurred on a very large scale. Many poor Kapu women have started making lace for exporters because of their growing pauperization. Increasing poverty has forced them to take recourse to wage labour for an invisible employer (an exporter based in town), but their involvement in production for the world market does not appear to have enabled them improve their standard of living. Both women who are dependent on waged labour only, and those who are simultaneously active as workers and small agents, suffer. Some summaries of case histories Mies presents follow.

> Mahalaxmi is an 80-year-old widow, belonging to the Kapu community. She has been doing *athukupani* work since her marriage at the age of 13. In her childhood, she remembers, the family could eat well. Her father owned six acres of land, so enough rice was produced for subsistence. They also could eat eggs, *ghee* and chicken regularly, and could earn extra from the sale of processed milk in the market. When her husband, who owned 10 acres of land, was alive, things went relatively smoothly. The money she received for lace-making sufficed to buy all the daily necessities, except the staples. Today, Mahalaxmi has to maintain herself largely through lace work, but she is unable to make ends meet. Free resources, like fish, are no longer available, for 'all the fish have died because of the fertilizers they use', and Mahalaxmi can no longer afford to eat chicken or *ghee*. While the level of the wages

for lace work has remained constant for many decades, the price of essential goods, like clothes, has shot up. 'Now if I have to buy a *sari* it will be Rs. 30 to Rs. 70. That time I could buy it for Rs. 1.50 . . . . Today we are at a loss and they [the exporters] are making money.'[30]

Lakshmi and Venkamma are lacemakers-cum-small agents. Both were married to *coolies* (agricultural labourers without land). They learned the trade of lace-making in their childhood, and started crocheting at the age of 12 and 6–7 years respectively. Although they are Kapu women subject to the rules of seclusion, they became small agents in the course of time, moving around to distribute and collect work. In describing their role, both refer to the payment of advance wages by the exporters who supply them with orders. Says Lakshmi, 'The exporter first gives only thread. After half the lace is produced, he gives 50 per cent of the wages. The rest of the money he only gives after he has received all the lace.'[31] The income they earn as agents varies. Venkamma mentions that when visiting four villages to give thread and collect lace for Jonah and Josef, she could do 30 gross per month, earning Rs. 90, which appears to be the maximum. Today Venkamma is a widow whose two sons are active as *coolies* and bonded labourers. Their combined income is not enough to prevent a constant deterioration in the family's standard of living. Their access to fish is limited, and rice breakfasts have had to be given up. 'Five to six years ago we used to eat left-over rice in the morning, but now we have only coffee.'[32]

Nagamma, who is 40 years old, is married to an agricultural labourer who has been leasing some land, but is mainly working for others. The couple has to depend on the income from her husband's wages and what they get for her lace work. Her husband gets work for only three or four months a year. In the peak season he earns Rs. 5–6 per day. Nagamma says she started making lace when she was 10 years old. Her task is mainly *chetipani*. She and her two daughters together make six bundles per month, which earns them Rs. 16 only. Mies has calculated the family's average monthly income to be Rs. 75.33, which is well below their requirement to buy staples. 'Every year we have to borrow for consumption. We repay when my husband gets *coolie* work in the peak season.'[33] Nagamma has pawned and lost most of her movable property. 'First I pawned my golden earrings and my silver anklets. Then my brass vessels went and the silver tumbler . . . Now nothing of the jewellery I got at my wedding is left.' Although Nagamma feels she is mainly a housewife and that her income is only supplementary to her husband's, both their incomes are necessary. 'When there is money, the control over it is in my husband's hands. When there is no money, the responsibility is mine. We have more than Rs. 1,000 debts.'[34]

The reverse side of this process of the pauperization of laceworkers is a rapid process of enrichment by a very small group of exporters. One example of a very successful venture is that of Shivaji and Sons, an exporting firm founded in 1948. Whereas the company's initial investment was no more than Rs. 800, which was borrowed from a private money-lender, today the firm is one of the big exporters in Narsapur. Its export volume, in the late 1970s, was reportedly about Rs. 3 million.[35] But the process of enrichment is best epitomized by the story of P. Venkanna, a thread stockist and exporter from the Palakol market, whose son was interviewed by Mies. According to the son, his father was originally a small agriculturalist owning five to six acres of land. Within a few years of becoming a lace agent, he managed to collect export orders through correspondence with importers in West Germany. Subsequently, he also got the distributorship for a thread factory. Due to this monopoly position, Venkanna and Son have now become one of the biggest, 'if not the biggest', lace exporters in the Narsapur area, challenging even the position of the oldest exporting firm. Venkanna's son mentions the company's increased capital strength since he himself entered the business, in 1971. 'My father's turnover was Rs 3 to 4 lakh in thread business and now it is Rs. 40 lakh. His turnover in the lace business was Rs. 4 lakh at that time, and now it is Rs. 40 to 50 lakh.'[36] Moreover, because of the lace business, they have also risen to the class of rich kulaks for, according to Venkanna's son, they have been able to buy 40 to 50 acres of land. This contrasts sharply with the position of the majority of the members of the 'backward' caste to which they belong—former toddy-tappers who have turned agricultural labourers.

The conclusion to be drawn from these and other examples, according to Mies, is that a clear class polarization has taken place, which is also a polarization along gender lines. All the women involved in production relations in the lace industry, including those who were agents, complained about a deterioration in their socio-economic position, and none of them had been able to accumulate any capital. They were 'downgraded rather than upgraded in their position'. On the other hand, the men involved in the lace industry, even if they had started very poorly, had been engaged in a 'rapid and spectacular process of capital accumulation', which enabled some of them to rise in class. While they had all come from landless, poor or middle peasant families, they not only became wealthy merchants, but 'all of them also became substantial landowners and capitalist farmers.'[37] While in the past, in the period preceding the introduction of the Green Revolution, women had controlled part of the marketing in lace, now they only occupied places at the bottom end of production relations in the sector. Polarization had pitted female producers against male non-producers. If looked at in isolation from its economic surroundings, class and gender positions in the lace industry virtually coincided: 'All women were *de facto* workers and all men were *de facto* or potential capitalists.'[38]

The Working Day: Women have no Leisure Time

A separate section in Mies' study is devoted to the working day of women producers. The distinguishing feature of their working day (which is shared with the women garment workers in West Bengal) is that it broadly consists of two kinds of toil—household labour and waged labour. The lacemakers, as Mies notes, are engaged in the production of both use value and exchange value (i.e., values which are directly consumed by the family and values which are intended for sale in the market). To understand the exploitation of these women, it is necessary to look at their whole working day, and not just at the time they spend in waged work, as Marx's economic theory proposed to do. The assessment made by Mies thus forms an illustration of what has been stated earlier: Marx's theory of labour value was too limited. A theory of women's labour needs to take account of women's whole labouring time, including all the time spent on household chores and other productive activities which do not take the wage form.

The first part of the working day of the lacemakers is devoted to a whole series of household activities, such as child care, cleaning, fetching water and preparing food. As Mies notes, 'for most of these work processes, the preparation and the transport of the raw material is also part of the activity.'[39] Since it is common for Hindu women to sprinkle their courtyard with *kallapi* (a mixture of water and cowdung), these components have to be collected and mixed. The courtyard is further decorated with *rangoli* (a white chalk powder), which is prepared by burning limestone and grinding it. In some of the work processes, the distinction between use value production and petty commodity production is blurred. This is true, for instance, of the production of cowdung cakes, which is a very elaborate process. The women make cowdung cakes as fuel for cooking, but they make an extra amount for sale. The domestic chores performed by women in Indian villages thus differs from the domestic chores performed by Western housewives. There is no clear demarcation between the spheres of production and reproduction in the Indian context.[40]

All the productive activities mentioned so far are concentrated in the morning. By about 10 a.m., the women start their second major task, which is the crocheting of lace. In many cases, household tasks and lace-making are carried out simultaneously. Tasks are generally divided between all the female members of a family, including young girls. If there are more women in the household, some would concentrate, for instance, on cooking in the morning, while others would be engaged in making lace. Taking account of variations for the number of women and girls in a household and the family's economic status, the average daily labour time devoted to lace-making is reportedly six to eight hours. This means that the total labour time of each lacemaker is exceedingly high: 'Grown-up women as well as their small female children work between 13 and 16 hours a day; 50 to 75 per cent of this time is spent on lace-making.'[41] And yet official sources, Mies charges, continue to define lace-making as a leisure-time activity or 'part-time' work. In practice, the producers of lace 'practically have no leisure time at all'. Their working day lasts from dawn until they go to sleep at night.

Finally, this evidence can be supplemented and corroborated with facts on the working day of women producers elsewhere. The findings reported for frock stitchers in Calcutta closely resemble those cited by Mies—the average, 'normal' working day of the stitchers turned out to be almost 15 hours, of which eight hours are spent on household chores. Whether they produce lace in Andhra Pradesh or clothes in West Bengal, the working day of homeworkers subjected to subcontract relations and the piece-rate system is equally divided between household tasks and waged work, and it is invariably long. Neither does the length of the piece-rate workers' labouring day differ widely from that of women garment workers in Bangladeshi factories who are subjected to a time-wage system. The difference is only that a much larger proportion of the latters' labouring day is covered by their waged work. In all three cases discussed, the owners of capital refuse to bear the full costs of reproduction of women workers' labouring strength.

Production for the World Market Embedded in a Rural Economy

I will now focus on some ways in which Mies' analysis of lace-making is distinct from, and moves beyond, the analysis of homeworking in garments production in West Bengal which I have made. One of these is the fact that Mies consciously highlights the lace industry's connection with agrarian relations. Her field investigation, as mentioned earlier, was carried out in both an urban setting (Narsapur town) where lace-making was originally concentrated, and in a village area some 9 km away from the town. Whereas the Christian and Agnikulakshatriya producers were town-based and had long since lost their relationship to the land, the Kapu women involved in crocheting in the village, being wives and daughters of poor peasants and agricultural labourers, formed a part of the structure of agrarian relations. In the West Bengal garments sector, we similarly analyzed production relations in an urban and rural setting. Yet we did not study the sector's interconnection with the village economy, even though the craft of tailoring first flourished in the countryside in Moheshtola–Santoshpur.

For Mies, it is very crucial to make an integrated analysis. As she points out, the more 'visible' agrarian relations, covering day labourers, small peasants, rich peasants and urban employers, have found considerable scholarly attention. But they are generally studied in isolation from other production relations, in particular reproduction relations, or the relations between women and men.

> Thus, the structural separation between these two spheres is reproduced and reinforced by research. Yet it should be clear by now that it is precisely this separation which leads to a mystified view

of the totality of social relations. As far as women's labour is concerned, it will always remain 'hidden', unless we abolish this separation.[42]

Thus, Mies devotes ample attention not only to relations between women's household tasks and their lace-making, but also to the way the totality of women's work is 'embedded' in the agrarian economy.

As has already been stated, this has resulted in the understanding that the expansion and transformation of the lace sector since the 1960s was intertwined with the spread of commercial farming under the impact of the Green Revolution. Many rich farmers chose to re-invest their profits not in agriculture but in the lace industry, where quick money could be made. This draining of the rural areas and the transformation of agrarian capital into merchant capital, Mies states, 'has led to a polarization in the villages', for 'the pauperization of peasants provides the lace exporters in Narsapur with an almost unlimited reservoir of very cheap female labour'.[43] Women belonging to poor village households simply had to take to lace-making to supplement the insufficient income of their husbands. Their pauperization, as a consequence of the new farming methods, serves as the pre-condition for the further enrichment of the rich kulaks who have invested in the export-oriented lace industry.

This exploitation of women laceworkers by a class of rich peasants is explained well in one of the sections dealing with reproduction relations. Here, Mies notes that

> the women work as workers not only for the lace merchants and exporters, but also indirectly for the rich peasants, because their income from lace is all spent on the reproduction of the family, including the reproduction of the men who may be jobless wage labourers, poor peasants or artisans.[44]

Thus, the productive activity of the male cultivators is made possible by the women performing household tasks and other subsistence activities in the home. Yet the landowners employing the men do not bear the costs for the reproduction of their labour power. In short, the labour of the laceworkers is not just a hidden source of accumulation in the world market-oriented lace sector, but also is a hidden source of accumulation in the agrarian sector of the rural economy.

This web of interconnections between the household industry and the agrarian economy was not analyzed in the foregoing discussion on the production of garments in West Bengal. To an extent this can be explained by the differential evolution of rural relations. In the rural area of Moheshtola–Santoshpur, agrarian production lost its predominant position long ago. Whole villages here are engaged in the manufacturing of single items, like trousers and *punjabis*. Yet, if we carefully scrutinize the position of the homeworkers in the villages surrounding the nerve centres of garments production (such as women doing *sabudana* and women buttonholers/fixers or *chukai* women, we can only admit that their toil, too, serves a function in relation to the agrarian economy. They, too, are wives and daughters of peasants and agrarian labourers responsible for the upkeep of their families. In short, Mies' framework of thinking has a broad relevance for the analysis of rural-based industries. To understand the mode of exploitation prevailing here, and remove the mystified view about such industries created by their male beneficiaries, the totality of the agrarian and non-agrarian production relations has, indeed, to be analyzed.

Dynamics of the Sexual Division of Labour—Interconnections with Changes in Class Relations

Mies' analysis regarding the sexual division of labour, and the changes it has undergone over time, is again embedded in her analysis of agricultural transformation. I have argued earlier, in the discussion on West Bengal, that the sexual division of labour in society is not fixed but varies. By comparing the situation in two distinct geographical areas, it was possible to show that there are different ways to ensure male dominance. What was fixed, and what was constant, was the fact that all women garment workers are home-based producers, and they are almost exclusively responsible for all household chores. Here, Mies' findings concur. The sexual division of labour, she says, is structured in such a way that 'men not only control certain means of production, but also the means of reproduction, namely their women.' Women carry the burden of all domestic tasks, including service tasks like preparing the bath water for their men, and washing their husbands' backs when they come home.[45]

Mies' historical approach enables her to bring out how the sexual division of labour has evolved over time, and how changes in women's social and economic status are closely linked to changes in class relations. Take, for instance, the changing position of the Kapu women who, as stated before, form the bulk of today's workforce in the lace industry. Their entrance into the sector first helped them to partially break their seclusion. Whereas previously they were *gosha* women who were not supposed to work outdoors, their status as wage workers made it necessary for them to contact the external world, the world of export business. This was particularly true of those women who were given tasks as agents and subagents, moving around to distribute thread and collect lace goods. These Kapu women were no longer homebound: they broke with traditional social norms to reach some degree of independence.

How were these changes related to changes in the class structure in the area? The massive entrance of Kapu women into lace-making was related to the 'overall process of pauperization' which affected many peasant families not sharing the benefits of the Green Revolution. 'The rise of the middle and rich peasants under the impact of the Green Revolution led to a polarization among the Kapu peasantry. Some became rich in this process and some lost their land and had either to migrate or become agricultural labourers.'[46] As Mies states, for peasant families with small holdings, the involvement in lace-making and trading was linked to their losing their status of independent cultivators and their getting de-classed. In order to understand the evolution of the sexual division of labour, therefore, an analysis of changing class relations is eminently relevant.

More recently, the changing composition of the group of merchants and agents in the lace business has, once again, had an influence on the position of women. It has deprived them of the little independence they had previously gained. I have already referred to the newest phase in which kulak peasants have become powerful participants in the accumulation process in the lace sector. The gender relations in the production process have concomitantly undergone a change, for the new generation of traders has replaced most of the former female agents with men. The excuse, according to Mies, has been the introduction of cycles to facilitate the work of the lace agents. This use of modern technology has served 'as an excuse to push women agents out of the trading sphere altogether'.[47] Once again, the transformation in class relations has affected the relations between women and men.

The dynamic process of transformation of production relations in the lace industry has ultimately resulted in a division of tasks between women and men which is much more polarized than what was observed for the garments sector in West Bengal. Here, all positions of economic power (of the *ostagars* and the merchants) are monopolized by males, but the actual production tasks (such as tailoring, finishing and ironing) continue to be the domain of both women and men. They are divided domains but, in Moheshtola–Santoshpur in particular, women do not stand alone as producers in opposition to male non-producers. In the case of the Narsapur lace industry, the situation is now almost fully polarized. As Mies argues, 'class polarization has also led to a polarization between men and women', for all lace producers are female and all lace traders are male.[48] In short, the dynamics of the sexual division of labour cannot be studied in isolation, but should be studied conjointly with the transformation in class relations in a given area.

The Housewifization of Lacemakers and its Effect on Women Workers' Consciousness

In her discussion regarding the lace industry of Narsapur, Mies repeatedly refers to the concept of 'housewifization'. She prefers this term to the term 'domestication', since it forms a clearer counterpart to 'proletarization' and the social definition of men as breadwinners.[49] When reading her text, it becomes evident that she is aware of the fact that the women are not in reality turned into non-earning housewives, as the bourgeois ideal of domesticated women prescribes. I would like to stress this from the start, since her approach significantly differs from that of Claudia von Werlhof, whose views will be referred to later. Mies, thus, notes the contradiction that exists between the appearance of lacemakers' position in society, and a reality which does not confirm with that appearance. She calls the lacemakers 'semi-domesticated'. 'This means', she states, that 'in their social appearance they are housewives. But in reality they are wage labourers, fully integrated into a world market-oriented production system.'[50]

This does not mean that the social definition of laceworkers as housewives has no economic consequences. It has, for it facilitates the ruthless exploitation of their labour by the lace merchants and the exporters of their produce. In a chapter on 'Profits and Exploitation', Mies points to the extreme underpayment of the laceworkers. *Chetapani* workers, on an average, got no more than Rs. 0.56 per day. With regard to the overall picture, Mies calculates the capital advanced by the exporter per day per worker to be Rs. 0.60. Even taking account of the difference in time (her investigation was carried out some 14 years before my own in West Bengal), the wage level in the lace industry is far below that of the worst-paid women workers in West Bengal's garments sector.[51] And although a precise calculation of the rate of exploitation is hardly possible, the approximate rate, according to Mies, is almost 300 per cent. 'This means that the exporters gain from one woman's daily production almost three times the amount they pay her as a wage.'[52]

To clarify how this works out for the women lacemakers themselves, Mies makes two further points. First, she looks at the daily consumption requirements of an individual *chetapani* worker (i.e., her minimum requirements for subsistence). These she calculates to be Rs. 1.60 per day. At the existing wage rate, a laceworker cannot even earn this meagre sum if she devotes her whole day of 14 hours work to lace-making alone. This illustrates the degree of underpayment of laceworkers. Mies refers to Marx's distinction between necessary and surplus labour (which I have also followed) where, as she also points out, necessary labour time only referred to the time required to earn money to buy daily necessities. The work that goes into the transformation of these commodities into use values for human consumption was ignored. Yet, if Marx's limited definition of necessary labour is followed, Mies states, it is clear that even this was not being paid for by the lace exporters. In short, the laceworkers were being 'robbed of their daily consumption fund'.[53]

Second, and to further underline the extreme underpayment of the laceworkers, Mies draws a comparison between their labour time and wages, and those of male agricultural labourers. Most of the latter have work for only six months a year, but their earnings are many times higher than those of laceworkers who toil all the year round. Whereas men's labour time (for six months) amounts to 1,440 hours, women's labour time (for 12 months, lacework and housework taken together) comes to 5,040 hours. A male agricultural labourer, earning on an average Rs. 5 per day, gets Rs. 600 in half a year, while a lace-making woman gets only Rs. 90 in the same period. There is a huge difference in earnings, and this in spite of the fact that capital accumulation in the lace industry is taking place very rapidly. Mies explains the difference between male and female wages by the fact that 'patriarchal institutions and ideology have become a material force', a form of structural violence 'by which women are robbed of their just remuneration as workers'. Women are treated as 'a natural resource' from which labour power may be extracted at will.[54]

Thus, Mies is keenly aware of the economic function which the construction of the housewife ideal has for the owners of capital, and for the husbands of the laceworkers themselves. As long as lacemakers are seen as 'housewives' and 'non-earning wives', they can be subjected to almost unlimited exploitation by the lace exporters, as if their labour power was a freely-available natural resource. Moreover, the exporters' view is shared by the husbands of the laceworkers who also have an interest in seeing them as housewives, for it allows them to hold property rights over women's labour. In short, 'the definition of women as housewives has precisely this function: to treat their labour power as natural, freely available to their husbands as well as to the exporters'.[55] To reiterate, it is not that the economic position of the lacemakers in Narsapur can be equated with that of the non-earning, middle-class housewife of Western societies. But, by defining them as housewives, patriarchal society deprives the women producers of both respect and status and the most minimal economic rights.

In several sections of her book, Mies further develops her analysis regarding 'housewifization'. The social definition of men as 'breadwinners' and women as 'housewives' influences the attitude of government officials and exporters. They generally expressed the opinion, Mies, states, that the laceworkers are just housewives 'who do this work in their leisure time and as a hobby'.[56] But the same ideology also has an effect on the thinking of the laceworkers themselves. They too appear to be influenced by the prevailing ideology, and by the way they are defined by those owning the fruits of their labour. Thus, Mies lays special emphasis on the effect of the ideology of 'housewifization' on the consciousness of the lace sector's female workforce.

First, she notes a contrast between the self-conception of the laceworkers belonging to the Kapu caste and the Untouchable (*harijan*) women who were active as agricultural labourers. The latter were 'not domesticated or defined as housewives'.[57] Although, Mies states, their wages were lower than those of male agricultural labourers, the *harijan* women earned considerably more throughout the year than the women laceworkers. 'This fact and the fact that they work collectively in the field has made them bolder and more self-confident. They talked with contempt about the women who sit in the house all day long and make lace for a few paisa.'[58] Even though the female agricultural labourers were outcastes, they did not feel inferior to the laceworkers positioned much above them in the caste hierarchy. Kapu women, on the other hand, expressed their inability to do fieldwork, reflecting a fear of getting de-classed.

Second, Mies observes, the atomization of the laceworkers, and their isolation as homeworkers, had a negative effect on their feeling of mutual solidarity. There was no basic unity between the women workers. Only the women of one family, daughters and mothers, worked together as a unit. 'By and large, production is individualized', and this, Mies observes, leads to intense competition between the laceworkers themselves. 'All women try individually to get better wages from an agent, to sell some lace on their own or become a sub-agent for a bigger agent, in any case to have an advantage over the other women.'[59] Mies even draws an analogy between the 'extreme competitiveness and jealousy' she says existed among the women lace producers, and the 'rat-race observed among the exporters'.

These findings are not fully corroborated by my later findings for the garments sector of West Bengal. In the Dumdum–Paikpara area of Calcutta, we found that many stitchers of cloth realize the need for a common trade union organization which reflects the existence of a collective consciousness. Some frock producers, in particular, were found to have been engaged in an attempt to raise piece-rates, through joint efforts, by striking work at a crucial time. Such an initiative would have been unthinkable, if the women did not conceive of themselves as waged workers. Nevertheless, it seems only logical that the ideology which propagates that women are mere 'housewives' creates barriers to the development of a collective consciousness. As long as homeworkers do not perceive that they share the same existence as other women engaged in waged work, it is only natural that their self-organization remains impeded. The ideology of 'housewifization' does have this function of mystifying women workers' existence to themselves.

The Limited Applicability of the Thesis on Housewifization

I will elaborate on the danger that reality is misinterpreted with the concept of 'housewifization', in particular given the way it is used by one of Mies' colleagues. But first I will try and explain how the thesis, as posed by Mies herself, already bears a certain risk of over-interpretation. The thesis is perhaps less generally valid than other concepts that have been put forward by contemporary feminists. First, Mies, like other feminists, argues that the concepts of the male 'bread-winner' and the female 'housewife' are intimately tied to the separation into two spheres—'production' and 'reproduction'. The dividing line between these two did not exist in the pre-capitalist era. As demonstrated by Mies for Andhra Pradesh, in the rural areas of most Third World countries, women today continue performing many productive tasks which involve the creation of use value and exchange value at the same time. As long as the production of commodities is not universalized, the capitalist drive to create two separate spheres of activity will remain incomplete.

Now, Mies' thesis is developed around a specific example—that of homeworkers in one geographic area of Andhra Pradesh. This case, as presented by her, brings out certain limitations to the concept of 'housewifization'. For although the housewife ideology facilitates the most ruthless exploitation, it struck roots because there was a whole pool of women available who, to a certain extent, fitted the prescribed ideology. As Mies points out, and as has been mentioned earlier, the large majority of laceworkers today are women belonging to the Kapu community, and they were already domesticated long before the foundations for the lace industry were laid. It was their preceding status as *goshami* women that made their incorporation as homeworkers in the industry feasible. The labour of other women, such as the *harijan* women who depend on wage labour in the field and who turned out to be comparatively more assertive, could not similarly be tapped.

How far is the thesis on 'housewifization' valid for cases other than the Narsapur workers specifically? Apart from lace-making, there are many more industrial sectors, both in countries of the North and the South, where women are working on piece-rates in their own homes. In some cases they are subjected to forms of commercial subcontracting, such as in the production of *beedis* in India and readymade garments in the West. In other cases female homeworkers are part of a structure of industrial subcontracting, such as in the automobile sector.[60] Yet, in numerous cases, the social definition of women as 'housewives' does not apply. Thus, women who are employed in plantations producing commercial crops, such as in the tea gardens in India and Bangladesh, should be called 'proletarianized'. They have been drawn into wage labour outside the home, and they toil together in large groups. In these cases, women's status approximates that of the collective worker rather than the domesticated wife. At times their status resembles, even more, that of the classical proletariat than the status of their own husbands.

Moreover, we should also note that historical developments have not been unilinear. In certain periods of time, industrial entrepreneurs, along with male-dominated trade unions, have succeeded in ensuring a massive expulsion of women from factory employment by pointing at women's domestic responsibilities. Yet there have also been trends in the opposite direction. As feminist historians have pointed out, during periods of war, for instance, massive numbers of women have been brought in to work in factories, including factories where arms and ammunition were manufactured, to replace men sent to the war front.[61] Thus, whereas the responsibility for household chores is almost universally women's, men have not consistently tended to monopolize waged work in factories, workshops or service sector establishments. In many countries of the North, in fact, a gradual increase in the wage labour employment of women outside the home has been observed in recent decades.

Thus, the thesis on 'housewifization' appears to be less broadly applicable than other concepts that have been put forward by women theoreticians since the second feminist wave. In order to analyze the process of capitalist accumulation, both the concepts of patriarchy and the sexual division of labour have proved to be of decisive importance. They have helped to lay bare general structures of domination and subordination which had hitherto been ignored in economic theory. The concept of 'housewifization' perhaps does not deserve the same status in a Marxist–feminist theory. For although the social definition of women as housewives is a convenient device eagerly applied by capitalist entrepreneurs when it suits their profit aims, in real life domestication has never been the general fate of women belonging to the classes producing society's wealth.

'Housewifization' Misinterpreted: The Analysis of von Werlhof

Before concluding this chapter, I wish to point to a further risk involved in using the concept beyond that of over-interpretation mentioned earlier. Over the last decade, and in particular since the crash at the international stock exchange in October 1987, monopoly companies worldwide have initiated a vast process of restructuring and reorganizing. One of the methods they use to maintain profit levels is to decentralize (i.e., disperse their production of automobiles, electronic equipment and other commodities to smaller factories, workshops, and even the home). This method, which has been devised and refined by Japanese companies long ago, and which is now applied in both the industrialized North and the South, is also known as 'informalization'.[62]

Another tendency is the by now well-known propensity, displayed by industrial companies, in particular since the late 1980s, for the replacement of fixed by flexible labourers. The number of male and female workers who enjoy the long-term security of jobs with additional fringe benefits (like pensions and health insurance) has been decreasing over the last two decades. Instead, companies prefer to recruit their workers on a temporary or seasonal basis, through manpower agencies and/or labour pools, so as to be able to discard them any time the company so desires. While trade unions tend to go along with the dictates formulated by monopoly companies, there is no doubt that the flexibilization of labour relations leads to an increase in the rate of exploitation. Both the trends of informalization and flexibilization help to strengthen corporate profits at the expense of the male and female members of the working class.[63]

How does one analyze the process just summarized? Claudia von Werlhof addressed this question in a provocative essay written when the process of informalization/flexibilization was just gaining momentum. She philosophically took the standpoint of the Western housewife: 'Housework is the most difficult phenomenon to understand. If we have understood housework, then we have understood everything.' Furthermore, 'the women's question is the most general, not the most "specific", of all social questions because it contains all others, and in contrast to all other questions, it leaves no one out.' Thus, only from the position of women, 'only from below—at the bottom—can the whole be seen as a whole'.[64]

Claudia von Werlhof adopted the position of the housewife, and from her vantage point it seemed that the free wage labourer was about to disappear. Whom did she consider to be this 'free wage labourer'? Here she referred to the worker who, since the 19th century, presumably has furnished the 'classical' figure of the exploited victim of capital. He was

> an alleged equal and adult contraot partner of the entrepreneur: protected by law against arbitrary action and violence, enjoyed social security, was a permanent employee in a factory or office, freely organized in a trade union, and received a wage which was sufficient for him and his family to maintain an average standard of living: the citizen, 'human being', the member of society, the free individual.[65]

This free wage labourer, von Werlhof argued, is going to leave the stage of history forever. The proletarian wage labourer, she assured her readers, was a minority phenomenon during a particular phase of capitalism. His prevalence, moreover, was limited to a few areas of the earth. In any case, contrary to what Marx and his followers had expected, it is not the principle of organization of the wage labourer which will determine humanity's future but that of housework. 'The wage will be abolished', von Werlhof literally stated, and the real model of work under capitalism is housework, not wage labour.[66] The German author depicted the free wage labourer and the housewife as 'two poles of a continuum' of capitalist conditions of work and relations of production. Though developments are not unidirectional, on the whole they veer towards the housewife, who is the model of the individualized, unpaid labourer, life-long at the service of the free wage labourer. Being imprisoned and deprived of any rights with regard to her labouring conditions, she is the model that determines the future of humanity. For the sake of capital, the proletariat is to be abolished. Long live the housewife!

What is one to make of von Werlhof's analysis of the present-day process of restructuring capitalist production relations? At first sight her viewpoint appears to be very apt and attractive—it puts anybody striving for justice on the defensive. What, after all, is nobler than to identify oneself with those at the bottom end? Yet, von Werlhof's specific presentation of the thesis on housewifization is flawed in several respects. First, she gives rise to a Babylonian confusion of speech by lumping together two distinct concepts: those of free and fixed wage labour. The concept of the free wage labourer was used by Marx, in a historic sense, to explain the position of those labourers who were no longer tied to the land, as feudal serfs in the European Middle Ages had been. 'Free labourers' then are not to be confused with the privileged working class which characterized Western, industrialized states in the decades after the Second World War.

The privileges enjoyed by major sections of the industrialized working class in the centres of the world economy, such as the United States, Western Europe and Japan, were not granted to waged labourers at the onset of the industrial revolution, but were the outcome of a long historical process. As Marx explained in *Capital*, initially capitalist entrepreneurs tried to extend the legal working day *ad infinitum*, and for much of the 19th century protective laws remained very few in number.[67] It was only through protracted struggle that industrial workers wrested more fringe benefits from the owners of corporate capital. As discussed here, an important milestone in the process of investing the fixed wage labourer with legal guarantees was the policy proclaimed by the owner of the American automobile company, Ford, shortly after the First World War. Since then, an aristocratic section of waged workers have enjoyed extensive fringe benefits. Thus, it is only the section of fixed wage labourers that constitutes an exception in the history of capitalism.

Second, while it is true that the position of the fixed wage labourers with their relative privileges is slowly being eroded, the new, flexible contracts being offered instead are wage labour contracts nonetheless. However individualized informal sector workers' labour, and however isolatedly homeworkers are forced to toil, the relation in which they stand to the class of manufacturers is that of waged workers. The piece-rate system, for instance, which prevails in much of the informal sector, while distinct from time wages, is nonetheless a capitalist form of exploitation.[68] Experience shows that the individualization of labour does not exclude payment of a wage, not even a fixed wage. Some women employed as homeworkers to do work behind computers in the service sector in the Netherlands, have fought for and won a contract which stipulates fringe benefits.[69] Thus, von Werlhof's thesis on the abolition of wages is decidedly wrong.

Finally, while it is correct to depict household labour as an extreme pole of isolated, hidden and unpaid labour, housewives in general cannot be depicted as being at the bottom end of society. My critique of von Werlhof's viewpoint thus extends beyond her interpretation of actuality, to her philosophical starting point. What is characteristic of women who are most severely oppressed under capitalist patriarchy worldwide is that they carry a double burden of toil: housework plus wage labour. To ignore one part of their work at the expense of the other means to do women workers injustice, and once again make a part of their toil invisible. As the concrete investigation of lacemakers in Andhra Pradesh by Maria Mies confirms, most informal sector women workers carry a double labouring burden, resulting in a 15-hour working day. It is only from this double vantage point—and not from the vantage point of the Western housewife—that 'the whole as a whole' can be understood.

Summary

This chapter has highlighted the thesis on 'housewifization', one of two major theses which have been put forward by Maria Mies, Veronika Bennholdt Thomsen and Claudia von Werlhof. Taking the debate within the international women's movement during the second feminist wave as their starting point, they have done substantial investigative work into the labouring conditions of women in Third World countries. All three women voice the same critique of Marxist economic theory, the focus of which, they argue, is too narrow. Instead of seeing the creation of an economic surplus as the outcome of the contradiction between capital and wage labour only, the German feminist school sees surplus value as the result of the exploitation of both waged and non-waged forms of labour. Without a broader conceptualization, the male bias in political economy cannot be overcome.

The most prominent representative of the German school, Maria Mies, has unravelled the social relations of production existing in the lace industry of the Narsapur area in Andhra Pradesh. The hierarchical relations in this sector, as pointed out, have much in common with those in the garments sector of West Bengal. In both cases, production is not concentrated in factories but organized along the lines of the putting-out system. In both cases, women are mainly involved as homeworkers. They are paid piece-rates for the dresses and lace goods which they fabricate. In both cases women's working day comprises household chores and waged work, and wage levels are too low to cover the value of women workers' labour power. Yet Mies has broadened the scope of analysis by including agrarian relations in her field research. Thus, the review of Mies' study on laceworkers has helped to carry forward the analysis of the sexual division of labour under conditions of commercial subcontracting, initiated in my earlier discussion on garments production in West Bengal.

In her book, Mies has dealt at length with the theme of 'housewifization'. Like women belonging to the working class in industrialized countries, women laceworkers in Narsapur are socially defined as housewives. In name they are not 'breadwinners' of their families, and their waged work is termed a 'pass-time' activity by the exporters employing them. This ideology facilitates the practice of an extremely high level of exploitation. While profit levels are high, the women homeworkers are not even paid a subsistence wage for the long hours they toil each day. As Mies argues, they are even robbed of a part of their consumption fund by the exporters and agents who control them through the putting-out system. Moreover, their social definition as housewives and their atomization negatively affect their consciousness.

However, while Mies' analysis of the lace industry concretely demonstrates the relevance of the thesis on 'housewifization', this thesis, if not carefully handled, could lead to a misinterpretation of today's economic realities. I have sought to illustrate this with the example of von Werlhof's interpretation of this thesis around the recent process of the restructuring of production relations. Through increased reliance on the subcontracting of product-parts to smaller companies and to women working at home, Japanese, American and European corporations seek to enhance their competitive advantages. The process entails a 'flexibilization' of labour relations, and means that fringe benefits formerly enjoyed by fixed wage labourers are taken away. But to interpret the process as the abolition of the class of 'free' wage labourers, to believe that more and more workers are hurled into an economic position approximating that of the housewife, is not correct. 'Housewifization' is primarily an ideological device which serves to make women's exploitation invisible.

Notes and References

1. von Werlhof (1988), p. 13.
2. Mies' introduction, in Mies, Bennholdt-Thomsen and von Werlhof (1988), p. 3.
3. Ibid. Mies explicitly states: 'Orthodox Marxism's theoretical and conceptual apparatus is, therefore, no longer adequate for the demands of this new critique of capitalism.'

4. Mies (1986b), pp. 100–10.
5. Ibid., p. 103.
6. Rogers (1980), p. 23.
7. Matthaei (1982), p. 158.
8. For details on Frederick Taylor's view, see Chapter 11.
9. Rogers (1980), p. 23.
10. Matthaei (1982), p. 165.
11. Ibid., p. 164.
12. Mies (1982), p. 97. The household survey was conducted among 150 women. Mies concluded that in 30 families of the sample, 'or in 20 per cent of the cases, the women were the main working and earning members of their families'.
13. Ibid., p. 29.
14. Ibid., p. 34.
15. Ibid., p. 33.
16. Ibid., p. 33.
17. Ibid., pp. 36–37.
18. Ibid., p. 39.
19. Ibid., p. 42.
20. Ibid., pp. 51–52.
21. Ibid., p. 52.
22. Ibid., p. 35. For a discussion on the *dadni* system, see also Singh (1991), pp. 21–22, 32. According to Singh (ibid.), p. 21, the Indian artisans under *dadni* were essentially 'independent' producers who were tied to the merchant companies through debt bondage since they were controlled through the advancement of cash money. 'The *dadni* system, through which the particular group or groups of craftsmen were bound to a merchant or European company, was so widespread in India that by the end of the seventeenth century virtually every commodity for the market was procured through this system'. The replacement of the *dadni* merchants by servants and agents of the East India Company is recorded by Mitra (1978), p. 45; Mukherjee (1974), p. 240; and Sinha (1956), pp. 6–7.
23. Mies (1982), p. 56.
24. Ibid., p. 53.
25. Ibid., p. 59.
26. Ibid., p. 57.
27. Ibid., p. 59.
28. Ibid.
29. Ibid., p. 63.
30. Ibid., p. 77.
31. Ibid., p. 86.
32. Ibid., p. 87.
33. Ibid., p. 81.
34. Ibid., p. 82.
35. Ibid., p. 92.
36. Ibid.
37. Ibid., p. 95.
38. Ibid.
39. Ibid., p. 119.
40. Ibid., p. 110.

41. Ibid., p. 121.
42. Ibid., p. 73.
43. Ibid., p. 173.
44. Ibid., p. 109.
45. Ibid., p. 112.
46. Ibid., p. 117.
47. Ibid., p. 118.
48. Ibid., p. 117.
49. Mies has made this clear (ibid., p. 180, note): 'I want to introduce the concept *housewifization* because it expresses more concretely the specifically modern form of control over women occurring in this case than does the term *domestication*. I define *housewifization* as a *process* by which women are socially defined as housewives, dependent for their sustenance on the income of a husband, irrespective of whether they are *de facto* housewives or not. The social definition of women as housewives is the counterpart of the social definition of men as breadwinners, irrespective of their actual contribution to their family's subsistence' (emphasis in original).
50. Ibid., p. 110.
51. Compare, for instance, the level of wages of the laceworkers with that of the *dagtolà* women in the Moheshtola–Santoshpur area of West Bengal in Chapter 5.
52. Mies (1982), p. 148.
53. Ibid., p. 150.
54. Ibid., p. 151.
55. Ibid.
56. Ibid., p. 54.
57. Ibid., p. 111.
58. Ibid.
59. Ibid., p. 60.
60. See, for instance, Mitter (1986).
61. See, for instance, Braybon (1982).
62. For details, see Chapter 11.
63. For the theme of 'flexibilization' see, for instance, Mitter (1986).
64. von Werlhof (1988), p. 168.
65. Ibid., p. 170.
66. Ibid., p. 171.
67. Marx (1977a), p. 252.
68. See Chapter 5. For a discussion on piece-rates, see Marx (1977a), p. 516.
69. Such contracts have, for instance, been obtained by tele-workers in the Netherlands, who do office administrative work behind computers at home.

PART 3

Women's Role as Agricultural Producers

8

Developmental Feminism and Peasant Women's Labour in Bangladesh

Developmental feminism was born from the recognition that male-dominated international institutions financing 'development' projects in the Third World were biased against women and tended to ignore women's contribution to economic production. In 1970, Ester Boserup highlighted the prominent role of women in field agriculture, particularly in Africa.[1] Since then, there has been a veritable wave of investigations into the productive activities of women in Third World countries. A school of developmental feminists emerged, whose research work is largely financed by Western aid and is geared towards 'integrating women in development'.[2]

Bangladesh is one of those Third World countries where women's labour has become the target of numerous feminist writings. Over the last 15 to 20 years, a series of publications have described and analyzed women's work in agriculture, particularly in the post-harvest processing of paddy.[3] The tone was set by a study commissioned by the Population Council, a private American foundation involved in developing contraceptives and promoting their use in the Third World. The study calls Bangladesh a class-divided and patriarchal society, and provides a materialist definition of patriarchy: 'the material base of patriarchy is men's control of property, income and women's labour'.[4]

In this chapter I will assess both the positive significance and the limitations of the research on village women in Bangladesh, that is financed with Western aid. On the one hand, I will show that developmental feminist research, in a sense, has 'outstripped' Marxist economic theory. While accepting, like Marxism, the need for a class analysis of rural economic relations, this research has brought into focus numerous home-based production tasks—such as the winnowing, drying and parboiling of paddy, and its husking on a foot-operated instrument, the *dhenki*—which have traditionally been overlooked by Marxist writers. At least one of the authors belonging to this school of feminism, Marty Chen, has given her own conceptualization of village women's work.[5]

On the other hand, I will explain how research that fails to question the fundamental causes of peasant women's pauperization, inevitably is limited in scope. For 'development' and 'modernization', as occurring in Bangladesh today, entail, amongst others, the enclosure of common property resources like water and fish, and the dispossession of peasant proprietors due largely to the 'skimming off' of the agricultural surplus by members of the country's commercial elite—processes which can be defined as 'original accumulation'. This chapter places both peasant women's pauperization and developmental feminist research against a background of original or 'primitive' accumulation in contemporary Bangladesh.

Embankment Construction and the Appropriation of the Commons

Bangladesh is an evergreen, deltaic country, whose agricultural wealth has been profoundly shaped by its rivers. These rivers, numbering 230 in all, include the mighty Brahmaputra (Jamuna), the Ganges (Padma), and their tributaries. In pre-colonial times, Bengal's rulers and peasants had developed a unique irrigation system, which has correctly been characterized as the 'overflow system of irrigation'.[6] To re-fertilize the land, peasants relied on a combination of flooding by muddy river water in the early period of the monsoons, and extensive monsoon rainfalls. Rich silt was distributed throughout the delta via canals that were broad, shallow and long, and were maintained by peasant labour. These canals ensured that the rain water in the later part of the monsoons was drained and flowed back into the major rivers (see Map 8.1). A British engineer, Willcocks, has described the irrigation system as one which 'ensured health and wealth to Bengal for very many hundreds of years'.[7]

Over the centuries, the peasants in Bengal developed their own knowledge system about agriculture. Some of their key practices were

Map 8.1
The River System of Bangladesh

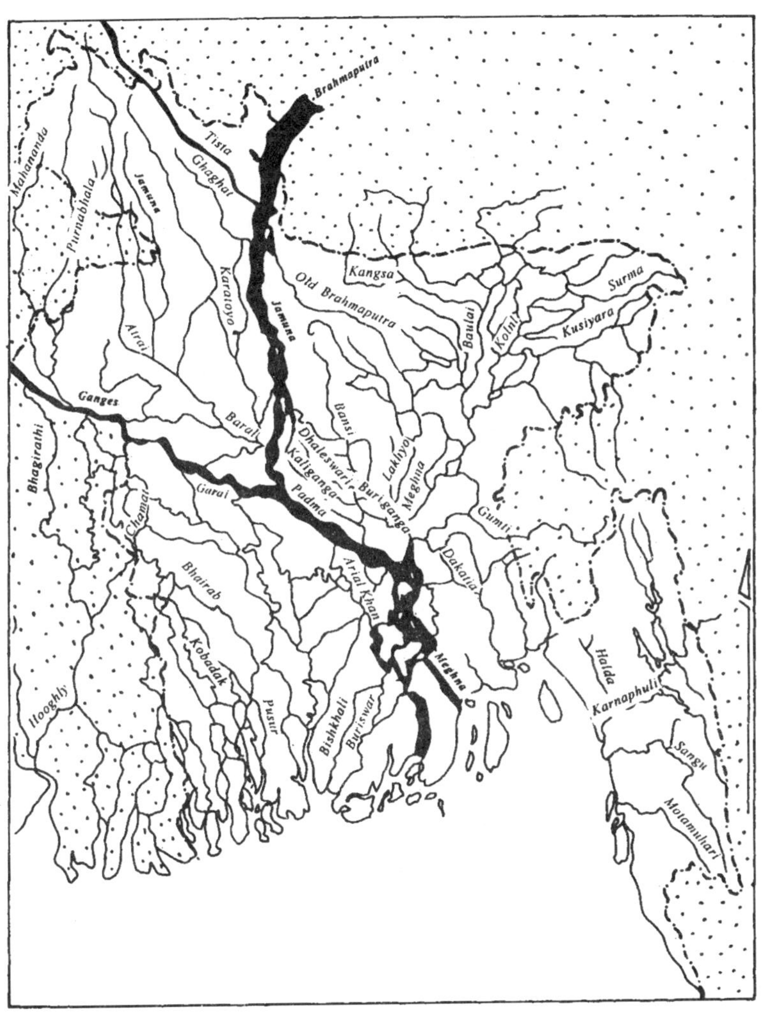

Source: Johnson (1982), p. 190

summed up by the peasant leader Abdus Sattar Khan in a briefing to the European Parliament in 1993.[8] In an extended parameter along the banks of the main rivers, tributaries and canals, elevations existed, which can be termed 'natural embankments'. These were slightly higher than the adjacent fields. The sloping parts of these elevations were used for the production of winter crops and vegetables, while the lower-lying plots were suitable for the cultivation of paddy. The peasants also devised a method to contain water for post-winter irrigation purposes. After the season for the cultivation of *aman* paddy was over, they would jointly close off the canals with small dams. The dams were breached after the month of *baishakh* (April–May), so that fresh flood water would once again spread its sediment as widely as possible over the fields. In short, the ancient system of irrigation in Bengal relied on a combination of numerous shallow canals, and small containment dams for the dry, spring and summer seasons.

From the period of British colonial rule onwards, this indigenous system of agriculture and irrigation was thoroughly disrupted. The British failed to properly maintain the comprehensive canal system, and they initiated the construction of 'watertight' embankments, for instance, along the river Ganges. As several professional engineers who were top-level functionaries of the colonial administration have argued, the embankments created more problems than they solved.[9] They impeded the natural re-fertilization of the soil and had a damaging effect on the natural production of fish (see the following description). Moreover, whereas the overflow system of irrigation helped to combat malaria, the construction of embankments did the opposite—it promoted the spread of malarial mosquitoes. In addition, the network of roads and railways built under the British administration also tended to disrupt the traditional system of water distribution as it created obstacles to the free flow of both flood and rain water.

Yet the construction of embankments was not halted when the British rulers left. Instead, the building of embankments and polders was given a fresh impetus during the Pakistani period, in the 1960s, with the founding of a separate government body, called WAPDA, responsible for construction works. Further, in the two decades that followed the formal independence of Bangladesh in 1971, a spate of separate flood control schemes were implemented with foreign aid.[10] Some of these, such as Chalan Beel Polder D in Rajshahi district, led to huge drainage problems, resulting in local peasant mobilization to breach the embankments. Yet, since 1989, Bangladesh's foreign donors have embarked on a multi-billion dollar comprehensive Flood Action Plan (FAP), aimed at building huge embankments and polder-like areas along the country's major rivers. While still in its preparatory phase, during which money is mainly being spent on studies and implementing pilot schemes, the plan has become the object of a fierce controversy, both within Bangladesh and abroad.[11]

Meanwhile, problems with old and new embankments are mounting. One example is the 20-km long embankment along the west side of the river Kangsa, not far from Netrakona town. According to newspaper reports, about 5,000 acres of field crops have been destroyed due to artificial waterlogging behind the embankment.[12] In response to people's complaints, the Bangladesh Water Development Board (the successor to WAPDA) constructed regulators as alternative drainage facilities, yet the waterlogging problem persists and paddy production suffers. Similarly, along two rivers bordering the Zakiganj area of Sylhet, embankments were built that have disrupted the traditional distribution of muddy water through canals into the interior. The rain water of the yearly monsoons could no longer be drained, and the area became permanently waterlogged. In July 1993, thousands of people tried to cut one of the embankments blocking entrances to the canals.[13] Clearly, non-indigenous structures (like watertight embankments and polders) are highly questionable methods of water management. Yet a powerful pressure exists to construct them at any cost. The question is: why?

Before venturing to answer this question, we need to discuss the effects of embankment and polder construction on the natural production of fish. Steve Minkin has pointed out that 'perhaps more than people in any other country, Bangladesh's citizens depend on natural wild fisheries resources for their food and livelihood'.[14] Approximately 80 per cent of animal protein in the Bangladeshi diet comes from fish. Fisheries rank only second to agriculture in importance in the Bangladeshi economy. Roughly 5 million people belong to the professional fishermen's community. Moreover, for many poor peasant families, fish capture is a crucial supplementary source of survival and/or income. Members of such families either add fish captured in rivers, distributaries and canals to their rice meals or sell the fish in the local market, earning some extra income.

Furthermore, among the various sources of fresh water fish captures, the flood plains hold a relatively important place. Whereas roughly a quarter of the yearly fish capture is gathered in the open sea, the remaining three-fourths hail from inland fresh water bodies. Here, flood plains are as important as rivers, taking up as much as 50 per cent of the inland fresh water captures. The yearly flooding of the rivers, as is common knowledge by now, stimulates the migration and spawning of fish, such as the famous *ilisha*. As Willcocks noted in the 1930s, the overflow system of irrigation ensured an abundant, natural production of fish for the peasantry of Bengal.[15] Since the traditional irrigation system has been undermined, the production of fish has fallen dramatically. The diversity of aquatic resources has been drastically reduced by embankments, and past flood control projects have left scores of fishing villages in decay. Quantitative data gathered by researchers under the Flood Action Plan (FAP) graphically illustrates this trend. In flood control projects reviewed under Component 12 of the FAP, losses of up to 75 per cent of the fish catch have been registered.[16]

Advocates of embankment and polder construction know well that the migration and spawning of fish is disrupted even where such structures are equipped with sluice gates. The Dutch environmental expert, Van Vierssen, has argued that even so-called 'submergible embankments' tend to have negative consequences since they disturb the timing of spawning.[17] Proponents of the Flood Action Plan suggest 'mitigating' the negative effect on fisheries by promoting fish production in ponds. Yet, as a report brought out by the Dutch Ministry for Development Cooperation points out, the expansion of fish-farming in ponds represents a shift, with crucial socio-economic consequences:

> Traditional fishing is done in freely accessible waters used by fishermen, landless people and small farmers. Fish farms are private property—the owner families are relatively rich. Whereas formerly fish was a common resource mostly for the poor, it is turning into a private resource of the larger farmers.[18]

In short, the shift from open fresh water captures to fish ponds has a multiple, negative effect. It leads to a steep fall in fish production, and it negatively affects the nutrition level and income of the rural poor, since the construction of embankments and polders implies the appropriation of common resources which traditionally helped landless families survive.

The enclosure of the commons has been identified as one of the key processes which historically laid the foundation of the capitalist mode of production.[19] In Britain, such enclosures took place from the 14th to the 16th centuries, and provided the raw material and labour force for the country's wool industry. Earlier, the system of 'open field'—of unfenced and communally-managed strips of land—had guaranteed access to the land for the bulk of the population. Here the rural poor could work their own plots after having performed labour services for the landlord. Further, on completion of the harvest, the villagers, for a part of the year, used arable land as collective pasture for their animals. The original or 'primitive' accumulation,[20] which formed the centuries-long prelude to the industrial revolution, was first and foremost a process of dispossession of peasant proprietors on a large scale. They were either evicted from their holdings, or saw their commons fenced off by sheep farmers. The process was intensely violent, and was supported by numerous state laws (i.e., some 4,000 Acts of Enclosure). Through this veritable onslaught, British agriculture was transformed, and the basis laid for an industrial proletariat.

The flood waters of Bangladesh, in a way, fulfil the same function as the 'open fields' and common pastures of the British peasantry before they were dispossessed. Traditionally, water resources constitute the most important form of common property resources for the deprived rural population of Bangladesh. As long as the muddy water of the major rivers freely flows across the land, and as long as water and manure need not be paid for, the re-fertilization of the peasants' soil is guaranteed and its irrigation greatly facilitated. Furthermore, the flood plains have another crucial function, since the landless are free to capture fish in flooded areas during the monsoon season. Like the British peasants in pre-industrial times, Bengal's peasants too have traditionally been able to survive because of access to the commons.[21]

The programme of construction of embankments and polders in Bangladesh, then, should be understood in these social terms—that it is part of a broader process of dispossession of the peasant population. The control of fishery resources is transferred from the public to the private domain, and is henceforth monopolized by rich farmers and money-lenders who become the owners of the fish ponds. These ponds are synonymous with enclosures, and imply the dispossession of the formerly free, landless fishermen and women. Simultaneously, the rural rich are provided the very real possibility to turn water into a commodity for their private use and sale. Whereas, earlier, no one needed to pay for the flow of irrigation water, and flood waters were a common property resource, the rural rich can now force peasant cultivators to pay for irrigation water. Contrary to freely flowing flood water, water entering polders via sluice gates can be privately managed and controlled. In this sense, even the polders along the coast of the Bay of Bengal, ostensibly intended for protection against storm surges and cyclones, are enclosures which strengthen the capital and power base of the rural rich at the expense of the masses of the rural poor.

Thus, whatever the rhetoric of 'development', and 'people's participation' in the design, building and maintenance of embankments and polders, these structures should be understood as part of a process of original accumulation taking place in Bangladesh. Just as the enclosures in pre-industrial Britain were sanctified by state laws, the building of embankments and polders too is legally protected by the state. According to a law promulgated in 1989, development projects cannot be challenged in court by the rural population, and where people question such projects (such as was done in Zakiganj in July 1993), they find the state armed forces blocking their way. Thus the appropriation of the commons, and of people's free access to water and fish resources, is as essential to paving the way for capitalist accumulation as is the expulsion of the peasantry from their privately-held plots of land. Unannounced by 'development' institutions, and hidden behind a barrage of rhetoric, the history of original accumulation repeats itself in Bangladesh.

Dispossession of the Peasantry: Land Alienation and the Structure of Rural Indebtedness

I shall now record a complementary process namely the expulsion of peasant proprietors from their own land. It is generally agreed in the literature on landownership in rural Bangladesh that the percentage of landless people has been growing phenomenally over the last three decades, both in absolute and relative terms. Whereas the number of landless peasants was less than 25 per cent in the early 1960s, today they are estimated to be 50 per cent or more. Some sources mention a figure of 70 per cent as 'functionally landless'.[22] An ever-increasing number of people thus have no means of production at their disposal. They have either to depend on the sale of their own labour power against a wage, or are forced to migrate elsewhere, to urban areas or neighbouring India, to escape from starvation and death.[23]

Secondly, the increased incidence of landlessness is clearly accompanied by a process of accumulation of land and other agricultural resources in the hands of the top layer of Bangladesh's rural population. This is confirmed by land occupancy surveys carried out by the Bangladesh Bureau of Statistics and USAID in the late 1970s. According to the 1978 survey, the bottom 75 per cent of the households owned only about 20 per cent of the total land, while the top 8.5 per cent of the households, owning more than 5 acres each, possessed 48 per cent of all agricultural land.[24] Surveys on peasant differentiation in two villages carried out by Atiur Rahman (1981–85) similarly showed that there has been a 'secular decline in the share of the bottom 60 per cent of households and a dramatic rise in the share of the top 10 per cent of the households in both villages'.[25]

These figures, further, indicate that the marginalization of the majority of Bangladesh's peasant population is not primarily caused by population growth and the division of landholdings via inheritance. In fact, both Atiur Rahman's study and other rural investigations confirm that many of the land transfers are a consequence of the inability of poor and middle peasant households to cover their consumption needs with what they produce. Eirik Jansen, in a detailed investigation into the economic relations in a village called Bhaimara, located not far from the junction of the Jamuna and Padma rivers, has highlighted the relationship between budget deficits of peasant households and the process of land transfers. According to him, 'about 50 of the 62 households in Bhaimara are persistently in deficit and have to take up loans in order to survive'.[26] The most important types of loans these households take are those for which agricultural land provides the collateral. Through credit obtained from the village rich, and often the mortgaging of their small plots of land, the village poor temporarily try and cover their deficits, but eventually are forced to give up their land.

A short review of the agricultural credit structure, furthermore, shows that indebtedness is a problem afflicting the vast majority of Bangladesh's peasant households today. Here we need to distinguish between private and institutional lending. Most peasants travel the road towards landlessness via a loan from a private, usurious money-lender or well-to-do peasant. Yet, in order to understand the structure of rural indebtedness in Bangladesh, it is instructive to look at the system of institutional lending (i.e., by banks). The banking system is entirely biased against landless peasants. Since land-ownership is a prerequisite for receiving a bank loan, and since only a literate person can fill up the necessary forms, landless families are structurally excluded from institutional loans. When the military government of Ziaur Rahman launched a credit programme in 1977, it officially targeted the rural poor. The programme was called off after a USAID study pointed out that it only reached the top 20 per cent of all peasants, and that the share obtained by poor and middle peasants was negligible.[27]

Investigations carried out by peasant organizations in the late 1980s similarly showed that 70 per cent of the credits issued by agricultural banks were absorbed by rich peasants and other members of the rural elite. Middle peasants (i.e., those relying on their own resources, like land, implements and labour to make ends meet) were the second main beneficiary—they formed roughly a fifth of the bank borrowers.[28] Yet most middle peasant borrowers could not transform their deficits into balanced budgets. Having taken credit for production purposes, a number of peasants failed to repay. By 1990, there were literally hundreds of thousands of 'certificate cases', (i.e., notices threatening peasants with a court case if they continued to default). Fearing arrest or detention, some sold their movable or immovable property, or fled from their own villages. Newspapers at the time abounded with stories of middle and lower-middle peasants with 'certificate cases' on their heads. Some of them, seeing no way out, committed suicide.[29]

The credit structure, thus, is a crucial link in the process of peasant eviction from the soil. A peasant facing the threat of a certificate case can act in two ways. One, he can sell his cattle and/or his land, which, to all accounts, has frequently occurred during the last decade. The other avenue open to him is to repay the bank by borrowing at usurious interest rates from a money-lender or Mahajan. But by borrowing thus, a peasant only obtains a 'delay of execution'. A Mahajan charges an extremely high interest rate of up to 350 or 400 per cent. Thus, in time, an indebted peasant is bound to lose his land and join the ranks of the rural proletariat. Whether he has lent from a bank charging a regular interest rate (12 per cent plus service charges) or from a Mahajan there is no way in which he can ultimately escape the consequences of the existing agrarian crisis which, as I will argue later, is at least partly caused by the market exploitation of the commercial elite.

Eviction of Peasants from the Soil and the Role of the Commercial Elite

Relatively little research has been carried out regarding the impact of market prices on agrarian relations in Bangladesh. Whereas Western and Bangladeshi academicians have systematically addressed issues like increasing landlessness, peasant differentiation and the role of the sharecropping system of production,[30] they have taken much less interest in analyzing the transfer of wealth from the peasant population to traders and other intermediaries living in market centres and in the country's cities and towns. It has been observed by de Vylder that the domestic terms of trade have moved against agricultural products throughout the post-Independence period.[31] On the whole, however, there is a dearth of statistics on the 'skimming off' of rural surplus by members of the commercial elite.

Nevertheless, news reports and personal interviews taken in 1991 and 1992 provide sufficient evidence to show that Bangladesh's peasants are at the mercy of traders buying off their products, and that the prices they receive for their crops are often not high enough to cover their production costs. Daily newspapers in August 1993, for example contained alarming stories of rice being smuggled to neighbouring India because of the 'extremely low price' of rice on the domestic market.[32] Around the same time, various newspapers reported that raw jute was being sold to local traders, or *fariyas*, at prices ranging from Taka 100 to 200 per maund, whereas the production costs were estimated to be at least Taka 300 per maund.[33] Data gathered during a field visit to Faridpur district in 1992 also indicated that peasants producing onions and other *rabi* (winter) crops received market prices below their production costs, while consumers in urban areas were stated to pay four or five times the price paid to the actual producers.

Undoubtedly, peasants belonging to different classes are not equally affected by the fluctuations in the market prices of crops. As Jansen, for example, points out, rich peasants are able to profit from such price variations through speculation, by hoarding paddy and other products until the sale price goes up.[34] Yet it seems clear that only a tiny section of the peasantry is able to engage in such practices, namely those who have substantial capital resources at their command. The vast majority of the village population (i.e., the landless, land poor, lower-middle and middle peasants), are adversely affected by the 'market squeeze'. Being unable to build enough financial reserves to repay the money they have borrowed, they are continuously at risk of losing their small pieces of land and even their homestead plots.

The dominant position which is held by the commercial elite in Bangladesh's economy can be further illustrated by referring to the evolution in the country's industrial sector in the 1980s. Although, as we will see in the following chapter, Bangladesh has seen a rapid expansion in the production of readymade garments since the late 1970s, this is by no means indicative of a general process of industrial expansion. On the contrary, the share of manufacturing output in the gross domestic product (GDP) 'has remained virtually unchanged in over two decades'.[35] It, reportedly, was 7.8 per cent in 1969–70 and 8.4 per cent in 1988–89. While a significant growth in manufacturing output was registered in the period 1976–81, the growth rate fell during the subsequent period from 1982 to 1989. According to the economist Rehman Sobhan, in three years during 1982–83, 1985–86 and 1988–89, it was stagnant or even negative.[36]

This industrial stagnation has not been due to a lack of investment resources, since development financial institutions and nationalized banks provided a vast amount of loans for 'industrial projects'. Sobhan has spoken of 'chronic financial indiscipline', citing a figure of Taka 10 billion of unserviced debts to these institutions.[37] The same problem was targeted by the then interim President, Shahabuddin, in a speech to Parliament in 1991:

> as to loans provided in the name of 'industrial establishments' by various nationalized banks—not even 10 per cent is being recovered .... Many people, using various names, have drawn huge amounts of lending money from industrial banks, from industrial lending institutions and other nationalized banks, stating that they will build industries. But they did not build industries, nor did they repay the loans. As a result, 10 thousand Koti Taka of industrial loans are to be recovered.[38]

Thus, the data confirms that the big borrowers of banking institutions in the 1980s were not interested in productive investments (i.e., they belonged to the commercial elite). Apart from their central role in the transfer of agricultural products from rural to urban areas, members of this elite engage in import and export business and absorb a major part of the monetary resources entering Bangladesh as foreign aid. They consume expensive luxury items, many of which are imported at high costs, and use their capital resources to speculate in the housing sector in Bangladesh and abroad. As Sobhan states, 'Trade, speculation, real estate investments and the export of capital, often using public resources, remain investments of choice for the new financial elite of Bangladesh.'[39]

Developmental Feminism and the Analysis of Women's Labour in Rice-processing

In what way are rural poor women particularly affected by the ongoing process of pauperization of Bangladesh's peasant population, of dispossession and the creation of enclosures? At least two trends may be mentioned at the outset—the growing participation of women in field labour and the replacement of brideprice by dowry payments. The traditional division of labour by sex prescribed that women's work be strictly limited to the home. While peasant men were responsible for all the agricultural tasks performed in the field, such as ploughing, transplanting and harvesting, women were burdened with all the household chores and with 'indoor' agricultural tasks (i.e., pre-planting and post-harvesting operations). They undertook to handle the seeds, and did arduous and labour-intensive tasks like winnowing, parboiling and husking. Toiling from dawn till dusk within their homes, women's scope for social intercourse was very limited.[40]

Now, under the impact of pauperization, women from the 1970s onwards have begun breaking down the age-old barriers against work outside the home. Several feminist authors have marked that, after Bangladesh was struck by famine in 1974, landless women were forced to look for outside employment. They started ignoring the rules of seclusion, or purdah, because of the need to ensure their own and their families' survival. As Chaudhury and Ahmed have noted, immediately after the 1974 famine, 30 per cent of the workers in foreign-financed food-for-work schemes were female:

> Without any formal encouragement, women came forward to take advantage of these rural work opportunities, where food in the form of wheat could be earned, in exchange for hard physical labour—digging and re-excavation of canals for drainage and irrigation, building of roads and flood embankments.[41]

While some joined food-for-work schemes, often related to the creation of enclosures, others tried to ensure their survival by joining production tasks in the paddy fields. Today, plowing remains a male preserve as in the past, but many landless women do tasks like sowing seeds, weeding the crops and cutting paddy stalks. Thus, the boundaries between men's and women's work are gradually changing. This change has not brought equality to women, and the value accorded to women's fieldwork is grossly unequal to men's. As Shamsun Nahar Khan, the president of the Peasant Women's Association (Kisan Sabha) notes, while male agricultural labourers are paid Taka 30 per day, plus meals, female labourers receive only half this amount (i.e., Taka 15, apart from food).[42] Nevertheless, their employment outside the home is hailed by women as a positive change.

Another change that has occurred since the 1970s is an indication of women's social degradation: the transformation of the payment system around arranged marriages. Amongst Muslims, the groom or his family traditionally used to pay a sum called *mahr* to the bride, in the form of gifts at the wedding and insurance money in the case of a divorce. The practice of *mahr* reflected, as has been stressed, the need for female labour in the groom's household. A woman's status was low, but the importance of her work was implicitly recognized. With pauperization in progress, however, the practice of *mahr* is rapidly being replaced by the system of dowry, more common among Hindus. Here, the bride's family pays money and/or goods to that of the bridegroom, in exchange for the latter's willingness to marry their daughter.

Quantitative data regarding the shift at the micro level is provided by Sarah White, in a study of a village in Rajshahi district. Whereas, in the British period, brideprice was paid in more than 90 per cent of Muslim marriages, by the 1980s 'there was an almost equal balance between dowry and non-dowry marriages' amongst the Muslims of the village.[43] The spread of the dowry system, which is not limited to a few villages but is a general phenomenon in contemporary Bangladesh, contributes to pauperization, since, as White notes, most dowries are not raised through saving, but by 'asset stripping' at the time of the wedding. The shift indicates that women, more than in the past, are considered a liability, and has been accompanied by an escalation of violence. Newly-married women are often put under pressure to bring in additional dowry, and if they fail to do so, can be murdered by their in-laws.

I shall describe, in the following, how developmental feminists have challenged male economists, particularly Marxist ones, by highlighting women's role in agricultural production. Developmental feminists have criticized official Bangladeshi statistics for vastly underestimating the number of women who work—who are 'economically active'. This male bias underlying statistical data is, of course, not unique for Bangladesh. Mies, for instance, has criticized Indian census data for suggesting that rural women, under the impact of the commercialization of agriculture, are transformed into non-earning housewives. Mies' field data shows that rural women, *de facto*, are forced to continue to work. Their work is only made invisible by statisticians and planners.[44]

Chen has analyzed the data put out by the Bangladesh government. She has made a crucial attempt to study women's labour from within the framework of a foreign-financed NGO (non-governmental organization). According to her: 'Micro-studies have begun to show that nearly all rural women work, but macro-data obfuscate this simple fact.' The census of Bangladesh shows that a total of 15.5 million women are 'housewives', and that over 3.5 million women are 'inactive'. Chen considers these quantifications to be deceptive because they hide the fact that nearly all village women are full-time workers in agriculture and animal husbandry. According to her, the 15.5 million housewives should be described as 'full-time workers'. She justly adds: 'Clearly, the definitions of work and of rural production systems in Bangladesh need to be re-analyzed.'[45]

This criticism is supported by Cain et al. in a study explaining the origin of the vast under-enumeration of women's work. The Bangladesh censuses adhere to the 'labour force approach', which largely limits enumeration of participation in the labour force to those employed in waged and salaried jobs.

> The labour force approach was developed in the United States during the depression in order to get better measures of current employment. This approach was designed for, and is best suited to,

> an economy in which the dominant form of economic activity is stable wage employment.[46]

This comment seems slightly off the mark, since it ignores the fact that the statistics of industrialized countries also gloss over part of the labour performed by women, (i.e., their household chores). Yet the authors rightly question the relevance of the 'labour force approach' in analyzing Bangladesh's economy which is family-based, where 40 to 60 per cent of the main staple food crop (i.e., rice) is produced for home consumption. As Cain et al. have observed, this approach 'yields categories and indexes that reveal little about the nature and extent of people's economic activity'.[47]

Developmental feminists have also given detailed descriptions of the range of agriculture-related productive tasks performed by village women. The central theme of their research is women's post-harvesting tasks, (i.e., their work in preparing the harvested paddy for consumption by the family or for sale on the market). Their descriptions tend to be of an empirical nature only, and contribute little to international feminist theorizing on the sexual division of labour between women and men. Nevertheless, their descriptive work is important, as it illustrates the facts on women's labour which traditionally have been ignored by male economists.[48]

Gudrun Martius von Harder, for instance, lists seven main processing tasks which need to be done after the harvesting of paddy from the field. Of these, two are primarily performed by men—threshing with bullocks or a pedal thresher, and storing the processed paddy. Men also carry the paddy to the place where the drying takes place, but women clean the yard, turn the kernels during the drying and keep a watch throughout. Other rice-processing activities are almost exclusively female tasks. Women winnow the paddy several times over, they steep the paddy and/or steam it before husking (parboiling), and they husk the paddy on a *dhenki*. Finally, it is the women who store the paddy in a basket which is sealed with a mixture of cowdung and mud.[49]

Though developmental feminists do not aim at throwing light on the rate of exploitation of village women's labour, some of their quantitative data is helpful precisely to those interested in this aspect. Thus, various articles mention that rural women's labouring hours are far longer than men's (up to 14 hours, compared to 10–11 hours for men). Moreover, women spend roughly an equal amount of time on agriculture-related tasks and household chores. Martin Greeley estimates that labour performed on post-harvest processing tasks adds 25 per cent to the value of the rice.[50] One can, therefore, conclude that village women's labour contributes directly and essentially to the value of rice and other field crops.

Moreover, rice-processing activities performed by women as wage labourers have also been taken into account by developmental feminist authors. Thus, it is stressed that the labour of husking in well-to-do-peasant homes is a key source of income for many landless women and their families. One source states that post-harvest work accounts for 25 per cent of employment in rice production.[51] But since all this work is done indoors and thus invisible, since it, like other post-harvesting work is done by women, and since it is not defined as 'social production', it falls beyond the scope of traditional Marxist economic analyses of labour exploitation in agriculture. Where women's wage labour is taken stock of by such sources, it refers foremost to their waged work outside the home.[52]

Another issue addressed by developmental feminist authors is that of class differences between village women. In this respect their research in fact contributes more to economic analysis than the research of the ecofeminist Vandana Shiva. Several authors, for instance, have shown that both the workload and the type of labour relations vary according to the class position a peasant woman holds. Thus, one study has illustrated that the rice-processing tasks of women belonging to subsistence, (i.e., middle peasant) households may be larger and more cumbersome than those of landless women who are deprived of a sufficient amount of harvested paddy to feed their families. Here, extreme poverty and the 'release' from agrarian production tasks, paradoxically, coincide.[53]

Marty Chen has redefined rural classes in terms of women's labour and income. She distinguishes between unpaid family labour, paid village labour and wage employment outside the village. The latter category, in her definition, comprises fieldwork too. Taking the type of labour relations women are subjected to as her clue, she (re)divides households into three categories, surplus, subsistence and below subsistence households:

1. Those below subsistence level: that is, households which cannot subsist even given their female paid village labour and must deploy

> all members of the family to seek wage labour opportunities. 2. Those at the subsistence level: that is, households which can subsist given their female unpaid family labour and paid village labour. 3. Those above the surplus level: that is, households which, for status reasons, can withdraw their women from paid village labour and, in some cases, unpaid family labour.[54]

Chen's scheme of peasant classes in Bangladeshi villages forms a mirror image of the traditional Marxist economic analysis of peasant classes. Whereas such analysis takes peasant households as given units and draws distinctions on the basis of the economic exploitation to which the male peasant head of the household and other male members are subjected,[55] Chen starts from the position of the subordinate female members of peasant families. As she states explicitly: 'The various classes of households . . . can be distinguished one from the other by the degree to which women's labour and/or income are required to meet the subsistence needs of the household.'[56] Her redefinition, then, at first appears as a welcome correction of the male bias in Marxist economic theory.

Yet, whereas Chen's analysis allows one to take account of certain effects of pauperization—of the process which forces landless women to seek non-traditional forms of waged work in order to survive—her classification is not satisfactory. For as a mirror image of Marxist classifications of the peasantry, Chen's conceptualization does not enable one to make a more comprehensive assessment of the exploitation to which the vast majority of village women and men are subjected. A full assessment of production relations in the Bangladeshi countryside can only be made by looking closely at the economic position of both. Moreover, her classification is limited to the labouring classes only. It leaves out of consideration those classes which do not engage in agricultural production tasks for their own livelihood, such as the *jotedars*, money-lenders and the class of market traders who, as indicated earlier, accumulate at the expense of the whole peasantry.

Finally, before discussing some of the major drawbacks of the developmental feminist approach, I shall draw attention to one further contribution of their research. An aspect which has not been touched upon yet, but which frequently appears in developmental feminist literature on Bangladesh, is the displacement of women's labour due to the introduction of rice mills. As noted earlier, landless and land-poor women were traditionally employed in the houses of rich peasant families to do paddy-husking on a *dhenki*. This work is heavy, seasonal in nature and very poorly paid. Landless and land-poor women were easily exploited by those who appropriate the agricultural surplus. And yet the work on the *dhenki* is an indispensable source of income for the rural poor.

Now, over the last two decades, an increasing number of women have lost their jobs as rich peasants, landlords and merchants have bought and installed rice mills. For a well-to-do peasant household, such mills represent clear advantages, because mechanized milling is both cheaper and more speedy than manual paddy-husking. It may even be true that some rich peasant wives benefit, as they are relieved of part of their toil. For landless women, however, the effects of such mechanization have been loathsome, and without a class differentiated analysis this might well be overlooked. Literally millions of women who used to be employed for paddy-husking have already been displaced by automated mills and custom mills.

Khaleda Salahuddin, who specifically deals with the impact of technological change in agriculture on women in Bangladesh, has calculated that each custom mill puts about 300 poor women out of work. According to her, the labour displacement effect of automatic mills is even more serious than that of custom mills, 'because it does away with the need of pre-milling manual operations, such as drying, parboiling, winnowing, etc., in addition to the husking operation'. Salahuddin estimates that 900 part-time employed women and 64 full-time (or 180 part-time) women employed in pre-milling processing work can be displaced by one automatic mill.[57] Khaleda Salahuddin concludes that 'the introduction of mechanized devices in the post-harvesting processing operations has created a devastating negative impact on the female wage-employment in rural areas'.[58] Some skilled male labourers do get employed by the mills, but at the cost of displacing a massive number of women.

Developmental feminist authors have commonly condemned this male-biased modernization. While they are all concerned with 'integrating women into development', enhancing women's 'output and productivity', and suggesting the best possible state policies for this, the introduction of rice mills is seriously questioned. They denounce the fact that the establishment of modern rice mills, instead of helping to lessen poverty, widens the gap between the rich and the poor.

The Limited Discourse of Developmental Feminism: Original Accumulation and Women

In the first part of this chapter I have summarized the process of pauperization which condemns the vast majority of Bangladesh's peasants to a life of misery. As in the case of Britain in the centuries preceding the industrial revolution, the basis for 'modernization' in Bangladesh is being laid through the dispossession of peasant proprietors on a massive scale.

Now, those being dispossessed primarily belong to the male section of the rural population. Although legally, Muslim women are entitled to some land property—a daughter may inherit half of what her brother inherits—in practice women hardly ever exercise their rights. 'Living law' here clearly diverges from 'lawyers' law'.[59] Thus, in Bangladesh it is men who own the land and who are in control of most agricultural means of production, while female owners of land are a rare exception. And it is the ownership of land and other means of agricultural production, such as ploughs, oxen and sickles, which enables men to dominate women. Unequal property relations lie at the root of the system of patriarchy. Consequently, the process of dispossession affects male peasants directly—it is they who are deprived of their status as proprietors.

At the same time, it is also true that female members of a peasant household feel the consequences of the process of original accumulation. Peasant women too are losing opportunities for subsistence labour, are uprooted and forced to migrate. Women also lose their limited source of security as much as men, a topic which is insufficiently addressed by developmental feminist researchers. While they refer to important aspects of the pauperization in Bangladesh (such as the fact that women are forced to throw off purdah customs and seek new forms of employment), they do not relate these concrete changes to the overall process of original accumulation.

This, then, is a significant limitation of developmental feminist analyses. While the issue of 'classes' and 'class hierarchies' is raised, such as in the writings of Marty Chen, the classes which form the main burden on the back of peasant women and men are hardly discussed. Developmental feminists draw attention to the negative consequences of rice-processing mills for village women. Yet they fail to draw attention to the most serious obstacles that male and female peasant producers face. Since their aim is to provide government and donor institutions with ideas for policy-making, they overlook the exploitation by Bangladesh's commercial elite.

Another issue of concern for women is the appropriation of common property, which I have already identified as a major form of original accumulation that has been sweeping the Bangladeshi countryside. Embankment schemes, flood control projects and irrigation schemes—most of which are financed by 'donor' institutions like the World Bank and the Asian Development Bank—involve the privatization of formerly free water and fish resources. At the same time, these schemes have a direct bearing on the labouring activities of women, and on their chances of surviving physically. For apart from the professional fishermen, women belonging to landless and land-poor peasant families, in spite of cultural constraints,[60] also engage in fresh water fish captures in the open waters accessible to all, such as rivers, canals and *beels*. In a district like Khulna, for instance, one can see innumerable women in the early morning taking cages and nets to the river to catch fish. When 8,000 landless families occupied four newly-emerged lands (*chars*) in Patuakhali district in January 1992, it was women who helped ensure their families' survival by catching fish with their bare hands from the Tetulia river.

The appropriation of the commons in the form of water management schemes has had a truly devastating effect on these survival strategies of women. Where natural fish production falls as a consequence of embankments and flood control projects (a causal connection noted earlier), women belonging to professional fishermen's families lose out in terms of food security. Further, women who used to catch fish themselves henceforth miss the opportunity for the production of both use values and exchange values, since the fish is either directly consumed or sold in the market. Thus, the enclosure of Bangladesh's commons directly and indirectly affects peasant women, and without an assessment of these consequences, the impact of foreign-financed development schemes cannot be complete.

Unfortunately, this issue has not formed an integral part of the research efforts of developmental feminist authors who have analyzed the labouring activities of women in Bangladesh. In some cases, such as the foreign-financed Dinajpur Fish Culture Development Project, the role of women in the cultivation of fish in village ponds has been studied.[61] Yet such a scheme does not constitute a genuine equivalent to fishing in rivers and flood plains. To draw a balance sheet of

Bangladesh's aid-financed economic strategy, an analysis of the social consequences of enclosures is equally necessary. The lack of field investigations into the consequences of enclosures for poor peasant women is a serious drawback.

Finally, the absence of the theme of original accumulation from the developmental feminist discourse on women's labour in Bangladesh can also be demonstrated by discussing the escalation of patriarchal violence against women. As elsewhere, the process of modernization in Bangladesh is being accompanied by an alarming increase in cruelty against women. Male violence takes the form of acid-throwing, which spells doom to a woman victim for the rest of her life; it takes the form of beatings or physical torture of married women; and it also takes the form of outright murder. Most frequently, the murder of a bride or wife is committed by her husband and/or in-laws when she fails to comply with extra demands for dowry. According to the publicized results of a survey of 48, mostly young women brutally killed in a period of eight weeks ending 21 January 1994, 25 of the murders were related to differences over dowry.[62] Another Dhaka press report, published in early 1994, claimed that 80 per cent of killings of married women are due to the dowry system.[63]

Developmental feminists have noted the historical shift from the *mahr* to the dowry system, but explain it with reference to the fragmentation of landholdings and the decreasing need for female labour in the processing of paddy. They do not emphasize that the trend is intrinsically related to the process of modernization. The dowry system was first adopted by landlord and rich peasant families, whose sons got access to urban education. It subsequently spread to all the rural classes, including the landless and land poor peasants. Further, in the course of time, the amount of dowry demanded has skyrocketed. Today, the rates vary from Taka 2,000–3,000 (the amount paid by a landless peasant for marrying off his daughter) to Taka 50,000 to 60,000 paid by well-to-do peasants.[64] If the bridegroom's family belongs to the class of urban commercial traders, the dowry will be fixed at several lakh taka, to which are added luxury goods like refrigerators and cars.

This escalation of dowry demands, and the accompanying patriarchal violence, are an expression of original accumulation. Where other avenues for gathering wealth have been closed off, where peasants are continuously threatened with eviction from their soil and where indebtedness is generalized, peasants seek to survive as agricultural producers by taking recourse to large dowry demands and violence against those who have least power. Tragically, the escalation of dowry demands in turn leads to the dispossession of peasant families, for in order to marry off their daughters, many peasants borrow money from usurious lenders; they are then forced to sell arable land, or even their own homesteads. Thus, the adoption of the dowry system in Muslim-dominated Bangladesh is related, like elsewhere, to the transition in the country's social system. As Mies has stated in the context of India, the 'economic rationale of the dowry system' is that it is 'a form of primitive accumulation' by men.[65]

Summary: Marxist Theory Superseded?

Developmental feminists who have analyzed the labouring activities of rural poor women in Bangladesh have posed an ideological challenge to Marxist economic theory. The classical Marxist view of peasant societies, as has been argued earlier, leaves out of consideration almost all women's toil, since rural classes are defined in terms of the position of the male head of the household.[66] This approach ignores both the labour of women that precedes the fieldwork of peasant men, and the various post-harvest processing tasks. It entails a gross underestimation of how much labour precedes the marketing, sale and/or consumption of agrarian goods.

Yet the developmental feminist literature on Bangladeshi women does not succeed in superseding Marxist theory. Though some attempts have been made to calculate women's workload, and though class differences existing between peasant women are pointed out, developmental feminist authors overlook the dominant process of class exploitation affecting village women, (i.e., the market exploitation by commercial traders). They do not relate the pauperization of the majority of rural women to the dominant mode of appropriation of the agricultural surplus. Nor do they question the appropriation of common property resources through flood control schemes. Due to the bias underlying their research work, they gloss over much of the displacement of women's labour. Enclosures which in the name of flood control negatively affect the subsistence and market-oriented labour of rural women form no integral part of their analytical work.

Ultimately, the labour of Bangladeshi peasant women can be better understood, and their rights defended, by combining the feminist concepts of patriarchy, the sexual division of labour and women's double workload with the insights provided by Karl Marx. In the first volume of *Capital*, Marx argued that 'the capitalist system presupposes the complete separation of the labourers from all property in the means by which they realize their labour'.[67] During the decades since Bangladesh's Independence, the process of original accumulation has involved the eviction of peasant proprietors from their land on a massive scale, and the appropriation of common water and fish resources to the detriment of peasant women and men. Since developmental feminism does not embark on a critical investigation of modernization, it is incapable of providing a truly comprehensive analysis. As Sarah White has stated about developmental feminism, 'the mystification of its highly contradictory origins lies at the roots of the unsubstantiality and analytical weakness of most of the discussion about women in Bangladesh up to now'.[68]

Notes and References

1. Boserup (1970).
2. A general critique of developmental feminism has been given by Simmons (1992), p. 16. Mies (1986b), pp. 117–18, notes the coincidence between increased reliance by multinational companies on the exploitation of Third World women, and the growing concern by international institutions 'to integrate women in development'.
3. Notably Abdullah and Zeidenstein (1982); Cain et al. (1979); Chen (1977, 1986a, 1986b); Feldman (1979); Sahela and Greeley (1983); von Harder (1975, 1978); Westergaard (1983a; 1983b).
4. Cain et al. (1979), p. 406. Referring to the feminist writer, Heidi Hartmann, the authors argued that their definition is a modified version of Hartmann's, which 'emphasizes the material base of male domination over women'.
5. Chen (1986a).
6. Willcocks (1988).
7. Ibid., p. 4.
8. Khan (1993), p. 121.
9. Willcocks (1988); Williams (1966).
10. About 17 of these have been critically evaluated under Component 12 of the Flood Action Plan (FAP), and five flood control projects were studied in depth. See FAP 12. FCD/I Agricultural Study, Huntington Technical Services Limited, January 1992.
11. See, for instance, Adnan (1991); Adnan et al. (1992); Bangladesh Agricultural Research Council (1989); Custers (1991c, 1992b); Dalal-Clayton (1990); Faaland et al. (1995); Pearce (1991).
12. See 'The Flood Control Embankment along the Kangsa River is Another Beel Dakatia', *Sangram*, 27 October 1993.

13. See 'BDR Fires on Mob in Zakiganj: 3 Killed', *The Telegraph* (Dhaka), 23 July 1993; also *Ittefaq*, 28 July 1993.
14. Quoted in Boyce (1990), p. 423.
15. Willcocks (1988).
16. See FAP 12. See also Faaland et al. (1995), p. 18.
17. van Vierssen (1991), p. 5. See also Faaland et al. (1995), p. 19.
18. Operations Review Unit (1993), p. 76.
19. *The Ecologist* (1992); Marx (1977a), p. 671.
20. The term 'primitive accumulation' was coined by Karl Marx. See Marx (1977a), Part VIII, p. 667.
21. This is observed, for instance, by White (1992), p. 50, in the context of modern irrigation methods: 'The poorest households are disproportionately dependent on common resources to eke out an income. Environmental changes therefore hit hardest those households which lack the means to purchase alternatives to hitherto free resources.' Further, Maal and Ali (1990), p. 5, comment on the importance of the commons in the context of an investigation on inland water bodies in Dinajpur: 'As long as the pond is inside and a part of the flood plain, all the people are entitled to fish in it. But when the water withdraws only the owner of the land has access to it.' A report on the Flood Action Plan, which explains the importance of water resources as common property, is the 'independent review mission' constituted by the UNDP: 'Substantial numbers of people in Bangladesh engage in subsistence fishing in contrast to full-time and part-time fishing for the market. Subsistence fishing by family members is typically based on a free common good resource in order to supply them with the majority of their animal protein. Subsistence fishing mainly applies to people who are too poor to buy fish in the market and who therefore enter a wageless labour system producing food for their families by catching fish. It is these people, unlike the full- and part-time fishermen, who are likely to suffer most due to the destruction of capture fisheries by FCD and FCDI schemes. Such poor and marginalized families will find it even more difficult to obtain an adequate level of nutrients.' See Faaland et al. (1995), p. 19.
22. For data on the number and proportion of landless peasants, see Alamgir (1981), p. 198; de Vylder (1982), pp. 9–10; Hartmann and Boyce (1983), p. 20; Hashemi (1991), p. 61.
23. For data on the rising proportion of agricultural labourers, see Atiur Rahman (1986), p. 175. The relationship between the dispossession of peasant proprietors and the extensive processes of migration is an important one in Bangladesh, and covers three sections of migrants: those who move to unsafe *char* lands along the coast, those who migrate to the capital Dhaka and other urban centres in search of odd jobs, and those who seek to survive by migrating to India. No comprehensive numerical data is available for all the migrants, but a figure of 20 million has been cited in the Bangladeshi press for migrants who have ended up in urban slums.
24. Ibid., p. 115. Comparable figures on land concentration are cited by Alamgir (1981), p. 197.
25. Atiur Rahman (1986), p. 110. According to Ashabur Rahman (1986), p. 137, the rate of increase in the number of landless households in Bangladesh is 3.1 per cent, which is higher than the annual growth of the population (2.5 per cent).
26. Jansen (1987), p. 111.

27. de Vylder (1982), p. 113. For a history of institutional lending, see also Hashemi (1991), pp. 62–63.
28. See the statement by Rashed Khan Menon at a press conference held on 9 November 1988, and published jointly by the Krishok Mukti Samity (Peasant Freedom League) and the Khet Majur Union (Union of Agricultural Labourers) as a booklet *What is and Why a Loan Arbitration Board?*
29. For figures on the number of certificate cases, see newspaper reports republished in *Kisan–Kisani* (Newsbulletin of the Bangladesh Krishok Federation), May 1990, pp. 18–20.
30. On the sharecropping system in Bangladesh, see Arens and van Beurden (1977), p. 120; Jannuzi and Peach (1980); Jansen (1987), p. 156.
31. de Vylder (1982), p. 36.
32. See 'Smuggling of Paddy', *Ittefaq*, 25 August 1993.
33. For reports on the sale of raw jute, see *Ittefaq*, 3 September 1993; *Sangbad*, 23 and 31 August 1993.
34. Jansen (1987), p. 146.
35. Sobhan (1991), p. 86.
36. Ibid., p. 85.
37. Ibid., p. 3.
38. Custers (1991), p. 19.
39. Sobhan (1991), p. 7. On the role of the commercial bourgeoisie, see also Umar (1986). Numerous instances of enrichment by members of the commercial elite via the banking system are mentioned by Rahman and Hoque (1987). One notable instance is that of Jahurul Islam, who built his initial wealth on the basis of a contract for the distribution of deep tubewells (ibid.), p. 11.
40. For details on the traditional sexual division of labour, see Chen (1986b), pp. 47–49.
41. Chaudhury and Ahmed (1980), p. 68. See also Chen and Ghaznavi (1977).
42. Statement by Shamsun Nahar Khan, chairwoman of the Bangladesh Peasant Women's Association (Kisani Sabha), at a seminar organized by the Bangladesh People's Solidarity Centre, Oslo, 27 April 1991. According to Jansen (1987), p. 185, when men are employed on a wage basis, their wages are 35–50 per cent higher than women performing the same job.
43. White (1992), p. 105.
44. Mies (1982), p. 3. For an extensive critique of 'definitional biases' in the census figures published by the Government of India, see Agarwal (1985), p. A 155. For a critical analysis of statistical data on changes in employment in Britain between the two World Wars, see Glucksmann (1990), p. 38.
45. Chen (1986b), pp. 52–53.
46. Cain et al. (1979), p. 412.
47. Ibid.
48. The traditional male bias in Marxist economics is typically reflected in the study by Atiur Rahman (1986) who derives his views from Lenin's analysis of class differentiation in pre-revolutionary Russia.
49. For a technical description of women's post-harvest activities in paddy production, see von Harder (1975), p. 66.

50. Greeley (1980), p. 8. For a quantification of the relative number of hours spent by village women on household- and agriculture-related tasks, see von Harder (1978), p. 169.
51. Greeley (1980).
52. See, for instance, Mujahidul Islam Selim's report to the Second National Conference of the Khet Majur Samiti, 13 February 1986, especially p. 20.
53. The differential effect of rice-milling on women of various peasant classes is described by Begum and Greeley (1983), pp. 2–3.
54. Chen (1986a), pp. 219–20.
55. Atiur Rahman (1986); Lenin (1977a); Patnaik (1976).
56. Chen (1986a), p. 220.
57. Salahuddin (1986), p. 11. On the same theme see Cain et al. (1979); Chaudhury and Ahmed (1980), pp. 77–78; Chen (1977), p. 32.
58. Salahuddin (1986), p. 22.
59. Rahman and van Schendel (1994).
60. For a discussion on cultural constraints, see Maal and Ali (1990).
61. Ibid.
62. See Kazi Montu, 'Crimes Against Women Increasing Alarmingly', *Holiday*, 28 January 1994.
63. See Ranjit Das, 'Ten *Fatwas*', *Khabarer Kagaz*, 25 January 1994, p. 17.
64. Based on personal interviews with village women, October 1992.
65. Mies (1986a), p. 125.
66. Lenin (1977a); Patnaik (1976); Atiur Rahman (1986).
67. Marx (1977a), p. 668.
68. White (1992), p. 21.

9

The Ecofeminist Discourse in India

Just like the developmental feminist current described in the previous chapter, ecofeminism as a distinct trend has emerged only recently, in the 1970s. The term ecofeminism reportedly was first coined by a French writer, Francoise d'Eaubonne, when in 1974 she called upon women to lead an ecological revolution to save the planet.[1] The concept was given further shape by feminists from different countries—by women based in the North, and by women belonging to various Third World countries. One of the most prominent representatives of ecofeminism today is an Indian scientist, Vandana Shiva, who combines a critique of Western, patriarchal science with a powerful indictment of the ecological destruction wrought by Green Revolution technology upon Indian agriculture.

Unlike developmental feminism, ecofeminism is grounded in women's experiences of struggles. It heralds the application of feminist ideas to problems of ecology, and explicitly claims to be 'an activist-based movement'.[2] In the West, the building of ecofeminist theory is linked to women's involvement in the peace and anti-nuclear movement, and in health and anti-pollution issues.[3] In the Third World, rural women's interest in defending the wealth of their natural surroundings and their role in maintaining the ecological cycle in agriculture have been important sources of inspiration for the growth of ecofeminist thought. A much-quoted reference point is the renowned Chipko movement of the 1970s in India. Following a centuries-old practice of women's resistance against the destruction of the forests, women in north India hugged trees in order to prevent them from being felled.[4]

Ecofeminists all draw parallels between the oppression of women and the destruction of nature, and trace both to the philosophical views that have dominated Western science since the 17th century. Yet ecofeminism, it needs to be stressed, is not a homogeneous trend but covers a variety of subcurrents of thought. A divide that has repeatedly been mentioned is that between cultural ecofeminism and social ecofeminism.[5] Cultural ecofeminism regards the exploitation of women and nature as a consequence of male domination. It sees women as having a superior relation to nature and emphasizes the quest for a new, spiritual relation between human beings and nature. Social ecofeminism disgrees. It traces the exploitation of both women and nature to the structure of capitalist patriarchy. According to Val Plumwood, 'perhaps the key political difference between the two approaches is that social ecofeminism does not attempt to reduce all forms of oppression to women's oppression, a feature characteristic of cultural feminism'.[6]

Plumwood believes that ecofeminism can claim to be a new, 'third wave or stage' of feminism. According to her, ecofeminism can overcome the conventional divisions in feminist theory and build a more complete theory if the question of dualism is addressed. Dualism is the process whereby contrasting concepts are formed which are hierarchical and exclusive, such as nature/human, rational/emotional and civilization/primitiveness. Western culture is pervaded by such concepts, and feminists in the past have questioned this dualism from various angles. A complete ecofeminism, Plumwood argues, would call into question 'the dualistic construction of both masculine and feminine identities'.[7] Given such a perspective, the third wave of feminism could succeed, she states, in connecting feminism with other contemporary social movements.

This chapter reviews some of the contributions of ecofeminism to economic theory and philosophy. First, I shall draw attention to two contributions to human thought which I consider to be basic, which are shared by many ecofeminists and which sharply distinguish this trend from developmental feminism, namely the critique of Western science and the privatization of common property resources. Subsequently, I will focus on the intellectual work of the Indian ecofeminist author, Vandana Shiva, who, within a short time, has emerged as a very influential thinker internationally. Her analysis of women's position in the food chain in India, to sustain their families and nature, provides fruitful material for comparisons with developmental feminism discussed in the previous chapter. This chapter is both a tribute to, and a critique of, Vandana Shiva's theoretical work.

Critique of Western Science

Perhaps the most decisive contribution of ecofeminism lies in the sphere of philosophy, in the critique that a number of ecofeminist authors have formulated modern, Western science as being patriarchal and biased against nature. This critical stance towards Western science is not unique to ecofeminism, but is shared by at least one other current within the ecological movement (i.e., 'deep ecology').[8] Yet it is conspicuously absent from the developmental feminist discourse. I will give a short summary of the ecofeminist stance later by covering three central themes: the mechanical worldview that has replaced the organic worldview since the scientific revolution of the 17th century; the patriarchal bias that has shaped the experimental method of Western science; and the reductionist nature of this particular form of science.

The charge that Western science, which was founded in the period when commercial capitalism spread, is reductionist has been elaborated and popularized by Vandana Shiva, following Carolyn Merchant and other feminist authors. Why does she and other ecofeminists speak of reductionism? According to Vandana Shiva, this science has created serious barriers to developing human knowledge and has disrupted the self-regenerating capacity of nature. It has reduced the human capacity to know nature 'by excluding other knowers and other ways of knowing'. In manipulating nature in laboratories and research institutions as 'inert and fragmented', Western science has also damaged 'the capacity of nature to creatively regenerate and renew itself'.[9] Thus she challenges Western science's claim to universal validity and questions its presumed objectivity and social neutrality.

Second, reductionist science, Vandana Shiva states, represents the needs of a particular form of economic and political organization. Being intimately tied to the needs of capitalist production, Western science takes account of only those properties of a resource system which generate profits through exploitation and extraction. Reductionism 'reduces complex ecosystems to a single component, and a single component to a single function', Shiva states. One of the examples she cites to substantiate her point is the exploitation of the timber resources of tropical forests, such as practised under British colonial rule in India. 'In the reductionist paradigm a forest is reduced to commercial wood, and wood is reduced to cellulose fibre for the pulp and paper industry.'[10] Contrary to the people who depended for their survival on the Indian forests, the British colonial authorities did not see the forests as an ecosystem fulfilling a variety of functions and needs. The living and diverse ecosystem 'is thus violated and destroyed by "scientific forestry"'.

Third, Shiva argues that thanks to the powerful political support it enjoys, reductionist science is, *a priori*, declared superior. According to her, reductionist science has displaced non-reductionist modes of knowing, not through cognitive competition but through political and financial support from Western state and developmental institutions. A pointed instance is that of the 'science' of the Green Revolution, the knowledge connected with the package of high response varieties of grain and paddy seeds and chemical inputs (i.e., fertilizers and pesticides). The introduction of such methods in place of organic farming methods has been achieved not through cognitive competition. The view that India should rely on its indigenous genetic resource base to develop its agricultural system was over-ruled through stiff financial and political competition against Indian research institutes by American research foundations, like the Rockefeller and Ford Foundations. The Green Revolution agricultural strategy got powerful backing in 1971 when, at the initiative of the then World Bank president, McNamara, a Consultative Group on International Agricultural Research (CGIAR) was formed to finance an international network of research centres.[11]

The fourth and 'ultimate' characteristic of Western science follows directly from its close links with the world of capital. As Vandana Shiva states, money has 'an asymmetric relationship to life and living processes'. Money can be used to exploit and destroy nature, but the profit motive can never become a source of nature's life and its life-supporting capacity. Thus Shiva's explanation of 'reductionism' results in a grave charge. For, in her view, it is the mentioned asymmetry that accounts for a deepening of the world's ecological crises: a 'decrease of nature's life-producing potential' has inevitably accompanied the process of capital accumulation of the last few centuries.[12] In short, Western reductionist science results in violence. Knowledge systems built by local communities of peasants and women are destroyed, people are converted into non-knowers through the 'expert/non-expert divide', and the integrity of nature which has always provided sustenance for human societies is also destroyed. For Shiva, Western science is not sacrosanct but a highly risky enterprise.

The origins of modern, Western science lie in the 17th century, when the experimental method was invented (i.e., the investigation of nature's processes within the confines of research establishments). To facilitate the application of this method, a new worldview was elaborated. The man who is known as the 'father of science' is Francis Bacon who, as the son of a middle-class employee of the British queen, was the originator of the idea of the modern research institute. Bacon himself followed a career as the king's attorney-general. At the same time, through his literary writings, he developed a new, oppressive conception of nature, which has remained the dominant view within Western science until today. Given the influence of Bacon's ideas, critics of Western science, including ecofeminists, have turned to the analysis of his writings so as to lay bare the social character of this science.

Whereas, preceding the 'scientific revolution' of the 17th century, the common view had been that nature is to be respectfully treated, Bacon believed that nature should be bound into service and made into a slave. He justified the severe testing of hypotheses through controlled manipulations in laboratories, by arguing that nature would exhibit herself more clearly 'under the trials and vexations of art (mechanical devices) than left to herself'.[13] Whereas cultural values preceding the scientific revolution had taught restraint in the use of natural resources, Bacon advocated openly that nature be conquered and subdued via the discipline of scientific knowledge. Bacon's philosophy meant a complete transformation in attitudes towards their own natural surroundings, not only by scientists but by human beings in general.

Moreover, Bacon's attitude towards nature was strongly coloured by his patriarchal views. Bacon's philosophy was drafted against the background of the witch trials which were taking place all over Europe in the early part of the 17th century. The witch-hunting aimed at annihilating women as holders of independent knowledge. As Carolyn Merchant has pointed out, much of the imagery used by Bacon in delineating his scientific method derived from the court room and the inquisition: 'it treats nature as a female to be tortured through mechanical inventions'.[14] One of the passages quoted by Merchant from Bacon's works strongly suggests the persecution of witches: 'For you have but to follow and as it were hound nature in her wanderings, and you will be able when you like to lead and drive her afterwards to the same place again.' Bacon even suggested that nature should be raped (i.e., he used the metaphor of men's most violent relationship to women).[15]

That the worldview of the father of Western science is anything but gender neutral is also evident from the utopia he drafted shortly before his death, *New Atlantis*. In the ideal, future society sketched by Bacon, politics is replaced by scientific administration. Decisions are made for the good of the whole by scientists whose judgement is to be trusted implicitly, for they alone possess the secrets of nature. According to Merchant, the social structure of Bacon's new society, Bensalem, was structured on the early modern, patriarchal family, with the man the master to other members, and the wife a subordinate partner. 'Bacon's Bensalem in the "New Atlantis" illustrated a patriarchal family structure in which the "Father" exercised authority over the kin and the role of women had been reduced to near invisibility.'[16] In short, the example of Francis Bacon well illustrates the ecofeminist view that under Western science the oppression of women and nature go hand-in-hand.

As mentioned earlier, the scientific revolution of the 17th century was accompanied by an unprecedented, complete transformation in the predominant worldview. Preceding the scientific revolution, the cosmos was understood as a living organism. The five elements (earth, air, fire, water and ether) were its material body, and the soul was the source of its animate daily motion. As Carolyn Merchant points out, the living character of the world organism meant not only that the stars and planets were alive, but that 'the earth too was pervaded by a force giving life and motion to the living beings on it'.[17] The earth was likened to a receptive, nurturing female, with the capacity to breathe. The earth's springs were akin to the human blood. 'As the waters on its surface ebbed and flowed, evaporated into clouds, and descended as dews, rains and snows, the earth's blood was cleansed and renewed.' Trees were the earth mother's tresses. This view of the cosmos and the earth taught people to treat nature with respect. As long as the earth was conceptualized as alive, there were strong inhibitions against any destructive acts against it.

This organic view, in the course of the scientific revolution, was replaced by an entirely new image of the world, the mechanistic worldview. Since then, the image of the cosmos and the earth has been thoroughly influenced by the philosophical assumptions of the natural physicists. From then on, nature has been viewed as a system of dead, inert particles moved by external rather than inherent forces.

The world, as understood by the first generation of mechanistic thinkers, was composed of atomic parts, of inert bodies moved with uniform velocity, unless forced by another body to deviate from their straight-line paths. The most powerful synthesis of the new mechanical philosophy was provided by Isaac Newton in *Mathematic Principles of Natural Philosophy*. Newton, throughout the evolution of his thought, 'clung tenaciously to the dualism between the passivity of matter and the externality of force'.[18] This new view of nature became the model of all knowledge, and it has permeated the day-to-day perceptions regarding the surrounding world of people living under capitalism ever since. Moreover, the new worldview taught that nature, instead of being treated with respect, should be conquered and dominated.[19]

The transformation in worldviews, further, went parallel with a transformation in the European economy, and with a spate of technological inventions. Medieval production relations were increasingly replaced by capitalist relations, as production aimed at subsistence of the peasantry and at supporting the luxurious lifestyle of feudal landlords was gradually replaced by more specialized production for the market. During the 16th century, mining operations expanded rapidly along with the expansion in the trading of metals. At the same time, the use of geared machines, such as water and windmills, became more common. They were the '*foci* around which new forms of daily life became organized', and symbols of the power to order human life and the natural surroundings. The clock, in particular, which had begun to govern civic life in European towns, became the symbol of 'cosmic order', a model of the ordered motion of the celestial spheres.[20] These technological developments accelerated the change in worldviews. As Merchant notes, 'the images and symbols associated with the machines of everyday life helped to mediate the transition between frameworks'.[21] The modern scientific view of nature is not that of a living organism, but that of order and power associated with the power of machines.

Moreover, according to Carolyn Merchant, the mechanistic approach to nature has never been thoroughly questioned since the 17th century, but remains the predominant view in physics at the end of the 20th century. Although natural physics has gone through moments of crisis, although some philosophers of science have attempted to return to a more organic view of nature, and although Einstein and others have claimed to have made obsolete the theoretical framework laid down by Isaac Newton, 20th century physics still 'views the world in terms of fundamental particles', such as electrons, protons and neutrons, Merchant states.[22] This analysis of Merchant's is disputed, but there is no doubt that the Western view that nature should be controlled and dominated is shared by many scientists in the Third World today. For instance, the Indian fisheries' specialist Ummerkutty, while depicting the 'limitless and countless variety of life in the sea', has recently stated that in the 'unveiling of the secrets of the marine realm', man's final aim is 'to conquer the sea, to colonize the submerged areas rich in food and mineral resources, thus alleviating the ever-increasing demand on the limited land available'.[23]

Appropriation of the Commons

Another important theme in ecofeminist literature is the destruction of common property resources, and their appropriation for capitalist profit. We saw in the previous chapter how the enclosure of the commons formed an intrinsic part of the original accumulation of capital in Britain, and how flood control schemes in contemporary Bangladesh can similarly be interpreted as so many attempts to privatize water and fish resources which, in the past, used to be commonly owned. This process of original accumulation has been largely overlooked by developmental feminists, though it severely affects, in particular, poor village women dependent on access to 'free' resources. Besides, the issue is of much broader relevance than has been stated so far: the privatization of common property is a worldwide strategy used to promote elite interests. Once again, the writings of Carolyn Merchant and Vandana Shiva contain rich, factual details to substantiate the point.

In her analysis of the commons, Carolyn Merchant first concentrates on European agricultural experiences in the long transition from the Middle Ages to the creation of capitalist agriculture. In *The Death of Nature* she describes the maintenance of ecosystems in European countries through the integration of crop planting with the raising of cattle for organic fertilizers.[24] As she sees it, peasants succeeded in preventing the disruption of nature's balance through the strict regulation of the use of common property resources, like forests, pasture and water. Officers elected or appointed by the members of peasant communities were entrusted with this task. Pressures for the expansion of arable land, at the expense of pastures for the grazing of animals, tended to build up due to population pressures. Yet peasants managed to maintain their ecosystems through closer cooperation.

It was the combination of population pressures with landlord taxation that 'led ultimately to the breakdown of the medieval agrarian economy and the ecosystem'.[25] Initially, the peasants' way of coping with the escalating demands of feudal lords was to strengthen cooperation amongst themselves. When more and more pastures and wastelands were converted into arable land, peasants, starting in Germany and Poland, developed a rotational system (the 'three field system') to facilitate the recuperation of the soil's fertility. The open-field system, according to Merchant, not only allowed for more intensive cultivation and higher crop productivity, 'but it also demanded greater cooperation and group regulation of water use, pasturing and wood gathering, as well as the sharing of oxen and horses for plowing'.[26] Thus, according to her, group regulation of the use of natural resources helped to ward off the danger of an ecological crisis.

Merchant also refers to the rights over the commons to explain the violent events that occurred in Germany in 1525. In that year peasants in Eastern Prussia rebelled against the power of the feudal lords in a war which has been described in rich detail by Frederick Engels. One of the causes of the rebellion, in Engels' view, was the inhuman treatment inflicted on the peasants by the landlord class. 'The lord reigned as he pleased over the peasant's own person, over his wife and daughters, just as he reigned over his property. He threw the peasant into the tower whenever he saw fit . . . . He killed the peasant, or had him beheaded, whenever he pleased.'[27] But, as Engels' account also makes clear, the peasants further sought to restore their rights over forests and pastures which the landlords had encroached upon. The restoration of the commons was one of the demands incorporated in the 'Twelve Articles' formulated at the height of the rebellion.[28] In Germany's famous peasant war, the cultivators of the soil sought to prevent the undermining of their ecosystem by the landlords' greed.

Another specific instance of the appropriation of common property described by Carolyn Merchant is that of the English fenlands (i.e., marshy lands which were drained with Dutch hydraulic technology over a period of three centuries). The fen country of England as it existed up to the 17th century was 'an extensive area north of London and Cambridge in the region of Peterborough, Ely and Bedford' which, in the Middle Ages, had been 'a region of marshes, meres, and meadows connected by open channels, affording pastures around its edges in the dry summers while almost entirely covered with water in the winters'.[29] Before drainage and reclamation of the marshy areas started, the fens had been 'well stocked with fish and fowl that afforded food for the people who made their home in the region'. Like other ecosystems,[30] the fenlands were 'multifunctional'. As opponents of drainage in the 17th century argued, the fens grew fodder for feeding cattle in winter. The manure of these cattle in turn was used to maintain the fertility of the peasants' soil.

This careful ecological balance was upset when technologies like windmills and sluices developed in Holland were introduced to drain and reshape the English fenlands. As Merchant notes, while the first windmills constructed as an energy source for drainage dated from 1406, by the early 17th century they were used in various European countries for pumping water out of inland lakes on a large scale. Inevitably, the drainage of such inland lakes was accompanied by the transformation of common property into individual ownership. Thus, the example of the drainage of fenlands shows how the loss of common property resources, at times, has been tied with the introduction of new technology. Furthermore, in England the drainage operations were clearly implemented to the detriment of the fenland dwellers who had survived on catching birds and fish; and the peasants who had had free access to the pastures located in the fenland areas. Those who benefited, according to Merchant, were the landlords who could lease the land after drainage, and those who had invested capital in the drainage operations. Whereas the majority of the previous users of the fens were displaced, 'only the wealthier peasants could afford to lease the newly drained pastures'.[31]

The case of the English fenlands also shows how social and environmental interests are often closely intertwined. According to Merchant, both the poor and the balance of nature suffered as a consequence of the drainage operations: 'Improvements in the productivity of the land were shared neither by the poor nor by the original inhabitants of the marshes—the fish, fowl, and marsh plant that over thousands of years had evolved a complex set of ecological interdependences.'[32] Finally the drainage operations enhanced the spread of market relations in the countryside and facilitated the production of raw wool for early British industry. Many of the former marshlands were transformed into pastures for sheep, owned by capitalist farmers. Thus, the drainage works were also linked to the process of original accumulation, referred to in the previous chapter. And, like their German counterparts in the peasant war, the inhabitants of the English fenlands reacted with resistance, although, apparently, on a much smaller scale. In 1631, fenland people rioted and took up arms against the drainers, breaking sluices and throwing down fences built around the newly-created pastures.[33] The rebellion was suppressed by the intervention of the British state.

Another ecofeminist, who like Merchant is keenly aware of the importance of the issue of common property resources, is Vandana Shiva.[34] According to the sources Shiva quotes, till the end of the last century, and in all historical periods before that, at least 80 per cent of India's natural resources were common property, with only 20 per cent being privately used. In Shiva's view, 'These free commons have historically been the survival base for rural India and the domain of productivity of women.'[35] Illustrative are the country's forest resources, which traditionally were used by the population for a variety of purposes: for food, fodder, organic fertilizers and water conservancy. When the British colonized India, they first colonized the forests, displacing local knowledge regarding the rich biodiversity of the forested areas.

In India, the destruction of forests has occurred in distinct phases. In the first phase, it was ordained by the British for military purposes and the building of a railway system. Teak from Malabar was extracted for the King's navy, while the teak trees of central India and the conifers of the Himalaya were exploited for the railway system.[36] Initially, till the British government took over supreme powers of administration in the Indian subcontinent, royalty rights for the felling of teak trees were vested in the East India Company. Subsequently, a special officer was appointed to oversee forest work, and given the task of improving the supply of teak for the navy's ship-building activities. Contrary to the needs of the Indian population living close to or in forest areas, for whom the forests served a multitude of functions, the British followed a 'reductionist' approach, seeing the forests only as a source of commercially valuable wood. They reduced the forests to a timber mine.

A new phase in the exploitation of the forests was heralded with the proclamation, in 1865, of the first Indian Forestry Act which authorized the government to declare forests and wastelands as reserved areas. Forest officials were given police and judicial powers—they could arrest forest dwellers without warrants and could also levy penalties.[37] As Shiva states, the introduction of this legislation marks the beginning of what is called 'scientific forestry' in India. The British government ignored the complex interrelationship between forests, agriculture and husbandry, and reduced the forests to a source of marketable value for industrial use. The 1865 Act was followed by fresh Forestry Acts (in 1878 and 1925), which further contributed to the erosion of both the forests and the rights of local people to forest produce. The encroachment of the Indian people's common property did not, however, go unchallenged—many forest satyagrahas and tribal insurrections over the last two centuries have sought to defend people's rights to forest wealth. According to Kelkar and Nathan, the tribal uprisings had the effect of, temporarily at least, preserving some forms of village ownership over the forests.[38]

Vandana Shiva believes that recent 'wasteland development' schemes in India should be understood within the same context of privatization/appropriation of people's common property rights. Thus, the World Bank's National Forestry Project for India (1984) aimed at the privatization of wastelands. The World Bank's Tropical Forestry Action Plan, floated in 1985, has the same underlying logic. In name, 'reforestation' is aimed at reversing the process started under British rule. Yet the schemes in no way help to re-generate biodiversity. 'Wasteland development schemes', for instance, aim at planting eucalyptus trees, a fast-growing tree which can be sold to industries, but which is known to impoverish the soil on which it is planted. Shiva cites the experience of people in Karnataka, who have protested against the taking away of village commons for wasteland development by uprooting large numbers of newly planted seedlings from these wastelands.[39]

The concept of 'wasteland' is clearly biased, since it does not take the needs of India's poor peasant population, but dominant capitalist interests, as its starting point. Historically, in British colonial days, Shiva reminds her readers, the concept of 'wastelands' was not an assessment of the biological productivity of the land. 'Wasteland was that land that did not pay any revenue because it was uncultivated.' Yet, as Shiva points out, such wastelands were, and are often, used for grazing animals. Small peasants and landless labourers can own livestock largely because of the existence of the commons. Thus, wasteland development projects threaten the life interest of the poor, for 'the last resource of the poor for fodder and fuel will now disappear through privatization'.[40] In short, the 'wasteland development schemes', after the 'scientific forestry' undertaken in British days, constitute a 'second robbery' of common property resources.

Finally, the accounts given by scholars like Vandana Shiva and Carolyn Merchant challenge the idea that the existence of the 'commons' is no more than a tragedy, since each individual making use of pastures, marshes and forests only exploits such resources to serve his or her own self-interest. In fact, the examples quoted from European and Indian history indicate that local communities, dependent on commonly-held natural resources, have acted with self-restraint for long to pre-empt the undermining of their ecosystems. As Mary Mellon has argued, the concept of 'common' is social by definition; 'it is understood as a boundaried and limited resource',[41] which is maintained through joint regulation. And instead of being the source of destruction of ecosystems, local communities of producers have frequently come to their defence.

The Productive Activities of Indian Women in Organic Agriculture

I shall now deal more specifically with the productive activities of Indian village women. While looking at some aspects of the transition from organic agricultural practices to 'modern' ones, based on the application of high-response varieties of seeds, I shall highlight Vandana Shiva's views on women's labour. But first I shall return to her views on science. We have already seen that Shiva considers Western science to be 'reductionist', since it dismisses other forms of knowledge as 'primitive'. The introduction of Green Revolution technology, of high-bred varieties of rice along with chemical inputs, well illustrates Shiva's point of view. According to her, it has implied the destruction, 'by a handful of white male scientists in less than two decades', of a system of people's knowledge evolved over four to five thousand years.[42]

First, Shiva draws on the writings of other authors who, before her, challenged the British colonial view that Indian agriculture was 'primitive'. She lists a number of central features which illustrate how well balanced the indigenous system was: Indian peasants relied, for instance, on organic manuring, and a combination of mixed and rotational cropping with leguminous crops to protect their soils.[43] As in the European agricultural system of the pre-capitalist era, farm animals played a central role in Indian agriculture. Indian peasants, moreover, developed the method of shallow and superficial plowing. This, Shiva states, came from the recognition that we cannot have an exploitative relationship with the earth—'it must be one of reciprocity'. The peasants recognized that 'too much cultivation and deep ploughing would oxidize the reserves of organic matter in the soil, and the balance of soil fertility would soon be destroyed'.[44]

The methods of mixed and rotational cropping were similarly based on the need to maintain the balance in nature. Thus, 'the method of mixed cropping is part of the adaptation of nature's ways in which cereal crops like millet, wheat, barley and maize are mixed with pulses, providing nutrition to each other, and thus a balanced diet to the people'. According to her, it was not until 1888, after a protracted controversy lasting 30 years, that Western science finally accepted the important part played by pulse crops in enriching the soil.[45] Facts cited earlier on the cropping patterns developed in the Gangetic delta of Bengal strongly corroborate Shiva's view that the South Asian peasantry had developed its own knowledge system, and its own approach to maintaining the balance of nature without the use of any fertilizers or pesticides.

Shiva's analysis of the Green Revolution in India amply illustrates that the impact of the package of modern seeds and chemical inputs has been negative in many invisible ways. Whereas in India's state of Punjab, a dramatic increase in cereal production could initially be scored, this increase involved a number of factors, such as an increase in the cropped area, a shift from mixtures of cereals and pulses to monocultures of wheat and rice, and a change from crop rotations to multicropping of rice and wheat.[46] Shiva's analysis illustrates that Western reductionist science, which narrowly defines 'productivity' as the output of one specific crop for the market, leads to the breaking of 'nature's food chains'.[47] And whereas, formerly, peasants could rely on their own agricultural knowledge, they now become dependent on external 'experts'. In short, the thrust of Western science's intervention in Indian agriculture has been to destroy a traditional knowledge system evolved over thousands of years.[48]

Another general comment should be made here. Over the last 15 years or so, a growing body of feminist literature has described and analyzed women's labour in Indian agriculture. The literature has shifted attention away from a theme that had dominated the intellectual debate on Indian agriculture in the 1970s, over the transition in class relations and the issue of the 'mode of production' (semi-feudal or capitalist). Starting from a critique of official statistics which defined peasant women incorrectly as 'housewives',[49] feminist authors have meanwhile laid bare the basic features of rural women's labour in different Indian states. They have also questioned the presumed beneficial effects of the introduction of technologies associated with the Green Revolution.

A central theme in the literature is the sexual division of labour between women and men. This division of labour is differently structured from what was discussed in the previous chapter. Fieldwork of peasant women is more common in India than in Muslim-dominated Bangladesh. Mencher and Saradamoni have, for instance, drawn attention to women's work in the transplantation of paddy, a task which in Bangladesh is traditionally done by men. They define transplantation as both hazardous and skilled. Consequently, peasant women contract various kinds of illnesses, such as parasitic infections, splitting of the skin of the heels and arthritis. In one village in Tanjavur, women told the interviewers that they make their children walk on their backs to massage them every night, to relieve the pain after transplanting. Some old women, who had spent 40 or 50 years of their life transplanting paddy, were permanently bent over and unable to stand straight.[50]

These descriptions help to counter the view that only male tasks, like ploughing, are heavy jobs. The second characteristic mentioned by Mencher and Saradamoni also goes counter to a well-known patriarchal prejudice, namely that skilled work can only be performed by men. The authors define transplantation as 'highly skilled' work, although knowledge is traditionally transmitted to young peasant women by their mothers. The task has to be done with great care. Transplanters have to pack down the earth cautiously after planting the seedlings. They also have to space the seedlings and avoid damage to the roots. 'If the seedlings are not put at the correct distance or deep enough, or if the ground is not patted down properly afterwards, the plants will not grow correctly.'[51] Thus, in the analysis of the sexual division of labour in Indian agriculture, women's field labour cannot be ignored.

Feminist authors have also pointed out the labour displacement effect of the Green Revolution. This process has, however, not been understood as unilinear. In Haryana and Punjab, the increase in the cropped area and the concomitant expansion of irrigation, initially at least, led to an increased demand for labour, including female labour.[52] Thus, extra labour was required for the harvesting of paddy. Yet, as the mechanization of farm operations took place (such as through the use of threshers and combine harvesters), labourers were displaced. Peasant women, in particular, lost out in terms of productive work. The use of chemical inputs obliterated tasks they had formerly performed. For instance, fertilizers took the place of manure, and the use of herbicides cut down on the weeding of the fields.[53] Thus, the multifarious consequences of the Green Revolution for the position of women in Indian agriculture have been the subject of a growing intellectual debate.

From what perspective does Vandana Shiva analyze women's labour? In the chapter 'Women in the Food Chain', Shiva looks at women's work in maintaining the ecological balance in traditional Indian agriculture. Women, she states, not only labour a large number of hours, but they also are productive in 'precisely those links in farm operations which involve a partnership in nature and are crucial for maintaining the food cycle—both in the soil and in the local food economy'.[54] In her view women have traditionally contributed much to maintaining the soil's fertility, yet their contributions are made invisible by the paradigm of Western science, which sees 'productivity' only in terms of output for the market.

Shiva looks at the types of activities undertaken by women in organic agriculture—at both their quantitative significance, and at the significance such activities have for the sustenance of nature. Thus, she quotes figures for the number of hours women toil in the hill areas of the Garhwal Himalaya. For 1 hectare of farmwork, women spend 640 hours in interculture operations like weeding, 384 hours in irrigation and 650 hours in transporting organic manure and transferring it to the field.[55] Moreover, as quantitative data from a study of agriculture in Himachal Pradesh illustrates, in percentage terms women also perform more than two-thirds of the tasks relating to the tending of farm animals (69 per cent). This work links up with the task of manuring, which is also essential to ensure the fertility of the soil in the traditional agrarian economy.

While describing women's various contributions to maintaining the fertility of the soil, Shiva draws a comparison between their invisible work and that of the earthworm, which too has been ignored for a long time in agricultural economics. As said, one of the key tasks of women is to fertilize the fields with organic manure derived from farm animals. This work, Shiva states, is supportive of the work of 'the decomposers and soil-builders which inhabit the soil'. Soils treated with farmyard manure have from two to two-and-a-half times as many earthworms as untreated soils, as farmyard manure increases the earthworms' food supply. And the work of the earthworm has varied significance—it ensures that the soil is more water-stable than unworked soils and facilitates drainage. Worm-worked soils, moreover, contain considerably more organic carbon and nitrogen than parent soils. Yet, in Western, 'scientific' agriculture, neither the work of the earthworm in building soil fertility, nor that of peasant women in support of the earthworm, is considered to be 'productive'.[56]

In consequence of the central importance she attaches to the work of maintaining the ecological cycle, Vandana Shiva gives special weight to the activities peasant women perform *before* the cultivation of the soil takes place (i.e., activities like the storing and selection of seeds, and manuring). In this, her approach differs significantly from the approach of developmental feminism discussed in the preceding chapter. For although such labouring activities are mentioned by developmental feminists, their primary attention is on the paddy-processing tasks of rural women (i.e., those tasks performed *after* the harvesting of crops from the field). Thus, Shiva's main aim is primarily to highlight the ecological significance of women's work—a theme which is ignored by Western science, and which does not hold much weight in developmental feminist discourse.

Another productive role of peasant women which Shiva stresses is that of 'custodians of the common genetic heritage' through the selection, storage and preservation of grain seeds.[57] As she points out, for 10,000 years agriculture has been based on the strategy of conserving and enhancing genetic diversity. In this experiment, millions of peasants all over the world have participated. They selected the best seeds, and they stored and replanted them. The results of their experimentation were never considered individual property. The knowledge regarding agricultural seeds, before the advent of the Green Revolution seed varieties, was always considered a common heritage. It was the common property of the producers of the soil.[58]

Moreover, in maintaining this genetic heritage, the role of peasant women was paramount. Women throughout South Asia, including

Bangladesh, were always responsible for storing seeds after the harvesting of the paddy.[59] Further, their role in seed selection was larger than that of men. Shiva cites a study of rural women in Nepal, where it was found that seed selection is primarily a female responsibility. In 60.4 per cent of the cases, women alone decided what type of seeds to use, while men decided in only 20.7 per cent of cases. Where a family decides to use its own seeds, women's predominant role is even larger: 'this work is done by women alone in 81.2 per cent of the households, by both sexes in 8 per cent of the households and by men alone in only 10.8 per cent of the households'. In India too, it is women who 'have carefully maintained the genetic base of food production over thousands of years'.[60]

With the introduction of high-response varieties of seeds under the Green Revolution, first, a common genetic resource has been turned into a commodity. Whereas, formerly, peasant families selected and stored their own seeds, they have now become dependent on centrally-produced seeds, which they need to buy in the market. Seed corporations and agricultural research institutes appropriate the control over plant seeds from the actual cultivators. At the same time, the transformation of agriculture leads to the displacement of genetic diversity in crops. As Shiva points out, 'uniformity is intrinsic to centralized seed production'.[61] Thus, the appropriation of common property resources (a key theme in ecofeminist discourse) and the loss of biodiversity go hand-in-hand.

The displacement of indigenous seeds, evidently, also eliminates women's role as custodians of the seed. Thus, the Green Revolution 'invisibly' undermines the productive role of peasant women in agriculture. This is not a unilinear process, as Shiva seems to suggest. Investigations regarding the effect of the Green Revolution on women's labour bring out multifarious effects. In the Indonesian island of Java, the replacement of the knife for cutting traditional paddy with the sickle, used for cutting high-responsive varieties of paddy, led to the displacement of women as paddy-cutters by men.[62] Yet the transformation of agriculture has also led to a more intensive use of female family labour for the performance of tasks like transplanting and weeding.[63] Still, Shiva's argument that the position of women as maintainers of the ecological cycle is undermined, holds. Both their tasks as guardians of the soil's fertility, and in the selection and storage of seeds, are scrapped.

Some Limitations of Shiva's Ecofeminism

In each of the previous chapters we have seen that the sexual division of labour is a central theme in feminist analyses of women's oppression and the structure of patriarchy. Whether it is the socialist–feminist or the developmental feminist school, each has devoted ample attention to the way men's and women's work is structured—both in the pre-capitalist and in capitalist modes of production—in such a way as to keep women in a subordinate position. In some cases male dominance is assured through men's monopoly over the use of machinery, whereas in other cases women's responsibility for all household chores and their double labouring burden are the 'organizing principle', the manner in which women's subordinate status is enforced. In any case, feminists belonging to different currents agree that the analysis of the sexual division of labour is the key to understanding the structure of patriarchy.

It is then surprising to note that the sexual division of labour between peasant women and men is largely glossed over in Shiva's analysis of women's work in the Indian countryside. While she highlights women's role in maintaining the ecological cycle in agriculture, she mentions various productive tasks performed by village women. Thus, in criticizing the absurdity of the 'white revolution', where Western 'developmental' institutions have sought to introduce Western-bred cows as milking machines in India, Shiva has stressed both how the integration of livestock with farming 'has been the secret of sustainable agriculture' in India, and has pointed out how women played a key role in nurturing cows, preparing cowdung as source of fuel and fertilizers, and processing cow milk into milk products for their family's subsistence needs.[64] Her analysis, then, is used to project women as the prime sustainers of nature, and as the main subsistence workers in society.

Shiva's work helps to highlight the productive tasks of women which are rarely accorded significance, in particular when she hails women as those who 'maintain the cyclical and sustainable flows of fertility between crops and cattle'. Other feminists would agree that much of women's work in this area has long been neglected in male analyses of agricultural processes. Thus, cattle-dung, known as *gobar*, is central to life in the Indian villages where up to 80 per cent of the households own cattle. Whereas men are the owners of the cattle, it is women who prepare the dung for a variety of uses, including dung-cakes for manure. The work is as backbreaking as it is crucial to agricultural processes.[65] Yet peasant women are not the only ones involved in maintaining soil fertility, since it is the male peasants who take the dung-cakes to manure the fields. Since Shiva does not consciously describe or analyze the sexual division of labour between male and female peasants, women appear as the sole agents of ecological sustenance.

When Shiva refers to the role of women in maintaining the water cycle in agriculture, she is similarly biased. As she rightly states, the paddy culture of South Asia has for centuries been possible through a careful use of available water resources to irrigate the land. The Green Revolution has led to severe water scarcity, 'water hunger' and numerous disputes over water between the Indian states,[66] because external 'experts', in their drive to transform Indian subsistence agriculture into market-oriented cash crop production, have ignored the indigenous knowledge system. The cause of the water crisis, as she states, is 'reductionist science and maldevelopment working against the logic of the water cycle'. For developmental experts 'fail to recognize that humans, like all living things, are participants in the water cycle and can survive sustainably only through that participation'.[67]

However, in stating that women are the 'invisible experts' and managers of the water resources, she does not base herself on a careful analysis of facts. Like Shiva, other Indian feminists have criticized 'development schemes' for increasing women's labouring burden. As women are responsible for gathering water for drinking and cooking purposes, the water crisis forces them to travel longer distances to collect this crucial household resource.[68] Yet the maintenance of the water cycle for the cultivation of paddy is a shared task, and not only the task of women. Whereas in villages of Andhra Pradesh, women peasants carry mud and stones, male peasants dig the small irrigation canals between the rice fields and construct the small *bunds* (dams) around the fields. Men are also responsible for irrigating the fields, both before and after the transplantation of the rice seedlings.[69]

In short, while the glossing over of the sexual division of labour allows Shiva to affirm that women are the prime sustainers of the ecological cycle, it does not enable us to understand either men's relation to nature or the operation of patriarchy. Shiva's depiction of women as soil builders and as experts of animal husbandry serves to repair an injustice against peasant women: their numerous productive tasks in traditional agriculture have long been neglected in economic theory. Yet the factual material she presents is incomplete. By ignoring the sexual division of labour, she makes it neither possible to fully understand labour relations in traditional agriculture, nor how these are transformed under the impact of Green Revolution technology. From a feminist perspective her analysis is flawed.[70]

One of the essential contributions of ecofeminist thinking in general, and of Vandana Shiva in particular, has been the recognition that nature is characterized by biodiversity, and that women play a crucial role in maintaining this diversity in nature. Nature consists of an infinite variety of life-forms, both in the forests and in the sea, in the world of plants and animals. In many Third World societies which have not yet been integrated, or only partly integrated, into the world economic system, 'biodiversity is simultaneously a means of production and an object of consumption'.[71] Capitalism with its homogenizing tendency has a destructive impact on this biodiversity, Shiva argues, and needs therefore to be fundamentally questioned.

The recognition of biodiversity in nature in Shiva's writings is, however, not accompanied by a conscious recognition of the diversity of social positions existing in contemporary class societies. While capitalism has historically both undermined the power of feudal landlords and the subsistence production of peasant communities, it has often led simultaneously to more class differentiation between peasant families. Their relationship to the means of production (land, cattle and instruments of labour) is increasingly diversified, such as between agricultural workers on the one hand, and wealthy peasants producing a surplus on the other hand. One Marxist author reputed for having drawn attention to this process of class differentiation is Lenin.[72] Now, as feminist authors have pointed out, the Marxist analysis of peasant differentiation is defective, since it does not lead one to bring out the diversified class position of peasant women. Yet feminist authors of various persuasions do not question the relevance of class analysis *per se*.

Shiva's approach is marked by a striking contrast. She argues that there is 'a general misconception that diversity-based production systems are low-productivity systems'; and further that 'the high productivity of uniform and homogeneous systems is a contextual and theoretically constructed category, based on taking into account only one-dimensional yields and outputs'.[73] Yet she does not extend her recognition of diversity to the analysis of social reality. In stating that 'diversity is the principle of women's work and knowledge' and that women's work and knowledge is 'central to biodiversity conservation and utilization', she obliterates the contributions of male peasants to maintaining the diversity of life and agricultural production. At the same time, she ignores the fact that women's own position, both in the diversity-based feudal production system and under modern-day capitalism, is far from homogeneous. Thus, whereas her approach to analyzing nature implies a serious critique of the dominant Western philosophy, her analysis of social relations is 'homogenizing'. It offers a retreat from the analysis of class relations which was the hallmark of Marxist economic theory.

In this chapter, where I have discussed the ecofeminist critique of Western science, I have mentioned Shiva's opposition to such science as 'reductionist': in line with dominant economic interests, it admits as productive only such activities and values which are marketable as commodities, and ignores the productive activities of nature and women that do not visibly promote capitalist accumulation. Here I wish to discuss the specific parallel Shiva draws between women and nature, which in my view could lead to a new 'reductionism'. In highlighting the productive role of women and nature, she elaborates on a theme proposed earlier by Maria Mies. According to Mies, women's relation to nature is different from men's because, although women appropriate nature, 'their appropriation does not constitute a relationship of dominance or a property relationship'. For Mies, women's work is the production of life, in the broadest sense.[74]

Shiva depicts both nature and women as the invisible creators of wealth. Thus, 'insignificant' plants create significant changes which shift the ecological equilibrium in life's favour. Similarly, women's invisible work provides sustenance and produces wealth for basic needs. In industrial society, the devaluation and de-recognition of nature's work and productivity has led to the ecological crisis; similarly, the devaluation and de-recognition of women's work has created sexism, sexual inequality and violence against women. This has occurred through the redefinition of 'productivity' in economic theory built to serve the needs of capitalist accumulation: '"Productive" man, producing commodities, using some of nature's wealth and women's work as raw material and dispensing with the rest as waste, becomes the only legitimate category of work, wealth and production. Nature and women working to produce and reproduce life are declared "unproductive".'[75]

It is true that capitalist institutions, and Western economic theory constructed from the 18th century onwards, have indeed redefined 'productivity' to the exclusion of those productive processes which do not take place directly under the sway of capitalist accumulation, in particular the life-giving activities of nature and women. The recognition of this reductionist bias is a crucial precondition for achieving women's liberation and the re-generation of nature. Yet it should not result in overlooking facts regarding women as producers of an economic surplus. In drawing a parallel between nature and women as 'sustainers', Shiva tends to overlook the fact that in both pre-capitalist and capitalist societies, women participate in forms of labour which cannot be defined as mere 'subsistence labour', since they involve the transfer of wealth, of a surplus, to classes which are not themselves the producers of such wealth.

In short, Shiva's neatly constructed scheme 'glosses over' all such forms of labour—slave labour, the services of male and female tenants to feudal lords, as well as wage labour under capitalism—which involve the transfer of products to classes of owners. One wonders whether her analysis does not harbour the danger that it will result in a new 'reductionism', that is, the non-recognition of all the labour, performed by women, which cannot properly be termed production for 'survival' or 'sustenance' (a standpoint which I will question later on theoretical grounds). In spite of the crucial new insights it provides, Shiva's analysis, like Mies', in the end raises critical questions of a theoretical kind.

Ecofeminism and Developmental Feminism: Comparison and Summary

Before concluding, I would like to draw a short comparison between the ecofeminism of Shiva, on the one hand, and developmental feminism, on the other. As the information presented here has shown, both have contributed towards our understanding of the role of women in South Asian agricultural practices. Developmental feminists have highlighted the productive work done by women belonging to different peasant classes. They have focused, in particular, on the processing tasks performed by various classes of women after the harvesting of paddy. Shiva, similarly, has given importance to the productive work of rural women. She has emphasized tasks like seed selection and manuring the soil, which are crucial to maintaining the ecological cycle, and the productive potential of traditional agriculture.

Yet, though both currents can be credited with having contributed to our understanding of rural women's work, the differences in the perspectives of these two feminist currents are vast. It is sufficient to mention two differences to indicate the gulf separating the two. First, their attitude towards the modernization of South Asian agriculture through Western, scientific methods varies. While developmental feminists are aware of the fact that certain elements in modernization, such as the mechanization of paddy-husking, are detrimental to the welfare of rural poor women, this current of feminism does not address the vast, ecological impact of the Green Revolution package of seeds and chemical inputs which is pushed in the name of 'development'. For the ecofeminist author Shiva, the ecological destruction wrought by the Green Revolution, and by other forms of modernization, is a paramount concern.

Second, as we have seen earlier, developmental feminists explicitly aiming to help 'the integration of women in development' fail to critically scrutinize the relationship between pauperization of the peasantry and the dominant process of economic exploitation (i.e., the original accumulation via the marketing of crops and the enrichment of a commercial class promoted by international finance capital). The ecofeminist author Shiva, on the contrary, does address the principal method of exploitation and its effects on women's labouring activities. For her, the driving force behind the loss of women's pre-eminence in sustainable agriculture is precisely the accumulation of capital, which is frequently equated with the 'patriarchal project'. Shiva questions precisely the dominant mode of appropriation of agricultural surplus. She seeks to criticize 'maldevelopment as a patriarchal project of domination and destruction'.[76]

Finally, while both currents pose questions that are relevant for economic theory, it is only ecofeminism that poses a fundamental challenge, and does so at a moment when the developmental process driven by Western science is threatening the very survival of the planet. This is because the ecological crisis caused by capitalist accumulation has reached worldwide proportions today,[77] and the process of environmental destruction can only be turned around if it is thoroughly exposed. Moreover, while developmental feminism's focus on rural women's work is far from unique within feminist literature, the parallels drawn by ecofeminist authors between patriarchal science's attack on women and nature form a crucial contribution to our knowledge about today's world. In short, the epistemological importance of what ecofeminism has to say far surpasses that of developmental feminism.

In this chapter I have made an assessment of the contributions made by ecofeminism to critical economic theory. One of the most valuable contributions is to have challenged the sanctity of Western science by bringing out both its internal, philosophical contradictions and its social roots. Western science claims to be 'objective', but its supremacy is based on financial and political support by Western-dominated international institutions rather than on cognitive competition. The close re-reading of texts written by the founding fathers of Western science by ecofeminist scholars reveals that this science is deeply biased against nature and women. Western science, in particular the natural science developed around Bacon's experimental method, through the period from the 17th century to date has, in fact, served the interests of capitalist accumulation and patriarchal men.

One of the most prominent representatives of ecofeminism, the Indian scientist Shiva, has researched the relationships between Western (in particular, American) research institutes, the spread of Green Revolution technology, and its effects on Indian agriculture. Indian agriculture, prior to the introduction of the so-called 'miracle seeds' and concomitant chemical inputs, was ecologically balanced. Its sustainability was ensured through an indigenous, people's knowledge system which, amongst others, stressed multiple and rotational cropping. In Shiva's view, much of the knowledge was located in women as the sustainers of traditional agriculture. The Green Revolution has created monocultures which, within a short period of time, have depleted both the soil and water resources in the selected areas where the foreign-imposed 'scientific' methods were tried.

The philosophical and social position taken by Shiva and other ecofeminists is clearly distinguishable from that of developmental feminists. Whereas the latter seek to integrate women in a capitalist process of accumulation which is presumed to bring 'development', ecofeminists expose the same process as 'maldevelopment'. Contrary to developmental feminists who, as stated, tend to ignore the dominant processes of exploitation of human beings (and of nature), ecofeminists focus largely on exactly these processes. Instead of taking the aims of international financial institutions, like the World

Bank and Western scientists, for granted, ecofeminists lay bare both their fundamental objectives and the ecological and social results (i.e., the destruction of biodiversity in nature and the undermining of the subsistence base, in particular of peasant women, in the Third World). The privatization of common property resources has both these effects.

However, in discussing Shiva's references to the labouring activities of rural women in India, I have questioned the narrow limits of her theoretical position. Her critique of Western science and her ecological insights are a welcome contribution to economic theory; they are formulated explicitly also as a critique of Marxism which has long accepted Western science's aim of controlling nature.[78] Her theoretical position, nevertheless, tends to culminate in a new 'reductionism'. Since she has largely glossed over women's differentiated class positions and the sexual division of labour, which forms a cornerstone of feminist thinking as developed since the second feminist wave, Shiva's theory can only be accepted with reservations. Without a specific theory of women's labour, her analytical contribution remains circumscribed.[79]

Notes and References

1. Merchant (1992), p. 184. See also Baker (1993), p. 4. According to Vål Plumwood's summary (1992), p. 10, the first ecofeminist book was written by Rosemary Ruether and published in 1976.
2. Plumwood (1992), p. 10. According to Baker (1993), p. 5, 'ecofeminism is . . . a philosophical critique as well as a political engagement'. It 'has its origins in political practice and forms part of the "new" social movements that have arisen within the late twentieth century' (ibid.), p. 14.
3. Merchant (1992), p. 183. Mary Mellon (1992), p. 1, traces her book's origins to her personal experience at the women's peace camp outside the American Air Base at Greenham Commons in Britain in 1983.
4. The Chipko movement in the Garhwal Himalaya in India is extensively discussed by Vandana Shiva (1988), pp. 67–77. According to her, in 1977 the movement became 'explicitly an ecological and feminist movement' (p. 76).
5. Plumwood (1992), p. 10. Merchant (1992), p. 190, distinguishes several more currents of ecofeminism.
6. Plumwood (1992), p. 10. For Merchant (1992), p. 184, what is characteristic of social ecofeminists is that they ask 'how patriarchal relations of reproduction reveal the domination of women by men, and how capitalist relations of production reveal the domination of nature by men'.
7. Plumwood (1992), p. 12. The author criticizes the second wave of feminism of the 1960s and 1970s for having 'attempted to fit women somewhat uncritically into a masculinist model of humanity and culture' (ibid.), p. 11.

8. See Jone (1987–88). Yet, while criticizing Western science like Vandana Shiva, for its 'reductionist' approach, Jone also believes that the latest paradigm of Western natural science (i.e., quantum theory) 'both complements and reinforces the message of the ecological movement'.
9. Shiva (1988), p. 22.
10. Ibid., p. 24.
11. Shiva (1991a), p. 43.
12. Shiva (1988), p. 25. A comprehensive critique of Vandana Shiva's views on reductionist science is provided by Nanda (1991).
13. Merchant (1980), p. 169.
14. Ibid., p. 168.
15. See also Shiva (1988), p. 16.
16. Merchant (1980), p. 173.
17. Merchant (1992), p. 42.
18. Ibid., p. 56. See also Einstein and Infeld (1938), Ch. 1. According to the authors, 'the connection between force and the change of velocity—and not, as we should think according to our intuition, the connection between force and the velocity itself—is the basis of the classical mechanics as formulated by Newton'.
19. A Marxist author who, to an extent, shares the mechanical worldview, is Caudwell (1989). According to Caudwell (ibid.), p. 23: 'We are criticising the bourgeois philosophy because its view of Nature is "mechanism". That does not mean we believe that Nature's laws are different in kind from those of a machine. In fact this would be an absurd suggestion; since a machine is constructed out of bits of nature, according to natural laws, the laws of the machine cannot be wholly different in kind from those of Nature.'
20. Merchant (1980), p. 217.
21. Ibid., p. 227.
22. Merchant (1992), p. 58.
23. Ummerkutty (1991), p. 96.
24. See Merchant (1980).
25. Ibid., p. 47.
26. Ibid.
27. Engels (1969), p. 39.
28. Ibid., p. 90.
29. Merchant (1980), p. 57.
30. For the multifunctionality of the oceans, see Ummerkutty (1991).
31. Merchant (1980), p. 58.
32. Ibid., p. 61.
33. Ibid., p. 59.
34. Shiva (1988).
35. Ibid., p. 83.
36. Ibid., p. 61.
37. Kelkar and Nathan (1991), p. 125.
38. Ibid., p. 126.
39. Shiva (1988), p. 87.
40. Ibid., p. 86.
41. See Mellon (1992), p. 233.
42. Shiva (1991a), p. 61.

43. Shiva (1988), p. 106.
44. Ibid., p. 107.
45. Ibid.
46. Shiva (1991a), p. 109.
47. Shiva (1988), p. 120. Similar criticism regarding the 'monoculture' approach of the Green Revolution has recently been expressed by the assistant director-general, FAO, A.Z.M. Obaidullah Khan. According to Martin Khor (1994), p. 14, when interviewed in 1994, the FAO functionary was very outspoken: 'Mr. Khan said that the apparent benefits of monoculture agriculture [where only a single crop is grown, as in the Green Revolution method] had been overestimated whilst the productivity of traditionally grown varieties had been understated. When comparisons were made between the two systems, only the yields of the single crop were measured. This, said Mr. Khan, neglected to calculate the value of other crops or other activities carried out in the same farm area in the traditional system, which no longer existed in the monoculture system.' See also Khan (1994).
48. It should be noted that Shiva's argument regarding the displacement of people's knowledge cannot be taken as the general and only way capitalism deals with such knowledge. As shown in Chapter 11, capitalist enterprises have also developed ways of incorporating and monopolizing knowledge formerly held by the actual producers.
49. See, for instance, Nayyar (1989), p. 234.
50. Mencher and Saradamoni (1982), p. A–149.
51. Ibid., p. A–150.
52. See Nayyar (1989), pp. 238, 243.
53. See, for instance, Mencher and Saradamoni (1982), P. A–150; see also Nayyar (1989), p. 243.
54. Shiva (1988), p. 114.
55. Ibid., p. 109.
56. Ibid., p. 108.
57. Ibid., p. 121.
58. Shiva (1991a).
59. For Bangladesh see Chen (1986a), p. 219; (1986b), p. 48.
60. Shiva (1988), p. 121.
61. Ibid., p. 122.
62. Wahyana (1994), p. WS–19, states: 'Due to the introduction of the short grains of HYV, the use of *ani-ani* knife for harvests has become obsolete. For the new varieties of rice, sickles are used. Sickles are considered men's tools as they are "big", "heavy", and "dangerous", therefore only men are supposed to use them. Men took over the task of rice-cutting. Indeed the use of sickles reduced the workdays necessary for rice harvest from 200 to 75 per hectare. Along with this it led to a massive displacement of rural women wage workers, who had worked as harvesters.' Wahyana (ibid.) also notes that women are gradually reclaiming their share in harvesting.
63. Ibid., p. WS–32.
64. Shiva (1988), p. 165.
65. Jeffery, Jeffery and Lion (1989).
66. For the last-mentioned development see, in particular, Shiva (1991a), p. 150.
67. Shiva (1988), pp. 182–83.

68. See, for instance, Kishwar and Vanita (1984), p. 3.
69. Mies (1986a), p. 61.
70. Based on her field research in the Himalayan hills of Himachal Pradesh, Gaul (1994), p. 28, has recently challenged 'popularized assumptions about "Indian women and the environment".' She also stresses (ibid.), p. 25, the existence of labour-sharing patterns between women and men: 'male and female youths and adults share and trade tasks of herding, grass, fodder and firewood cutting and carrying, and the collection of other materials from the forests (such as herbs for teas, or plants and fruits for eating)'.
71. See Shiva (1993), p. 164.
72. Lenin (1977a), p. 70. Lenin connected this process of differentiation with the development of capitalist relations in the countryside: 'The sum total of all the economic contradictions among the peasantry constitutes what we call the differentiation of the peasantry. The peasants themselves strikingly characterize this process with the term "depeasantizing". This process signifies the utter dissolution of the old, patriarchal peasantry and the creation of *new types* of rural inhabitants' (ibid.), p. 173, emphasis in original. See also Atiur Rahman (1986), p. 12, for the effect of the Green Revolution on class polarization in India. Also Huizer (1980), p. 202; Sharma (1973), p. 77.
73. Shiva (1993), p. 165.
74. Mies (1986b), pp. 49–62; Shiva (1988), pp. 42–48.
75. Shiva (1988), p. 43.
76. Ibid., p. 14.
77. As Kelkar and Nathan have argued, the global nature of the ecological crisis is characteristic of the capitalist system only whereas, previously, ecological crises were localized. For their critique of Shiva's views, see Kelkar and Nathan (1991), pp. 110–19, 136–38.
78. Mies and Shiva (1993), p. 157: 'The Left, particularly, clings to the Hegelian and Marxist philosophy of history, according to which the development of productive forces, man's progressive domination over nature constitutes the precondition for political and economic emancipation from obsolete relations of production.'
79. For another critique of ecofeminism, as represented by Shiva and Mies, see Jackson (1995), p. 124.

10

The German Feminist School and the Thesis of Subsistence Labour

In an earlier chapter, I have presented the thesis of the German feminist school on 'housewifization'. This, however, is not the only thesis shared by Maria Mies, Veronika Bennholdt-Thomsen and Claudia von Werlhof. I will now review their second major proposition, namely, that women's labour worldwide should be understood as 'subsistence labour', defined as the production of life in its widest sense.[1] We will see that the implications of this thesis are more far-reaching than those of the earlier-mentioned thesis. The thesis on subsistence labour, in fact, shapes the fundamental view of the German authors regarding the process of capitalist reproduction and accumulation. A review of this thesis is, therefore, decisive for an evaluation of the contribution made by the German feminist school to economic theory.

To begin with, I shall briefly recall the process of development of this thesis, which occurred, as Maria Mies has recorded,[2] in course of a series of seminars held at the University of Bielefeld, (West) Germany, during the second half of the 1970s. Here, the continual dependence of Third World countries on the industrial world was re-debated and linked with the discussion on housework. The members of the German feminist school argue emphatically that the women's question is related to the colonial question, that women and the colonies serve as the 'unseen foundation for the entire edifice of industrialism', and that both are an area of reality which has 'systematically' been excluded from existing theories regarding the world capitalist system. Both women and the colonies are appropriated through direct violence, and both are subjected to robbery and the destruction of the basis of their life.[3]

Second, Mies, Bennholdt-Thomsen and von Werlhof underline the similarities between the position of Third World peasants and women, and this is done explicitly in their thesis on subsistence labour. Both women in general, and peasants in the Third World, constitute a vast mass of 'subsistence producers', whose labour is a hidden source of accumulation for capital. Both peasants and women share as a common characteristic the fact that 'they are forced to [also] produce goods for their own direct consumption without payment, as they would be unable to survive on their often minimal wage labour, much less without it'. Women and peasants might earn an additional wage, but they are, so state the members of the German school, in essence non-capitalist producers and consumers. They are, thus, subject to a continual process of original or 'primitive' accumulation.[4]

Third, we should note from the start the broad definition given to the term 'subsistence labour'. Here two types of activities are cited which are 'presupposed by all human history', namely the production of the means of subsistence and the production of new life or procreation.[5] Thus, Mies follows Engels in terming both types of human activities 'production'. She speaks of the combination of the production of human life and of living–working capacity, of a continuum between 'subsistence production and reproduction'. Subsistence production, then, involves 'a variety of human activities ranging from pregnancy and the birth of children, to production, processing and the preparation of food, clothing, making a home, cleaning as well as the satisfaction of emotional and sexual needs'. According to Mies, 'In all this activity human energy is spent to transform 'nature' into human life. Therefore, I shall call this activity subsistence work. Most of the work is done by women.'[6]

In practice, the interrelationship between the two forms of subsistence activities (i.e., procreation and the production of working capacity) is not elaborated upon. This, in my view, is a limitation not only in the theorizing by the German feminist school, but in most feminist discourse on women's work (including in the treatment of women's work in this study).[7] In practice, the members of the German feminist school use a definition of subsistence work which, in a sense, is narrower than that of Marx. Reviewing the literature produced by Mies, Bennholdt-Thomsen and von Werlhof, I conclude that their common view can concisely be stated thus: subsistence labour consists of the production of use values for day-to-day sustenance.[8] In this chapter I will look at both the theoretical ramifications of the thesis on subsistence labour and its application to women's work in India.

Luxemburg's Theory of Imperialism as Viewed by the German Feminist School

In developing their thesis on subsistence labour, the three German feminist authors have taken as a common reference point the theory of imperialism formulated by Rosa Luxemburg. The nature of European domination over the continents of Asia, Africa and Latin America, as well as its causes, formed the subject of heated debate between Marxist theoreticians in the years that preceded and covered the period of the First World War. The Polish-born theoretician and revolutionary, Rosa Luxemburg, was one of the participants in this debate. In *Die Akkumulation des Kapitals* (The Accumulation of Capital), she sought to provide a 'strictly scientific explanation of imperialism and its contradictions'.[9] Rosa Luxemburg believed she had discovered the internal causes, within the capitalist system, for the need to dominate non-capitalist regions of the world.

What then was Luxemburg's specific explanation, and how did her theory differ from that put forward earlier by Karl Marx? In *Capital*, Marx had analyzed the process of 'social reproduction' (i.e., the reproduction of the relation between capital and wage labour on an ever-widening scale). For Marx it was clear that the capitalist system cannot survive unless the conditions for continual self-expansion are present. These cannot be guaranteed by individual entrepreneurs, but must be ensured through mechanisms created by the system as a whole. In searching to find a solution to the question he posed, Marx looked closely at the two departments of production—that of the means of production and that of the articles of consumption—and their interrelation.[10] Marx viewed the capitalist system as a self-contained one. According to Rosa Luxemburg, that is why he ultimately could not explain how 'extended reproduction', meaning the process of expansion of the scale of production, is 'realized' (i.e., how ever larger quantities of commodities can be sold).

Rosa Luxemburg sought a different solution to this problem of extended reproduction, in which she simultaneously gave her own economic explanation of imperialism. She agreed with Marx that the capitalist system consists of basically two departments, but in her view the surplus value produced in the two departments can only be realized if possibilities to market commodities exist outside these two departments.[11] Thus, she argued that 'Marx's scheme of extended reproduction does not enable us to explain the process of accumulation as it takes place in reality and historically proceeds.' Further, 'This scheme presents the process of accumulation under the presumption that capitalists and workers are the only representatives of social consumption.' Yet, in reality, 'there nowhere has existed or exists a self-sufficient capitalist society with exclusive dominance of capitalist production'.[12]

Agreeing that the 'realization of surplus value is in fact the life-and-death question of capitalist accumulation',[13] Rosa Luxemburg suggests that the possibilities for the realization of profits are provided in the consumption of new commodities by non-capitalist layers and societies. 'The determining point is that the surplus value can neither be realized by workers nor by capitalists, but only by social layers or societies which themselves do not produce capitalistically.'[14] In short, the solution to the problem of extended reproduction lies outside capitalism: 'The solution lies, in the sense of Marxist theory, in the dialectical contradiction that capitalist accumulation, in order to proceed, requires non-capitalist social formations as its environment; that it moves forward in constant material exchange [*Stoffwechsel*] with these formations, and that it can only exist as long as this milieu is available.'[15] Capitalism, Luxemburg concludes, cannot survive without an environment of other economic systems as its medium of exchange.[16]

How has Luxemburg's theory been revived and applied to women's labour? What exactly is its relevance for the thesis of Mies, von Werlhof and Bennholdt-Thomsen on subsistence labour? In their writings, all three German feminist authors state that Rosa Luxemburg's theory of imperialism anticipated their discussion on non-waged forms of labour. For instance, Mies refers to the debate which she and her colleagues carried on in the 1970s in the following manner: 'In the discussions that took place between Claudia von Werlhof, Veronika Bennholdt-Thomsen and myself in these years on the various forms of non-wage labour relations and their place in a worldwide system of capital accumulation, Rosa Luxemburg's work on imperialism played a decisive role.'[17]

Mies, Bennholdt-Thomsen and von Werlhof are convinced that Rosa Luxemburg had started a crucial debate on the limitations of Marx's scheme for extended reproduction. Although Luxemburg's reconceptualization was heavily criticized in the Soviet Union-oriented international communist movement of the 1920s, the three contemporary feminist authors believe that she should be praised for her 'clairvoyance'[18] in pointing out Marx's incorrect presupposition, his neglect of subsistence work. Thus the members of the German feminist school agree that the capitalist system, for its own survival, needs access to non-capitalist areas of production. They agree with Rosa Luxemburg that capitalism has never been a closed system, but has throughout its historical evolution needed the exploitation of non-capitalist strata and milieus.

In two respects, however, the German feminist authors seek to move beyond Luxemburg's conceptualization of the world economic system. They do not directly question Luxemburg's anti-feminist view on household labour, as I have done in Chapter 3 on the mass movement of German women workers in the decades before the First World War. Nor do they criticize her for having failed to base her theorizing on the concrete experiences and factual material brought out in the course of that movement. Nevertheless, they are aware that Rosa Luxemburg was not specifically concerned with women's labour. Thus, they argue that Luxemburg's theory regarding the two-tier structure of capitalist reproduction can only be used as a broad framework which helps to incorporate hitherto neglected spheres of production and exploitation.

Second, the members of the German school also do not seem to share Luxemburg's so-called 'self-destruction thesis'. As stated, according to Luxemburg the process of capital accumulation would be unthinkable without a non-capitalist milieu, especially for the sale of commodities. Yet the historical tendency of capitalism being to transform all non-capitalist relations into wage relations, capitalism ultimately destroys its own basis for realization. Bennholdt-Thomsen argues against Luxemburg's 'perspective of unlimited generalization of wage workers'. She states, 'In the present we cannot close our eyes any more to the historical evidence that the tendency towards transforming every work into wage work will not be realized.' Against Luxemburg she argues that 'capital itself reproduces its own "non-capitalist" surroundings, in the imperialist as well as in the dependent countries'.[19]

In a rudimentary manner, however, the German authors uphold Luxemburg's significance for contemporary feminist theorizing. Maria Mies has summed up their view of Luxemburg's contribution thus:

> what her work opened up for our feminist analysis of women's labour worldwide was a perspective which went beyond the limited horizon of industrialized societies and the housewives in these countries. It further helped to transcend theoretically the various artificial divisions of labour created by capital, particularly the sexual division of labour and the international division of labour by which precisely those areas are made invisible which are to be exploited in non-wage labour relations and where the rules and regulations governing wage labour are suspended. We consider it the most important task of feminism to include all these relations in an analysis of women's work under capitalism, because today there can be no doubt that capital has already reached the stage of which Rosa Luxemburg spoke.[20]

'Subsistence Labour' in India: Mies' Focus on Female Agricultural Labourers

In assessing the thesis on subsistence labour in the following sections, I will take as my starting point, once again, a field investigation carried out by Maria Mies in India. In 1978, Mies and two research assistants spent several months reviewing production relations in three villages of an administrative unit (*taluk*) called Bhongir, in Nalgonda district of Andhra Pradesh. As when doing their investigation about lace-making, they used a combination of methods to gather their data, such as interviews with individual women, group discussions and selected household surveys. The prime focus of the village research was on those women who had to rely on the sale of their labour power to make ends meet. According to Mies' sources, 'in 1971 54.7 per cent of the female labour force in the taluk were agricultural labourers and 58 per cent of all the agricultural labourers were women'.[21]

One of the things Mies pointedly highlights is women's overall lack of control over the means of production, which contrasts sharply with the picture for men. The vast majority of women in the three villages had no control over the main means of production—land—nor did they possess other key means necessary for agricultural operations, such as wells, ploughs and draught animals. The only tools and implements in the possession of women were sickles—'the universal female tool'[22]—baskets and winnowing fans. Contrary to men's tools, which involve 'the use of other-than-human sources of energy',[23] women's tools are usually dependent on their own physical energy. Again, huts and tenements belonged to the heads of the households (i.e., men) while women only owned the household utensils used for cooking. Thus, women were 'virtually excluded from control over all means necessary for exchange value and surplus value production'. What they owned were typically the means necessary for 'subsistence work'.[24]

Mies' study may be called pioneering, as she drew attention to a category of women workers in India who have subsequently become the focus of much more academic research. For one, the Indian Census of 1981 has confirmed the increasing importance of agricultural workers among the rural workforce of women. It gave these figures for 'occupational distribution': 50 per cent agricultural labourers, 37 per cent cultivators, 4 per cent women workers in household industries, and 9 per cent in the category of 'other workers'.[25] Moreover, the share of female agricultural labourers in India's total female 'workforce' had almost doubled compared to the census data of 1961. It has been disputed whether these statistical figures are precise. Yet there seems no doubt that the proportion of women wage workers in India's villages has dramatically increased at the expense of female cultivators.[26]

In the villages of Andhra Pradesh studied by Mies in 1978, the predominance of female agricultural labourers was striking in other comparative terms as well—women carried a far larger burden of farm work than men and formed the bulk of the force of agricultural labourers. Thus, Mies calculates that 70–80 per cent of all fieldwork was done by women and that, more generally, women did 80 per cent of all agricultural operations.[27] Moreover, Mies' findings are that no less than two-thirds of all *coolies*, or all persons employed as day labourers in agriculture, were women.[28] How does one explain this state of affairs, what was the nature of women's workload, and what are the implications of Mies' research for the thesis of the German feminist school that women's work can be equated with subsistence labour?

Map 10.1
Districts in India where the Number of Female Agricultural Labourers Equals or Exceeds Male Agricultural Labourers, 1961

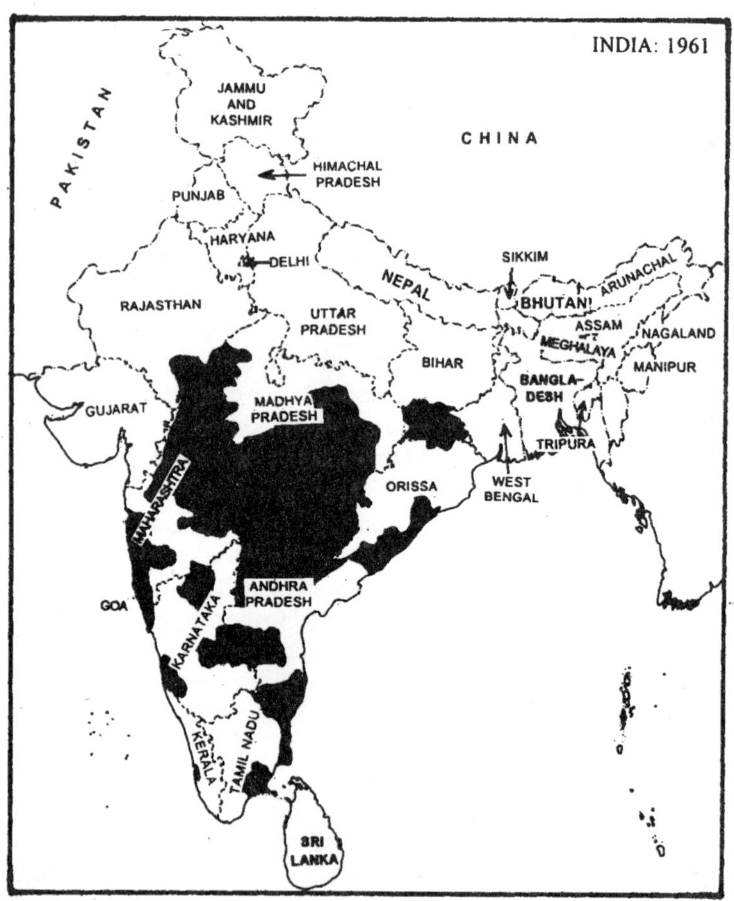

Source: Jose (1989), pp. 104–5.

When discussing the organization of the work process of female agricultural labourers, Mies mentions a crucial distinction between their work processes and those of men. Whereas men's work processes (such as ploughing, harrowing and irrigation) were rather individualized, women's work was more collectively organized. A

Map 10.2
Districts in India where the Number of Female Agricultural Labourers Equals or Exceeds Male Agricultural Labourers, 1981

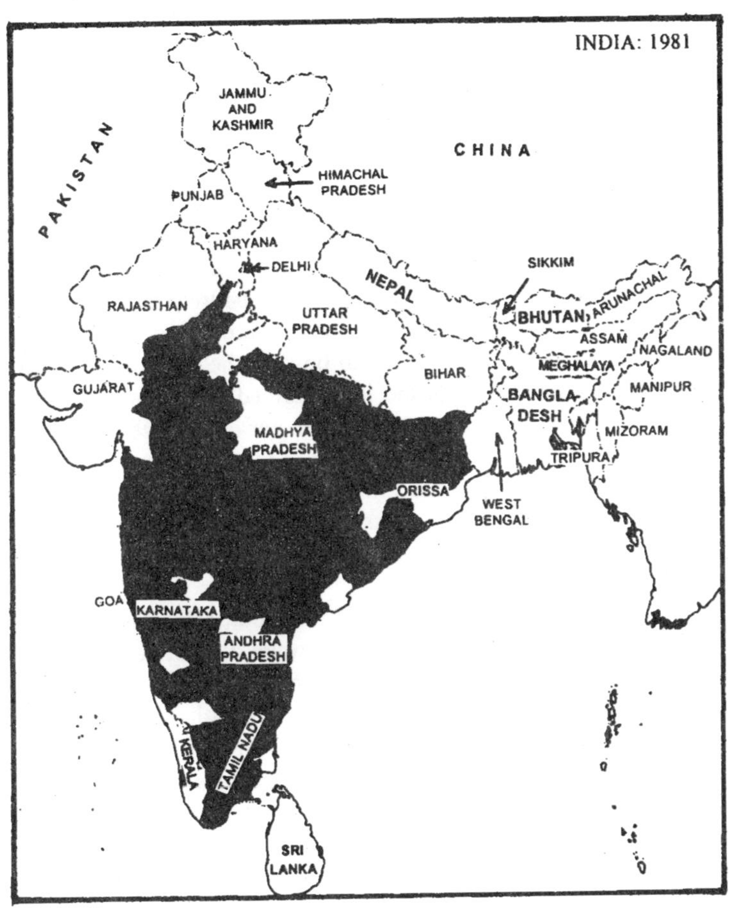

Source: Jose (1989), pp. 104–5.

pointed instance is that of rice transplanting which, as stated earlier, is a key task performed by women in Indian agriculture.

> In transplanting rice seedlings, teams of 20 to 30 women had to work simultaneously, wading through the mud and putting individual

> plants into the soil. They worked in a row, all bending down and moving forward slowly as they worked.... All workers performed the same movements: in one hand they held the seedlings, with the other they stuck them into the mud. All followed the same work rhythm.[29]

This nature of the work process resulted in a collective consciousness, as reflected in the instance of struggle Mies describes. The struggle was centred around the low wages which landlords paid to the female *coolies*. This practice was common among all the landlords in the area, but it led to resistance by women in the village of Kunur, after the formation of a women's association in the locality. 'On a day in the month of August, 1978, all the labourers assembled at a point where they usually meet in teams before going to their daily work.'[30] The women then decided to boycott the work on the farms of the rich landlords, unless the latter agreed to increase women's agricultural wages from Rs. 2 to Rs. 2.50 per day. Since the women threatened to strike at a crucial moment in the agricultural cycle, the landlords had to give in. And although they subsequently took revenge by increasing the work pressure, the action effectively demonstrated the existence of a collective consciousness amongst the female agricultural labourers.

In her study of the lace industry of Narsapur, Mies found that the women doing crocheting at home for a wage did not generally conceive of themselves as workers, but as housewives. Mies' findings about female agricultural workers in the Bhongir area of Andhra Pradesh are qualitatively different. In terms of their economic position, the *coolies* shared much with the lacemakers in and around Narsapur: both were labourers with a double workload, both were paid below subsistence wages. Yet the social existence of the two groups differed widely, for whereas the crocheters were individualized producers, the female *coolies* worked collectively. This fact, Mies notes, 'fundamentally influenced their consciousness, their self-perception and their interpretation of social relations'.[31] In other words, neither the economic nor the social position of the female *coolies* approximates that of the (Western) housewife.

Further, unlike the ecofeminist author Shiva, Mies devotes considerable attention to the sex-wise division of labour between peasant men and women. This is a theme she consistently addresses in her writings on women's labour. Thus, in her book on village women in

Andhra Pradesh, she reviews the male and female tasks in the field cultivation of three crops, millet, rice and tobacco. In the growing of millet, *jawar*, which still bears the characteristics of production for immediate use (see the following), men plough and harrow the fields, while the sowing is done either by women or jointly. Where the primitive seed-drill is still being used (an implement with three bamboo pipes drawn by bullocks) men drive the bullocks and hold the drill while women put the seeds into the bamboo pipes by hand.[32] The harvesting of millet is considered a female task (see Table 10.1).

In rice cultivation, which has partly been commercialized, men again are responsible for the tasks of field preparation, including the levelling of the fields with a wooden plank drawn by bullocks. Men are also responsible for the irrigation of the fields, 'Where there are wells they work the *mota*, a metal container with a leather hose attached to it by which the water is lifted from the wells and poured into the small irrigation canals with the help of bullocks.'[33] Women's role in the ecological cycle, as mentioned before, is to maintain the fertility of the soil. They put cow and buffalo dung on the seedbeds and the field. Women's role in rice transplantation—which is 'purely manual labour and does not involve any tools'—has already been referred to. The harvesting of paddy is done by men and women together, while men do the threshing by driving the animals over the paddy.

The account of tobacco cultivation—the third main crop, which is a purely commercial one—does not add much to the foregoing description of rice. Like paddy, the growing of tobacco involves tasks like irrigation and transplantation, and the sexual division of labour follows basically the same pattern. Again, men's work is mostly done with implements and draught animals, while female workers are employed for manual operations. This includes tasks like the spreading of fertilizers, weeding and the cutting of tobacco leaves. Mies devotes a separate section to the sexual division of child labour in which she mentions boys' and girls' tasks in rice cultivation. Little boys help their fathers to plough and water the fields, or have to graze cattle, while girls assist their mothers in practically all the female tasks. They join in transplanting rice seedlings from their earliest childhood.[34]

Mies' detailed account of the sexual division of labour emanates in an explanation as to why men's and not women's work is being displaced under the influence of the commercialization of agriculture, and why there are fewer male than female agricultural labourers. As

Table 10.1

Sexual Division of Labour in Kunur, Raigir and Sikandarnagar for Three Major Crops

Crop	*Operations*	*Work done by*		*Period*	*Crop*	*Work done by*		*Period*	*Crop*	*Work done by*		*Period*
		Women	*Men*			*Women*	*Men*			*Women*	*Men*	
Rice					*Jowar*				Tobacco (Virginia variety)			
	Field preparation											
	Field-cleaning	X	–	May		X	–	May		X	–	May
	Ploughing	–	X	March–April		–	X	March–April		X	X	March–April
	Harrowing	–	X	May		–	X	May		–	X	May
	Levelling	X	X	June–July		–	–	–		–	X	June–July
	Bunding	X	X	June–July		–	–	–		–	–	–
	Digging canals	X	X	June–July		–	–	–		X	X	June–July
	Putting manure	X	–	July		X	–	June–July		X	–	September–October
	Putting fertilizer	–	X	August		–	–	–		X	–	September–October
	Seed-bed preparation											
	Levelling	X	–	June–July		–	–	–		X	–	June–July
	Putting manure	X	–	June–July		–	–	–		X	–	June–July
	Sowing	X	–	June–July		X	–	June–July		–	X	June–July
	Weeding	X	–	July–August		–	–	–		X	–	August–October
	Watering	–	X	June–July		–	–	–		–	X	August–September
	Irrigation of fields	–	X	August–September		–	–	–		–	X	September–October

Transplanting	X	–	August–September	–	–	–	X	–	September–October
Weeding	X	–	September	–	–	–	X	–	October
Harvesting	X	X	October–November	X	–	October	X	–	January–February
Threshing	X	X	October–November	X	–	October	–	–	–
Transport	X	X	October–November	X	–	October	X	–	January–February
Processing of grain	X	–	November–December	X	–	October–November	–	–	–
	15	11		7	2		11	7	
Total no. of operations									53
Operations done by women									33
Operations done by men									20

Source: Mies (1986a), p. 65.

Note: The operations done by women total 34, rather than 33 as shown in the original, and work done by women in tobacco totals 12, rather than 11 as shown in the original.

the forementioned facts show, 'women's work involves hardly any tools or work instruments, whereas practically all men's work is performed with the help of agricultural implements and draught animals'. Women's work, Mies argues, is more easy to maintain, because 'their labour does not necessitate investment in any other means of production'.[35] To illustrate the displacement of men's work that occurs as the rural rich re-invest the profits they reap from market-oriented paddy cultivation, the author mentions the case of the introduction of motor pumps. Due to the mechanization of irrigation, many men, who formerly irrigated the fields with the aid of metal containers and bullocks, have lost their work.[36]

This explanation does not suffice to explain the predominance of female wage labour, since mechanization has also affected agricultural tasks which traditionally were the women's domain. I have noted here the displacement of female labour in rice-husking due to the introduction of rice-mills. Such mills, as Mies states, have also made their appearance in the Bhongir area of Andhra Pradesh. The other example she cites regarding the displacement of male labour is different from the displacement resulting from the mechanization of agricultural operations. The loss of opportunities for artisans like cobblers is due to the availability of cheap shoes in the urban market.[37] Thus, the reality of men's monopoly over implements and machinery appears to be of limited relevance in explaining the quantitative predominance of women among the day labourers in south Indian agriculture today.

Two other factors, then, need to be considered to understand the reasons for the wide prevalence of female agricultural labour, and both are of relevance for discussing the thesis of Mies and her colleagues on subsistence labour. Both these factors are also referred to by Maria Mies. One factor is on the demand side (i.e., it is a factor influencing the recruitment policies of the landlords). Following a worldwide patriarchal practice, everywhere in Indian agriculture there are substantial wage differentials between women and men. Government statistics confirm that the average daily earnings of women are much lower than those of men in all major agricultural operations, such as sowing, transplanting and harvesting.[38] This is also true of the villages of Andhra Pradesh studied by Mies. She mentions that men received Rs. 3 to Rs. 5 for all types of work, whereas women received only Rs. 1.50 to Rs. 2 as wages per day.[39]

Given such discrimination along gender lines, it is not surprising that landlords prefer female to male agricultural labourers.

The other factor is a supply-side factor, and it parallels the evolution in Bangladesh and other parts of Andhra Pradesh. In this book, I have referred to the pauperization taking place under the impact of 'modernization' of agriculture. Pauperization (i.e., impoverishment and the loss of hereditary possession over land)[40] forces people who were formerly 'self-employed cultivators' and artisans to seek employment as waged workers. Yet pauperization affects men and women differently. Whereas men may seek jobs outside agriculture, it is women who join the ranks of the rural proletariat. Thus, the literature on the dramatic increase in the number of female agricultural labourers appears to confirm that this development is related to the pauperization of the Indian peasantry.[41] Mies describes, in particular, the experience in the village of Kunur. Here, the former male artisans—such as blacksmiths, toddy-tappers and carpenters—have migrated to nearby towns, but the women of all the artisan families 'have joined the army of agricultural labourers who, during the agricultural seasons, competed with the Harijan women for employment.'[42]

Production of Use Values: Non-waged Subsistence Activities by Women

I will now initiate a discussion on 'subsistence labour' (i.e., the production of use values for immediate consumption). It is, of course, ironic that a study which elaborates a thesis regarding forms of labour which are non-waged, should in fact pose the primacy of waged work. Nevertheless, non-waged forms of work play a significant part in the life of the women in the Nalgonda villages studied by Mies. I will review these varied forms of work in the following. One typical instance of use value production is that of the cultivation and processing of millet or *jawar*. According to Mies, whereas women in Kunur buy their staple food (rice) from the market, peasant families in Sikandarnagar village depend on millet they themselves grow for their daily survival. One of the factors apparently responsible is the fact that in Sikandarnagar all the families still own some land and cattle (i.e., they are more or less independent smallholders).[43] And although their agriculture is cash crop-oriented, they keep some land for their subsistence crops, mainly millet. They thus are able to follow traditional food habits.

Mies' description focuses on the tasks that need to be performed after the *jawar* has been harvested. Many of these tasks are similar to those enumerated elsewhere for the processing of paddy. After the *jawar* ears have been taken home and dried, women beat them with simple sticks until most of the grain has come out; they winnow the millet with a hand winnowing fan; do the pounding in a big metal bowl, either together with their husbands or with another woman; and wash the millet three or four times, until all the husk and chaff come out. While a part of rice processing (i.e., pounding and grinding) has been mechanized in the area, the processing of millet in Sikandarnagar still is done without any labour-saving technique (i.e., manually).

The example of *jawar* further demonstrates Mies' point that in traditional agricultural societies there is no clear dividing line between 'production' and 'reproduction'. The cultivation of millet, its processing and preparation for consumption, are one continuum. The millet is eaten by the peasants as a thick porridge called *sankati*. Consequently, after the washing, most of the millet grains are pulverized into flour. This flour is mixed and cooked with half-broken, partly cooked millet, until it becomes one mass. According to Mies' calculations, millet processing and the preparing of *sankati* takes about five and a quarter hours and needs at least two persons, if not four. The process is repeated day after day, in one unending routine that consumes much of women's energies.

For Mies, this is one example of a 'pure subsistence-oriented production process',[44] and it does indeed demonstrate the persistence of production for immediate use within an environment of growing commercialization. Yet one wonders what will happen when capitalist agriculture spreads further. As Mies' account indicates, the production of *jawar* for peasants' family consumption is bound up with the fact that they possess their own plots of land. So far, their traditional style of living has not yet been disrupted, but for how long will they be able to preserve their old customs? Will their production not be ultimately affected by the process of class differentiation and pauperization which has accompanied the commercialization of agriculture in the area? In other words, the example of *jawar* does not conclusively prove that the production of use values will continue forever, and that in the future it will remain unaffected by the dominant process of the accumulation of capital.

The preparation of *sankati* was not a practice observed among agricultural labourers' families. Mies also describes a whole series of non-waged, 'subsistence' activities performed by outcaste (Harijan) women and by other women belonging to the class of day labourers. Some of these tasks are similar to, or close to, the domestic chores of housewives in industrial societies; others Mies identifies as 'remnants of the gathering stage of human development';[45] and some activities are characterized as forms of 'petty commodity production'.[46] In any case, these tasks absorbed a large part of a woman's working day in the slack season. During the peak season, they occupied all the time of a woman before and after her toil in the field.

The daily routine of Somira, a field agricultural labourer in the village of Kunur, illustrates how much work is involved in household tasks. While a number of categories, such as child care, cooking and cleaning, are familiar to women in Western societies, most categories imply a far heavier burden of work. Thus, to be able to cook, Somira regularly has to collect twigs and branches from thorny shrubs on fallow land. Somira also has to fetch water for the family's drinking purposes, for cooking, for washing and for her buffalo. Each time she goes to the well, she fills 14 big vessels with water and oarries them home.[47] As commercialization of agriculture proceeds, water scarcity increases and people lose control over common property resources, India's poor village women are forced to travel many more miles than they used to in the past, to collect water and fuel for their daily use.[48]

Another series of activities which 'do not fit into the modern categories of work', Mies ranges under the heading of 'gathering activities'. Apart from having to collect firewood, agricultural labourers and other village women also have to go out to stretches of barren land to gather grass to feed their buffaloes. In the summer, they go to the forest and collect leaves. These leaves, Mies reports, 'are dried and stitched together with a thin twig into a plate. The women sell these leaf-plates to a middleman who gives them Rs. 2–3 for 100 plates.'[49] In other words, although this activity is associated with the prehistoric foraging mode of production, it cannot properly be termed 'production of use values'. This is because some of the gathering activities, such as the collection of leaves and, to an extent, firewood and grass, are market-oriented (i.e., they are also production of exchange values).

The production work of women connected with the dairy scheme set up by the Andhra Pradesh government to distribute milk to urban centres is decisively market-oriented. Under this scheme, and due to the efforts of a local non-governmental organization, 10 members of the women's association in the village of Kunur have been given credit to purchase one hybrid buffalo each. To feed their buffaloes, these women have to cut grass twice a day around the fields and on fallow land, and prepare a feed-mix of water and rice husk. As is true for the other gathering activities mentioned, the collection of grass is difficult, since it is no longer available from the village commons and since landlords now claim all the grass available on and around their own land. 'If they want to avoid constant harassment by the land-owners, the women have to walk for miles to areas covered with shrubs and bushes which are unfit for cultivation.'[50]

The introduction of the dairy scheme, Mies notes, has meant an increased workload for the women agricultural labourers. Women are almost exclusively responsible for all the tasks related to the production of milk, including milking the buffaloes. If we follow Mies' analysis, it is highly doubtful whether the scheme has led to a genuine improvement in the living conditions of the women participants. One of the women, Abbamma, by tending to her buffalo, succeeds in earning, on an hourly basis, no more than about a third from what she receives as an agricultural labourer.[51] And although, as milk producers, the women are not paid a wage, their work cannot be considered production of use values for immediate consumption either: the buffalo milk is transported to urban centres to be sold as a market commodity. According to Mies, the money from the milk is often collected by husbands of the women producers.[52]

The foregoing enumeration of the activities listed by Mies as 'subsistence work' shows that the workload of female agricultural labourers is not by any means limited to their wage work. It is clear that, like the lacemakers of Narsapur, they have to perform many other activities in order to ensure their own and their families' survival. Yet the forementioned description also illustrates that a significant number of their tasks involve both the production of use values and exchange values. The participation of female agricultural labourers in the dairy scheme, in fact, is wholly market-oriented. In short, whereas Mies is right in putting the spotlight on the range of non-waged work of female *coolies*, the conceptualization of subsistence work provided by the German feminist school does not give a satisfactory framework for understanding the economic nature of this work.

The Two-tier Structure of Capitalism: Conceptual Contradictions in Mies

Mies' book contains a brief but significant discussion on the issue of bonded labourers and permanent farm servants. Such labourers are known as *jitagallu* in the region and, according to Mies'information, they are always men. *Jitagallus* are clearly distinguished from daily wage labourers or *rojukulis* (coolies). Whereas the latter are not bound to a particular master but are 'free' to sell their labour power to whomever they want to, bonded labourers and farm servants are tied to a particular master. Peasants are often forced to accept such bondage because they have fallen into debt and see no way of repayment, except by agreeing to a contract as a *jitagallu*. They are, Mies states, usually paid in kind.[53]

At first glance the issue of bonded labour does not appear to be relevant to the subject of subsistence labour by women. The divide which Mies marks when discussing bondage is one between two different kinds of exploitation, capitalist and 'feudal', structured more or less along gender lines. In all the villages the daily wage work is performed mainly by women, including and 'particularly' in the production of commercial crops, such as tobacco and chillies. On the other hand, non-waged labour for payment in kind is mainly performed by men. In any case, neither forms of labour can be termed independent production of peasants for their own, immediate subsistence. In both cases, the production of surplus value, appropriated by the landed classes, takes place.

Still, Mies' account is relevant for the debate on the conceptualization of a two-tier structure of capitalist accumulation. Thus, Mies notes the following apparent contradiction inherent in the persistence of forms of economic servitude:

> Contrary to the common belief that capitalist development would do away with these 'feudal' remnants, the progressive capitalist farmers in this area were, rather, strengthening this type of labour. By the introduction of modern farm technology, above all oil pumps and electric pumps, they were able to reduce the number of male *coolies* who had to be paid in cash.[54]

In other words, non-capitalist forms of exploitation are clearly preserved in spite of the expansion in the production of commodities for market sale.

This shows that the idea of a two-tier structure of capitalist accumulation, as perceived by members of the German feminist school, is relevant. Examples from Bangladesh could be added to substantiate this point. Thus, the introduction of power pumps for irrigation there has led to the creation of a class of 'waterlords', who use share-cropping arrangements when renting the pumps to peasant cultivators. Here, again, a non-waged form of exploitation has been strengthened along with the introduction of modern technology. Yet the example cited by Mies also brings out the fact that the 'secondary' layer of production relations does not just comprise people engaged in production for their own sustenance. It includes toilers producing a surplus, which is consumed or re-invested by those owning the major means of production, such as water and land.

The criticism of Mies' presentation can be further elaborated. The book *Indian Women in Subsistence and Agricultural Labour* is primarily concerned with the position of women wage labourers employed by landlords to do fieldwork. The villages studied were found to have reached different stages of commercialization. Yet women agricultural labourers were basically producing cash crops, such as rice and tobacco, and, as stated, they formed the bulk of the waged workers. This means that these women were engaged in producing exchange values (i.e., goods to be traded in the market). Thus, their economic role diverged from that of producers of use values (i.e., from subsistence producers as originally defined by the three authors of the German feminist school).

Still, there is no doubt that the wage labour of female agricultural labourers is essential for the survival of their families. As Rohini Nayyar has argued, with reference to the Indian Census data of 1981 on the high incidence of women agricultural labourers, women's participation rates are 'highly correlated to poverty and landlessness in rural India', and 'women belonging to poorer households work in order to supplement male earnings'.[55] Mies also relates women's waged work to their survival needs. She argues that in the case of the families of women agricultural labourers, 'the bulk of the income was undoubtedly from wages' (i.e., of the husband and wife), and that the women 'spend all their earnings on the immediate family consumption needs, their daily wages being used to buy the daily food'.[56] In other words, although waged work results in the production of agricultural commodities for exchange, and though it results in a surplus, such work is essential for the survival of village women and their kin.

This conceptual contradiction is also reflected in the definition of subsistence production which Mies uses. For, on the one hand, she states that 'subsistence production, as it is understood in this text, means the production of life in its widest sense, the production of *use values* for day-to-day sustenance as well as the production of new life'.[57] Yet, on the other hand, she includes producers of exchange value into her definition of subsistence labourers, for instance, when she argues that women's 'subsistence production does not only include wage work but also various kinds of non-wage work in the form of housework and other services, sometimes including sexual services'.[58] Mies' definition, in short, is not consistent.

The inconsistency in Mies' views can, paradoxically, be solved by returning, at least partly, to the conceptualization of Karl Marx. Marx's view was limited: he ignored the sexual division of labour and numerous productive tasks performed by women in pre-capitalist and capitalist societies. Yet he understood well that a certain proportion of the values produced—whether under slave owners, landed proprietors or commercial farmers—is paid to the labourers for their maintenance. The contradiction cited can only be fully solved by re-including this labour—which Marx also terms 'necessary labour'—into our definition of subsistence work. For what happens otherwise is that, after having tried to widen the scope of analysis, economic analysis is narrowed down in a new manner, and at the expense of toiling women.

The Nature of Subsistence Labour: Bennholdt-Thomsen and Marx

I shall now point out certain flaws in the thesis on 'subsistence labour' as presented by Veronika Bennholdt-Thomsen. Bennholdt-Thomsen's views on Rosa Luxemburg's theory have been briefly referred to in the foregoing. Here I will first address the distinction drawn by Bennholdt-Thomsen between extended reproduction (i.e., capital accumulation) and subsistence reproduction.[59] Is it correct, as Bennholdt-Thomsen states, to speak of a clear 'separation' taking place between these two spheres as the capitalist system expands? From her analysis of the two spheres, it follows that all subsistence reproduction (i.e., work related to pregnancy and child birth, the production/transformation of food and clothing, and other women's work) is carried out under non-capitalist production relations. But is this really true? Can the dividing line really be drawn the way Bennholdt-Thomsen does?

Let us once again return to Marx and use his explanation of capitalist exploitation as the starting point for our discussion. In a crucial section of *Capital*, where Marx explains his theory of the working day, he first reminds his readers that capital has not invented surplus labour:

> Wherever a part of society possesses the monopoly of the means of production, the labourer, free or not free, must add to the working time necessary for his own maintenance an extra working time in order to produce the means of subsistence for the owners of the means of production.[60]

No matter whether the proprietor is a slave owner, feudal lord, modern landlord or capitalist entrepreneur, the labourers' productive activities fall into two parts, one of which is surplus production accruing to the owner of the means of production.

Marx goes on to explain the exact difference between exploitation under capitalism and exploitation as it occurred under preceding modes of production. He discusses in detail the exploitation which peasants were subjected to in the Danubian Principalities, territories which, by the time Marx wrote, had been incorporated in the Romanian state. Under the legal regulations proclaimed in 1831, the Danubian peasants had to perform 56 working days a year as *corvee*, consisting of fieldwork, carrying wood and other forced labour services for their landlords. Marx calculates the relation of this surplus labour to necessary or subsistence labour (which according to him amounted to 84 days) to be 66.67 per cent. However, in practice the number of days which peasants toiled for the landlords was far greater, since the legal stipulations had been drawn in such a way as to facilitate their evasion.

Now, the key point which Marx makes is that under feudalism surplus and necessary labour time were clearly demarcated from each other. 'The necessary labour which the Wallachian [i.e., Danubian] peasant does for his own maintenance', Marx literally states, 'is distinctly marked off from his surplus labour on behalf of the *Boyard* [i.e., landlord]'. There could be no confusion about the distinction between the two forms of labour, for 'the one part he does on his own field, the other on the seigniorial estate. Both parts of the labour time exist, therefore, independently, side by side one with the other.' In other words, 'in the *corvee* [system] the surplus labour is accurately marked off from the necessary labour'.[61] Thus, in Marx's view, it was under the mode of production which preceded capitalism that necessary labour, which term for him is equivalent with subsistence labour, formed a separate sphere of activity.

All this changes with the capitalist mode of production, and Marx raises the example of the working day of the industrial workers in English factories to illustrate his point. Marx's theory of the working day has been reviewed repeatedly in this book, and I need not repeat his views in detail. The working day consists of both necessary and surplus labour, which could amount to six hours each. What is important for the discussion here, however, is how Marx explains the difference between exploitation under the capitalist and pre-capitalist modes of production. Whereas the latter is easily identifiable because it is demarcated in space and time, the same is not true for exploitation under capitalist ownership. How much the industrial labourer exactly toils for the entrepreneur is not evident on the surface, since 'surplus labour and necessary labour glide one into the other'.[62] Under capitalism, necessary or subsistence production does not constitute a separate or distinct sphere.

Let us now compare Marx's views with those of the German feminist Bennholdt-Thomsen. Bennholdt-Thomsen presumes the 'basic contradiction' within the capitalist mode of production to be 'the separation of subsistence production from social production'. This thesis, as will now be clear, does not just form a correction of what Bennholdt-Thomsen calls 'male chauvinist Marxism': it is not just an extension of the labour theory of value developed by Marx, but stands diametrically opposed to his. The two theoreticians, Marx and Bennholdt-Thomsen, propose qualitatively different theses regarding the character of subsistence labour under capitalism. Whose thesis then should be supported, and whose views most closely approximate the contradictory reality of the present world economic system?

First, there can be no question of going back and supporting Marx's theory without qualifications. Bennholdt-Thomsen has developed a critique of the patriarchal bias underlying the labour theory of value in a specific direction, but that critique stands. To repeat once again what participants in the debate of the second feminist wave have stated so eloquently: Marx ignored domestic labour, he did not explain that the reproduction of labour power involves labour, and that this unpaid labour is necessary labour, performed by women in the home. The full extent of exploitation under capitalism can only be understood if economic theory takes full stock of child-bearing and child-rearing, and of the other reproductive activities women universally perform. 'Subsistence reproduction', as Bennholdt-Thomsen rightly insists, must be given a place at the heart of a theory of the capitalist system. Without it, the political economy cannot possibly be comprehensive, and fails to lead to the full emancipation of humankind.

Yet my re-reading of Marx's explanation regarding the distinction between capitalist and pre-capitalist exploitation also clarifies how Bennholdt-Thomsen's views have their own specific bias. Her thesis is that subsistence production and reproduction are subsumed under capitalism, yet remain non-capitalist in form. The implication is that all production which obtains the wage form should not be defined as subsistence or necessary labour. Thus, Bennholdt-Thomsen does not just supplement and correct Marx's labour theory of value; her thesis in fact poses a challenge to Marx's basic theory. By defining subsistence production under capitalism as a distinct sphere, instead of a sphere which 'glides over' into surplus production, Bennholdt-Thomsen's thesis in turn makes part of subsistence production invisible. By replacing Marx's thesis regarding the 'non-separation', the merging of two spheres, with her own thesis on the 'separation' of extended production and subsistence reproduction, Bennholdt-Thomsen eliminates Marx's path-breaking discovery.

My view, then, is different from Bennholdt-Thomsen's. A comprehensive view of labour relations under the present world capitalist system is achieved not by formulating an antithesis to Marx's labour theory of value, but through a synthesis between his view on the 'non-separation' of necessary and surplus production and Bennholdt Thomsen's view on the 'separation' of the two spheres. In reality, I propose, subsistence production and reproduction form a continuum, with one part (as wage labour) being performed directly under capitalist ownership, and the other being taken for granted and performed under family relations in and around the home (non-waged labour). Both are made invisible by bourgeois economic theory, and both are essential for the survival of the capitalist mode of production. Moreover, women are subjected to both.

The Worldwide Process of Encroachment on Common Property Resources

A further objection to the thesis of the German feminist school on subsistence labour follows from what I stated earlier about the appropriation of common property resources in the chapters on developmental feminism and ecofeminism. For women to be able to continue the production of use values for immediate consumption, they require non-capitalist surroundings (i.e., access to resources outside the market system). One of the bases to continue subsistence labour, in the sense in which the members of the German feminist school use this term, is the existence of common property resources. As long as these are not turned into private resources, forests, fallow lands and wetlands can be used by local communities for immediate sustenance. The direct access to plants, trees, fowl and fish greatly facilitates women's production of food for family use.

Historically speaking, the amount of resources which people held in common was vast all over the world. Shiva quotes an Indian author, Chattrapati Singh, who has given the following assessment of the importance of common property in India's past:

> It is evident that till the end of the last century, and in all historical periods before that, at least 80 per cent of India's natural resources were common property, with only 20 per cent being privately utilized . . . . This extensive common property has provided the resource base for a non-cash, non-market economy. A whole range of resources has been freely available to the people.[63]

Singh mentions amongst others the availability of wood, shrubs and cow dung for cooking and heating, and of wild grass and shrubs as animal fodder. Instead of having to procure such material through purchase on the market, they could, throughout the ages, be appropriated by peasants for subsistence use.

The appropriation of common property by the dominant classes has historically occurred in a variety of ways, and the process started well before the advent of industrial capitalism. The ecofeminist author, Carolyn Merchant, as mentioned earlier, has shown how in Europe feudal landlords in the transitional period from the Middle Ages to commercial capitalism laid claim to people's common property through taxation and the use of violence. Conflicts over common property were a key element in the class struggles during this epoch. Karl Marx, in his description of the exploitation of peasants in the Romanian provinces, has raised the same point. According to him, the original mode of production here was based on community of the soil. Land was partly cultivated as freehold, and partly by peasants jointly. 'In the course of time military and clerical dignitaries usurped, along with the common land, the labour spent upon it. The labour of the free peasants on their common land was transformed into *corvee* for the thieves of the common land.'[64]

In India, the British colonial administration played a key role in the transfer of right over common property to both the Indian landlord class and commercial traders. Through the Permanent Settlement proclaimed in 1793, it vested ownership rights over land in a class of feudal landlords, the zamindars, who had earlier been responsible for the collection of taxes.[65] As mentioned earlier, with regard to the appropriation of forest resources, it was the British administration which was instrumental in undermining the rights of the local communities, through the introduction of 'scientific forestry' and the enactment of legislation on the management and use of the Indian forests. As in the case of the enclosure of the English commons, the state helped in accelerating the process of the dispossession of the peasantry and the transfer of community resources to commercial interests.

What needs to be stressed in the context of the thesis on subsistence labour of the German feminist school is not only that this process of encroachment on common property rights is continuing full-scale, but also that today it is being backed by international institutions representing the interests of multinational companies and the industrial states of the North. I have already mentioned the example of the World Bank-coordinated Flood Action Plan which aims at building embankments and polders along Bangladesh's main rivers, and the World Bank-sponsored wasteland development projects in India. In order to underline the fact that the most powerful economic institutions at the world level are central participants in this process of the encroachment of common property, I shall add another example, namely the appropriation of peasants' rights over seeds through regulations under GATT (General Agreement on Tariffs and Trade).

Once again, it is Shiva who has stated the case in very clear terms. As she has argued, for 10,000 years farmers and peasants had produced their own seeds, on their own land, selecting the best seeds, storing them, replanting them, and 'letting nature take its course in the renewal and enrichment of life'.[66] For instance, Indian peasants never needed to procure paddy seeds from the market. The traditional production of seeds thus is an example of the production of use values for peasants' immediate sustenance and, as mentioned in the previous chapter, in the past it was mainly a women's domain. The Green Revolution formed an outright attack on this use value production. For peasants were no longer to be the custodians of the common genetic heritage—they were to be displaced as 'custodians of the planet's genetic wealth', to enhance the profits of transnational corporations and 'First World control over the genetic resources of the Third World'.[67]

The issue of the rights of Third World peasants over seeds has come up in the trade negotiations called the Uruguay Round under GATT, which were concluded in December 1993. Under a regime entitled TRIP (Trade Related Intellectual Property), the patenting of parts of animals and plants is allowed, and Third World governments are being forced to adapt their laws in order to protect the rights over animal and plant life established through genetic manipulation by companies of the industrial North. As Shiva and Holla-Bhar have commented, the text of TRIP will 'send every country down the slippery slope of patenting life forms'.[68] Indian peasants have protested massively against the provisions of GATT, since they consider them an encroachment on their traditional rights, 'an expropriation of their immediate surroundings and an attack on their way of life'.[69] Like the World Bank, GATT too is a party to the undermining of the subsistence base of peasant women and men in the Third World.

What significance does this recapitulation of the worldwide encroachment on common property have for our evaluation regarding the thesis of the German feminist school? People's joint control over resources, like land, water and forests, and their access to a common heritage like agricultural seeds, enables them to engage in subsistence labour as defined by Mies, von Werlhof and Bennholdt-Thomsen. As long as such resources are not turned over to wealthy classes interested in production for the market, they can be employed for the production of use values. Given the overwhelming importance of common property in human history, the fate of these resources cannot be left out in a discussion regarding the 'subordination of subsistence reproduction under capitalism'. In fact, it is one way of testing the validity of the thesis on subsistence production and reproduction.

In discussing the relation between 'extended reproduction' and 'subsistence reproduction', Bennholdt-Thomsen argues, in opposition to Rosa Luxemburg, that production for subsistence or 'small peasant production' is reinforced or even re-introduced 'by bourgeois agrarian reforms and eventually sponsored by the World Bank itself'.[70] Rosa Luxemburg had argued that capitalism for its own survival needs non-capitalist surroundings but destroys the basis for its own reproduction through its process of worldwide expansion. Bennholdt-Thomsen agrees that capitalism needs a second sphere of subsistence production, of non-capitalist relations, but believes that this sphere is reproduced by capitalism itself. She concludes that 'capital itself reproduces its own "non-capitalist" surroundings, in the imperialist as well as in the dependent countries'.[71]

This conclusion is based on the consideration, primarily, of the fact that wage labour has not been generalized in the contemporary world economic system. Bennholdt-Thomsen refers to the 'increasing consolidation of an industrial reserve army', to the existence of a marginal mass of people, both in countries of the Third World and in the industrial North, which is 'in charge of its own reproduction'.[72] In any case, her basic presumption is that capitalism leaves scope for the production of use values, that people who are not absorbed as wage labourers can survive by independently producing their own means of sustenance. Her presumption is that capitalism helps to maintain a sphere which is not commoditized, a sphere beyond commodity production which is not touched by capitalist institutions. Hence, she proposes 'a new reproduction scheme where extended reproduction as well as subsistence reproduction are included'.[73]

Bennholdt-Thomsen's two-tier structure can be questioned on the basis of the evidence presented in the foregoing on the encroachment of common property resources. As the World Bank promotes schemes to turn water into a resource controlled by private, elite interest, as the scope for the natural production of fish is slowly but steadily narrowed, and as people are deprived of their free access to forestry resources, the basis for use value production shrinks simultaneously with the expansion of the sphere of commodity production. In other words, Bennholdt-Thomsen admits that the 'society of commodities has imposed itself universally'.[74] Yet it is difficult to account for the expropriation of the commons within the scheme which she proposes. For the continual attack by the World Bank, GATT and other international institutions on the sphere of common property in Third World countries, in practice, limits the sphere of use value production.

Marx's analysis of the capitalist system had started from his observations on generalized commodity production, which, as he saw it, had been established in 19th-century England.[75] One of the ways—and a crucial one, in view of World Bank and GATT policies—in which the area of commodity production is incessantly expanded, is through the expropriation of people's common property. As examples cited here and elsewhere illustrate, this process of encroachment stretches over many centuries, from the European Middle Ages to today's realities in the Third World. It is my view that the thesis of the German feminist school needs to be questioned on the basis of the evidence regarding the destruction of common property resources. For the given process severely limits the scope for use value production in the interest of 'extended reproduction', the dominant mode of operation of world capitalism.

Subsistence Production and the Creation of Commodities

Finally, I wish to return to the definition of subsistence production and reproduction of the German feminist school cited here. To reiterate, it signifies 'the production of life and of living–working capacity'. Defined thus, subsistence labour consists of a variety of activities, which, in agreement with what has been stated earlier, can broadly be divided into the following three categories of work women perform under capitalism: (*a*) that of procreation, that is, child-bearing, the process of giving birth to new life; (*b*) reproductive work, that is, all those activities needed to restore the capacity of human beings to participate in social production; and (*c*) necessary labour performed in waged employment, which is also needed for working class families to be able to survive.

The question that arises now is whether or to what extent any of these productive activities involve, exclusively, the creation of use values, as the narrow definition of subsistence labour by the German feminist school prescribes. First, it need not be disputed that even under contemporary capitalist relations in countries of the North, the production of use values continues to be required. Thus, cooking (that is, the preparation of staples, vegetables and meat or fish for consumption by family members) continues to involve the creation of use values, at least, the transformation of commodities bought in the supermarket into warm meals. Yet, what is more remarkable is that, now, each of the categories of subsistence work also comprises the production of commodities. More material that serves to dispute the equation of subsistence labour with the production of use values follows.

For clarity, I will illustrate my point for each category separately. The 'necessary labour', which women and men perform as wage labourers, results both in a payment from which they can procure their daily necessities on the market, and in the creation of a variety of commodities for market sale. Whatever the nature of these industrial goods, whether they are articles for consumption (like soaps, medicines or automobiles) or means of production (such as threshing machines and printing presses), they need to be 'realized' through purchase by capitalist owners or other members of society. Thus, this labour aimed at securing the survival of wage employees emanates not just in use values, but in exchange values. The equation as proposed by the German feminist school does not hold.

The second category of subsistence work termed 'reproductive labour' (i.e., the work to restore the physical energy of male and female employees) also results in the production of commodities. This has been pointed out by Dalla Costa, a participant in the debate on household work.[76] This is the commodity 'labour power', which is also offered for sale. As Marx has stressed, labour power is a very special commodity, but it is a commodity nevertheless. Like other commodities, it carries a price tag (the wage), signifying the exchange value of human, manual and mental energy that can be bought by the owners of capital. Here, again, we see that subsistence reproduction cannot be equated with the production of use values, for by doing so we would negate a part of what happens in real life, under the system of capitalist relations.

The category of procreation has, for a long time, been the one area where capitalist intervention appeared to be most limited. Yet, with the rapid growth in reproductive technologies, this production of life is also being subjected to the rules of commodity production. This has been well explained by Mies.[77] She discusses the implications of the standpoint formulated by an American feminist, Lori Andrews, about contract law on surrogate motherhood. In the case of surrogate motherhood, a woman's reproductive organs are used to breed a child who, after birth, is turned over to the couple that had engaged the woman. The surrogate mother's womb is used in exchange for a considerable sum of money.[78] In other words, the surrogate mother sells her capacity to give birth.

Mies does not discuss the consequences of what she says for the conceptualization of the German feminist school on 'subsistence labour', yet the consequences exist. For she states that Lori Andrew's view on the legalities of surrogate motherhood means that women engaged as breeders 'have to be forced into accepting that what they produce is a *commodity*, not something of their own and that they are doing alienated labour'.[79] Mies believes that feminist concepts like reproductive autonomy 'are used now to open up women's procreative power and bodies for total commercialization in the hands of profit- and fame-seeking industries and "technodocs".'[80] In short, with the spread of new reproductive technologies, women's work in birth-giving, too, is transformed, from an integrated and natural activity into the production of commodities. A sphere of productive work which had for long evaded the rules of the market, with the social acceptance of new reproductive technologies, is gradually being incorporated into the market sphere. Even this third form of subsistence reproduction is gradually being commoditized.

Summing Up

In formulating their thesis on women's labour as subsistence labour, Mies, Bennholdt-Thomsen and von Werlhof have drawn inspiration from Rosa Luxemburg, who questioned Marx's scheme on extended reproduction. Like her, the three contemporary feminists believe that the process of capitalist accumulation cannot be understood by looking merely at the relation existing between the owners of capital and those who sell their labour power, the wage workers. In the eyes of the members of the German feminist school, the non-waged form of exploitation on which capitalism thrives can be identified as 'subsistence labour', and this work is primarily performed by women engaged in the production of use values, both in the industrialized world and in the Third World.

In this chapter I have raised questions regarding the validity of the thesis on subsistence labour. For instance, I believe it is difficult to accommodate the destruction of common property over natural resources within the framework of this thesis. Ever since the birth of capitalism, propertied classes and states representing their interests have sought to undermine people's ownership over land, water and forest resources. Today, powerful institutions at the world level, like the World Bank play an active role in the drive to turn such natural resources into sources of private accumulation, and they do so at the behest of multinationals and well-to-do classes in the Third World. This privatization of common property severely limits the scope for production of use values. Rather, the effect is incorporation of these common resources into the process of extended reproduction, at the expense of non-capitalist relations of production.

On the other hand, is it correct to equate subsistence labour with the production of use values, as all three members of the German feminist school tend to do? My impression is that this equation has not led to theoretical clarity, but has given rise to considerable confusion. Ever since the dawn of class societies, a part of subsistence labour, of production for survival, has been carried out under the direct control of, first slave owners, subsequently feudal landlords, and now multinational enterprises. Today, a part of the reproduction of people's immediate life occurs under the sway of capitalist farmers and industrialists worldwide (i.e., via the wage system). As the examples from India and Bangladesh highlighted in this book indicate, many millions of women have been absorbed into this system, both in agriculture and industries. A conceptualization which equates women's labour with the production of use values faces the difficulty that a part of the economic exploitation of women is, ultimately, made invisible.

Nonetheless, I do consider the ideas elaborated by Mies, Bennholdt-Thomsen and von Werlhof as an important stage in the development of a feminist conception regarding labour under capitalism. Theirs forms a decided departure, a farewell to orthodox Marxism. During the 1970s, many discussions in the women's movement in the West revolved around questions such as whether household labour is 'productive', and whether it contributes to 'value creation'. The members of the German school have continued the line of thinking of those participants in the movement who insisted that housewives do produce value, and they have justly tried to broaden the debate to include the labour of (peasant) women in the Third World. A more profound conceptualization of labour and exploitation than that elaborated by Marx—as Mies, Bennholdt-Thomsen and von Werlhof have argued—can only be reached if the various contemporary production relations, which do not have the wage form, are taken stock of by economists.

Notes and References

1. Mies (1986a), p. 5. For Mies' discussion regarding the 'production of life', see also Mies, Bennholdt-Thomsen and von Werlhof (1988), p. 27.
2. See Mies (1988), p. 49, n. 30.
3. See Mies (1988), pp. 1–10.
4. See von Werlhof (1988), p. 16.
5. See Mies (1988), pp. 27–28.
6. Ibid.
7. In her more recent writings, Mies has drawn attention to the consequences of the new reproductive technologies for women. See Mies and Shiva (1993), pp. 174, 277.
8. For definitions cited by Mies' colleagues, see von Werlhof in Mies, Bennholdt-Thomsen and von Werlhof (1988), pp. 9, 151–61. For Bennholdt-Thomsen's definition, see her article (1981), pp. 16–29.
9. Quoted in Nettle (1969), p. 165.
10. Marx (1967), p. 399.
11. Luxemburg (1981a), p. 107.
12. Ibid., pp. 296–97.
13. Ibid., p. 300.
14. Ibid., p. 301.
15. Ibid., p. 315.
16. Ibid., p. 411. For a Marxist critique of Rosa Luxemburg's realization theory, see Sweezy (1972), p. 239.
17. Mies (1986b), p. 36.
18. See Bennholdt-Thomsen (1981), p. 23: 'Rosa Luxemburg, in her reformulation of Marx's reproduction schemes, focused precisely on this point—the total neglect of subsistence production in Marx's theory of extended reproduction.'
19. See Bennholdt-Thomsen (1981), p. 24.
20. Mies (1986b), p. 34.
21. Mies (1986a), p. 29.
22. Ibid., p. 55.
23. Ibid.
24. Ibid., p. 57.
25. Nayyar (1987), p. 2212.
26. Jose (1989). Jose gives somewhat different figures from Nayyar, but the trend indicated is similar: 'the ratio of female agricultural labourers to cultivators was 0.42 in 1961 and by 1981 it had increased to 1.19' (ibid.), p. 74. See also Chhachhi (1989), p. 571: 'There has been a dramatic increase in the number of agricultural

workers, within which section the number of women is higher and increasing faster than the number of men'.

27. Mies (1986a), p. 57.
28. Ibid., p. 52.
29. Mies (1986a), p. 88.
30. Ibid., p. 87.
31. Ibid., p. 91.
32. Ibid., p. 62.
33. Ibid., p. 61.
34. Mies (1986a), p. 67.
35. Ibid., p. 64.
36. Ibid., p. 66. See also p. 114, where a participant in the group discussion in Kunur is quoted: 'Earlier our men used to go to pull water from the wells to irrigate the fields and to make the small irrigation canals in the fields. Now they [the Doras, or the landlords] have motors.' According to Mies (ibid.), p. 117, in the village of Raigur, male labour to some extent had also been replaced by motor pumps.
37. Ibid., p. 66.
38. See Nayyar (1987), p. 2213, chart from the Ministry of Labour.
39. Mies (1986a), p. 84.
40. Maria Mies uses the same definition of pauperization. See Mies (1986a), p. 113.
41. See, for instance, Jose (1989), p. 77. According to Nayyar (1987), p. 2214, 'female participation rates are highly correlated to poverty and landlessness in rural India'.
42. Mies (1986a), p. 116.
43. Ibid., p. 73.
44. Ibid., p. 74.
45. Ibid., p. 76.
46. Ibid., p. 79.
47. Ibid., pp. 71–72.
48. See, for instance, Kishwar and Vanita (1984), p. 3: 'Over the years the task of fuel and fodder collection has become more and more onerous for women, as the government has appropriated the entire forest wealth of the country.'
49. Mies (1986a), p. 77.
50. Ibid., p. 81.
51. Ibid., p. 122.
52. Ibid., p. 120.
53. Ibid., p. 59. Compare Mies' analysis with Breman's discussion (1985), p. 263, of farm servants in Gujarat.
54. Mies (1986a).
55. See Nayyar (1987), pp. 2212–13.
56. Mies (1986a), pp. 98, 109.
57. Ibid., p. 5, emphasis added.
58. Ibid., p. 6.
59. Bennholdt-Thomsen (1981).
60. Marx (1977a), pp. 226–27.
61. Ibid., p. 227. See also Lenin (1977a), pp. 191–92.
62. Lenin (1977a); Marx (1977a).
63. Shiva (1988), p. 83.
64. Marx (1977a), p. 228.

65. Sen (1979), p. 1. See Umar (1978), p. 20 for a description of the village community system which existed in India prior to the British conquest. See also Mukherjee (1974), p. 140; Ray (1990), p. 161.
66. Shiva (1991a), p. 63.
67. Ibid.
68. Shiva and Holla-Bhar (1993), p. 227.
69. Ibid.
70. See Bennholdt-Thomsen (1981), p. 25.
71. Ibid., p. 24.
72. Ibid., pp. 26–27.
73. Ibid., p. 28.
74. Ibid., p. 24.
75. For Marx's discussion on generalized commodity production, see in particular Marx (1977a), Part I, p. 43.
76. For the analytical distinction between social reproduction, the reproduction of labour power and biological reproduction, see Barrett's discussion (1980), p. 21, of the contribution made by Edholm, Harris and Young.
77. Mies and Shiva (1993), p. 198.
78. See also Corea (1988), p. 250.
79. Mies and Shiva (1993), p. 205, emphasis added.
80. Ibid.

PART 4

Japanization and Women's Labour

11

The Japanese Style of Management and Fordism Compared

Is Fordism 'a new mechanism of accumulation and distribution of finance capital, based directly on industrial production'? Does Americanism constitute a distinct phase, a new epoch, in the history of capitalist production? These questions were posed by the Italian revolutionary thinker, Antonio Gramsci, in his well-known *Prison Notebooks*, drafted while in prolonged detention under fascism. At that time, new American production methods—the workers enchained to the assembly line, and the stop-watch as a means to closely regulate their movements—were rapidly gaining prominence. Outside the prison walls, these methods formed the object of fierce debate between academicians belonging to various currents of thought. Ultra rightist Italian intellectuals, for instance, discussed how Fordism could be adapted to Italian conditions; they propagated a marriage between American-style organized mass production and the corporatist state.

Gramsci's views, formulated in the desolation of his prison cell, are an eloquent testimony to his sharpness of mind. They do not merely prove that he was a keen observer of social trends in his own days. Some of his views retain their value even today, 60 years later, and help explain why Fordist methods are now being superseded. Gramsci, for instance, dwelled on the dilemma which the introduction of the conveyor belt posed for entrepreneurs. The capitalist, so he argued, can mechanize the physical movements of the labourer, but this does not prevent the latter from using his brains. 'One walks automatically, and at the same time thinks about whatever one chooses.'[1] American industrialists, according to Gramsci, were conscious of this 'dialectic' underlying the mechanized mode of production and its possible consequences. Notwithstanding the spread of Fordism, assembly line workers in the United States and Western Europe have continued resisting the despotism of the factory system. Consequently, multinationals have continued searching for ways to obtain maximum control over the factory workers' thinking processes.

Roughly 80 years have passed since the American company owner, Ford, introduced the conveyor belt system and concomitant management techniques (derived from Taylor) in his automobile factories. These methods enabled Ford and other American enterprises to temporarily gain hegemony within the world economy. Today, a new production model has risen to prominence, which stipulates 'quality circles' and 'subcontracting' as its key concepts. This model is closely identified with one Japanese corporation, Toyota like Ford a giant company belonging to the automobile sector. Throughout the industrialized North, as well as in Third World countries like India,[2] multinationals, and even smaller, local companies, are frantically studying the Japanese model. They feel compelled to re-adapt the organizational structure of their companies in the worldwide rush for super profits.[3]

Analogous to Gramsci's initial conceptualization of the previous phase of world capitalism, Japanization can be understood as a new phase in the history of capitalism, as the present phase is distinct from the period when the views of Ford and Taylor held sway. Further, the emergence of specifically Japanese management techniques invites a re-examination of the fundamental critique of the capitalist system. Today's developments should encourage us to critically re-assess the relevance of the views put forward by capitalism's most powerful critic, Karl Marx. In order to grasp the reasons for the international trend towards Japanization, we need to adopt a creative Marxist approach.

Features of Toyotism: Internal and External Decentralization

To start, I shall briefly highlight an important aspect in the history of Japanese industrialization: the more or less direct transition from commercial subcontracting to vertically organized, industrial subcontracting, as was imposed by fascism. In the middle of the 19th century

Japanese society, as is well-known, was still largely characterized by feudal relations. There existed a rising commercial bourgeoisie which was composed of intermediaries, called *tonyas*, who increasingly operated as entrepreneurs, since they had started regulating the production of craftsmen. The *tonyas* distributed raw materials, and sometimes equipment, to self-employed craftsmen and homeworkers, and they brought the final products to the market. Under these conditions of infant capitalism, the Meiji Restoration was launched from the year 1868 onwards. The process of the modernization of society was facilitated by the fact that it was favoured by members of the traditional elite of *samurai* warriors. Delegations were sent to Europe and the US 'to learn from foreign countries'. Machinery and expertise were imported to prepare the founding of the first silk-spinneries and textile factories. Thus, from the later part of the 19th century onwards, the factory system of production rapidly superseded craft production dominated by the *tonyas*.[4]

Yet it would be wrong to believe that the Meiji Restoration ended the role of home-based industries and traditional intermediaries. They were only partly supplanted by the factory system. Many small producers adapted to the new conditions, by installing electrical motors in their own workshops—mechanization reached the drawing room of the craftsmen—and by taking to the manufacturing of modern goods, like bulbs, rubber products and Western umbrellas. In the footsteps of the *samurai*, the *tonyas* too transformed themselves. Instead of continuing to function as the link between craftsmen and the market, they now became suppliers of half-finished goods. They henceforth chose to fulfil the task of subcontracting for industrial enterprises, to act as intermediaries between homeworkers and the factory. It is only when the fascist regime enforced 'rationalization' of production during the 1930s, that their role came under serious threat. Those *tonyas* who failed to provide technological guidance to the small producers were eliminated, under the joint pressure of the fascist government and monopoly companies.

During the period from 1935 to 1945, the system of subcontracting was built which, more recently, has enhanced Japan's reputation amongst entrepreneurs worldwide. Partly as a consequence of the brutal wars fought, the country suffered from a severe lack of raw materials. The government introduced a system of rationing industrial raw materials and imposed price regulation on intermediaries. Most far-reaching was the government's attempt to unify the subcontractors of major companies, via horizontal cooperation. When the desired result was not obtained, corporate enterprises themselves streamlined the structure of subcontracting. They selected the most efficient clients and brought them under corporate control. Small supplier firms were patronized through instructors, and by providing them with instruments to improve product quality. Moreover, a mutual division of labour was promoted between the subcontractors. Thus arose the typically Japanese pyramid-shaped structure of production.

The period after the Second World War merely brought a further refining in the methods of control over subcontractors. Thus, the transfer of knowledge regarding financial accounting and management techniques were added to the range of regulatory mechanisms. In recent decades, the proportion of production which is subcontracted has greatly expanded. This is true in particular of the automobile sector, where the share of production that is subcontracted amounts to at least 70 per cent. In short, and contrary to Marx's expectations, the factory system of production has not completely replaced the network of small producers, but rather has subordinated them, and adapted this network to the needs of corporate capital.

Before discussing the effects of this elaborate system of subcontracting on labour, I shall comment on the second central aspect of Japanese-style company management: 'labour groups' or 'quality control circles'. Again, a historical review is helpful, for Japanese companies have employed labour groups for the purpose of enhancing productivity for many decades. Examples can be traced in reports regarding working conditions in the spinneries and weaving mills, where women, a century ago, worked to lay the foundations of Japan's industrialization. Thus, groups of female labourers, employed in textile companies and organized by their district background, in the beginning of the 20th century engaged in sports competitions initiated by the management. The same groups were encouraged to undertake production competition by offering them little prizes in reward. As early as the late 19th century, then, entrepreneurs tried to devise clever means to influence the thought processes of the overwhelmingly female workforce.

Today, the system of labour groups, now termed 'quality circles', has become a common phenomenon in almost all Japanese factories. They are to be found in the large enterprises of key industrial sectors, such as automobiles and electronics, but also in the smaller subcontracted firms. During my visit to Japan in 1990, a woman employed in a company producing temperature regulators for Toyota trucks, described how the women workers during off-time are forced to jointly ponder over possibilities for raising productivity. For individual women there is simply no escape: the company manager does not just own the wage workers' labour time, but a part of their 'free time' as well. And when visiting the multinational chips producer Fujitsu Electronics, managers in blue uniforms self-confidently stated that the factory's labour groups provide a guarantee for production without an undue number of errors. Due to the quality circles, the workers are perfectly disciplined. In other words, the ideal of the 'trained gorilla', which American corporations earlier tried to approximate through the use of the stopwatch, has to a frightening extent been realized in contemporary Japan.

In Western countries, the discussion about labour groups is not completely new either, as is evident from the postscript to Benjamin Coriat's book on the history and significance of Fordism. In many enterprises, such groups were introduced in the late 1970s and early 1980s, in the name of 'the humanization of labour'. The significance of the system is as follows:

> Place him, or the migrant worker or the female labourer, in a team or 'collective' which itself decides on speed and working rhythm. 'Time-and-motion' experts, with their stopwatches in their pockets, are no longer required, nor are foremen who watch you, the worker, from behind. You yourself can decide how you want to work and how fast.[5]

In other words, the formation of labour groups eliminates the need for detailed supervision. Contrary to the Fordist/Taylorist approach, the individual is no longer the basis of the labour process; it is the group that is considered its foundation. Moreover, 'since the income of the team, i.e., of all its individual members, is dependent on the productivity of each separate member, there is little chance that the group will show benevolence towards a "lazy" worker'. The structure of the quality circles, in other words, ensures strict self-discipline on the part of the exploited workers.

The new method which Japanese companies are teaching to their competitors, however, consists of more than the forementioned trend towards what can schematically be termed 'internal decentralization'. At issue is a phenomenon on the borderline between internal and external decentralization: various powers are transferred to smaller production units within the factory complex. Such units tend to be granted a close-to-independent status. Responsibilities are delegated and flexibility is promoted, while profits continue to flow towards the corporation itself. The extent of influence the model has gathered internationally can be illustrated by citing the example of the Dutch steel foundry Hoogovens. The territorial size of this foundry's complex—its production structure until recently was an integrated one—is equal to a whole town. According to the masterplan formulated by the Hoogovens management some years ago, the factory complex is to be restructured along the model of the Japanese company Nippon Steel, which means the granting of far-reaching autonomy for the various sections/departments, and the devolution of tasks even with regard to the marketing and sale of steel products.

The key question remains, of course, whether such decentralization really leads to 'the humanization' of labour relations. According to a trade union researcher interviewed in 1990 about the consequences of the trend described, the splitting up of production into smaller units, aspired to by many Dutch companies, leads to the side-tracking of trade unions. Relations between the management and unions become increasingly nebulous, as union officials are in doubt at what level negotiations about labour conditions should take place, which trade union a specific group of workers should join, and so on. In short, the major danger is decreasing solidarity between the workers, and the further weakening of their collective power.

Like internal decentralization, external centralization also affects the workers negatively. The corporation's relations with small supplier firms today are primarily regulated through the principle of *kanban*, which means the delivery of components or product parts just-in-time. This principle, as I will explain later, can be understood within the framework of classical Marxist economic theory. What I wish to elaborate on first, are the immediate social and economic consequences of subcontracting organized on Japanese lines. We should realize, above all, that a large degree of dependence is engendered by the system. In the typical Japanese company, the *keiretsu*, only the first line of subcontractors is directly owned by the mother company. Smaller supplier firms, on the contrary, are formally independent. Yet, since in practice they are generally up to 100 per cent dependent on the orders of one particular corporation, they are virtually subject to the latter's arbitrary rule.

Subcontracting of product components, in essence, means that Japanese automobile corporations and electronic companies are exempted from the fluctuations of the domestic and international market. Since small subcontractors are independent, the corporations are in a position to transfer market risks: in times of crisis not they, but the smaller companies, are made to pay the price. Thus, many Japanese industrial enterprises during the oil crisis of the 1970s imposed delivery-on-credit on their supplier firms, by simply delaying the payment of components obtained. And when the yen suddenly rose in value in relation to other currencies, raising the price of crucial Japanese export products like automobiles and electronic gadgets, a price reduction was imposed upon the dependent and rather powerless firms supplying components. In the Tokyo area, a reported 45 per cent of all firms were made to face the consequences of the 'yen spiral'.[6]

Yet, the ultimate victims having to face the brunt are the male and female labourers employed in the subcontracted firms. They are forced to make many hours of overtime, and in times of crisis are the first to be threatened with lay-offs. The secondary status faced by the majority of the Japanese labour force is well illustrated by the working conditions applying to part-time labourers in Japan. From interviews taken of women workers in Japan it clearly emerges that many subcontracting companies, employing 100 persons or less, make extensive use of 'part-time labourers'. Such women perform wage labour up to 7 and a half hours per day, earn wages calculated on an hourly basis, and are paid less than half the amount earned by male employees in fixed service. The wage rate of part-time women workers is a maximum of ¥500–600 per hour. Many middle-aged women, in particular, belong to this vast labour reserve. Since they can be dismissed any time, they are called 'throw-away-articles' in the Japanese press, analogous to the throw-away-sticks used by Japanese consumers to eat their meals.

The Japanese government, major corporations and right-wing trade unions, all actively work to maintain these deplorable labouring conditions in subcontracted firms. They jointly ensure that the method of transferring risks to the workers remains firmly entrenched. The corporations themselves transmit knowledge about the quality circles, and they put pressure on the 'independent' suppliers to ban any trade union activities. The government contributes its share by issuing laws in favour of part-time work, and by promoting the growth of a system of 'manpower agencies'. Similarly, the powerful trade union federation,

Rengo, has implicitly accepted the prohibition on trade union work in small supplier firms. This is confirmed by functionaries representing Rengo. A regional secretary defended the fact that Rengo only protects the interests of the relatively privileged layer of fixed employees, by citing as argument that union organizing in subcontracted firms would lead to the loss of orders for such firms. In other words, the decentralization of production and the silencing of the most severely exploited groups in society are a part of the very same Japanese 'model'.[7]

From Americanism to Japanization: Appropriation of Workers' Independent Knowledge

During the 1960s and 1970s, progressive authors studied and analyzed the Taylorist/Fordist system—management methods which, as explained earlier, were introduced in the early part of this century in order to promote the mass production of commodities. The French author, Coriat, for instance has given a lively description of the features and advantages to capital of the Fordist/Taylorist system. One of the key advantages he ascribes to the assembly line and the stopwatch is the 'breakdown of the independent knowledge of the trained craftsmen over the production process'. In the period of capitalism's ascendance, entrepreneurs realized that the independent knowledge of the workers over their own production provided them with considerable power. This power limited, Coriat argues, the control entrepreneurs could exercise in the historical first phase of capitalist production. It made them dependent on the physical presence, in the locality of their operation, of people knowing the ins and outs of the given trade.

This dependence on craftmen's knowledge forms the background to the struggle waged in England during the 19th century, over the (proposed) lifting of the ban on emigrations. Many skilled cotton workers in the Lancashire region wished to leave in the second half of the century, since they were starving due to temporary unemployment. Their impending exodus was fiercely resisted by the manufacturers, and triggered a debate in the British lower house—a debate which was won by those advocating that the emigration ban be maintained, for the owners of British textile factories could not dispense with a skilled workforce. Manufacturers are quoted as having stated: 'Could one imagine a more disastrous plan for all classes of the country than to weaken the nation by exporting its best labourers?' The presence of many unskilled workers in the United States, on the other hand, facilitated the introduction of the methods propagated by Taylor and Ford, the chronometer and the assembly line. During the period 1885–1915 alone, 15 million people migrated to the United States, most of them semi- or unskilled workers. Thus, American entrepreneurs could easily launch an offensive against skilled workers who temporarily tried to defend their jobs by relying on the principle of the exclusive workshops ('closed shops'), and on labels which in name guaranteed the quality of the commodities ('blue labels').[8]

The Taylorist phase of mass production has caused a fragmentation of production tasks and an accompanying breakdown of skills—changes which enhanced the power of entrepreneurs over the whole production process. According to Coriat, the time-and-motion studies of experts used to discipline the workforce were explicitly aimed at facilitating the massive integration of unskilled immigrants into the industrial production process. They were aimed at making craft-workers superfluous. The system, however, was not bereft of disadvantages. Its main drawback was that the remaining knowledge possessed by the workers, their creativity, could not be optimally used. 'Japanization', in my view, signifies that a solution has been found to this drawback of Fordism. Male and female workers organized in labour groups, both in the large corporations and in subcontracted companies, are forced to concentrate on production problems. They are made to constantly ponder over ways to increase production efficiency. It is often said in Japan that workers, employed by Toyota, think 24 hours a day about production. Japanization thus signifies the effective appropriation of the remaining knowledge and insights of the workers. 'Their knowledge is permanently tapped'.

Since both Taylorism/Fordism and Japanization are crucially concerned with the effective use and control over human knowledge and behaviour, it is useful to further elaborate on this theme. Harry Braverman, the American author of a classical study regarding the work processes under monopoly capitalism, has minutely analyzed the evolution of technical knowledge and its application by capitalist corporations up to the 1970s. Just like Coriat, he stresses that at the dawn of capitalism the skilled worker was the repository of human techniques required in the labour process of his/her particular branch. The craftsman/woman—the potter, the tanner, the smith and so on—combined in mind and body 'the concepts and physical dexterities of the speciality', and his/her technique was 'the predecessor and progenitor of science'.[9]

The history of the conquest of technical knowledge, its appropriation by the capitalist from the skilled worker, has long been burried by modern science. Yet the aim of this conquest, and the methods to achieve it, were quite explicitly stated by Frederick Taylor. Taylor's crusade was aimed at convincing the American entrepreneurs of his day that they should develop a complete 'monopoly' over knowledge, so as to 'control each step of the labour process and its mode of execution'. He advised that, first, the managers should 'assume the burden of gathering together all of the traditional knowledge which in the past had been possessed by the workmen', and, second, that 'all possible brain work should be removed from the shop and centred in the planning and pay-out department'.[10] Indeed, Gramsci's interpretation was very precise: the purpose of Americanism was to break up the old psycho-physical nexus of qualified professional work.[11]

The separation between conception and execution, proclaimed by Taylor as a cardinal principle of capitalist control, has historically given rise to the creation of a new profession—that of the technical engineer. In the US as Braverman records, there existed as few as 30 engineers or quasi-engineers in 1816. The first census which distinctly mentioned the profession showed a number of about 2,000 engineers, 'few of whom had gained their titles through academic training, and most of whom were engaged in canal and railroad construction'. It is only in the last two decades of the 19th century that the number of engineers rapidly expanded, and only in the 20th century did theirs become a mass occupation: there were some 1.2 million technical engineers bearing the responsibility for the conceptualization and planning of production in 1970.[12]

Seen against this background, it is more than ironic that in the last quarter of the 20th century, industrial corporations have abandoned Taylor's insistence on the strict separation between conception and execution, his open advocacy of dehumanized labour. Whereas, on the one hand, the engineering profession is being undermined partly by the development of computer technology and the growth of an army of data workers, engaged, like engineers, in the task of conception and planning, on the other hand Japanese companies have commonly instituted 'quality control circles' of shopworkers engaged in studying work processes and potential improvements in work methods. Yet before concluding, as monopoly capital would like us to, that what is at stake is the 'humanization of labour', we should take a closer look at the functioning of Japanese quality circles.

The spread of quality control circles—a system that has greatly contributed to the superiority of Japanese automobile concerns and other multinationals over their European and American competitors—is a rather recent development. It is true, as argued earlier, that 'labour groups' engaged in production competition have existed in Japan since the founding period of industrialization. In the late 19th and early 20th centuries, textile companies organized speed-up campaigns (i.e., they sought to intensify exploitation through competition between groups of women workers). Yet the idea of quality control, in the form of zero-defect drives, has reportedly originated in the US missile industry. It was brought to Japan in the late 1950s, by the Japan Productivity Centre. According to Muto Ichiyo, who has specialized in Japanese industrial relations since the Second World War, the idea was 'wedded' to the pre-existing 'small group concept'.[13]

As Ichiyo and other sources confirm, the quality control circles mushroomed during the 1960s and 1970s. In 1962, there were just 23 such circles. By 1980 the number had increased to well over 100,000! The Japan Productivity Centre held a survey in 1976 which showed that 71 per cent of the country's companies had instituted quality control circles. In big enterprises employing 10,000 workers or more, the figure for workers' participation in the given groups reportedly was as high as 91.3 per cent. One sector where quality control circles gained early ascendance was steel: the Kawasaki plant of Nippon Kokan Steel had implemented quality control drives already in 1963. By the 1980s, the same plant, then reportedly employing 8,000 persons, counted 1,320 quality control circles, indicating that the company's whole workforce had been mobilized to participate.[14]

Through the quality circles, Japanese companies have in a sense broken with the tradition of Taylorism, which had hoped to reduce workers to virtual animal extensions of the machine. To a very limited extent, and in a distorted manner, Japanese companies have restored the nexus between the workers' physical and mental activity: once again, as in pre-Taylorist days, workers are permitted to hold some knowledge over their immediate labour process. Still, it would be very wrong to conclude that capitalism is bent on restoring the workers' original craft knowledge, for the workers' domain of knowledge is carefully delineated by the enterprise. And whereas the quality circles are forced to provide the management with scores of suggestions on how to cut production costs, on how to reduce production errors to the barest minimum, the power to decide, to use the workers' knowledge, remains entirely the management's.

Finally, let us note the following contradictions between the ideology and practice of Japanization. Proponents of Japanese management styles argue that the quality control circles represent 'participation by the workers in management'—a form of 'self-management' (*jishu kanri*). The reality is that the quality circles help to further undermine whatever workers' autonomy had formerly existed in Japan. The groups are instructed to convene and discuss problems of production efficiency after the official working time. In general, the labourers are not paid any overtime wage for participating in the groups. In other words, the quality circles represent an unpaid extension of the labour day—an increase in exploitation. Most alarming is, as Ichiyo notes, that the quality control circles have usurped the role of workers' activism. 'There is no room left for union activity to intervene, since all the available time and energy of workers are absorbed by the company.'[15]

Fordism and Toyotism: Further Comparisons

One purpose of the Fordist/Taylorist system was to ensure workers' loyalty to large corporations by paying them relatively high wages, and by introducing various additional benefits, such as pensions and social security. Ford, the owner of the American automobile company, was an outspoken proponent of making economic concessions to a select group of workers in order to counter the tendency towards resistance in key sectors of the capitalist system. Coriat has concretely depicted how Ford conceived of his 'high wages' idea.[16] In 1915 he announced a big increment in the nominal level of wages; the pay rise involved no less than a doubling of wage rates, up to $5 per day (hence the slogan 'Five Dollar Day'). The immediate background to this policy change was a huge turnover in workers at Ford and other companies in the automobile city of Detroit. In 1913 alone 53,000 persons were recruited to fill 15,000 jobs. Moreover, the city was beset with rebelliousness, which Ford sought to deflect by increasing the level of wages.

This last-mentioned motive of Ford's was well understood by Gramsci. He discusses the Fordist 'ideology of high wages', and argues that the American companies could only pay their high wages because they held a position of monopoly, which was not to last forever. High wages, besides, were not being paid to all American workers, but only to those belonging to the 'labour aristocracy'; and high wages were paid with the sole motive of keeping the workers in line. Though the entrepreneurs, according to Gramsci, intentionally strived to transform the workers into 'trained gorillas', into a species without workers' consciousness, they nevertheless continued functioning as thinking human beings, which the entrepreneurs understood.

> And not only does the worker think, but the fact that he gets no immediate satisfaction from his work and realises that they are trying to reduce him to a trained gorilla can lead him into a train of thought that is far from conformist.[17]

In a 'Japanized' production structure, the need for a labour aristocracy remains. Thus, there exists in Japan a sharp divide between the male workers in life-long employment, and the mass of 'throw-away' female labourers. Further, in a structure with extensive subcontracting relations, the individual responsibility of industrialists to maintain a reasonable standard of living is greatly reduced. The payment of a 'high wage' after all only applies to a very select group of fixed workers who undertake final assembly tasks in the main factory hall. All the remaining categories of workers, in particular female workers, are paid low wages, and like the automobile workers in Detroit at the beginning of this century, they can be laid off at any time.[18]

One of the advantages of Ford's system of the assembly line, which is frequently overlooked, is that in such a system the turn-over time of capital is accelerated. Surely, an entrepreneur's chances of reaping super profits are enhanced by the speed with which his money is re-invested. Marx had underlined the importance of the theme of the turn-over time of capital.[19] In connection with capital's turn-over time, he made a distinction between production time and working time: the first is generally longer than the second. If wood, for instance, first needs to be laid to dry before being used, or in case the production time comprises a period of fermentation of grapes, it means that a part of capital is temporarily stored and the turn-over time of capital is extended. A similar phenomenon was observed in

Japan in a tobacco company in 1990. Tobacco leaves remained stored for one year in huge cauldrons before being considered suitable for the production of cigarettes. A part of the company's capital thus was 'stored' in the form of tobacco leaves.

Like the production time of capital, the circulation time—the time required for purchasing raw materials and selling the commodities produced—can pose complications for the entrepreneur. The more time it takes to find buyers for the goods, the more expenses are incurred, as a consequence of the storage of these goods after the completion of production. Marx called the period of sale the decisive part of the circulation time. On the other hand, the entrepreneur may require extra financial resources, since certain raw materials are auctioned at a few occasions in a year. What is involved here is the lengthening of the purchasing time, the starting period of capital. According to Marx, entrepreneurs in capitalist countries wage a perennial struggle to reduce the turn-over time of their capital, to accelerate capital's circulation. Fordism and Toyotism both aim at shortening the turn-over time of capital, but in the two systems this aim is realized differently. Let us, once again, refer to the French author Coriat: 'Ford introduced the production without stocks', he wished to 'counter the loafing of production materials' through a well-regulated supply and conveyance of all necessary materials. Ford himself is reported to have used the image of the river and its branches: the assembly line, in his view, served to promote a 'well-coordinated flow' of goods in the course of the process of production. He was concerned primarily with reducing 'losses' in terms of money, capital, as a consequence of the storage of goods in between various phases of production in the factory. By adopting his system of the conveyor belt, many costs in connection with transport–labour were eliminated, as well as expenses for the maintenance of stocks.[20]

The same aim of reducing storage costs is also pursued in the Japanese structure of decentralized production. Here, however, the savings are not realized by pressing down the costs of storage during the production process itself, but by cutting down on expenses for holding stocks before and after the production time in the factory. The target of Toyotism is precisely the circulation time of capital. A concept which as mentioned earlier, is wholly identified with the Japanese style of management is *kanban*: delivery just-in-time. Since it is demanded from supplier firms that they deliver precisely on the minute, and on the second, stipulated by the company issuing the order, the corporation is no longer burdened with the necessity of maintaining stocks of product components. In short, *kanban* is a contemporary Japanese concept that can easily be understood on the basis of Marx's classical *Capital*.

The Turn-over Time of Capital and the Need to Extend Marx's Theory

In this section I shall further underline the actual relevance of Marx's analysis regarding the problem of the turn-over time of capital. When preparing for his theoretical and practical analysis, Marx, during the winter of 1857–58, wrote a series of notebooks for self-clarification. Published only a century later, they have justly been termed a 'sourcebook of inestimable value for the study of Marx's method of inquiry'.[21]

Two of the notebooks contain extensive passages on the theme of the turn-over time of capital. First, how did Marx define the term? For Marx, the turn-over time of capital refers to the whole cycle which capital completes. It refers to the composite of production time and circulation time (i.e., to the various phases capital passes through before, during and after the end of the production of a commodity).[22] Preceding the initiation of production, for instance, raw materials have to be procured, and after the commodity has been readied it has to be brought to the market. The time to cover these steps belongs to the circulation time of capital.

The key question that Marx asks himself is the following: What influence does circulation time exert on the creation of value? 'The question which interests us here is this: Does a moment of value determination enter in *independent of labour*, not arising directly from it, but originating in circulation itself?'[23] Marx's answer is positive—circulation time does exert an independent influence, and in order to illustrate the point, Marx draws a comparison. If a value four times smaller realizes itself as capital four times in the same period in which a four times greater value realizes itself as capital only once, then the smaller capital's gain—production of surplus value—is at least as great as the larger's.[24] It can even be greater, Marx says, because the surplus value can itself again be employed as surplus capital!

Thus, the calculation of circulation time proper, and of the total turn-over time of capital, requires specific analysis. In order to understand an entrepreneur's capacity to accumulate, it does not suffice to know the rate of exploitation of his workforce, or the surplus time extracted from his male and female labourers. We also need to take a look at the turn-over time of his capital.

> The sum total of values produced or the total realization of capital in a given epoch . . . is determined . . . not simply by the surplus time realized in the production process, but rather by this surplus time [surplus value] multiplied by the number which expresses how often the production process of capital can be repeated within a given period of time.[25]

Marx then discusses whether circulation time is a positive or negative value-creating element. Given that a moment enters into value determination, circulation time, which does not come out of the direct relation of labour to capital, what influence precisely does circulation time exert? Marx considers circulation time to be a 'natural barrier'; it is a time of devaluation. The more the circulation of capital can be speeded up, the greater the speed with which the production process can be repeated, and the better this is for the owner of capital. In other words, 'circulation time in itself is not a productive force of capital. All that can happen through the acceleration and abbreviation of circulation time—of the circulation process—is the reduction of the barrier posited by the nature of capital'.[26]

The foregoing explains several major contemporary trends of international capital, in particular the specific mode of operation of Japanese companies (*kanban*), and capitalism's drive to further develop the means of communication. The time needed to maintain stocks of commodities produced, for instance, is influenced by the time required to transmit orders. Whereas originally these needed to be conveyed by courier or letter, with a transmission time of several days or more, the invention of the telegraph system, and more recently the fax system, have brought the transmission time down to nearly zero. Thus, the development of telecommunications serves capital's need to reduce the circulation time to the barest minimum. To quote Marx once again 'Capital by its nature drives beyond spatial barriers. Thus the creation of physical conditions of exchange—of the means of communication and transport—the *annihilation of space by time*—becomes an extraordinary necessity for it.'[27]

Marx's analysis also helps us understand the enormous popularity among entrepreneurs of the Japanese principle of *kanban.* Capital is interested in limiting to a minimum both the time capital lies idle before the start of production (in the form of raw materials and product components) and the period that stocks of commodities have to be held after their production has been completed. One of the ways in which the circulation of capital can be accelerated is precisely by forcing subcontracted firms to deliver components strictly on time. The managers of Japanese corporations, and their international competitors, know fully well that the time needed for the circulation of commodities exerts an influence on the mass of values they can produce. *Kanban* serves to eliminate barriers to the realization of capital, at least for those who can impose this rule. Here, as in the case of the development of communications, capital's target is to bring down the circulation time as close as possible to zero.

The era of Japanization further compels us to re-appraise our fundamental understanding of the capitalist system. Marx presumed that industrial entrepreneurs would unwillingly dig their own grave by bringing together thousands of workers under one roof, in one factory complex. Marx argued, as is well-known, that capitalism itself created the collective worker who, more or less spontaneously, would strive to overthrow the capitalist system and build a socialist society. In fact, Marx did not hesitate to equate the gathering together of workers in one building or space with the new mode of production:

> A great number of labourers working together, at the same time, in one place (or, if you will, in the same field of labour), in order to produce the same sort of commodity under the mastership of one capitalist, constitutes, both historically and logically, the starting point of capitalist production.[28]

Yet, in the modern Japanese model which has heralded a new phase in late capitalism, the number of workers corresponding to Marx's ideal of the collective worker is brought back to a minority of the working class, and to a minority also of the industrial labourers. Moreover, Japanese capitalists have upset Marx's very conceptualization of the stages in capitalist production. Marx, it may be recalled, conceptualized three stages. The historical phase of home industries, with its small, 'independent' producers working under the putting-out system, was followed by the phase of manufacturing, in which specialized craft-workers under the leadership of one boss laboured in the same workshop. This system of manufacturing, according to Marx, was to be replaced by the industrial system where workers were reduced to a mere extension of the machinery. Marx realized that home industries and manufacturing would not be immediately abolished, but would temporarily survive. Thus, the production of clothing in England was characterized by 'a medley of transitional forms'. Yet history would favour the factory: 'the variety of transitional forms, however, does not conceal the tendency to conversion into the factory system proper'.[29]

Today's reality (i.e., conditions more than 100 years later) does not support the schematic view propounded by Marx. Home industries and mini enterprises have not disappeared in the economically most powerful, over-industrialized country of the world, Japan. In fact, the continued existence of small subcontractors is purposefully aimed at by this country's large corporations. And although the mode of production in subcontracted firms admittedly cannot be equated with the one that prevailed in the sweatshops in the earliest phase of industrial development, any profound understanding of Japanization cannot be acquired without analyzing the comprehensive network of subcontractors maintained by multinational companies. It is indeed a crucial task for political economists today.

Should one conclude then that Marx is outdated, or that his understanding of capitalism was wrong? The tendency to reject Marxist economics is great at a time when the 'death' of Marxism is proclaimed in the Western press. Anybody who continues upholding this theory is branded an 'anachronist'. I nevertheless hold that the outright rejection of Marxism merely leads to intellectual disarmament—it leads to subordination under a system producing 'trained gorillas' and 'throw-away labourers' instead of producing liberated human beings. As illustrated in the forementioned example of Marx's analysis of the turn-over time of capital, his conceptualization provides essential attributes for grasping recent developments in world capitalism. In fact, we can apply to the system of subcontracting the same analytical approach that I am applying to women's labour: in order to fill blind spots, the legacy of Marxism should be extended.

Mass Production of Consumer Goods and the Position of Women

So far few references have been made to the impact of Fordism and Toyotism on women. Yet these two methods for the mass production of consumer goods have not left women unaffected. On the contrary. As we will see in the following, since the introduction of the assembly line and the conveyor belt in modern industries, women workers in fact have occupied a central place in the process of capital accumulation. They have been crucially affected by the two differential approaches to accelerate the turn-over of capital. Still, the literature on methods of mass production has for long failed to differentiate between the consequences for male and female workers. Only recently have feminists started to investigate the sexual division of labour in factories producing mass consumer goods.

One author who has undertaken a remarkable study on women assemblers is Miriam Glucksmann. As recorded earlier, Glucksmann has interviewed women who, during the 1930s, were employed in British factories producing household appliances and processed food. According to her, the introduction of the 'continuous flow' process of production in Great Britain differed significantly from the US. Whereas, in the US, the use of assembly lines in the motor industry 'preceded their widespread adoption in the light consumer goods industries', in Britain this was not the case.[30] Here women were the first to be subjected to assembly lines and machine-pacing through the conveyor belt system (namely, in the sectors of electrical engineering and food-processing). Thus, 'women were the first to pioneer the class relations of assembly lines'. According to Glucksmann, it was only after the Second World War 'that male workers in the British motor industry were subjected to the class relations of assembly line work on a large scale'.[31]

Moreover, even in the automobile sector, women from early onwards occupied a key position, which has also been overlooked by male researchers of Fordism and Toyotism. According to Glucksmann, during the 1930s women workers formed the bulk of the manual workforce in the manufacture of components and accessories for automobiles, and component industries 'were often further ahead than the assembly firms' in their use of mass production methods.[32] Yet the literature on 20th-century management methods has for long tended to concentrate attention one-sidedly on the final assembly of cars in factory halls. Since final assembly has always been a male preserve, the literature has one-sidedly focused on men. Thus, Glucksmann, along with other feminist authors,[33] has criticized the trend set by Braverman: 'ever since Braverman's *Labour and Monopoly Capital* was published in 1974, the central preoccupations of his followers have been firmly fixed on men. Not only have women workers been made no more visible than they were in traditional labour history, but the one-sided portrayal of the labour process distorts history by obscuring some of its most significant developments.'[34]

Glucksmann studied the evolution in five factories in detail. These included two producers of packaged food (Peak Frean of biscuits; and Lyons and Co. of cakes, bread and ice cream); a producer of gramophones (Electrical and Musical Instruments, EMI); a manufacturer of electrical irons (Morphy Richards); and, finally, a producer of vacuum cleaners (Hoover).[35] Each of them adopted Fordist principles. In some cases, the rudimentary type of assembly line work, where operators sat in a row, attached components and passed them on by hand, were introduced well before the 1930s. An intermediate stage could consist of the transportation of the product, still by hand, from operator to operator via a belt or band. But the 'ultimate goal' to which employers in mass production industries aspired was the introduction of the moving conveyor belt, the speed of which could 'externally' be controlled, (i.e, by the management).[36]

Further, as in the case of the assembly of automobiles, the aim of introducing this form of mechanization was quite clearly to shorten the turn-over time of capital. The moving belt system and the control of its speed, as Glucksmann states, gave the owners total control over production and permitted planned output to be automatically achieved.[37] Glucksmann consistently refers to the 'continuous flow process' of production to pinpoint the essence of the new system: 'all impediments to the smooth and uninterrupted through-flow of work from beginning to end of the production process were to be eliminated along with all sources of waste (time, labour, physical effort)'.[38] Clearly, as was the case in Ford's factories turning out cars, entrepreneurs in British factories turning out light consumer goods sought to eliminate 'any potential source of lost seconds or minutes'[39] in between the various stages of the production process.

Moreover, Glucksmann's account illustrates that it was women, not men, who in the given mass production of electric apparatus and packaged foods were subjected to time-and-motion studies and machine-pacing, so characteristic of Taylorist management. Although the mentioned companies did employ male workers, none were subjected to the given methods of control, for in all the cases of the production of consumer goods recorded by Glucksmann, the assembly work was exclusively performed by female operators. Through time-and-motion studies production targets were set, and bonus schemes were devised to encourage women to work at maximum speed. Women who were employed in the packing section of the Peak Frean biscuit factory, interviewed by Glucksmann, for instance, recalled how the *Bedaux* system was introduced in the early 1930s. Under this system, a basic rate had to be achieved and all work in excess was paid at an extra rate, in the form of a group bonus. 'This meant that the faster the belt moved and the more tins were packed, the more the group earned as a whole, since each received the same bonus.'[40] In Lions and Co., a time-and-motion bonus system was similarly imposed after *Bedaux* time-study engineers had been brought in.[41]

In the chapter on garments' production in West Bengal, it has been illustrated for a sector at a low level of technical development, that the sexual division of labour intersects with the detailed division of labour. To understand the process for the production of *punjabis*, for instance, both the detailed division of labour, and the allocation of product tasks to women and men, were scrutinized. The same point is brought out by Glucksmann for highly mechanized industries. The author not only throws light on the hitherto ignored role of women in the production of mass consumer goods; she specifically analyzes the sexual division of labour in these industries. According to the British author, 'in practice the sexual division is always embedded in and interlocked with the prevailing technical division of labour'.[42]

The pre-existing situation on which the Fordist methods of production were grafted differed from sector to sector. Electrical engineering had been a male preserve, but sectors like clothing and food-processing had had a mixed labour force. Yet, according to Glucksmann, the outcome of the transformation that took place in the 1920s and 1930s was, in all cases, quite similar: women ended up being the direct producers on assembly lines, whereas men were given responsibility for all indirect (i.e., servicing) tasks, such as arranging for the supply of components, the setting and repairing of machinery, and inspecting of the final product. Whereas the new system did engender new jobs, such as the 'progress chaser', which were allocated to men, all assembly tasks were exclusively allocated to women who held no other responsibilities. Thus, the first characteristic of the new sexual division of labour, according to Glucksmann, was that it coincided with that between direct and indirect producers in the factories.[43]

Two other features of the sexual division of labour are noted by Glucksmann. First, women workers constituted a homogeneous group, whereas the male part of the workforce was heterogeneous.

> Women formed a homogeneous group who were all in the same grade, with the same level of skill, all performing similar tasks and all receiving the same level of wages. Men, in sharp contrast, were in a much more heterogeneous position, spread throughout all the occupations and all the levels in the division of labour, possessing various degrees of skill, engaged in many different kinds of work and being paid accordingly more or less.[44]

Glucksmann uses the phrase 'women assembled' to transmit the fact that women held similar positions in the production process. Women were assembled as 'collective workers', and shared interests as a group, whereas men were divided by their position in the division of labour in the factory.

Finally, the system of the conveyor belt also affected the patriarchal control which men as foremen and supervisors exerted over women. As Glucksmann recalls, and is confirmed by other feminist studies on British industrial history, 'in traditional manufacturing industry women machine operators had worked directly under the supervision of a male setter who held individual authority over her'.[45] Under the assembly line industries of the new era, women were still in a subordinate position, but the form of their subordination changed. Rate fixers, quality controllers and other men acted as agents of the control exerted through the conveyor belt. Thus, women 'were much more directly subordinate to technical control than had been the case in earlier or other systems of production'.[46]

Glucksmann's study is, as stated, a historical one and is not concerned with the evolution of the sexual division of labour under the latest (i.e., Japanese) style of management. Yet her analysis could form a starting point for a comparative analysis of the sexual division of labour under the two mass production systems, Fordism and Toyotism. In the next chapter I will briefly refer to the sexual division of labour in Japanese electronic companies today. As in the case of the British factories analyzed by Glucksmann, women here continue to be relegated to tasks defined as 'semi-skilled'. It remains to be assessed whether other aspects of the sexual division of labour, mentioned by Glucksmann (i.e., the divide between direct and indirect producers, and between a homogeneous female and a heterogeneous male workforce), apply to companies run along Japanese principles.

Summing Up: The Need for an Innovative Trade Union Strategy

In this chapter I have described and analyzed Japanization/Toyotism, and have drawn comparisons with the Fordist system of mass production which emerged in the US in the early part of this century. I have argued that the Japanese style of management possesses two decisive characteristics: the quality control circles of male and female labourers intended to mentally subject them to the corporation's rule, and the structure of subcontracting which entails the transfer of production risks to the manufacturers of components and to the workforce employed by them. These two elements are as characteristic of Toyotism as were the conveyor belt and the stopwatch for Fordism/Taylorism.

A comparison with Fordism further shows that some 'bottlenecks' which entrepreneurs have been trying to solve ever since the industrial revolution, are 'solved' in an original manner under the system of Toyotism. Ford and Taylor hoped to do away with the rebelliousness, the spirit of resistance of the working class, once and for all, through the introduction of the chronometer and the assembly line. They were out to regulate factory production in a way that would help uproot from the factory the struggle against capital—the struggle for a humane world. They succeeded only partly—witness, for instance, the wave of socialist-inspired class struggles which engulfed Western European countries like France and Italy during the 1960s and 1970s. Hence the attraction exerted by the Japanese style of management: the physical expulsion of the bulk of the male/female labourers from the factory halls and the splitting up of the collective workers into numerous small, geographically separated units.

The Japanese regime, and its application by multinationals worldwide, has already heralded a new phase in the process of capital accumulation. For the future of the struggle for a viable world it is of crucial importance that this be fully recognized. The serial production of mass commodities is not abolished in a Japanized structure; on the contrary. The Japanese automobile and electronic companies, just like their American competitors, aim at the standardized manufacture of mass products on the largest possible scale.[47] But, in order to reach this goal, the internal, hierarchical relations within enterprises, and external relations, are being profoundly restructured. 'The terrible strength of Fordism', Benjamin Coriat wrote, 'lies in its enormous speed'. In companies that are ruled by the norms of *kanban*, speed and inhuman pressure are raised to unprecedented levels.

For the trade union movement of industrial workers (and here I not only have in mind the over-industrialized countries, but Third World countries like Mexico, Brazil and India as well), Japanization has far-reaching consequences. 'Trade unions could be completely outmanoeuvred', a Dutch trade union official states. An exclusive orientation towards the labour aristocracy, or the collective worker, as trade unions, including progressive ones, have traditionally done, is not tenable. In such a strategy, the interests of only the most privileged section of male employees in fixed service are defended, while those of seasonal labourers, of temporary workers, and in particular of the world's largest industrial reserve army, women, remain structurally neglected. This strategy is self-defeating, for through external decentralization entrepreneurs succeed in undermining the power of the whole working class. In short, the capitalist strategy of *kanban*, of quality circles and subcontracting, poses the need to fundamentally reconsider trade union strategies, as is happening in several Asian countries.[48]

Notes and References

1. Gramsci, p. 309.
2. A striking instance of the application of the Japanese model of subcontracting is the company Hindustan Lever in India, which is controlled by the British/Dutch Unilever corporation. In recent years, Hindustan Lever has increasingly taken to subcontracting, partly as a reaction to factory workers' resistance. See the results of the academic investigation carried out by Fransen (1991).
3. The globalization of Japanese management methods is briefly described in Transnationals Information Exchange (1991), p. 2: 'On the international market North American and European multinationals began to feel the squeeze of the Japanese and others using these organizational principles. At the beginning of the 1980s Japanese firms brought Toyotism to the USA with their "transplants". At the same

time American companies, impressed with Japanese efficiency and competitiveness, started to introduce elements of Toyotism. By the end of the 1980s, Toyotism had become the dominant new management philosophy all over the world.'

4. A good description of the historical transition from commercial to industrial subcontracting in Japan is provided by Annavajhula (1989), p. M–23.
5. Quoted from the postscript by Hugo Klijne, Grahame Locke and Hans Venema, in Coriat (1980), p. 115.
6. See Annavajhula (1989), p. M–19.
7. It may be noted at this point that my interpretation of Japan's success story differs significantly from the analysis provided by Paul Sweezy (1980) at a time when the globalization of Japanese management techniques was just starting. Sweezy discusses factors like the effect of the Korean War (1950–53) on the recovery of the Japanese economy, and the massive growth in both Department I (the sector producing means of production) and Department II (producing means of consumption), but does not address the specific Japanese methodology of industrial exploitation.
8. For details regarding the destruction of the craft knowledge of the workers and the rise of Fordism, see Coriat (1980), pp. 18–32.
9. Braverman (1974), p. 109. It may be noted that Marx discussed the appropriation of the workers' knowledge as the absorption of this knowledge in the instruments of production, in machinery. Thus: 'The development of the means of labour into machinery is not an accidental moment of capital, but rather the historical reshaping of the traditional, inherited means of labour into a form adequate to capital. The *accumulation of knowledge and of skill*, of the general productive forces of the social brain, is thus absorbed into capital, as opposed to labour, and hence appears as an attribute of capital, and more specifically of fixed capital, in so far as it enters into the production process as a means of production proper' (Marx, 1973b), p. 694, emphasis added.
10. Braverman (1974), pp. 112–13.
11. As Gramsci (n.d.), p. 302, stated: 'Taylor is in fact expressing with brutal cynicism the purpose of American society—developing in the worker to the highest degree automatic and mechanical attitudes, breaking up the old psycho-physical nexus of qualified professional work, which demands a certain active participation of intelligence, fantasy and initiative on the part of the worker, and reducing productive operations exclusively to the mechanical, physical aspect'.
12. Braverman (1974), p. 241.
13. Ichiyo (1987), p. 35.
14. Figures on the quantitative increase in the number of quality control circles are in Mankidy (1984), p. M–57.
15. Ichiyo (1987), p. 36. According to the Transnationals Information Exchange (1991), p. 9, 'the fundamental contradiction of Toyotism' is that workers, on the one hand, are involved in thinking about production structures and processes, but on the other hand are refused 'the right to true self-determination'.
16. Coriat (1980).
17. Quoted from Gramsci (n.d.), p. 310. In his essay, Gramsci (ibid.), pp. 310–13, devotes a specific section to the theme of 'high wages'.
18. The Transnationals Information Exchange (1991), pp. 3–4, notes that the introduction of Japanese management techniques is often accompanied by factory

closures, the dismissal of trade union activists, and a reduction in wages. Examples discussed are those of NUMMI (New United Motor Manufacturing Inc.), a joint venture between General Motors and Toyota in Fremont, California, which 'became a model for other companies worldwide', and the Ford–Cuautitlan factory near Mexico city.

19. A major part of Marx's *Capital*, Vol. II, is devoted to the theme of the turn-over time of capital (Marx 1967a), p. 156.
20. The point is noted by Coriat (1980), p. 57.
21. See the Foreword by Martin Nicolaus to Marx (1973b), p. 7.
22. Marx (1973b), pp. 520–21, 618–19.
23. Ibid., p. 519, emphasis added.
24. Ibid.
25. Ibid., p. 544, emphasis added.
26. Ibid., p. 545.
27. Ibid., p. 524.
28. Marx (1977a), p. 305.
29. Ibid., p. 442.
30. Glucksmann (1990), p. 263.
31. Ibid.
32. Ibid., pp. 90–91.
33. For an elaborate critique of Braverman, see Beechey (1987), p. 73.
34. Glucksmann (1990), p. 278.
35. Ibid., p. 93.
36. Ibid., p. 148.
37. Ibid., p. 152.
38. Ibid., p. 148.
39. Ibid., p. 152.
40. Ibid., p. 105.
41. Ibid., p. 128.
42. Ibid., p. 198.
43. Ibid., p. 154.
44. Ibid., p. 205.
45. Ibid., p. 207.
46. Ibid., p. 208.
47. For a lively account of the intense pressure experienced by Japanese workers employed to work on the assembly line, see the diary of the Toyota worker Satoshi Kamata (1986). As the author notes (ibid.), p. 142, the system of assembly line production is extended to the subcontracted firms, and the system of *kanban* provides the connecting link: 'The assembly lines in the supplying firms are synchronized with the assembly lines in the Toyota factories. This *kanban* method, which has been hailed in the media, is actually intended to ensure the deliverance in time by the subcontracted firms. It forms a further proof of the increasing synchronization in industry. Even the streets between the supplying firms and the Toyota factories are considered to be assembly lines which connect the actual assembly lines in the factories with each other'. This quote well illustrates the close interconnection between the Fordist reduction of stocks and the Toyotist reduction of stocks!

48. The history, of Fordism indicates that the victory of Toyotism over the trade union movement may well be temporary. As the Transnationals Information Exchange states (1991), p. 4, it took several decades for American unions to catch up with Fordism: 'Until the sit-in strike at General Motor's Flint car plant in 1937 [during which the United Automobile Workers Union was born], it was thought impossible to organize the deskilled and semi-skilled assembly line workers into a union.'

12

Japanese Women as a Vast Reserve Army of Labour

'Women have been the potential industrial reserve army, whose working power is absorbed or rejected according to the accumulation cycles and epochs, since the capitalist mode of production came into existence.'[1] Although Bennholdt-Thomsen did not refer to women in Japan, this statement can well apply to the experience of Japanese women workers during the various phases of the industrial evolution. At every stage, entrepreneurs have treated women as a disposable labour reserve.

Japan has long been projected as a country where workers enjoy life-long employment with job security and steadily increasing incomes. Benevolent company managers, so it was argued, ensure that workers never need to worry about the stability of their jobs. The previous chapter has already shown that this image is highly deceptive, for in the subcontracted companies which supply the product components to Japan's major corporations, workers' life-long employment does not exist. Moreover, although it is true that a major section of the male labour force of corporations like Toyota, Mitsubishi and Nissan are permanently employed, such corporations also rely on seasonal and temporary labourers drawn, for instance, from the Japanese countryside.[2]

In this chapter I will show that the bulk of Japanese women workers have always been deprived of benefits associated with the system of 'life-long employment'. They have never benefited from such 'benevolence' on the part of Japanese entrepreneurs. On the contrary. Throughout the era of the country's rapid ascendance as a capitalist nation, industrialists have abundantly made use of women as a source of labour power. Thus, they recruited young and illiterate village women as a workforce for the early textile factories. More recently, in the post-Second World War period, they have opted to employ pre-marriage high school graduates, and ultimately middle-aged, married women as well. But women's labour has always been transient and disposable. If any, this has been its permanent characteristic.

Taking Japan as a concrete example, in the last chapter I will address myself to both the practice of using women as a secondary, disposable labour force, and to the theoretical conclusions which feminist authors have drawn from this reality. In the previous chapters I have sought to extend Marx's theory of labour value to account for women's domestic work under capitalism. In this chapter I will show that his theory of the 'relative surplus population' (i.e., of the 'reserve army of labour') similarly needs to be extended in order to clarify why unmarried, young women and middle-aged housewives are tapped by capitalist companies as a vast labour reserve.

The Exploitation of Women Workers in the Early Silk and Textile Factories

It is useful to start my overview with a brief review of the history of Japan's industrialization, since it brings out well that women's waged labour from the very start has been crucial to the process of capital accumulation. As I have mentioned in the previous chapter, modernization was initiated in Japan in the second half of the 19th century, after the Meiji Restoration of 1868. The members of the traditional elite of *samurai* who, in the face of the pressure exerted by foreign powers on Japan, decided to adapt to the external environment, chose textile production to spearhead the process of modernization. Well into the 20th century, the textile sector overshadowed other Japanese industries, in terms of both the number of workers employed (a reported 62.8 per cent of all factory workers in 1899) and value of output.[3]

In the initial phase, the textile sector was mainly composed of silk and cotton yarn production. Silk-reeling was done in small-scale, rural-based factories. According to Harui, this industry brought in the foreign currency required to buy raw materials like cotton and iron ore, and the machines needed for developing heavy industries. The cotton-spinning mills, which were established in the urban areas, on the other hand, formed an import-substitution industry: they helped to prevent the outflow of foreign currency as a consequence of the import of textile clothes.[4] For several decades, the two sectors together completely dominated Japan's foreign trade: in 1913 cotton and silk comprised almost two-thirds of the country's exports. Moreover, as more and more cotton-weaving factories were established, Japan captured an increasingly large share of the world market in textile fabrics. By 1937 this share (by weight) amounted to 37 per cent.[5]

While this side of the story of Japan's successful transformation has frequently been told, much less known is the fact that the early industrialists relied primarily on women as their workforce (see Table 12.1). This is true for both the owners of silk factories and cotton mills. According to Gary Saxonhouse, if a comparison is drawn with other textile production centres in the world (for instance, with Lowell, Massachusetts, in the mid-19th century, or with Bombay in the late 19th century), the percentage of female labourers was highest in the Japanese textile mills. His data shows that in 1909, women constituted as much as 83 per cent of the whole workforce in such factories. In his words, the young female workers were 'the integral force in the fifty-year drive of the Japanese cotton textile industry to world dominance'.[6] I will, then, start my analysis of women's labour in Japan by looking more closely at the conditions of exploitation faced by these early female factory workers.

The exploitation practised by the owners of the silk-reeling and cotton-spinning mills in critical ways resembled that practised by upstart capitalists elsewhere (for instance, in Britain at the time of the industrial revolution, and in Bangladesh today). In the chapter on Bangladeshi garment workers, I have observed that in the early stages of industrialization, entrepreneurs display a distinct propensity to extract surplus value from their workers at any cost. They show a preference for the cheapest labour, including that of children, and tend to extend the working day beyond what is physically sustainable. All efforts are geared towards reaping a maximum profit in the shortest possible time.

The early Japanese entrepreneurs displayed the same ruthless attitude. First, the working day in the textile mills was exceedingly long. Female labourers in silk factories had to toil 14 hours a day. The first strike erupted in Japan when an attempt was made to extend the working day from 14 hours to 14 and a half hours.[7] The working time

Table 12.1

Percentage of Females in the Cotton Textile Labour Force in Japan

Japan		*United States*		*United Kingdom*		*India*		*France*	
1909	83.0	1830	66.0	1835	55.1	1884	22.5	1886	53.0
1914	83.3	1850	63,0	1847	58.7	1894	25.9	1896	50.0
1920	80.0	1890	54.5	1867	61.3	1909	22.1	1906	45.5
1925	80.6	1910	48.3	1878	62.7	1924	21.6		
1930	80.6	1919	42.4	1895	62.3	1934	18.9		

Source: Saxonhouse (1976), p. 100.

Table 12.2

Percentage of Employees in Different Manufacturing Sectors in Japan (1909–30)

	1909	*1915*	*1920*	*1925*	*1930*
Textiles	60.8	59.9	55.5	52.3	47.7
Metals	2.3	2.9	4.7	5.4	5.3
Machinery	5.8	7.8	12.3	13.2	12.5
Chemicals	3.2	4.0	5.9	5.6	6.0
Food-processing	11.1	8.2	6.5	9.5	8.1
Others	16.8	17.2	15.1	14.0	20.5

Source: Saxonhouse (1976), p. 100.

Table 12.3

Length of Service in Cotton Textile Industries in Japan as a Percentage of the Total Labour Force

	Japan (1897)	*Japan (1918)*	*Lowell, Mass. (1845)*	*American South (1925)*	*Bombay, India (1890)*	*Bombay, India (1927–28)*
Less than 1 year	46.2	50.3	25.0	27.3	–	–
1 to 2 years	23.3	18.4	13.0	13.2	–	–
2 to 3 years	13.3	11.1	11.0	12.7	–	–
3 to 4 years	7.7	9.3	11.0	9.6	–	–
4 to 5 years	4.7	9.3	9.0	6.4	–	–
Total (less than 5 years)	95.2	89.1	69.0	69.2	72.2	46.5
5 to 10 years	4.6	7.0	25.5	19.1	11.1	24.3
More than 10 years	0.2	3.9	15.5	11.7	16.7	29.2

Source: Saxonhouse (1976), p. 101.

of women in cotton spinneries was slightly shorter (12 to 13 hours a day). But the two-shift system, which was introduced by the owners of spinning mills from 1885 onwards, forced women and children to work in regular night-shifts, and at times to toil for 25 hours continuously.[8] Thus, the principal method used to maximize profits was the extraction of 'absolute' surplus value (i.e., extension of the length of the working day).

Further, like Bangladeshi owners today, Japanese mill-owners devised various methods to reduce the costs spent on variable capital. They also instituted a fines' system which increased workers' exploitation. As Kidd reports, the cotton-spinning mills set strict standards regarding the quality and amount to be produced by each worker, and if the quota was not met at the end of the day, the worker was fined, and the fine was subtracted from her monthly pay. Each worker was also required to deposit with the company, every month, a sum equal to his or her earnings for one day, and this deposit was liable to confiscation in the event of any infringement, however slight, of the labour contract or the factory regulations. Like in Bangladeshi garment factories today, this system of fines was used to bring down workers' earnings.[9]

Equally characteristic of the Japanese textile mills was the employment of child labour. Kidd gives figures by age for women and children employed in the cotton-spinning mills: 49 per cent of the workforce consisted of women under 20 years, and children less than 14 years represented 13 per cent of the total workforce.[10] Children worked the same long hours as the adults. After 40 years of unlimited exploitation of child labour, a Factory Act was promulgated in 1911, which in name prohibited the employment of children under 12 years. Yet, far from providing effective protection, the Act legalized inhuman treatment, as it reportedly permitted children under 15 years and female workers of all ages to be employed for as much as 12 hours a day.[11]

We have seen earlier that one of the ways in which the government supports the factory owners is by ignoring legal regulations against child exploitation. The Japanese authorities in the early 20th century, driven by the same desire to protect their own foreign currency earnings, went further. They legally permitted the employment of children for an inhumanly long period of 12 hours a day. Moreover, one of the loopholes the Factory Act contained was that industrialists could ask their workers to put in more than 12 hours as 'over-time'.[12] Thus, throughout the era when the basis was laid for Japanese accumulation, the entrepreneurs' boundless thirst for surplus value, and their urge to extend the working time of women and children *ad infinitum*, remained virtually unchecked.

The Transient Nature of the Workforce and the Methods of Control in Cotton-spinning Mills

Two features which require special attention are the recruitment methods and the transient nature of women's labour in the textile industry. After an initial period in which they themselves went out to find young workers, the owners of the cotton mills started commissioning free-lance agents. These agents travelled around the countryside to recruit the daughters of impoverished peasants for labour in the mills. Since famine conditions prevailed in the countryside and since numerous families were in debt, the agents faced few difficulties. They frequently acted as moneylenders, providing peasants with loans to be repaid from the factory wages of their daughters. Until the 1930s, young village women constituted 80 to 90 per cent of the workforce of Japanese textile mills.[13]

While parents were enticed into signing labour contracts with stories about a rosy future for their daughters, the actual conditions in the mills were unbearable. Apart from demanding long hours of work, the owners ignored the health needs of the women labourers. Particularly notorious was the lack of fresh air inside the weaving departments, which were set up from 1898 onwards. The dust problem was severe since tiny particles of cotton fibres were constantly whirling in the air. So was the problem of moisture, as the owners thought it necessary to keep the air damp to ensure the quality of the cotton clothes. Thus, the dark factory halls surrounding the machines were filled with steam, water would drip down from the ceiling, and the windows were kept tightly shut. The female workers had to endure such conditions for 12 long hours every day.[14]

Due to these and other circumstances, the incidence of illnesses among textile workers was very high. According to government sources, a common ailment was stomach trouble, which was caused by poor food and the fact that many women relied on excessive amounts of sweet to sustain themselves throughout the long working day. A major illness was colds, especially among the cotton weavers. But the foremost killer of female labourers was tuberculosis, like in Germany around the turn of the century. According to a government survey during 1898–1902, a quarter of all deaths in dormitories, where the women workers of the textile mills were housed, were caused by tuberculosis.[15] Other studies claimed even higher figures for tuberculosis victims. One report stated that as much as a sixth of the female workers in the industry succumbed to the illness.[16]

It is not surprising then that many women tried to, literally, escape from their inhuman existence as labourers. As already mentioned, the women were lodged in mill-owned dormitories, which were virtual prison camps. Yet many women workers simply disappeared long before their three- to five-year contracts expired. They knew they were taking a great risk by trying to flee because, if they were caught, they were beaten and forced to march naked through the factory premises. Yet most women saw escape as the only possible road to freedom. Thus, according to a survey carried out by the cartel of the textile industry in 1897, 44 per cent of the recruits to the Hyogo mill, owned by Kanebo, left within six months.[17] Similarly, a government investigation into a factory near Osaka showed that 'altogether more than half of the workers escaped from the mill in 1900'.[18] Thus, stability of employment did not exist in the early textile factories, and the transient nature of the overwhelmingly female labour force was one of the main characteristics of the sector that spearheaded Japan's industrialization. As Saxonhouse states, on an average women stayed at work for no more than two years.[19]

A historical review further reveals that the methods to control the workforce, which today are standard practice in factories operated by Japanese companies, were tested about a century ago in the cotton textile mills. Since the beginning of the 1970s, Japanese investments overseas have rapidly expanded, especially in the countries of East and South East Asia. In their external drive, both multinationals and medium-sized companies rely heavily on women's labour. They commonly draw their workforce from the very same source that was tapped by the early cotton textile mills (i.e., from among young, unemployed village women).[20] Moreover, they use methods to control the workers which have been developed long ago, namely, small group competition, fenced dormitories, and a system of forced savings. I will briefly review how each of these methods was applied around the turn of this century.

In the previous chapter on Fordism and Toyotism I traced the idea of quality control circles to the sports competition promoted by the 'grandfathers' of today's corporations. 'Group competition among mill workers', Kidd notes, 'began as informal games pitting one group of workers from the same prefecture against a group from another prefecture'.[21] Taking advantage of the competitive spirit created, the textile mill owners also initiated production contests among groups of women. They offered paltry prizes, like flags, towels and cosmetics, to the victors. Since the contests were held through the year, they caused a lot of stress. Worse, according to Wakizo, whose book is reputed to be the only first-hand account of workers' lives in the cotton spinning mills, women workers were virtually forced to participate in the contests, so that many collapsed from exhaustion or sickness.[22]

The structure of fenced dormitories is a second pioneering idea which multinationals like Toyota have borrowed from their predecessors. The dormitories, where the young women from the villages were brought together, were generally located inside or near the factory compound, and were all 'constructed in such a way as to make it difficult for women to escape or leave unnoticed'.[23] Thus, many mills were surrounded by high fences or walls, behind which broken glass, sharpened bamboo sticks and barbed wire were placed. Half the mills were reportedly built so that the back of the dormitories faced water barriers, such as the ocean, a river or a marsh. Clearly, the compound structure of the early textile factories itself indicates how serious the problem of women labourers trying to escape was.

The third concept still in practice is that of forced savings. Along with the dormitory system, it has been introduced in Taiwan, for instance, by the textile multinational Toray,[24] and it too can be traced to the learning phase of the Japanese capitalists. Like company owners today, the early mill owners would pose as surrogate parents. Ostensibly to enable the girls to help their families, they were obliged to save a fixed amount of money. This was deduced from their wages and kept in the capital fund of the mill. In practice, the system served more to tie the female labour force to the factory and to enhance company profits, than to support the girls' families. The savings generally could not be freely withdrawn and, as we have seen, more women fled from their jobs than stayed on during their contract term. Thus, many mills 'were able to reap a windfall of confiscated earnings'.[25]

In practice, the system of forced savings was one more source for the extraction of surplus value.

Growth of the Electronics Sector: Feminization and the Gender Division of Labour

Since the 1960s, the electronics sector has increasingly taken the place earlier occupied by the textile sector (i.e., it is now spearheading the Japanese process of capital accumulation). I shall cite data on the sector's international expansion which I have procured from the headquarters of Denki Roren, the national trade union federation of company-based unions in the sector. According to the representative of Denki Roren's research department, who refers to government figures, in the period from 1982 to 1988, the number of investments by Japanese electronics companies abroad has doubled, while the value of these investments has increased five-fold.[26] Examples of corporations which have sought external expansion are M. Electronics which, reportedly, was the leader in foreign production in 1983,[27] and Fujitsu Electronics, which claims a worldwide network of plants and research establishments.

The external drive, further, was preceded by a 'flight', beginning in the late 1960s, to Kyushu, an island located in the southern corner of the archipelago which, until then, had been on the periphery of the Japanese economy. Companies like Mitsubishi and National Electronics Corporation (NEC) opened their first factory premises for the manufacture of integrated circuits (ICs) near Kumamoto city, in 1967 and 1969 respectively. Other electronic giants followed suit. Kyushu developed into a replica of the Silicon Valley in the US, which for years has been seen as the Mecca of successful entrepreneurship. According to the Japanese researcher, Fujita Kuniko, in 1988 44 per cent of all ICs in Japan were produced on this island, which is 10 per cent of the world's production of ICs compared to Silicon Valley's 25 per cent.[28]

The new industrialization heralded a process which is similar to that noted by Mitter for Scotland. 'Over the last 10 years', Mitter wrote 'Scotland has lost over 200,000 manufacturing and mining jobs'.[29] The decimation of the steel, ship-building and mining sectors caused high levels of unemployment among male workers in industrial zones. Yet the electronic companies which invested in the manufacture of wafers (i.e., the first production stage of semi-conductors) did not recruit their workforce from redundant shipyard workers and coal miners, but from among their wives and daughters. Thus, the 'feminization of industry', where nearly 50 per cent of the workforce and the majority of production line workers became women, was 'the most significant effect' of the expansion of the electronics industry in Scotland.[30]

In Kyushu, companies producing semi-conductors showed an even higher preference for female labour. In the Kumamoto prefecture, for instance, female high-school graduates made up 95 per cent of the whole workforce of electronics companies in the early 1970s. Their tasks were related to the assembling and testing of ICs (i.e., the final processes of production). 'Abundant female labour at low wages', Kuniko states, 'was an enormous attraction to IC manufacturers'.[31] The picture, however, has subsequently changed, and Kuniko uses the terms 'polarization' and 'the marginalizing of women' to describe developments in Kyushu during the 1980s. According to her, the percentage of female workers had declined to 50 per cent in 1986, the basic reason being the fact that the number of newly-recruited male employees by far exceeded that of new women employees. While the absolute number of women workers continued increasing, the rate of increase of male workers was much higher.[32]

The analyses presented by Mitter for Scotland and Kuniko for Kyushu concur in that both indicate a polarization between female and male workers. Thus, Kuniko relates the relatively decreasing role of women to the transformation that has taken place in the manufacture of ICs since 1980, from the originally labour intensive to highly automated and capital intensive production.

> The nature of the IC industry tends to severely polarize its workforce as the industry becomes highly automated, with highly skilled, highly paid male workers, such as researchers and engineers, on the one pole—and abundant, semi-skilled female production workers on the other, constantly eliminating the middle strata. As the number of skilled labourers increases, the role of semi-skilled labourers diminishes.[33]

The situation in the factories manufacturing wafers in Scotland is equally polarized. Mitter speaks of a 'chasm' between the work of 'semi-skilled, largely female operatives' and that of 'emerging multi-skilled technicians or graduate engineers', which has entailed the elimination of the middle rank of blue collar workers.[34] According to her, in the electronics industry, as elsewhere, skill has increasingly been defined against women—skilled work is work that women do not do. Women are recruited to do minute tasks, like fixing chips on to small aluminium plates, a job requiring manual dexterity. This dexterity is supposed to be a 'natural' attribute of women, and not of men, and is simultaneously given a low grade. The result is that skilled work tends to be identified with factory jobs performed by men.[35]

A striking example of the hierarchical gender division of labour is found in the factory compound of Fujitsu Electronics near Kagoshima, employing 600 men and 400 women. The managers in blue uniforms openly talked about the strict division between men's and women's tasks.[36] Cutting wafers is exclusively done by men, as is the maintenance of machines. Quality control of the chips, on the contrary, is performed by women, in a dust-proof room. Women in synthetic dresses stare through microscopes, checking whether the thin wires of the chips have been properly fixed to tiny plates. Why is this quality control exclusively done by women? The response is stereotype. One of the uniformed bosses told us: 'This work is very suitable for women, since they are used to doing stitching and embroidery. The work requires enormous concentration, and men are not fit for such monotonous labour.'

The experience of women in the electronics sector in Japan illustrates what has been stated earlier on women garment workers in Bangladesh. In both cases, a strong 'sectoral' sexual division of labour operates, with men performing the tasks that are defined as 'skilled', and women being relegated to jobs marked 'semi-skilled' or 'unskilled'. In both these cases, and in conformity with established international practices, managers rely on women to do production tasks requiring manual dexterity, a skill which women acquire through informal training. By recruiting women who already possess these skills, managers can cut training costs; and by defining the work as 'semi-' or 'unskilled', which is by definition poorly paid, they further save on labour costs. In short, the issue of skill, and the ideological biases built into its definition, are crucially relevant for the analysis of women's exploitation.

Another issue, which is central for women workers employed in electronics companies, is that of occupational diseases, such as the loss of eyesight, and neck, shoulder and arm pain. During the investigation carried out in Japan in 1990, the issue figured briefly in discussions with female workers at Fujitsu Electronics. Under the watchful eyes of the bosses dressed in blue, we interviewed five women, four of whom did quality control tasks in a dust-proof room. After posing our regular questions about their labouring burden—30 hours of overtime per month appears to be quite normal—we tried to touch on the theme of occupational hazards. What kind of diseases do women suffer from as a consequence of monotonous work? 'Sitting is most tiresome, I wish I could move. Because I am constantly chained to my chair, my shoulders are tense,' said one of the women. Although one of the other women formally denied that peering through microscopes day after day caused eye problems, there did seem to be an on-going controversy within Fujitsu over the question. According to one of the women workers, 'Just recently, the director has assured me that if the microscope is adjusted well, it can do no harm to my eyes.'

While the evidence collected through interviews conducted in Japan is hardly conclusive, there in fact is ample written proof to show that many women, employed to do assembly work and quality control tasks in the production of ICs, suffer from serious occupational hazards. At an international seminar held in Manila in 1986, Saida, a woman who was employed by a US-owned multinational electronics company to do the bonding of chips with a microscope, testified about women workers' health problems. According to her, many of the women in her factory lost the capacity to see things at a distance and had to get spectacles.[37] In a survey of women's experiences in assembling chips in American electronics companies in South East Asia, Hancock also found that the daily use of microscopes frequently causes eye problems, along with headaches. 'After two to three years' work, up to 50 per cent of the women assembly workers complain of deteriorating eyesight and headaches.'[38]

In Japan, the issue of occupational diseases and the manifest negligence of electronics companies, in several recorded cases, has led to the formation of independent unions by women workers. For instance, M. Electronics Company was founded in 1955 and expanded its capital initially by making transistor radio parts. Subsequently, it entered the market for the production of ICs, where it relied on women for the task of bonding. In one of the examples recorded by Hiroki, numerous health hazards were revealed in 1972. The company, instead of responding to women's complaints about constant eye strain, and shoulder and back pain, issued dismissal notices. The sick workers were considered a nuisance. The workers successfully fought back, both to have the dismissals rescinded, and to force the company to start rehabilitation programmes.[39] Elsewhere, women employees of M. Electronics also struggled to obtain recognition for occupational diseases, and tried to find ways to eliminate such diseases, taking this issue up to the Japanese parliament.[40]

The M Curve: Official View on Women's Employment

Let us look at the overall employment figures for women to get a more complete picture of women's status in the labour market in Japan. In official statistics and graphs, the employment of women of various ages is shown as an M-shaped curve. Millions of girls, on graduating from high school, are employed for several years as full-time workers in the service and retail trading sector (i.e., in banks, offices and shops). When they marry or bear their first child, most of them disappear from the labour market, only to return once their children have grown up. Many middle-aged women in Japan are part-time labourers, and constitute the second peak in women's employment. As the Ministry of Labour (1989) states, 'Women's employment rate forms an M-shaped curve, with those aged 30–34 forming the bottom and those aged 20–24 and 45–49 forming the right and left peaks.'[41]

What the M curve brings out well is the transformation that has taken place in employment practices over the last approximately 25 years. Earlier, the majority of the Japanese women were active as 'self-employed' workers on farms, as industrial homeworkers or housewives (i.e., they mainly performed productive tasks in and around the home). But the overall picture has drastically changed in the course of the 1970s and early 1980s. The number of part-time women labourers, in particular, has grown phenomenally (see Figure 12.1). It rose to about 8 million by the late 1980s. According to government figures, they formed 75.7 per cent of non-regular female workers in 1988, and they appear to have constituted about half the total number of women performing waged work in that year.[42] As for

Figure 12.1
Age-wise Ratio of Working Women in Japan

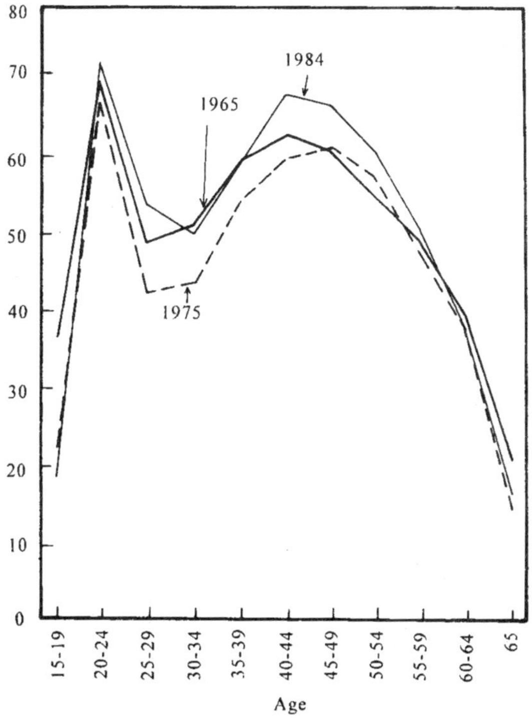

Source: Bureau of Statistics, Management and Coordination Agency, *Labour Force Survey*, Japan.

the age composition of female part-timers, about two-thirds belonged to the age 35 to 53 years.[43]

Several critical comments may be made about the M curve. First, if one only looks at the peaks, one tends to ignore the fact that apart from the categories mentioned, there is a significant and increasing number of women who are engaged as 'temporary labourers', through 'manpower agencies'. The expansion of manpower agencies is actively promoted by the government. After a law was introduced to regulate their operations, in 1985, the number of such agencies within a single year more than tripled from 2,000 to over 7,000. The law exempts the ultimate employers from any responsibility for people they recruit through manpower agencies. An investigation carried out by trade unions has concluded that women engaged as 'temporary workers' in the service sector (two-thirds of the workforce in this sector are women) are deprived of any supplementary allowances. They do not even receive a bonus, though the length of their working time often hardly differs from that of full-timers.[44]

Nor does the M-shaped curve properly highlight the wage labour which many Japanese women continue to perform as homeworkers. The number of outworkers sewing for an entrepreneur, making toys, assembling electronics components or packing parcels, seems to have tumbled during the last 20 years. Estimates today range from 1 to 2 million women.[45] Homeworkers, however, do constitute a separate age category, for the group is largely composed of women with small children (i.e., those whose age forms the down-turn in the M curve). Homeworkers' wages, moreover, are undoubtedly the lowest of all categories of female labourers in Japan. According to Hayashi in Fukuoka city, the average is ¥357 per hour, or about half that of a part-time woman labourer, and merely a quarter of the wage drawn by a male employee in fixed service.[46] Annavajhula cites figures indicating an even larger discrepancy (i.e., that female homeworkers' earnings are merely a fifth of that of full-time employees).[47]

The M-shaped curve, if taken at face-value, thus tends to present an incomplete picture. And yet it does give us an indication of the secondary position held by women in the hierarchy of wage labour. As stated before, Japan has for decades prided itself on, and is praised for, maintaining a system of life-long employment, with security of jobs and steadily increasing incomes. The forementioned facts show that the story about the 'life-long employment system' is highly propagandistic and gives a very selective idea of reality. It applies to a section of male labourers only, while excluding almost all women labourers. To summarize, when young women marry, they are generally induced to leave their office jobs, or if necessary are forced to resign. And when, after raising children for 10 or 15 years, they wish to rejoin a paid job outside the home, they have no other choice but poorly-paid work as part-time labourers.

Now, the question that arises is: When and how did the phenomenal growth in the number of women part-time labourers come about? First of all, from interviews conducted in Japan and from written sources, it emerges that this growth has specifically occurred from the early 1970s onwards. At that time, companies had to cope with the fact that fewer and fewer high school graduates were available as new recruits. Thus, capitalist entrepreneurs had to start looking for fresh sources of cheap labour. This was noted, for instance, in a report issued in 1969 by a study commission of the Joint Committee of the Council on the Labour Force in the Economy: 'In order to maintain an annual rate of economic growth of 10.6 per cent, there will be a demand for additions to the labour force of 16.42 million between 1968 and 1975.'[48]

Both this and other governmental reports explicitly suggested tapping middle-aged women as a flexible source of new labour. As far back as 1960, the Economic Council, an advisory body to the Prime Minister, devised a plan in which the employment of women 'who constitute half of the national population' was advocated. Moreover, the authors of the plan opined that women should resign from their jobs at marriage or at the birth of the first child. Here we have a clear indication that the Economic Council devised the trend shown in the M curve. As we are further informed by a booklet on discrimination against women workers in Japan, the plan of the Economic Council emphasized the need to utilize the capacities of middle-aged women who 'wished to work again'.[49] The Council on the Labour Force similarly stated that the balance of over 8 million new employees required up to 1975, which would not be available through school graduates, should be recruited 'from a labour force which has not yet been drafted, mainly housewives'.[50]

The same thinking has further been enshrined in laws and legal amendments enacted by the Tokyo government. In April 1986, an Equal Opportunities Law became operative. This new law was a necessary outcome of the signing, by the Japanese government, of the United Nations Convention on equal opportunities between women and men. The Convention, amongst other things, contains clauses about 'equal remuneration' and the 'equal valuation of labour of equal value', but Japanese researchers and women's groups complain that their government's Equal Opportunities Law was not designed to achieve this. One of their criticisms is that the law ostensibly seeks to curb discrimination from the moment people are employed, for instance through changes in advertisement practices, but does not contain clauses regarding promotions and the allocation of functions within enterprises. In practice, women still end up in routine and low-paid jobs, for instance through a 'multi-track' system of employment which separates 'executive track' from 'clerical track' workers.[51]

Moreover, the revision of the Labour Standard Law which was passed in the Japanese parliament, the Diet, at the same time when the law on equal opportunity was adopted, reportedly pushes more women into part-time jobs. The amendment has relaxed bans on late night work for women and restrictions on over-time. Consequently, women who are unable to work long hours or late at night tend to be excluded from full-time employment and are forced to work as part-timers.[52] Japanese tax laws too are said to discourage married women from working full time, since a wife with a high salary loses her status as her husband's dependent and has to pay more taxes.[53] In short, the Tokyo government, since the late 1960s, has actively sought the entrance of middle-aged, married women into the labour market as a new labour reserve. And although in name it is committed to equal employment opportunities for women and men, in reality its laws have been designed to encourage the employment of part-time women labourers with a secondary status and comparatively low pay.

Reproductive Labour and Day Care Centres

In Chapter 4 where the feminist debate on household labour was reviewed, I recalled that Marx (like his precursor David Ricardo) took labour time as the basis for calculating the value of commodities. As stated then, and further applied in my chapters on lace-making and garment production in India, Marx's theory of value needs to be extended in order to comprehensively assess the exploitation of women under capitalism. Women workers perform two kinds of unpaid labour—waged work (partly unpaid) and domestic work (wholly unpaid)—and a calculation of the time they spend on both is required in order to illustrate how much women contribute to capitalist profits.

In the course of the interviews conducted in Japan in 1990, 'housewifization' (i.e., the patriarchal ideology which defines women as housewives) proved to be a double obstacle to the assessment of women's exploitation. First, many part-time women labourers do not see themselves as workers, but as housewives. For instance, women who as part-timers had been employed by the electronic company Shin Shirasuna in Nagoya, and who after their dismissal started a protracted legal battle against their former employer, stated that they used to consider themselves 'housewives' and not workers. In the eyes of the company and of full-time employees, they had taken up part-time jobs as 'pass-time', obscuring the real reasons that had driven them to the factory, such as the need to repay housing loans and the high educational expenses of their children.[54]

Their identification as 'housewives' thus facilitated a more intense exploitation of their labour than was the case for full-timers. The actual length of the working day of Shin Shirasuna part-timers was almost the same as that of full-timers, yet differences in pay were very substantial.[55] Meanwhile, the domestic labour which is performed by these and other women workers in Japan too remains unrecognized. To the question 'How many hours of household work do you do per day?', we got the routine answer: 'Those I have never calculated.' Thus, not only is domestic work wholly unpaid, but the time which women devote to it daily is never calculated, and this further contributes to the degradation of women's work, and to the obscuring of their double exploitation. Beyond intensification of the rate of wage labour exploitation, 'housewifization' also tends to facilitate the exploitation of non-waged labour.

In practice, the length of the combined working day of Japanese women does not seem to differ widely from that registered for women lacemakers and garment producers in the informal sector in India. Women with jobs in factories stated that they would spend an hour and a half to two hours on tasks like preparing meals before leaving home early in the morning, and another four to five hours on domestic chores after returning exhausted from their toil at the assembly line. In particular, women with children calculated high figures for their total labouring burden. For Kawanosan, a full-time quality control worker at a cigarette-producing company, the amount was 15 hours; for Ombesan, a part-time assembly line inspector at Shin Shirasuna, the amount was six and a half hours of waged work plus six hours of household work (i.e., 13 and a half hours).[56] And although systematic data is lacking, the relevance of calculating women's total labouring time was amply demonstrated through the interviews held in Japan.

The Japanese state in the post-Second World War period has, to an extent, relieved women's burden of domestic work by bearing a part of the costs relating to child care. Throughout the 1970s, the government has spent an increasing amount of money on the maintenance and operation of child care centres. This means that the state took upon itself the financing of some of the costs for the production of future labour power (i.e., of the future employees of Japan's entrepreneurs). Yet, more recently, attempts are under way to transfer responsibility back to the children's parents. Since 1980, the government has repeatedly slashed the budget for social welfare, which has notably affected day care centres.

After the Second World War, in particular during the 1950s and 1960s, a movement began in Japan demanding the establishment of public nurseries financed by the state. In some cities, women, with crying children on their backs, staged protests in front of municipal buildings. Elsewhere, mothers hung diapers to dry in the town hall. Where possible, negotiations were held with local bureaucrats, and in some cases a mayor who refused to talk to the protesters was faced with sit-down strikes. 'By the early 1970s, the nursery issue was taken up at local assembly meetings all over the nation as an important issue.'[57] This movement, under the motto 'There should be as many day care centres as mailing boxes', forced the government to contribute its share to the operating costs of day care centres.

Thus, under the pressure of agitating women, and perhaps also to facilitate the re-employment of married women, the state took the responsibility for paying as much as 80 per cent of the running costs of the nurseries.[58] For mothers with small children, it meant that they could more easily take up jobs. It signified, as said, that a part of the burden of reproducing labour power, which capital in principle leaves to the private responsibility of their workers, was henceforth carried by the state. While child-rearing, if performed by mothers–housewives, remains unpaid under capitalism, the partial transfer of this work to publicly-financed nurseries implies that the state, not workers, bears the cost.

In recent years, however, this achievement of the women's movement is slowly being eroded. On the one hand, military expenses are continuously on the rise while, on the other hand, a declining amount of money is available for social welfare in general, and for child care centres in particular. Under the slogan 'payment by the user', the government has twice reduced its contribution to running the centres, from 80 to 70 per cent of child care unit costs in 1985, and further down to 50 per cent in 1986. Between 1980 and 1986, the Tokyo government's total financial contribution declined at an expanding rate. Local municipalities in turn raised nursery fees.[59] This evolution puts added pressure on married women, more specifically on those married women who, as homeworkers, temporary workers and part-timers, are part of the labour reserve.

Women Part-timers Employed in a Retail Trading Company

A concrete description of the position held by part-time workers in Japan is provided by Tamura Katsuko, who for 15 years has been a salaried employee of the retail trading company Sunny. At the time of the interview in 1990, she was responsible for training cashiers at the company's headquarters in Fukuoka, a city located on Kyushu island. Katsukosan herself is not a part-time labourer. She enjoys a full-time job with a decent salary: the net amount is 170 to 180 thousand yen per month (roughly US$ 900 at 1990 currency rates). Yet she is very conscious of the unjust, secondary economic position of most Japanese women. To make her own husband, who according to her has 'very stereo-typed ideas about male and female roles', share in the burden of household tasks, she has waged a prolonged struggle inside the family. Proudly smiling, she tells us that at one time she simply forced him to wash and cook, by refusing to do any domestic chores. Katsukosan's consciousness has been influenced both by her own family background (her father was married into her mother's family) and by her membership of a women's group, Agora.

Tamura Katsuko explains that Sunny consists of some 60 supermarkets spread across Kyushu. A total of 1,500 persons, including staff members and non-staff personnel, are employed by the company. The majority are sales persons and cashiers, and no less than three-fourths (i.e., 1,200 persons) are part-timers. As for the company's profits, it is difficult to give precise figures. According to Katsukosan, 'Just like other Japanese retail traders, Sunny does not disclose profit figures. Whereas the company of course has to report its data to the tax office, the workers are not informed. My own estimates are that the total turn-over is ¥50 billion per year, and that Sunny's average yearly profit margin is 20 per cent.'

What about the wages of the 1,200 part-time labourers?

> The wages of the part-timers clearly differ from those of full-timers, but there also exist differences between part-timers themselves. For example, the wages of cashiers who are on their jobs in the morning are lower than those of cashiers who work in the evening. Part-timers who have to serve fish and meat receive more money than part-timers serving ordinary food. For a newly recruited part-timer, the average wage lies between ¥490 and 620 per hour [$2.5 to 3]. The wage level of an experienced part-timer is slightly higher. After one year, wages rise by ¥15 . . . . Eighty per cent of the workforce of part-timers receive less than ¥550 per hour.

This data is in accordance with the general data cited in the literature on wage levels and wage differentials in Japan. The official fact sheet brought out by the Ministry of Labour for 1988, for instance, stated that 'female part-timers earned about 70 per cent of the pay of regular female workers in 1987, thus evidencing a fairly wide disparity in wages between the two segments'.[60] The fact sheet also admitted that these disparities have tended to grow since the middle of the 1970s. The difference in wage levels between women and men cited by various sources are even larger. According to a booklet of the Fukuoka-based women's group Agora, 'women earned only 52.8 per cent of what males earned in 1983'.[61] In the famous suit brought against the Shin Shirasuna Electric Company, women part-timers demanded an end to the inequality in wages.[62]

A circumstance which seriously affects the wage levels of part-timers in Japan is the fact that they are deprived of most supplementary payments which regular employees are entitled to. The structure of the Japanese wage is rather complicated. It consists, except for a basic wage, of a series of allowances (like a holiday allowance or a family allowance). Part-time labourers are only paid a bonus at the year's end, which is a paltry sum. According to Katsukosan, in Sunny's supermarkets 'they generally receive just ¥1,000 after one year's service, ¥1,200 after 10 years [i.e., $5 to $6]. Besides, women part-timers are given a small summer bonus. Those who have not yet completed a full year's service are handed out a small present at the year's end.'

In addition, the working hours of these women labourers are much longer than what would be expected given their designation as part-timers. A part-timer's working week is assumed to last maximally 35 hours in Japan, but in practice the status of such employees often hides the real length of their labour time. Thus, even the forementioned fact sheet of the Labour Ministry admitted that 'approximately 10 per cent of women part-time workers work almost the same number of hours as full-time workers'.[63] Often, they toil barely half an hour less than full-timers. A survey carried out by a private labour research institute revealed that the average working week of women part-timers in 229 companies was 5.3 days.[64] In the Shin Shirasuna factory near Nagoya, full-timers started at 8.30 a.m. and finished work at 5.20 p. m., while the working time of part-timers lasted from 9.00 a.m. till 5.15 p. m.[65] Clearly, in such cases status as a part-timer signifies nothing but a higher rate of labour exploitation.

At Sunny, the working hours of different categories of part-timers vary greatly. According to Katsukosan,

> Part-time women labourers work under a contract which is valid for one year. Each contract is signed on an individual basis, via negotiations between the management and each individual woman from the moment when she enters employment. Most of the women work four hours a day, but some do as much as eight hours. Those with the longest working hours serve 22 to 25 days a month, five or six days per week.

Thus, while for Sunny the picture is not uniform, here too there are women who for all practical purposes are full-time on their jobs, but are called 'part-timers' in order to avoid paying them a decent salary.

Has an attempt ever been made to negotiate labour contracts collectively? What is the role of the trade union, and does it fight for improvements? Katsukosan states:

> Within the trade union based at Sunny, there indeed exists a section for part-time labourers. Those whose service period exceeds one year automatically become members. But the union is a company union and it closely cooperates with the management. The fact that women part-timers are admitted is a consequence of a rumour which earlier circulated that Sohyo [a former trade union centre linked to the Socialist party of Japan] was planning to float a trade union of part-time labourers. Sunny's management then got frightened and decided to allow part-timers join the company union.

Katsukosan finally broaches the subject of the large turn-over in personnel. Part-time labourers, Katsukosan states, mostly do not stay with Sunny for more than a couple of years. One is reminded of the transient nature of women's work in Japan's early textile factories. What are the reasons for the high rate of drop-outs from part-time work in the supermarkets? Katsukosan says: 'They find better jobs or it happens that they drop out due to human conflicts, because of friction with other women labourers. Strong and weak characters tend to clash.' But after further probing, in particular into the work pressures that women have to bear, Katsukosan explains:

> Cashiers are trained so as to be able to handle customers. The instruction guidebook contains detailed prescriptions about how to address customers, how to hand over money, how to behave when a customer passes the counter, and so on. The management has

calculated everything, even the number of seconds a cashier should devote to one customer. The work schemes are arranged in accordance with these data. Surely, some women part-timers object and it probably is one of the reasons why so many of them leave.

In short, human communication has been mechanized in Sunny's supermarkets, and even here methods of speed-up, common for workers on the assembly line in factories, are applied so as to increase the company's rate of profits.

Japanese Women as a Labour Reserve: Marx versus Bennholdt-Thomsen

After reviewing practical data on the employment experiences of Japanese women, I will look at the theoretical implications of the data. I have already referred to Marx's concept of the industrial reserve army (i.e., a 'relative surplus population' which is recruited by capitalist entrepreneurs on an irregular basis). Marx never spoke of women as a category of the labour reserve, nor did he discuss how patriarchy influences women's status as waged labourers. Yet if we once again list the major ways in which Japanese women have been employed in the various phases of the country's modernization, we find that they have always borne characteristics which Marx mentioned for the three major categories of the industrial reserve army—the latent, the stagnant and the floating.[66]

To start, let me recall the young girls who slaved in silk-reeling and cotton-spinning factories in the last quarter of the 19th and the first quarter of the 20th centuries, and who formed the bulk of the industrial workforce. One of the categories described by Marx is that of the latent reserve. This is formed by the constant flow from the countryside of former labourers in agriculture who have sunk into the morass of poverty and look for alternative employment in towns.[67] The flow of young Japanese girls to early textile mills was similarly influenced by the conditions of misery in the countryside; the female factory workers were mainly migrants. Moreover, as stated earlier, few stayed in their factory jobs for long, and their wage employment was highly transient.

Another category of women who have contributed crucially to capital accumulation in Japan are the homeworkers, whose numbers have tumbled in recent decades, but whose labour continues to be an extremely cheap source of accumulation. In *Capital*, Marx specifically referred to 'domestic industry' as the chief form of the stagnant section of the reserve army of labour, which is characterized by 'a maximum of working time, and a minimum of wages'.[68] That married women doing homework by the piece form a section of the labour reserve has been observed both by 'Marxist emancipationists' such as Bebel in Germany and, more recently, by socialist–feminist authors. Thus, the socialist–feminist historian Leydesdorff, who has analyzed the contribution of married women homeworkers (producing umbrellas, processing peas, and so on) to the Dutch economy at the beginning of this century, has argued that they constituted a specific category of the industrial reserve army. 'Married women and their families working at home . . . could not join factory production but manifested all characteristics of the industrial reserve army.'[69] Leydesdorff explicitly referred to the economic role of married women in the family to explain why they are part of the reserve army of labour.

The section of Japanese women, which today most clearly holds the function of a labour reserve, is that of married, middle-aged women employed as part-time workers. First, part-timers fulfil the general criterion stipulated by Marx for the labour reserve. Being paid an hourly wage at low rates, their employment probably exerts a downward pressure on the overall level of wages in the Japanese economy. Part-timers can also be shifted between various industrial and service sectors, since the owners of capital can dismiss them at any time. In Marx's categorization they could be called the floating form of the labour reserve. In the Japanese press, part-timers have been likened to chopsticks which, after the daily meal, are disposed of without further thought: 'Like disposable chopsticks, throwaway lighters and pocket cameras, part-time women workers have often been regarded in the past as being "easily disposable".'[70]

The fact that married women are a part of the reserve army of labour has been stressed by socialist–feminist authors who, since the second part of the 1970s, have re-investigated women's waged work in Western, industrialized societies. One such author is the British researcher, Veronika Beechey. She argues that married women should be defined as a specific form of the labour reserve, different from those described by Marx. They can be made redundant more easily than men because, for example, they are less likely to be strongly unionized and because they do not appear in unemployment statistics. Moreover, women are more likely to be a flexible labour force, she states, since they are horizontally mobile and are willing to take on part-time work. And since women's wage rates are substantially lower than men's, female employment poses a particularly intense pressure on wages.[71]

Thus, Beechey has pointed to the specific role of married women within the labour reserve, and she has also initiated the analysis of part-time work. She has, moreover, explained why married women form a separate category. The basic reason, she states, lies in the patriarchal structure and ideology of society. Women's primary economic task under capitalism is domestic labour. The sexual division of labour is presumed by society and is embodied in the policies of industrial states. In Beechey's view, Marx inadequately recognized this reality, and he was unable to theorize it satisfactorily. Since his work lacked a theory of the family and the sexual division of labour, he was unable to provide an adequate explanation of female labour in general, and could not elaborate on women's role as part of the labour reserve.[72]

The evidence that I have gathered on part-time work in Japan broadly confirms what Beechey states. For the whole idea behind the M curve is to split up women's lives in such a manner that women's responsibility for reproductive work is preserved. The presumption which underlies the re-employment of middle-aged, married women as part-timers is that they first fulfil their responsibility as mothers and housewives during the period when children grow up. Clearly, the Japanese owners of capital, in employing women as part-timers, take full advantage of the unequal, sexual division of labour in society. Traditional relations between women and men are taken for granted, and the whole structure of part-time work is based on it.[73] Without preservation of patriarchy, the strategy for the continued accumulation of capital in Japan probably would not work.

One of the members of the German feminist school, Veronika Bennholdt-Thomsen, has addressed the theme of the 'relative surplus population'.[74] Here she has given the following view regarding the origins of a superfluous population in relation to capital. Through the constant revolution in technology, she argues, a part of the wage-working population becomes superfluous and is 'banished' from the process of capital accumulation. Thus, in highly industrialized countries, a 'marginal mass' is created which is 'in charge of its own reproduction'. Members of the surplus population 'sell their products and labour for less than minimum subsistence'.[75]

Bennholdt-Thomsen's view, to some extent, helps explain what has happened in Western Europe during the last two decades. Ever since the mid 1970s, most countries of Western Europe have suffered from structural employment, with millions of people available for waged work, more or less permanently, unable to find paid jobs. And while the state, to some extent, pays for the subsistence needs of this 'marginal mass' in the form of unemployment rates, it is also true that the relative surplus population seeks additional sources of survival through non-waged forms of labour. The contradictory evolution of capitalism, to some extent, does lead to the re-appearance of production for immediate consumption—of subsistence production as defined by members of the German feminist school.

Yet Bennholdt-Thomsen's analysis hardly helps us understand the expansion in women's part-time labour which has occurred over the last 25 years in Japan. For this process has not involved the banishment, but rather the incorporation, of millions of women in the process of capitalist production. Women who formerly were 'merely' in charge of reproductive tasks, as housewives, were drawn into the labour market. Their labour power was newly tapped by capital. And while this incorporation has not signified that married women received permanent employment (their inclusion was organized so as to ensure the availability of a disposable labour reserve), it was consequent upon capital's need for additional labour, as explained earlier.

The key to analyzing the expansion of women's part-time labour in Japan does not lie in technological innovation, but in the structure of patriarchal relations which relegates women to a secondary position in society. The state, industrial entrepreneurs and companies in the service sector from the early 1960s onwards started consciously looking for a new source of flexible labour that could be extracted at low costs. In opting for the employment of middle-aged married women, they took full advantage of women's permanent responsibility for child-rearing, and of patriarchal ideology which defines women's waged work as supplementary. And although the employment of women part-time workers, as stated, is never permanent, its emergence seems to have signalled a substantial increase in the number of people who sell their labour power to the Japanese owners of capital.

Summary

As the foregoing description and analysis shows, women's labour has been crucial for capital accumulation all through the history of Japan's industrialization. Already, in the phase when the first silk-reeling and cotton-spinning factories were established, their owners preferred young village women as wage workers. Through strict rules of factory life, by ignoring women's health, and by ruthless extension of the working day, the early capitalists were able to harvest quick and rich profits. Thus, the basis for Japan's modernization was laid through the production of absolute surplus value and through the exploitation of an overwhelmingly female force of factory workers.

However, women's labour has not only been important in a bygone era. The multinationals that dominate Japan's economy today continue to rely on women's labour, in particular for tasks that are monotonous, require 'nimble fingers' and patience, qualities which supposedly are women's natural attributes. Although the proportion of male employees in the electronics sector, which has taken over the role of textiles as the motor of the economy, has increased during the 1980s, many manual tasks continue to be performed by women whose labour is defined as 'semi-' or 'unskilled'. Thus, in the production of ICs, a strict sectorial division of labour between women and men is maintained, with women relegated to such strenuous tasks as bonding and quality control of chips through microscopes.

An overview of women's role in the contemporary economy further illustrates that Japanese companies (both in the industrial and in the service sector) consider women to be a vast labour reserve. Whether they are young girls recruited by banks and supermarkets, or temporary workers recruited through 'manpower agencies', married women with small children doing work at piece-rates in their homes, or middle-aged women employed as 'part-timers', all categories of women workers are paid low wages, and are easily disposable. Of all these listed categories, that of part-timers appears to be the numerically largest one today. Not coincidentally, this form of employment has been designed in order to provide Japanese companies with a cheap labour reserve.

Marx's theory of the reserve army of labour, as stated, can be used to explain the function which women's labour fulfils within the Japanese economy, but needs to be elaborated. The employment of middle-aged, married women as part-timers, who are paid hourly rates and are deprived of supplementary allowances, is only possible because of patriarchy. They are available as a cheap reserve precisely because of their forced absence from the labour market throughout the period of their life when they have to bear and rear children (i.e., capital's future labour force). The socialist–feminist analysis regarding the status of married women as a specific segment of the labour reserve is best able to explain .the reality faced by contemporary women in Japan.

Notes and References

1. Bennholdt-Thomsen (1981), p. 27.
2. See, for instance, Bouwman (1986), p. 157; Ichiyo (1987), p. 39.
3. Harui (1985), p. 51; Kidd (1978), p. 1; Saxonhouse (1976), p. 97.
4. Harui (1985), pp. 51–52.
5. Saxonhouse (1976), p. 97.
6. Ibid., p. 101.
7. This first strike is noteworthy. According to Tanaka (1977, p. 23), women workers of a silk-reeling factory locked themselves in a temple. The action reportedly sparked off a wave of strikes in textile mills throughout Japan, heralding the awakening of a new class. As Tanaka notes, 'The strikes in this early stage almost always resulted in a victory for the women workers, because the owners had as yet no strategy to suppress these strikes.'
8. Harui (1985), p. 54; Kidd (1978), p. 31.
9. Kidd (1978), pp. 25, 27.
10. Kidd (1978), p. 19.
11. Ibid., p. 22.
12. Ibid., pp. 22–23.
13. Harui (1985), p. 54; Kidd (1978), p. 9.
14. Kidd (1978), p. 34.
15. Ibid., p. 45.
16. Ibid., p. 44. See also Harui (1985), p. 55.
17. Saxonhouse (1976), p. 103.
18. Kidd (1978), p. 18.
19. Saxonhouse (1976), p. 98.
20. See, for instance, Harui (1985), p. 63.
21. Kidd (1978), p. 39.
22. Ibid., p. 40.
23. Ibid., p. 51. See also Harui (1985), p. 55.
24. Harui (1985), p. 69.
25. Kidd (1978), p. 29.
26. Personal communication, Tokyo, February 1990.
27. Hiroki (1986), p. 26.

28. Kuniko (1988).
29. Mitter (1986), p. 89.
30. Ibid., p. 91.
31. Kuniko (1988), p. 47.
32. Ibid.
33. Ibid.
34. Mitter (1986), p. 92.
35. Ibid., p. 93.
36. Personal communication.
37. Proceedings of the International Consultation on Micro-Chip Technology (1986), p. 27.
38. Hancock (1983), p. 142.
39. Hiroki (1986), pp. 18–19.
40. Ibid., p. 32.
41. Ministry of Labour (1989a), p. 11.
42. Ibid., p. 6. See also Ministry of Labour (1989b), p. 4. For recent data on the evolution in the number of 'working women', see Nakano (1995), p. 35.
43. Ministry of Labour (1989a), p. 9.
44. For a report on the Temporary Workers' Employment Act, see the newsletter, *Resource Materials on Women's Labour in Japan*, No. 3, June 1988, p. 3.
45. According to the Ministry of Labour (1989a), p. 10, of Japan, 'outworkers in the home' numbered 998,000 in 1989, but this figure is probably an understatement.
46. Personal communication, February 1990.
47. Annavajhula (1989), p. M–23.
48. Carney and O'Kelly (n.d.), p. 23.
49. Shiozawa and Hiroki (1988), p. 19. According to the same source, laws like the Womens' Welfare Act and the Employment Insurance Act were adopted in 1972 and 1974 specifically to promote the employment of women along the pattern of the M curve.
50. Carney and O'Kelly (undated), p. 23.
51. See *Resource Materials on Women's Labour in Japan*, (1987), p. 5. Nakano (1995), p. 37, states: 'Companies introduced a dual-career tract employment system when the EEOL (Equal Employment Opportunities Law) was enforced. The aim of this system was to divide workers into two groups—managerial and general clerical—at the time of employment. This system soon proved to be a mere pretext for stabilizing and even expanding the existing sexual discrimination against women by simply placing women into the subsidiary group at the start, or by excluding women workers from the managerial group by imposing transfers to faraway places and long working hours, knowing it would be virtually impossible for most women to accept these conditions.'
52. Agora (n.d.), p. 7.
53. Ibid., p. 4. According to Glucksmann (1990), p. 43, 'the mass entry of married women to the waged labour market' in Britain was strictly a development that occurred after the Second World War and was 'closely associated with the possibility of working on a part-time basis'.
54. Interview with former part-time employees of Shin Shirasuna, Nagoya, February, 1990.

55. Harui (1985), p. 67. 'The part-timers were only working 35 minutes a day less than the full-timers, yet receiving half the wage (¥50,000 to 70,000 a month). On top of this, the full-timers received ¥400,000 as bonuses compared to the ¥60,000 received by part-timers.'
56. Figures from both women were obtained through personal communication, February 1990.
57. Hiroki (1988).
58. Ibid., p. 11.
59. Ibid., pp. 11–12.
60. Ministry of Labour (1989b), p. 4.
61. Agora (n.d.), p. 4.
62. Interview with the former part-time employees of Shin Shirasuna, Nagoya, February 1990, on wage differentials between women and men. See also Nakano (1995), p. 37.
63. Ministry of Labour (1989b), p. 4.
64. See *Resource Materials on Women's Labour in Japan*, (1989), p. 9.
65. Personal communication by former Shin Shirasuna part-time workers, February 1990.
66. Marx (1977a), p. 600.
67. Ibid., p. 601.
68. Ibid., p. 602.
69. Leydesdorff (1977), p. 123. Speaking specifically about British women part-time workers, Bruegel (1986), p. 49, argues: 'it is part-time women workers who form an increasing proportion of women workers (40 per cent are now part-time), who conform most closely to the model of women as a disposable reserve army'.
70. Marx (1977a), p. 600. See also 'Part-Time Women Workers', *Mainichi Shimbun*, Tokyo, 26 February 1990, editorial, p. 2, and Chapman (1987), p. 11.
71. Beechey (1987), pp. 48–49.
72. Ibid., p. 9.
73. Nakano (1995), p. 35, states, 'Companies operate under the pretext that women, who bear the brunt of family responsibilities, cannot sacrifice their family life as men do. By so doing they confine women primarily into part-time employment where unstable position and bad working conditions are a given.'
74. Bennholdt-Thomsen (1981).
75. Ibid., p. 26. For a critical review of the thesis on the reserve army of labour as applied to women, see Barrett (1980), p. 158.

13

Conclusion: Capital Accumulation in Contemporary Asia

In the preceding chapters, I have reviewed the economic experiences of three Asian countries—Japan, Bangladesh and India—and I have taken the labouring activities of women in agriculture and industry as my point of departure. In my investigation, I have assessed the relevance of Marxist economic concepts, such as the concept of the original accumulation of capital, Marx's theory of the working day, his analysis of the turn-over time of capital, and his concept of the 'reserve army of labour'. In Marx's own days, the economies of Asia were marginal to the world economic system, and his theory was primarily anchored on the experience of Britain, then the centre of the system. My investigation shows that the process of capital accumulation in Asia has 'progressed' up to the point where Marx's tools of analysis have become highly applicable to the realities in this continent.

In reviewing the labour of women in Bangladesh, India and Japan, I have tried to assess the significance of concepts which have been proposed by participants in the international feminist debate. Here I have concentrated, in particular, on the views of four distinct currents. First, I have drawn attention to authors belonging to developmental feminism who, in researching rural women's labour, have sought to support women's 'integration in development'. Further, I have contrasted their views with those of the ecofeminist author, Vandana Shiva, who questions the existing economic growth process as 'maldevelopment', leading to ecological destruction, loss of common property resources and the marginalization of women. The third current, of which I have reviewed books and articles, is the German feminist school. The theses of Maria Mies and others on 'housewifization' and 'subsistence labour' were especially relevant to my discussion, since they have precisely been devised for the analysis of women's work. Finally, in my chapters on 'Japanization' and women in the Japanese economy, I have briefly referred to socialist–feminist analytical work.

Original Accumulation and the Economy of Bangladesh

The process of original or 'primitive' accumulation is one of the historical processes analyzed by Marx. Marx has argued that

> capitalist production presupposes the pre-existence of considerable masses of capital and of labour power in the hands of the producers of commodities. The whole movement, therefore, seems to turn in a vicious circle, out of which we can only get by supposing a primitive accumulation [previous accumulation of Adam Smith] preceding capitalist accumulation; an accumulation *not the result of the capitalist mode of production, but its starting point.*[1]

How did Marx view this process for England, the environment from which he drew much of his investigative material? In subsequent chapters, Marx described in detail the violent manner in which the English peasantry, from the 15th century onwards, was driven from the soil. Capital was created by depriving the agricultural population of its means of production, primarily land. A key aspect of the process of dispossession, as analyzed by Marx, was the enclosure of the commons: fields which, in earlier centuries, were held in common and used as pasture for the peasants' animals, were fenced off and used for the grazing of sheep. These sheep were owned by capitalist farmers, who were interested in producing raw wool for England's growing wool industry. The enclosure of the commons was supported by 'bloody legislation' enacted by the British state.

Thus, Marx's analysis of the original accumulation that preceded the industrial revolution was very concrete. For him, the road to capitalist accumulation was paved through dispossession of the agricultural producers: 'The expropriation of the agricultural producer, of the peasant, is the basis of the whole process.'[2] This dispossession helps to pave the way for the formation of both the class of wage labourers, and the class of capitalist entrepreneurs. For Marx, the two developments were clearly interconnected. In one violent sweep, the social means of subsistence and production previously held by the peasants were transformed into capital, while the immediate producers were turned into wage labourers. 'The so-called primitive accumulation, therefore, is nothing else than the historical process of divorcing the producer from the means of production.'[3]

In the chapter on women's labour in Bangladeshi agriculture, I have sought to explain how the concept of original or 'primitive' accumulation is crucial to understanding the expropriation of the Bangladeshi peasantry under the impact of 'modernization', which has taken place in the last two decades in particular. Here, I have pinpointed two key developments. On the one hand, millions of former, small peasant proprietors have been turned into landless peasants as a consequence of the dominance of commercial traders, who 'skim off' the agricultural surplus through the method of buying cheap and selling dear. Underpayment of the producers of agricultural commodities, the spread of peasants' indebtedness, and the loss of arable land on a vast scale have been consistent and interrelated features of the Bangladeshi rural economy throughout the period since the country's formal political independence in 1971.

On the other hand, the rural poor are increasingly being deprived of their access to common property resources, in a process which is broadly comparable to the historic enclosure of the commons in England. For the agenda underlying the drive to build embankments and polders throughout the country's fertile delta, is the desire on the part of the World Bank, Bangladesh's major 'donor', and the country's own rural and urban elite, to privatize natural resources which have always been held in common. Although this is never explicitly stated, and remains hidden under a barrage of propaganda about 'people's participation', the effect of the construction of embankments is to restrict the free access of peasant women and men to water and fishery resources. In order to create the basis for capitalist accumulation, the immediate producers in the countryside of Bangladesh have to be separated from their means of subsistence and, as it seems, at any social or ecological cost.

Prominent Marxist theoreticians in the 1960s and 1970s, like André Gunder Frank, have elaborated on the continued occurrence of original accumulation long after capitalism has been established as a world economic system. Frank has argued that there surely was a long period of original accumulation that preceded self-sustaining capital accumulation through the production of surplus value by wage labourers.[4] He, however, disputes whether this process stopped after the industrial revolution. Moreover, the occurrence of 'primitive' accumulation has not been limited to Great Britain. Peasant producers in the Third World in the colonial and post-colonial period have been, and continue to be, robbed of part of their consumption fund in the interest of capital accumulation in the centres of the world economy. The dispossession of the immediate producers, the appropriation of their means of production, is a worldwide and persistent phenomenon.

The evidence gathered on Bangladesh, thus, broadly supports Frank's conclusion that 'the process of divorcing owners from their means of production and converting them into wage labourers was not only primitive, original, or previous to the capitalist stage, but also continued during the capitalist stage, as it still does'.[5] Though Bangladesh has been incorporated into the world economy, its agriculture continues to bear many features of the pre-capitalist mode of production, including the fact that peasant producers have access to natural resources which have not yet been turned into commodities for market sale. The evidence on the effects of embankment and polder construction illustrates well that original accumulation is taking place in full swing. Such accumulation is being promoted by the very institutions, such as the World Bank, which also staunchly defend surplus production in its 'proper' capitalist form.

Marx's Theory of the Working Day and the Garments Sector in Bangladesh

Bangladesh's experiences, however, cannot only be used to demonstrate the present-day occurrence of original accumulation, but can also illustrate the nature of capital accumulation proper. Marx's understanding regarding the basic character of capitalist production has been referred to repeatedly in this book, and there is no need to restate his labour theory of value *in extenso*. The accumulation of industrial entrepreneurs is made possible through the appropriation of what Marx called surplus value—of that value which the waged labourers produce on top of the value required for their subsistence. This distinction between surplus labour and subsistence or 'necessary' labour makes it possible to explain modern-day exploitation. It is the very cornerstone of Marx's system of economic thought.

One of the two major ways in which the appropriation of surplus value by the owners of capital is achieved is through the prolongation of the working day, a method which was amply used by British factory owners in the period during and after the industrial revolution. Marx calls this method the production of absolute surplus value: 'the production of absolute surplus value turns exclusively upon the length of the working day'; he considers it 'the groundwork of the capitalist system'.[6] Thus, Marx defines absolute surplus value as: 'The prolongation of the working day beyond the point at which the labourer would have produced just an equivalent for the value of his labour power, and the appropriation of that surplus labour by capital, this is *production of absolute surplus value*.'[7]

Historically speaking, the proponents of the capitalist mode of production in England had to wage a protracted struggle to enforce a gradual extension of the working day. As Marx indicates, up to the epoch of modern industry and machinery, capital in England had not succeeded in seizing for itself the whole week of the labourers, and the struggle to compel them to toil the whole six days in the week continued throughout the greater part of the 18th century. It was only in the last third of that century that 'all bounds of morals and nature, age and sex, day and night, were broken down'.[8] Only then, only with the birth of modern industry, were all limitations to the length of the working day removed. The 'boundless thirst for surplus value' of the entrepreneurs, Marx remarks in characteristic language, was reflected in an extension of the time wage labourers had to work—beyond even what could physically be borne.

In the chapter on the export-oriented garments' sector in Bangladesh, we have seen how Marx's theory of the working day can be applied to industrial relations in a Third World economy today. This sector, as stated, was founded only in 1977, and over a period of some 15 years has grown into the principal industrial sector of Bangladesh's economy, employing more than three times the number of wage workers in the second-largest sector—that of jute. Like their British predecessors of the late 18th and early 19th centuries, the owners of Bangladeshi garment factories have waged a relentless struggle for the extension of the working day. Neither the traditionally strong jute sector, nor the agrarian sector which still employs the vast majority of the country's producers, is characterized by similarly long hours of toil. It is only in the sector of readymade garments that the working day is exceedingly long. In some cases, working time is stretched up to 48 or 72 hours (i.e., beyond what is physically sustainable for the mainly female workforce of the factories).

The practice of the limitless extension of the working day was illustrated through a description of violations of government laws, in particular the Factory Act of 1965. The Factory Act and other regulations had sought to limit the exploitation of industrial workers through prescriptions, such as regarding the normal length of the working day, the maximum length of overtime work, the number of hours that children may be set to work in factories and the working time of women. The practice of forced overwork for which the workers receive no pay, prolongation of the probationers' period far beyond the legally fixed maximum, children being obliged to do overtime work like adults, and many other illegal practices amply demonstrates the owners' drive to appropriate as much labour time as possible, and increase the rate of workers' exploitation to the maximum.

Thus, Marx's view regarding the extraction of 'absolute' surplus value remains as relevant to understanding conditions in Third World industries today as it was for the analysis of conditions in Britain in the 19th century. The existence of phenomena like a labouring day of 14 to 16 hours and overtime work of 70 hours or more per month, with pay rates of 40 to 60 per cent of the normal hourly rate, can best be analyzed within the theoretical framework devised by Marx. The distinction between necessary and surplus labour time, which is hidden from the eye of the workers because it is never made by the owners who buy their labour power, is the key to laying bare, and quantifying, the exploitation garment workers are subjected to. Without Marx's distinction, the causes of the 'medieval' slavery in modern, world market-oriented garment factories, remain a mystery.

Finally, it should be mentioned that there is one crucial difference between the economic position of contemporary Bangladeshi garment workers and that of 19th-century industrial workers in England. Unlike the surplus value produced by the latter, the surplus value produced by Bangladeshi garment workers does not wholly accrue to the immediate owners: the lion's share of profits from readymade garments is appropriated by retail trading companies in countries of the North. It is they who are partly responsible for the fact that the

Bangladeshi workers are robbed of part of their consumption fund. A comprehensive assessment of the production relations in Bangladesh's garments' sector, in short, needs to take account of this double structure for the appropriation of surplus value—of the 'skimming off' of value through unequal trade relations side by side with the appropriation of value by the immediate owners of the factories.

Japanization and the Turn-over Time of Capital

In the chapter on Japanese methods of industrial management, the relevance of Marx's analysis regarding the turn-over time of capital has been discussed. Turn-over time, as defined by Marx, comprises both the time of the actual production of commodities, and the circulation time before and after production (i.e., the time needed to purchase raw materials and that needed for the sale of the produced goods). This turn-over time plays an important role in the calculations which the owners of capital make. 'From the point of view of the capitalist', Marx explained, 'the time of turn-over of his capital is the time for which he must advance his capital in order to create surplus value with it and receive it back in its original shape'.[9]

In elaborating further on the importance of the theme of turn-over time, Marx raised and answered two basic questions which retain all their actuality today. The first is whether the length of turn-over time exerts an independent influence on the amount of value that can be created. Does the duration of production and circulation time combined have an effect on the accumulation process, independent from the value-creating power of labour, which Marx considers the source of value? Marx argues that the answer should be 'yes', and proves it through precise calculations. The owner of a mass of capital which is four times smaller in size than the capital of another entrepreneur can nevertheless gather at least as much surplus value as the latter, if the turn-over time of his capital is one-fourth in duration.[10] The greater velocity of his capital makes up for its relatively small size.

The second question discussed by Marx is whether the impact of turn-over time on value creation is positive or negative. Marx repeatedly states that the part of turn-over time in which the owner is busy with the tasks of procuring raw materials and getting his commodities sold (i.e., circulation time), constitutes a time of devaluation.[11] This time thus exerts a negative influence, and is, in Marx's words, a 'natural barrier' to value creation. The longer the circulation time lasts, the costlier it is for the owners of capital. Consequently, they are engaged in a continuous battle to reduce the circulation time to the barest minimum, and bring this time as close as possible to zero.

This explanation given by Marx in the middle of the 19th century is helpful to analyse the key developments that have taken place in the world economy during the 1980s. Let us look once again at the circulation time of capital, at the period before and after the time in which the industrial goods are actually produced. The length of these timings is influenced by the speed with which orders to and from the producing company can be transmitted. Whereas, at the time of the industrial revolution, factory owners needed to rely on couriers to transmit messages to suppliers or buyers, they could later accelerate their communication through the post and telegraph system. Since the introduction of computers and faxes, transmission time has been brought down to nearly zero. Following Marx's explanation regarding the role of circulation time, it is easy to understand the interest which capitalist enterprises have in the development of telecommunications.

In the chapter on Japanization, I have pointed out that the issue of the turn-over time of capital has been one of the factors influencing the devising of both Fordism (Americanism) and Toyotism (Japanization)—the two management methods that have shaped industrial relations in the key sectors of the world economy in the 20th century. In devising both, the desire to shorten the turn-over time of capital has been a key element. In the case of Fordism, efforts have focused primarily on eliminating 'unproductive' time intervals between different stages of the production process. For one of the effects of the introduction of the assembly line was to reduce the time required for transportation (for instance, component parts of automobiles) in between the manual tasks performed by the workers to assemble the cars.

In the case of Toyotism, the desire to abbreviate the turn-over-time of capital has, perhaps, had an even more decisive impact. One of the obstacles to the circulation of capital, Marx explains, is that there must always be a greater accumulation of ready raw materials, and so on, at the place of production than is used up, say, daily or weekly. Hence the demand 'for a greater rapidity, regularity, and reliability in furnishing the necessary raw materials, so that no interruption will ever occur'.[12] Capital's urge to restrict the time of storage has played a key role in the devising of Toyotism. The Japanese word which concisely expresses this urge is *kanban*, meaning the demand that subcontracting companies deliver their components strictly on time so that the company or corporation does not need to keep stocks, and faces no interruption in its own production process.

Finally, it may be objected that the principle of *kanban* is not the only one involved in Japanization. As my own analysis has brought out, the differential manner in which Japanese companies treat workers' knowledge, indeed, is no less important to our understanding of Toyotism. The institution of 'quality control circles' was analyzed as a 'correction' to Taylorism—the management style which has held sway since the beginning of this century where the aim was to completely monopolize knowledge in a separate department of engineers. This aspect of Toyotism surely cannot be analyzed on the basis of Marx's theory laid down in the 19th century. Still, Marx's elaborate discussion regarding the issue of turn-over time, and his view that entrepreneurs have an interest in removing all barriers to the speediest possible circulation of capital, is relevant to our analysis of the recent innovations in industrial management.

Marx's Thesis of the Industrial Reserve Army Applied to Japanese Women

In the chapter on the position of women in the Japanese economy, I have tried to demonstrate how the employment policies pursued in relation to women in Japan can best be understood on the basis of Marx's theory regarding the 'relative surplus population' or 'reserve army of labour'. Marx observes that the capitalist mode of production does not only give birth to a new class, that of the collective workers, but also produces an excess population. He argues that 'it is capitalistic accumulation itself that constantly produces, and produces in the direct ratio of its own energy and extent, a relatively redundant population of labourers'.[13] Marx speaks in this context of a 'a law of population peculiar to the capitalist mode of production'.[14]

This relatively superfluous section of the working class, Marx further states, becomes 'the lever of capitalist accumulation, nay, a condition of existence of the capitalist mode of production. It forms a disposable industrial reserve army, that belongs to capital quite as absolutely as if the latter had bred it at its own cost'.[15] The key function of the floating reserve, of people who are employed and dismissed by the owners at will, is to press down the general level of wages and hold the 'pretentions' of regular wage employees in check. Marx even believed that the general movement of wages is 'exclusively regulated by the expansion and contraction of the industrial reserve army', a process which corresponds to the periodic changes in the industrial cycle.[16]

Marx illustrates his views with extensive data on the situation at the time in England. He calls England explicitly the 'classical example' of capitalism, because of its leading position in the world economy and because capitalist production 'is here alone completely developed'.[17] Thus, he records the undernourishment of the worst-paid section of the British industrial working class; the deplorable health conditions of persons belonging to the 'nomad population' (i.e., migrant workers whose origins lie in agriculture); and he also details the decreasing standard of living among agricultural workers. While the reserve army of labour can be divided into various categories, they have a shared role for the process of capital accumulation (namely, to keep the level of wages in society in check).

Marx's theory, at least its essential traits, can well be applied to contemporary Japan, to explain the secondary economic position held by women waged labourers. Alongside the United States and the countries of the European Union, Japan today occupies centre-stage in the world economy. Of all the states of Asia, it is undoubtedly the country where the capitalist mode of production has most fully been developed. And although the rate of unemployment is low compared to other industrialized countries, the Japanese economy nevertheless harbours a large reserve army of labourers. Typically, the 8 million middle-aged women who toil as part-time workers, can be disposed of, dismissed, any time the company owners employing them choose to do so.

Following what Marx did for England, I have looked at the different categories of Japanese women workers belonging to the labour reserve. The position of women recruited as temporary workers through 'manpower agencies' is highly insecure: they are 'sometimes repelled, sometimes attracted' (i.e., they clearly form a floating section of the labour reserve.[18] The category of women homeworkers could be called a 'stagnant' section: while their numbers have decreased, they are definitely the lowest paid of all Japanese women performing waged labour. The most significant section, as we have seen, is that of women 'part-time' workers. Although they work an almost equal number of hours as 'full-timers', their wage is only two-thirds that of regular women workers, and they are deprived of most extra payments which regular employees in Japan are entitled to.

The institutionalization of part-time work in the Japanese economy, perhaps, most clearly shows that the existence of a labour reserve is a matter of life and death for the process of capital accumulation. As mentioned, the Japanese state played a very active role in promoting the employment of middle-aged women as part-timers. It was a governmental body, the Economic Council, which devised the M curve that helped to institutionalize the idea of part-timers in the 1960s. And although the government in name promotes 'equal opportunities' for women and men, in practice it has facilitated the emergence of a new, female workforce in the Japanese economy, which is characterized by its cheapness and disposability. Japanese women who are part-timers, in short, show the classical features of members of the reserve army of labour, as defined by Marx.

The idea that women in capitalist countries form part of the reserve army of labour is in no sense new. It has been put forward both by orthodox Marxist authors, such as Bebel,[19] and by contemporary feminist writers, like Bennholdt-Thomsen.[20] What the example of part-time workers in Japan clearly brings out is that women's role as part of the labour reserve is conditioned by patriarchy and the sexual division of labour it prescribes. For it is women's responsibility for the bearing and rearing of children, the fact that they are excluded from participation in wage labour for a whole period of their lives, which has made it possible for the Japanese state to define middle-aged women as a readily available labour reserve. Thus, while Marx's concept of the industrial reserve army of labour is relevant to our analysis of the position of women part-timers in Japan, the feminist analysis regarding the sexual division of labour in the family is its necessary correlative.

Non-waged Labour of Women and the Extension of Marx's Labour Theory of Value

Though many of Marx's ideas, as illustrated, are still relevant for the understanding of Asian economies today, his labour theory of value, which formed the cornerstone of his economic thought, cannot be uncritically accepted. Ever since the first wave of feminism, the non-inclusion of women's domestic chores, and of other non-waged work performed by women in Marx's economic theory, has been questioned by leading feminist spokeswomen. Just as Marx's own theory was anchored on the experience of the European proletariat in the 19th century, the debate about household labour for analogous historical reasons too tended to be Eurocentric in the beginning. Thus, it tended to largely ignore the productive activities of rural women in the Third World. Nevertheless, the debate has resulted in an important extension of Marx's labour theory of value, with universal implications.

I have argued in this book that to understand the evolution, strengths and weaknesses of feminism during its first and second waves, we need to be aware of a striking contrast: between the organizational achievements of the German proletarian women's movement in the beginning of this century, and the theoretical achievements of the women's movement which emerged in industrialized countries during the 1960s. The German proletarian women's movement showed, at the practical level, how to mobilize both female wage workers and proletarian housewives, yet its theoretical achievements were meagre. From the experiences during the second feminist wave, on the contrary, few positive, organizational lessons can be drawn. Still, it is during this second wave that the 'riddle' regarding household labour was basically solved at the level of theory. Here one can speak of uneven development between theory and practice recurring twice in history.

The proletarian women's movement under the leadership of Clara Zetkin developed a remarkable, quantitative organizational strength. It was characterized by a significant degree of autonomy vis-à-vis the male leadership of the official, working class party, the Social Democratic Party, and conditions of repression forced it to be very flexible in organizational methods. Given the need to ensure the broad participation of women in all three 'departments' of women's labour (the formal sector, the informal sector, and the sector of household labour), the movement learnt to rely on a combination of action forms, including strikes and political boycotts. Meanwhile, the investigations into the exploitation of working-class women carried out at the time resulted in rich perceptual knowledge, but failed to enhance the conceptual understanding of the leaders of the proletarian women's movement, and of thinkers belonging to the Social Democratic Party's left wing.

The experiences gained during the second wave of feminism, as mentioned, did not give rise to powerful new organizational ideas. The movement was hampered because of the narrow focus on women performing domestic chores. The debates tended to create a divide between housewives and women doing wage labour in the formal and informal industrial sectors. Yet a conceptual breakthrough was achieved with far-reaching consequences, in particular when Dalla Costa put forward the view that household labour does not just create use values, but exchange values in the form of the commodity labour power as well. Women at home produce, Dalla Costa argued, when they give birth to children and raise them (future labour power), and they produce when they restore the strength, the labouring capacity, of living workers (present labour power). With this conceptual framework laid down, it is possible to visualize that women's labour under capitalism is more all-embracing than men's.

In this book I have applied this feminist extension of Marx's labour theory of value to women's labour in Asian economies. Marx stated that value is determined by labour time, but in calculating labour time he only looked at the time which wage labourers spend producing commodities for capitalist entrepreneurs. In my investigation into the labour of women part-time labourers in Japan, I have calculated both the time they toil in the factories, and the time they do domestic chores: their average working week turned out to be 90 hours or more. Again, when interviewing homeworkers stitching garments at piece-rates in West Bengal, equally dramatic results were obtained: women perform 15 hours of labour per day, out of which more than half is non-waged. Given the fact that women's reproductive work is necessary, and essential, to the maintenance of their own working capacity and that of their family members, it needs to be included when calculating the degree of exploitation which women workers are subjected to.

Women's creation of both use and exchange values has also been brought out in this book. The view that women labourers create both kinds of values was, for instance, powerfully demonstrated by Mies in her investigation into the lace industry in Narsapur, India. While the work of Indian women cannot be equated with that of housewives in the West, many of the activities they perform (such as the production of cowdung cakes and milk) clearly have a double, value-creating nature since they are often intended both for family consumption and market sale. Thus, in spite of sharp differences between the economic circumstance of Third World countries and the industrialized North, the critique and extension of Marx's labour theory of value formulated during the second feminist wave can well be applied to women's labour in the Third World. It provides a fruitful, basic framework for assessing women's contribution to the creation of values.

The Sexual Division of Labour and the Experience of Asian Economies

An interrelated theme which also calls for a criticism of Marx's views is that of the sexual division of labour. Marx tended to dismiss the question of the division of labour between women and men as 'naturally given'. As explained here, in his view the first social division of labour in history was the division of labour between towns and villages. Participants in the contemporary debate on women's labour have judged otherwise. Except for the ecofeminist Shiva, the writings of women belonging to all other currents of international feminism accord great importance to the theme of the sexual division of labour and its varied manifestations. It is, in fact, now considered to have been the first division of labour established in human history.

For a concrete discussion of the given theme, a broad distinction can usefully be made between the 'social' and the 'sectoral' division of labour between the sexes.[21] The social division of labour between women and men refers to the fact that, throughout society, women are held responsible for domestic tasks like cooking, cleaning and raising children, whereas men are exempted from such tasks. The sectoral division of labour refers to the fact that within specific sectors of a given economy—whether the production of crops (i.e., sector of agriculture) or the industrial sector—a hierarchical division of labour between women and men also operates. Whereas the former, sexual division is 'fixed' and is of a universal character, the latter changes over time according to the need to preserve male power over women.

The flexibility of the sectoral sexual division of labour has figured in several chapters of this book. For instance, in the chapter on rural women's labour in Bangladeshi agriculture, I have shown how the traditional division of labour between women and men is changing under the impact of modernization. Whereas patriarchy in the past prescribed that women's work should be limited to processing tasks, which can be implemented within the courtyard and the home, such as paddy parboiling and husking, pauperization since the 1970s has forced women from landless and land poor peasant families to increasingly seek outside employment, including employment as field labourers. This development has not led to the emancipation of village women, as is evidenced by the persistence of wage discrimination against women. Yet women's employment is a landslide social change, evoking highly contrasting responses.[22]

Another striking example of the flexible, sectoral division of labour between the sexes has been described in the chapter on women home-workers involved in producing *punjabis*, trousers, frocks and other readymade garments in West Bengal. Here the issue is not primarily one of an evolving gender division of work, but one marked by territorial contrasts. In Moheshtola–Santoshpur, men monopolize all machine operations, including recently mechanized work which formerly, as manual operations, used to be women's domain. In Dumdum–Paikpara, on the contrary, the main task requiring the use of machines (i.e., the stitching of garments) is performed by women. As stated, the difference between male and female wage workers in this geographic area is that men do the tasks located at the owner's residence, while all women producers are home-based. Here, the spheres of men's and women's waged work coincide with the dividing lines set by the social sexual division of labour.

Nevertheless, men's monopoly over the instruments of technology is frequently and justly identified by feminist authors as a means to enforce male dominance. Highly significant in this respect is the account given by Mies of the sexual division of labour in the production of three field crops—millet, paddy and tobacco—in Andhra Pradesh, India. As she shows, women's work in agriculture hardly involves the use of any tools or equipment, whereas most of the labouring activities of men are performed with the help of agricultural implements and draught animals. Mies' factual account further makes clear that, unlike what is implied by the ecofeminist Shiva, men do play an active role in the maintenance of the ecological cycle in agriculture. However, the sexual division of labour is structured in such a way that the ecological role of men is well differentiated from women's role.

Apart from the divide between home-based/outside labouring tasks, and the divide between manual operations and those involving the use of major tools/equipment, a third 'structuring principle' for the sexual division of labour has been identified in this book—that between skilled and semi-skilled or unskilled tasks. The divide between male jobs that are termed skilled and female ones termed less skilled has been referred to in the chapter on garment production in Bangladeshi factories. Neither the work of male employees, such as of cutters and ironers, nor that of female employees, like operators of sewing machines, is purely manual; the tasks of each gender require the mediation of some tools or mechanical equipment. And yet factory management, in its wage scales, invariably evaluates men's contribution to garments production as far higher than women's. As feminist research on the issue of skill has brought out, the manipulation of skill definitions is yet another method by which a hierarchical division of labour between the sexes is maintained.[23]

In short, my investigation into the economies of Asian countries confirms that one cannot ignore the sexual division of tasks when trying to assess women's oppression and exploitation. For a systematic analysis, both the social and sectoral division of labour between women and men have to be looked at. The experiences of women also confirm that the sexual division of labour varies (for instance, the striking contrast between the traditional allocation of paddy transplantation tasks in Andhra Pradesh and Bangladesh), and changes over time. While the sexual division of labour is not determined by nature, but by social circumstances, there are identifiable methods (such as skill definitions and men's monopoly over machines) by which the subordinate position of women is maintained.

Strengths and Limitations of the Theses of the German Feminist School

The mission of Mies, Bennholdt-Thomsen and von Werlhof, the three members of the German feminist school, has been to transcend the limits of the household labour debate of the second feminist wave, and make it relevant to the analysis of women's labour in the Third World. In this, they have drawn inspiration from Luxemburg's theory of imperialism, which held that capitalism cannot survive without a non-capitalist milieu (i.e., that capitalist accumulation thrives on the existence of non-capitalist forms of production and exploitation).

Though Luxemburg's theory did not focus on the productive activities of women specifically, the members of the German feminist school argue that it can and should be used to explain the importance of women's household work and other non-waged work for the ceaseless growth of the capitalist world system.

How significant are the views of the German feminist school for our understanding of Asian economies? One of the two theses of the school concerns the social definition of Western, and increasingly also Third World, women as housewives. By defining women in census reports and statistical accounts as housewives, and by propagating the ideology that the man is the 'bread-winner' and that the work of women as 'non-earners' is of little importance, proponents of the capitalist system make much of women's productive work in the Third World invisible, and facilitate the ruthless exploitation of women's labouring capacities. The social definition of women as housewives thus is an important ideological devise—it helps to perpetuate and strengthen the subordinate position of women within the hierarchical structure of production relations.

In the chapter on the lace industry in Narsapur, India, I have highlighted Mies' application of this thesis to a specific case—that of women homeworkers producing for the world market. The women crotcheters are at the bottom end of a hierarchy of subcontract relations, stretching through small agents and export traders to retail trading companies in countries of the industrialized North. By defining the home-based wage labourers as housewives whose lace-making is just an activity to 'pass time', and by denying the necessity of their waged and non-waged work, the owners of capital are able to enforce an extremely high level of economic exploitation. I have argued that, although one should guard against over-interpretation, Mies' investigation into the exploitation of lace workers has established the importance of the housewife ideology. By masking women's real identity as wage workers, rich profits can be reaped from their labour.

Much more critical than my assessment of the thesis on 'housewifization' has been my assessment of the second thesis of the German feminist school on subsistence labour. According to this thesis (which is close to the view propounded by Benston at the outset of the household labour debate in 1969),[24] women worldwide are basically producers of use value, more broadly the producers of life. In this context, Mies has spoken of a continuum between subsistence production and reproduction. Bennholdt-Thomsen has elaborated the thesis by arguing that the capitalist system should be understood as a two-tier structure. It is composed of what Marx called 'extended reproduction' and 'subsistence reproduction' (i.e., a second sphere occupied by women worldwide).

In trying to assess the validity of this thesis I have, once again, taken a concrete investigation of Mies as my starting point, (i.e., the fieldwork which, in the late 1970s, she undertook on female agricultural labourers in Andhra Pradesh). The facts cited by Mies, such as on the production of millet, fuel collection and the gathering of grass to feed buffaloes, show that village women in India today continue to engage in the production of use values, and that these are very time-consuming. Yet her evidence also reveals that women perform numerous market-oriented production activities. The growth in the number of rural women employed as *coolies* in commercial agriculture, in fact, shows that women's participation in the production of exchange values has been expanding steadily.

In questioning the thesis on subsistence labour, I have raised two fundamental objections. One, I have argued that this thesis risks making part of women's productive work invisible. In reality, the work performed by women worldwide has since the dawn of class societies not been limited to production for their family's immediate use, but has for thousands of years included surplus labour for the benefit of slave owners, feudal landlords and other exploitating classes. Two, I do not believe that the capitalist system is simply leaving the sphere of non-capitalist production relations untouched. The policies pursued by the World Bank and other international institutions leads to the further erosion of common property resources in Third World countries. And the consequences are not only that the bourgeois system of private property relations is imposed everywhere, but also that exchange value production is ever-growing.

In conclusion, I believe that, in order to understand women's labour under contemporary capitalism, it is necessary to uphold Luxemburg's evaluation that the capitalist system is self-contradictory by nature. As she stated some 80 years ago, the expansion of the system, the process of accumulation, requires the existence of non-capitalist spheres of production. Yet the inevitable outcome of the self-expansion of aggregate capital is that, like an octopus, it grasps and incorporates ever-greater parts of non-European, pre-capitalist economies. The material presented in this book on the economies of Bangladesh, India and Japan sufficiently proves the point. Thus, the assessment of women's labouring activities, whether in Asia or elsewhere, ultimately cannot be complete without taking stock of the self-contradictory process of capitalist expansion.

Notes and References

1. Marx (1977a), p. 667, emphasis added.
2. Ibid., p. 669.
3. Ibid., p. 668.
4. Frank (1982), particularly p. 238.
5. Ibid. See also Luxemburg (1981a), p. 313, for similar comments on the question of 'primitive' accumulation.
6. Marx (1977a), p. 477.
7. Ibid., emphasis added.
8. Ibid., p. 264.
9. Marx (1967a), p. 159.
10. Marx (1973b), p. 519.
11. Ibid.
12. Marx (1967), p. 145.
13. Marx (1977a), p. 591.
14. Ibid.
15. Ibid., p. 592.
16. Ibid., p. 596.
17. Ibid., p. 607.
18. Ibid., p. 600. See also Luxemburg (1981a), p. 311, for her interpretation of the meaning of the 'reserve army of labour' for capital accumulation.
19. Bebel (1979), p. 182.
20. Bennholdt-Thomsen (1981). See also Beechey (1987), pp. 48–49; Bruegel (1982); Young (1986), p. 43.
21. For a comparison, see the discussion on the sexual division of labour in Mies (1982), p. 110.
22. The increasing employment of village women outside the home has evoked angry reactions from orthodox Muslim sections of Bangladesh's society.
23. See, for instance, Elson and Pearson (1986); Phillips and Taylor (1976).
24. See Benston (1980).

Glossary

Agnikulakshatriya: fisherman caste.
aman: main paddy crop, harvested in November–December.
athukupani: joining together various patterns in the lace-making process.
aus: early monsoon crop harvested in July and August.
baishakh: April–May.
beedis: small cigarettes.
beel: marshy area or lake.
bigha: about one-third of an acre.
boro: rice crop transplanted from December to February and harvested from late March to the end of June.
char: newly emerged land.
chetipani: elementary work in lace-making, consisting of making one pattern or 'flower'.
chira: puffed rice.
chopai: making the waist of trousers.
chukai: finishing tasks (button-holing, button-fixing and the removal of loose threads) performed by women.
coolies: day labourers in agriculture.
dadni: putting-out system used by Indian merchants in the early colonial period.
dagtola: a woman employed to remove stains from newly-produced *punjabi* dresses.
daleej: production workshop in the tailoring sector, frequently also the dwelling place of an *ostagar*.
darjee: a tailor.
dhenki: a foot-operated paddy-husking device.
dholai: washing of old pants with soap, and starching with arrowroot.
doras: traditional landlords.
fariya: a local intermediary trader.
furan: the piece-rate system.
ghee: clarified butter.

ghunti: ornamentation (see *sabudana*).
goshami: women observing the custom of seclusion.
haat: a weekly or bi-weekly market.
harijan: an Untouchable.
ilisha: a variety of fish.
jawar: millet.
jitagallu: bonded labourers and farm servants, usually paid in kind.
jotedar: a petty landlord.
joutuk: dowry.
kajbotam: button-fixing.
kajghar: button-holing.
kallapi: a mixture of water and cowdung used to sprinkle the courtyard.
Kapu: originally a caste of agriculturalists.
karigar: a skilled producer (also tailor).
kazakattu: fixing lace borders to pieces of cloth or joining several cloth pieces into a whole piece.
khasland: government-owned fallow land.
kholai: undoing the stitching of old pants.
lakh: One hundred thousand.
Madigas: a caste of Untouchables.
Mahajan: a usurious moneylender.
mahr: brideprice, or the amount a groom promises to pay his wife in case of a divorce.
Malas: a caste of Untouchables.
matji: a cutter, directly employed by the *ostagar*.
maund: a unit of weight, approximately 37.5 kg.
mistri: an ironer.
mota: a metal container with a leather hose by which water is lifted from wells for irrigation purposes.
ostagar: the owner of a manufacturing unit.
paisa: one-hundredth of a rupee.
phulwala: an embroiderer.
punjabi: men's wear, traditionally used by Bengali Muslims.
puvvalu: literally 'flowers', a term used to denote patterns.
purdah: system of seclusion for women.
rabi: a winter sown and spring harvested crop.
rangoli: decoration of the courtyard with white chalk powder.
rojukulis: day labourers in agriculture paid by wages.
sabudana: ornamentation, an aspect of the manufacturing process specific to *punjabi* production.
samiti: association.
sankati: thick porridge made of millet.

sinthechopai: folding at the waist.
taluk: a small administrative unit.
tatal: drill-like machine used to burn holes into embroidered clothes.
turpai: hemming.

Bibliography

Abdullah, Tahrunnessa and **Zeidenstein Sondra**. 1997. 'Rural Women and Development', in *ADAB News*, newsletter of Agricultural Development Agencies in Bangladesh, Vol. 4, No. 6, June.

———. 1982. *Village Women of Bangladesh: Prospects for Change*. Oxford: Pergamon Press.

Adnan, Shapan. 1991. *Floods, People and the Environment*. Dhaka: Research and Advisory Services.

Adnan, Shapan, Alison Barrett, S.M. Nurul Alam and **Angelika Brustinow**. 1992. *People's Participation: NGOs and the Flood Action Plan—An Independent Review*. Dhaka: Research and Advisory Services.

Afanasyev, V., A. Galchinsky and **V.B. Lantsov**. 1980. *Karl Marx's Great Discovery—The Dual Nature of Labour Doctrine: Its Methodological Role*. Moscow: Progress Publishers.

Agarwal, Bina. 1985. 'Work Participation of Rural Women in the Third World—Some Data and Conceptual Biases', *Economic and Political Weekly*, Vol. 20, Nos 51, 52, 21–28 December.

———. 1988. 'Who Sows? Who Reaps? Women and Land Rights in India'. Paper presented at a workshop on Women in Agriculture, Trivandrum, Centre for Development Studies, 15–17 February.

Agora. n.d. 'Hanako—A Japanese Working Woman', Fukuoka, Agora, Fukuoka Women's Group.

Akhtar, Farida. 1992. 'The Garments Industry and the Future of Women Workers in National and International Perspective'. Paper presented at the Seminar on Women Workers, Dhaka, October.

Akhtar, Shireen. 1992. 'Women Workers and the Policy of Trade Unions'. Paper presented at a seminar on Women Workers, Dhaka, October.

Alam, Sultana. 1985. 'Women and Poverty in Bangladesh', *Women's Studies International Forum*, Vol. 8, No. 4.

Alamgir, Muhiuddin Khan (ed.). 1981. *Land Reform in Bangladesh*. Dhaka: Centre for Social Studies.

Alavi, Hamza. 1988. 'Pakistan: Women in a Changing Society', *Economic and Political Weekly*, 25 June.

Albistur, M. and **D. Armogathe**. 1977. *Histoire du Féminisme Francais du Moyen Age a Nos Jours* (The History of French Feminism from the Middle Ages up to Our Times). Paris: Editions des Femmes.

Alim, A. 1982. *Bangladesh Rice*. Dhaka: Urmee and Abu Bakar.

Allen, Sheila and **Carol Wolkowitz**. 1986. 'Homeworking and the Control of Women's Work', in Feminist Review (ed.), *Waged Work—A Reader*. London: Virago Press.

Amin, Samir. 1974. *Accumulation on a World Scale—A Critique of the Theory of Underdevelopment*, Vols 1 and 2. New York and London: Monthly Review Press.

Annavajhula, J.C.B. 1988. 'Subcontracting in Electronics—A Case Study of Keltron', *Economic and Political Weekly*, 27 August.

———. 1989. 'Japanese Subcontracting Systems', *Economic and Political Weekly*, 25 February.

Arens, Jenneke and **Jos van Beurden**. 1977. *Poor Peasants and Women in a Village in Bangladesh*. Oxford: Paupers' Press.

Arora, Dolly. 1994. 'NGOs and Women's Empowerment', *Economic and Political Weekly*, 2 April: 792–93.

Baader, Odilia. 1905. '*Bericht der Vertrauensperson der Genossinnen Deutschlands*' (Report of the Trusted Person of the Female Comrades of Germany), *Die Gleichheit*, Supplement, 23 August.

Baker, Susan. 1993. 'The Principles and Practices of Ecofeminism: A Review', *Journal of Gender Studies*, Vol. 2, No. 1.

Bandopadhyay, Bela. 1997. '*Kajer Meera*', *Parichay*, December.

———. 1985. 'The Value of Women's Daily Chores', *Point–Counterpoint*, No. 58, 25 August.

Banerjee, Nirmala. 1985. *Women Workers in the Unorganised Sector—The Calcutta Experience*. Calcutta: Sangam Books.

———. 1989. 'Trends in Women's Employment, 1971–1981—Some Macro-level Observations', *Economic and Political Weekly*, Vol. 24, No. 17, 29 April.

———. 1983. 'Working Women in Colonial Bengal: Modernisation and Marginalisation', in Kumkum Sangari and Sudesh Vaid (eds), *Recasting Women—Essays in Colonial History*. New Delhi: Kali for Women.

———. (ed.). 1991. *Indian Women in a Changing Industrial Scenario*. New Delhi: Sage Publications.

Banerjee, Nirmala and **Devaki Jain** (eds). 1985. *The Tyranny of the Household— Investigative Essays on Women's Work*. New Delhi: Shakti Books.

Bangladesh: Country Study and Norwegian Aid Review 1986. Bergen: The Chr. Michelsen Institute.

Bangladesh Agricultural Research Council (BARC). 1989. 'Floodplain Agriculture'. Policy brief based on a discussion meeting on 30 November, Dhaka.

Bangladesh People's Solidarity Centre (ed.). 1994. *Proceedings of the European Conference on the Flood Action Plan in Bangladesh, European Parliament, 27–28 May 1993*. Amsterdam, January.

Banu, Fazila. 1985. 'Garment Industry and its Workers in Bangladesh', in *Industrial Women Workers in Asia*. Hong Kong: ISIS International and the Committee for Asian Women, September.

Barrett, Michele. 1980. *Women's Oppression Today—Problems in Marxist Feminist Analysis*. London: Verso and New Left Books.

Barrett, Michele and **Mary McIntosh**. 1987. The 'Family Wage', in Elisabeth Whitelegg et al. (eds), *The Changing Experience of Women*. London: Basil Blackwell.

Bauer, Karin. 1978. *Clara Zetkin und die Proletarische Frauenbewegung*. (Clara Zetkin and the Proletarian Women's Movement). Berlin: Oberbaum.

Baxandall, Rosalyn, Linda Gordon and **Susan Reverby**. 1976. *America's Working Women—A Documentary History, 1600 to the Present*. New York: Vintage Books.

Bebel, August. 1979. *Die Frau und der Sozialismus* (Women and Socialism). Berlin: Dietz Verlag.

Beechey, V. 1987. *Unequal Work*. London: Verso.

Beechey, V. and **T. Perkins**. 1987. *A Matter of Hours—Women, Part-time Work and the Labour Market*. Polity Press.

Behal, Monisha. 1984. 'Within and Outside the Courtyard—Glimpses into Women's Perceptions', *Economic and Political Weekly*, Vol. 19, No. 41, 13 October.

Bennholdt-Thomsen, Veronika. 1981. 'Subsistence Reproduction and Extended Reproduction—A Contribution to the Discussion about Modes of Production', in K. Young et al. (eds), *Of Marriage and the Market*. London: Routledge and Kegan Paul.

———. 1988a. 'Investment in the Poor: An Analysis of World Bank Policy', in Maria Mies et al. (eds), *Women: The Last Colony*. London: Zed Books.

———. 1988b. 'Why do Housewives Continue to be Created in the Third World Too?', in Maria Mies et al. (eds), *Women: The Last Colony*. London: Zed Books.

———. 1991. '*Overleven in Mexiko—Ekonomische Krisis en de Waardigheid van Mensen*', *Konfrontatie* (monthly magazine), Zero Issue, 1 March.

Benston, Margaret. 1980. 'The Political Economy of Women's Liberation', in Ellen Malos (ed.), *The Politics of Housework*. London: Allison and Busby.

Bernstein, Eduard. 1899. *Die Voraussetzungen des Sozialismus und die Aufgaben der Sozialdemokratie* (Preconditions of Socialism), trans. Henri Tudor. Cambridge: Cambridge University Press.

———. 1988. *Marxism and Social Democracy*. Cambridge: Cambridge University Press.

Bhasin, Kamla. 1993. *What is Patriarchy?* New Delhi: Kali for Women.

Birnbaum, Lucia Chiavola. 1986. *Liberazione della Donna: Feminism in Italy.* Middletown, Connecticut: Wesleyan University Press.

Bono, Paula and **Sandra Kemp** (eds). 1991. *Italian Feminist Thought: A Reader*. Oxford: Basil Blackwell.

Borneman, Ernest (ed.). 1981. *Arbeiterbewegung und Feminismus: Berichte aus Vierzehn Ländern* (Workers' Movement and Feminism: Reports from Fourteen Countries). Frankfurt am Main: Ullstein Materialien.

Bortolotti, Franca Pieroni. 1963. *Alle Origini del Movimiento Femminile in Italia—1848–1892* (On the Origins of the Women's Movement in Italy). Turin: Einaudi.

———. 1974. *Sozialismo E Questione Femminile in Italia—1898–1922* (Socialism and the Women's Question in Italy). Milan: Gabriela Mazzotta.

Bose, A.N. 1978. *Calcutta and Rural Bengal: Small Sector Symbiosis*. Geneva: International Labour Organisation.

Boserup, Ester. 1970. *Women's Role in Economic Development*. New York: St. Martin's Press.

Bouwman, Theo. 1986. '*Over Saturn, Toyota en Mensen*' (About Saturn, Toyota and Human Beings), in Satoshi Kamata, *Japan aan de Lopende Band.* Amsterdam: Jan Mets.

Boyce, James. 1990. 'Birth of a Megaproject: Political Economy of Flood Control in Bangladesh', *Environmental Management*, Vol. 14, No. 4.

Braverman, Harry. 1974. *Labour and Monopoly Capital—The Degradation of Work in the Twentieth Century.* New York: Monthly Review Press.

Braybon, Gail. 1982. 'The Need for Women's Labour in the First World War', in Elizabeth Whitelegg et al. (eds), *The Changing Experience of Women*, Oxford and New York: Basil Blackwell.

Breman, Jan. 1976. *Een Dualistisch Arbeidsbestel? Een Kritische Beschouwing over het Begrip 'De Informale Sector'* (A Dualistic Labour System? A Critical Review Regarding the Concept of the 'Informal Sector'). Rotterdam: Van Gennep.

———. 1985. *Of Peasants, Migrants and Paupers: Rural Labour Circulation and Capitalist Production in West India*. Delhi: Oxford University Press.

Brinker-Gabler, Gisela (ed.). 1979. *Frauenarbeit und Beruf—Die Frau und der Gesellschaft. Fruhe Texte*. Frankfurt am Main: Fischer.

Brow, Monica and **Hiroe Gunnarsson**. 1982. *Frauen in Japan—Zwischen Tradition und Aufbruch* (Women in Japan—Between Tradition and Break-up). Frankfurt am Main: Fischer Taschenbuch Verlag.

Bruegel, Irene. 1982. 'Women as a Reserve Army of Labour: A Note on Recent British Experience', in Elizabeth Whitelegg et al. (eds), *The Changing Experience of Women*. Oxford: Open University.

———. 1986. 'The Reserve Army of Labour, 1974–1979', in Feminist Review (ed.), *Waged Work: A Reader*. London: Virago.

Cain, Mead, Syeda Rokeya Khanam and **Shamsun Nahar**. 1979. 'Class, Patriarchy and Women's Work in Bangladesh', *Population and Development Review*, Vol. 5, No. 3.

Carney, Larry S. and **O'Kelly, Charlotte G.** n.d. 'Women's Work and Women's Place in the Japanese Economic Miracle', Rhode Island College and Providence College, mimeo.

Carroué, Laurent. 1993. '*Dumping Social et Délocalisations—Le Naufrage des Industries Textiles Européennes*', *Le Monde Diplomatique*, December.

Caudwell, Christopher. 1989. *The Crisis in Physics*. Calcutta: Baulmon Prakashan.

Chandigarh Women's Conference. 1986. 'Women in the Informal Sector—To Keep on Keeping On', *Economic and Political Weekly*, 20 December.

Chapkis, Wendy and **Cynthia Enloe** (eds). 1983. *Of Common Cloth—Women in the Global Textile Industry*. Amsterdam: Transnational Institute.

Chapman, Christine. 1987. 'Throwaways Seek a Better Deal for Part-time Women Workers', *International Herald Tribune*, 24 March.

Chattopadhyay, Paresh. 1994. 'Marx's First Critique of the Political Economy, 1844–1994', *Economic and Political Weekly*, Vol. 29, No. 31, 30 July.

Chaudhury, Rafiqul Huda and **Nilufer Raihan Ahmed**. 1980. *Female Status in Bangladesh*. Dhaka: Bangladesh Institute of Development Studies.

Chen, Marty. 1977. 'Women Farmers in Bangladesh: Issues and Proposals', *ADAB Newsletter*, Dhaka, Vol. 4, No. 6, June.

———. 1986a. 'Poverty, Gender and Work in Bangladesh', *Economic and Political Weekly*, Vol. 21, No. 5, 1 February.

———. 1986b. *A Quiet Revolution—Women in Transition in Rural Bangladesh*. Dhaka: BRAC Prokashana.

Chen, M. and **R. Ghaznavi**. 1977. *Women in Food-for-Work: The Bangladeshi Experience*. Dhaka: BRAC.

Chhachhi, Amrita. 1989. 'The State, Religious Fundamentalism and Women in South Asia: Conceptual Issues and Trends', *Economic and Political Weekly*, Vol. 24, No. 11, 18 March.

Clairmonte, Frédéric F. 1994. 'Malaysia: The Unstoppable Tiger?' *Economic and Political Weekly*, Vol. 29, No. 37, 10 September.

Clairmonte, Frédéric F. and **John Cavanagh**. 1981. *The World in their Web—The Dynamics of Textile Multinationals*. London: Zed Press.

Commins, Saxe and **Robert N. Linscotts**. 1954. *Man and the Universe: The Philosophers of Science*. New York: Modern Pocket Library.

Conference of Socialist Economists. 1977. Pamphlets on the Political Economy of Women. London: Stage 1.

Coontz, Stephanie and **Petra Henderson** (eds). 1986. *Women's Work, Men's Property: The Origins of Gender and Class*. London: Verso Books.

Corea, Gena. 1988. *The Mother Machine: Reproductive Technologies from Artificial Insemination to Artificial Wombs*. London: Women's Press.

Coriat, Benjamin. 1980. *De Werkplaats en de Stopwatch: Over Taylorisme, Fordisme en Massaproduktie* (The Workplace and the Stopwatch: Regarding Taylorism, Fordism and Mass Production). Amsterdam: Van Gennep.

Coulson, Margaret, Branka Magas and **Hilary Wainwright**. 1975. 'The Housewife and her Labour under Capitalism—A Critique', *New Left Review*, No. 89, January–February.

Custers, Peter. 1987. *Women in the Tebhaga Uprising: Rural Poor Women and Revolutionary Leadership (1946–47)*. Calcutta: Nayaprakash.

———. 1991a. 'Gulf Crisis and World Economy', *Economic and Political Weekly*, Vol. 26, Nos 1 and 2, 5–12 January.

———. 1991b. 'Women's Labour in the Japanese Economy', *Economic and Political Weekly*, 1–8 June: 1415–22.

———. 1991c. 'Floods and Disasters—A History of Mismanagement'. Lecture at a seminar held at the Agricultural University of Wageningen, the Netherlands, September.

———. 1992a. 'Cyclones in Bangladesh: A History of Mismanagement', *Economic and Political Weekly*, Vol. 25, No. 7, 15 February.

———. 1992b. 'Banking on a Floodfree Future? Flood Mismanagement in Bangladesh', *The Ecologist*, Vol. 22, No. 5, September–October.

———. 1992c. *Nari Sram: Oitihashik O Tattik Prekhapot* (Women's Labour—Historical and Theoretical Perspectives). Calcutta: Shilpa Sahitya.

———. 1993. 'Bangladesh's Flood Action Plan: A Critique', *Economic and Political Weekly*, Vol. 28, Nos 29 and 30, 17–24 July.

Cutrufelli, Maria Rosa. 1977. *Operaie Senza Fabrica* (Workers Without Factory). Rome: Editore Riuniti.

d'Héricourt, Jenny. 1856. 'M. Proudhon et la Question des Femmes', *Revue Philosophique et Religieuse*, 1 December.

———. 1857. 'Réponse de Mme Jenny d'Héricourt á M. P.J. Proudhon', *Revue Philosophique et Religieuse*, 1 February.

D'Mello, Bernard. 1992. 'Thinking About the Labour Process—Some Clues from Western Studies', *Economic and Political Weekly*, Vol. 27, May.

Dalal-Clayton, Barry. 1990. *Environmental Aspects of the Bangladesh Flood Action Plan*. London: International Institute of Environment and Development.

Dalla Costa, Maria Rosa and **Selma James**. 1972. *Die Macht der Frauen und der Umsturz der Gesellschaft* (The Power of Women and the Subversion of the Community). Berlin: Merwe Verlag.

Darby, H.C. 1956. *The Draining of the Fens*. Cambridge: Cambridge University Press.

Das, Ranjit. 1994. 'Ten *Fatwas*', *Khabarer Kagaz*, 25 January, p. 17.

Davis, Angela. 1982. *Women, Race and Class* London: Women's Press.

de Marco, Clara and **Manlio Talamo**. 1976. *Lavoro Nero—Decentramento Produttivo e Lavoro a Domicilio* (Black Work—Decentralisation of Production and Homeworking). Foro Buonaparte, Milan: Gabriele Mazzotta.

de Vylder, Stefan. 1982. *Agriculture in Chains: Bangladesh: A Case Study in Contradictions and Constraints*. London: Zed Press.

Desai, Dolat (ed.). 1990. *All India Directory of Readymade Garment Dealers*, August.

Desai, Neera and **Maithreyi Krishnaraj**. 1987. *Women and Society in India*. New Delhi: Ajanta Publications.

Deshpande, Sudha and **I.K. Deshpande**. 1992. 'New Economic Policy and Female Employment', *Economic and Political Weekly*, 10 October.

Dharmalingam, A. 1993. 'Female Beedi Workers in a South Indian Village', *Economic and Political Weekly*, Vol. 27, Nos 27, 28, 3–10 July.

Diamond, Irene and **Gloria Feman Orenstein** (eds). 1990. *Reweaving the World: The Emergence of Ecofeminism*. San Francisco: Sierra Club Books.

Dietrich, Gabriele. 1983. 'Women and Household Labour', *Social Scientist*, Vol. 11, No. 2, February.

———. 1992. *Reflections on the Women's Movement in India: Religion and Ecological Development*. New Delhi: Horizon India Books.

Draper, Patricia. 1975. '! Kung Women: Contrasts in Sexual Egalitarianism in Foraging and Sedentary Contexts', in Rayna R. Reiter (ed.), *Towards an Anthropology of Women*. New York: Monthly Review Press.

Dubois, E.C. 1978. *Feminism and Suffrage: The Emergence of an Independent Women's Movement in America, 1848–1869*. Ithaca: Cornell University Press.

Dunayevskaya, Raya. 1982. *Rosa Luxemburg, Women's Liberation, and Marx's Philosophy of Revolution*. Sussex: Humanities Press, Harvester Press.

Easton, Loyd D. and **Kurt H. Guddat**. 1967. *Writings of the Young Marx on Philosophy and Society*. New York: Anchor Books.

Ecologist. 1992. 'Development as Enclosure: The Establishment of the Global Economy', Vol. 22, No. 4, July–August.

Economists Interested in Women's Issues Group (EIWIG). 1984. 'Women, Technology and Forms of Production', *Economic and Political Weekly*, 1 December.

Ehrenreich, Barbara and **Deirde English**. 1976. 'The Manufacture of Housework', in *Capitalism and the Family*. San Francisco: Agenda Publishing Company: 7–42.

———. 1979. *For Her Own Good: 150 Years of Expert Advice to Women*. London: Pluto Press.

Eisenstein, Zillah. 1979. *Capitalist Patriarchy and the Case for Socialist Feminism*. New York and London: Monthly Review Press.

Einstein, Albert and **Leopold Infeld**. 1938. *The Evolution of Physics*. Cambridge: Cambridge University Press.

Ellickson, Jean. 1975. 'Rural Women', in *Women for Women* Series. Dhaka: Women for Women Research Group, University Press Limited.

Elson, Diana and **Ruth Pearson**. 1986. 'Third World Manufacturing', in Feminist Review (ed.), *Waged Work—A Reader*. London: Virago Press.

Engels, Dagmar. 1986. 'Female Labour Migration in the Organized Industrial Sector in Bengal, 1890–1930'. Paper presented at the International Conference of Historians of the Labour Movement, Linz, September.

Engels, Frederick. 1969. *The Peasant War in Germany*. London: Lawrence and Wishart.

———. 1975. *The Conditions of the Working Class in England: From Personal Observation and Authentic Sources*. Moscow: Progress Publishers.

———. 1976. *Dialectics of Nature*. Moscow: Progress Publishers.

———. 1977. *Anti-Dühring: Herr Eugen Duhring's Revolution in Science*. Moscow: Progress Publishers.

———. 1979. *The Origin of the Family, Private Property and the State*. New York: Pathfinder Press.

Erler, Brigitte. 1985. *Tödliche Hilfe—Bericht von Meiner Letzten Dienstreise in Sachen Entwicklungshilfe* (Aid that Kills—Report of My Last Official Visit Regarding Development Aid). Freiburg: Dreisam Verlag.

Ettinger, Elzbieta. 1986. *Rosa Luxemburg: A Life*. Boston: Beacon Press.

Evans, Richard. 1976. *The Feminist Movement in Germany, 1894–1933*. London: Sage.

———. 1977. *The Feminists—Women's Emancipation Movements in Europe, America and Australasia, 1840–1920*. London: Croom Helm.

———. 1979. *Sozialdemokratie und Frauenemanzipation in Deutschen Kaiserreich, 1870–1918* (Social Democracy and Women's Emancipation in the German Empire). Berlin: Dietz Verlag.

Faaland, Just, Rounaq Jahan, Fashiuddin Mahtab, Patricia Almada-Villela and **Geoffrey Wood**. 1995. *Flood and Water Management: Towards a Public Debate*. Report by the Independent Flood Action Plan Review Mission. Dhaka: United Nations Development Programme.

Feldman Shelley. 1979. 'Rural Women in Bangladesh', *ADAB Newsletter*, Vol. 6, No. 12, December.

Frabotta, Biancamaria. 1973. *Feminismo e Lotta di Classe In Italia (1970–1973)* (Feminism and Class Struggle in Italy). Rome: Saggestica.

Frank, André Gunder. 1981. *Reflections on the World Economic Crisis*. New York: Monthly Review Press.

———. 1982. *World Accumulation: 1492–1789*. London: Macmillan Press.

Fransen, Jan. 1991. *Subcontracting and Inequality—The Case of Hindustan Lever in India (A Unilever Company)*. Nijmegen, The Netherlands: Third World Centre.

Fuentes, A. and **B. Ehrenreich**. 1984. *Women in the Global Factory*, Inc. Pamphlet No. 2. Boston: South End Press, November.

Gain, Philip. 1990. 'Women Workers in the Clothing Industry of Bangladesh', Dhaka: Manobadhikar Samannaya Parishad.

Gandhi, Nandita and **Nandita Shah**. 1992. *The Issues at Stake—Theory and Practice in the Contemporary Women's Movement in India*. New Delhi: Kali for Women.

Ganguly, Basudev and **Peter Custers**. 1993. 'Bengal's Tailoring Industry: The Little Money Machine (I and II)', *Frontier*, 1 and 8 May.

Gardiner, Jean. 1975. 'Women's Domestic Labour', *New Left Review*, January–February.

Garments. 1993. 'The Current Labour Law and the Garment Industry'. Dhaka: Bangladesh Workers and Employees Federation.

Gates, Hill. 1995. 'Foot Binding, Handspinning and the Modernisation of Little Girls', Stanford: Stanford University, April, mimeo.

Gaul, Karen. 1994. 'Exploding Myths: Women, Men and Work in a Himachal Village', *Manushi*, No. 81.

Geras, Norman. 1976. *The Legacy of Rosa Luxemburg*. London: New Left Books.

Glickman, Rose L. 1984. *Russian Factory Women—Workplace and Society, 1880–1914*. Berkeley: University of California Press.

Glucksmann, Miriam. 1990. *Women Assemble: Women Workers and the New Industries in Inter-War Britain*. London: Routledge.

Goldschmidt-Clermont, Luisella. 1982. 'Unpaid Work in the Household', *Women, Work and Development*, Series No. 1. Geneva: ILO.

Gothoskar, Sujata. 1989. 'Part-time Work for Women', *Economic and Political Weekly*, 18 November.

Gough, Kathleen and **Hari Sharma** (eds). 1973. *Imperialism and Revolution in South Asia*. New York: Monthly Review Press.

Gramsci, Antonio. n.d. 'Americanism and Fordism', *Selections from the Prison Notebooks*. New York: International Publishers.

Greeley, Martin. 1980. 'Rural Technology, Rural Institutions and the Rural Poorest', September, mimeo.

Grubitzsch, H. and **L. Lagpacan**. 1980. *Freiheit für die Frauen, Freiheit für das Volk: Sozialistische Frauen in Frankreich, 1830–1848* (Freedom for Women, Freedom for the People: Socialist Women in France). Frankfurt: Syndikat.

Guérin, Daniel. 1970. *Anarchism—From Theory to Practice*. New York: Monthly Review Press.

———. 1982. *Rosa Luxemburg et la Spontanéité Revolutionnaire*. Paris: Spartacus Publications.

Gulati, Leela. 1984. 'Technological Change and Women's Work—Participation and Demographic Behaviour—A Case Study of Three Fishing Villages', *Economic and Political Weekly*, Vol. 19, No. 49, 8 December.

Gunew, Sneja (ed.). 1990. *Feminist Knowledge: Critique and Construct*. London: Routledge and Kegan Paul.

Hall, Catherine. 1987. 'The Home Turned Upside Down? The Working Class Family in Cotton Textiles 1780–1850', in Elisabeth Whitelegg et al. (eds), *The Changing Experience of Women*. Oxford: Basil Blackwell and The Open University.

Hancock, Mary. 1983. 'Transnational Production and Women Workers', in Annie Phizacklea (ed.), *One Way Ticket*. London: Routledge and Kegan Paul.

Harding, Sandra. 1986. *The Science Question in Feminism*. Ithaca: Cornell University Press.

Harrison, Faye V. 1991. 'Women in Jamaica's Urban Informal Economy: Insights from a Kingston Slum', in Chandra Talpade Mohanty et al. (eds), *Third World Women and the Politics of Feminism*. Bloomington and Indianapolis: Indiana University Press.

Hartmann, Betsy and **James Boyce**. 1983. *A Quiet Violence—View from a Bangladesh Village*. London: Zed Books.

Hartmann, Heidi. 1981. 'The Unhappy Marriage of Marxism and Feminism: Towards a More Progressive Union', in Lydia Sargent (ed.), *The Unhappy Marriage of Marxism and Feminism: A Debate on Class and Patriarchy*. London: Pluto Press.

Harui, Tono. 1985. 'Japan's Industrialisation and Women Workers', in Women's Journal, *Industrial Women Workers in Asia*, ISIS International/Committee for Asian Women, Rome and Hongkong.

———. 1989. 'Women Workers and the Multinationals: The Shin Shirasuna Case', *AMPO–Japan–Asia Quarterly Review*, Vol. 20, No. 4, and Vol. 21, No. 1.

Hashemi, Syed M. 1991. 'The Agricultural Sector in Bangladesh: Productivity and Equity Issues', in Rehman Sobhan (ed.), *The Decade of Stagnation: The State of the Bangladesh Economy in the 1980s*. Dhaka: University Press Limited.

Hegel, G.W.F. 1987. *Logic*, trans. by William Wallace from the *Encyclopedia of Philosophical Sciences*. Oxford: Clarendon Press.

Hiroki, Michiko. 1986. *In the Shadow of Affluence—Stories of Japanese Women Workers*. Hongkong: Committee for Asian Women.

———. 1988. 'Child Care and Working Mothers', *Resource Materials on Women's Labour in Japan*. Tokyo, No. 3, June.

Huizer, Gerrit. 1980. *Peasant Movements and their Counter-forces in South East Asia*. New Delhi: Marwah Publications.

———. 1993–94. 'Some Thoughts on Global Marxism in the Next Millennium', *Economic Review*, December–January.

Huws, Ursula. 1984. *The New Homeworkers*. London: Low Pay Unit.

Ichiyo, Muto. 1987. 'Class Struggle and Technological Innovation in Japan since 1945', *Notebooks for Study and Research*. Amsterdam: International Institute for Research and Education.

Itoh, Makoto. 1983. *Waarde en Krisis: Een Bijdrage aan de Marxistische Politieke Ekonomie*. Groningen: Uitgeverij Konstapel.

Jackson, Ben. 1992. *Threadbare—How the Rich Stitch Up the World's Rag Trade*. London: World Development Movement.

———. 1992b. 'Hard Work—But there is Hope', *Spur*, September–October.

Jackson, Cecile. 1995. 'Radical Environmental Myths: A Gender Perspective', *New Left Review*, No. 210, March–April.

Jannuzi, F. Thomassen and **James T. Peach**. 1980. *The Agrarian Structure of Bangladesh: An Impediment to Development*. Boulder: Westview Press.

Jansen, Eirik G. 1987. *Rural Bangladesh: Competition for Scarce Resources*. Dhaka: University Press Limited.

———. 1991. 'Processes of Polarisation and the Break-up of Patron–Client Relationships in Rural Bangladesh', in Reidar Gronhaug a.o. (ed.), *The Ecology of Choice and Symbol*. Bergen: Alma Mater Forlag AS.

———. 1992. 'Interest Groups and Development Assistance: The Case of Bangladesh', *Forum for Development Studies*, No. 2.

Jayawardena, Kumari. 1986. *Feminism and Nationalism in the Third World*. London: Zed Books.

Jeffery, Roger, Patricia Jeffery and **Andrew Lyon**. 1989. 'Taking Dung-Work Seriously—Women's Work and Rural Development in North India', *Economic and Political Weekly*, 29 April.

Jhabvala, Rehana. 1985. 'From the Mills to the Streets—A Study of Retrenchment of Women from Ahmedabad Textile Mills', *Manushi*, No. 26.

Johnson, B.C.L. 1982. *Bangladesh*. London: Heinemann Educational Books.

Jone, Alwyn. 1987–88. 'From Fragmentation to Wholeness: A Green Approach to Science and Society (Parts I and II)', *The Ecologist*, Vol. 17, No. 6 and Vol. 18, No. 1.

Jose, A.V. (ed.). 1989. *Limited Options—Women Workers in Rural India*. Geneva: International Labour Organisation.

Kabeer, Naila. 1988. 'Subordination and Struggle: Women in Bangladesh', *New Left Review*, No. 168, March–April.

Kamata, Satoshi. 1986. *Japan aan de Lopende Band* (Japan on the Passing Line). Amsterdam: Jan Mets.

Katayama, Sen. 1918. *The Labour Movement in Japan*. Chicago: Charles Kerr.

Kelkar, Govind and **Dev Nathan**. 1991. *Gender and Tribe—Women, Land and Forests in Jharkhand*. New Delhi: Kali for Women.

Khan, Abdus Sattar. 1993. Speech on the World Bank-coordinated Flood Action Plan (FAP) to the European Parliament in Strasbourg, 28 May, published in Bengali by the Krishok (Peasant) Federation, Dhaka.

Khan, A.Z.M. Obaidullah. 1994. 'The Earth does not Belong to Man: Man Belongs to the Earth', *Holiday*, 29 July.

Khondker, S.M. 1993. 'Axe Comes Down on Garment Workers', *Holiday*, 1 January.

Khor, Martin. 1994. 'Back to Basics—Goodbye to the Green Revolution', *Frontier Weekly*, 11 June, pp. 13–14.

Kidd, Yasue Aoki. 1978. *Women Workers in the Japanese Cotton Mills: 1880–1920*. East Asia Papers, No. 20. Ithaca and New York: Cornell University Press.

Kishwar, Madhu and **Ruth Vanita** (eds). 1984. *In Search of Answers—Indian Women's Voices from Manushi*. London: Zed Books.

Kollontai, Alexandra. 1977. 'Social Democracy and the Women's Question', in A. Kollontai, *Selected Writings*. London: Alison and Busby.

Korsch, Karl. 1970. *Marxism and Philosophy*. London: New Left Books.

Kossler, Reinhart and **Mammo Muchie**. 1990. 'American Dreams and Soviet Realities: Socialism and Taylorism, A Reply to Chris Nyland', *Capital and Class*, No. 40, Spring.

Krishnaswamy, G. 1989. 'Dynamics of the Capitalist Labour Process—The Knitting Industry in Tamil Nadu', *Economic and Political Weekly*, 17 June.

Kuhn, Annette and **Annemarie Wolpe** (eds). 1978. *Feminism and Materialism: Women and Modes of Production*. London: Routledge and Kegan Paul.

Kulkarni, Sumati. 1994. 'Dependence on Agricultural Employment', *Economic and Political Weekly*, Vol. 29, Nos 51 and 52, 17–24 December.

Kuniko, Fujita. 1988. 'Women Workers, State Policy and the International Division of Labour: The Case of Silicon Island in Japan', *Bulletin of Concerned Asian Scholars*, Vol. 20, No. 3.

Langlois, Jacques. 1976. *Défense et Actualité de Proudhon*. Paris: Petite Bibliothêque Payot.

Leacock, Eleanor Burke. 1981. *Myths of Male Dominance: Articles on Women Cross-culturally*. New York and London: Monthly Review Press.

Lee-Wright, Peter. 1990. 'The Sun Never Sets: The Legacy of Empire in Bangladesh', in P. Lee-Wright (ed.), *Child Slaves*. London: Earthscan.

Lenin, V.I. 1972. 'The Taylor System—Man's Enslavement by the Machine', *Collected Works*, Vol. 20. Moscow: Progress Publishers.

———. 1973. *Collected Works*, Vol. 38. Moscow: Progress Publishers.

———. 1976. *Marx*. Peking: Foreign Languages Press.

———. 1977a. *The Development of Capitalism in Russia, Collected Works*, Vol. 3. Moscow: Progress Publishers.

———. 1977b. *The Three Sources and Component Parts of Marxism*. Beijing: Foreign Languages Press.

Lewenhak, Sheila. 1980. *Women and Work*. Glasgow: Fontana Paperbacks.

Leydesdorff, Selma. 1977. *Verborgen Arbeid—Vergeten Arbeid: Een Verkenning in the Geschiedenis van de Vrouwenarbeid rond Negentien-Honderd* (Hidden Labour—Forgotten Labour: An Exploration into the History of Women's Labour around Nineteen Hundred). Amsterdam: Van Gorcum.

Liddington, Jill and **Jill Norris**. 1978. *One Hand Tied Behind Us: The Rise of the Women's Suffrage Movement*. London: Virago.

Liebknecht, Karl. 1973. *Militarism and Anti-militarism—With Special Regard to the International Young Socialist Movement*. Cambridge: Rivers Press.

Lim, Linda. 1985. *Women Workers in Multinational Enterprises in Developing Countries*. Geneva: United Nations Centre on Transnational Corporations, ILO.

Luxemburg, Rosa. 1971. *Selected Political Writings*, ed., with an introduction by Dick Howard. New York and London: Monthly Review Press.

Luxemburg, Rosa. 1972. *Schriften über Kunst und Literature* (Writings on Art and Literature). Dresden: VEB Verlag der Kunst.

———. 1974. *Reform or Revolution?* New York: Pathfinder Press.

———. 1981a. *Die Akkumulation des Kapitals—Ein Beitrag Zur Ökonomischen Erklärung des Imperialismus*. First Published in 1913. Reprinted in *Gesammelte Werke* (Collected Works), Vol. 5. Berlin: Dietz Verlag.

———. 1981b. 'Einführung in die Nationalökonomie', in *Gesammelte Werke*, Vol. 5. Berlin: Dietz Verlag.

———. 1981c. *Die Akkumulation des Kapitals oder Was die Epigonen aus der Marxschen Theorie Gemacht Haben. Eine Antikritik*, in *Gesammelte Werke*, Vol. 5. Berlin: Dietz Verlag.

———. n.d. *The Junius Pamphlet—The Crisis in Social Democracy*. First published in 1915. Republished. London: Merlin Press.

Maal, Bodil. 1989. *Fish Cultivation for Landless Groups in the Water Bodies of Kurigram District*. Dhaka: Rural Employment Sector Programme.

Maal, Bodil and **Shahid Ali**. 1990. *Women's Participation in Fish Culture in Greater Dinajpur District—Constraints and Possibilities*. Dhaka: Centre for Development Studies, University of Bath and Bangladesh Centre for Advanced Studies.

Malos, Ellen (ed.). 1980. *The Politics of Housework*. London: Allison and Busby.

Mandel, Ernst. 1972. *Der Spätkapitalismus—Versuch Einer Marxistischen Erklärung* (Late Capitalism—Attempt at a Marxist Interpretation). Frankfurt am Main: Surkamp Verlag.

Mankidy, Jacob. 1984. 'Human Resource Management—Relevance of the Japanese Model for India', *Economic and Political Weekly*, Vol. 19, Nos 20 and 21, 19–26 May.

Marx, Karl. 1967. *Capital: A Critique of Political Economy*, Vol. 2. Moscow: Progress Publishers.

———. 1973a. *The Economic and Philosophical Manuscripts of 1844*, ed., with an introduction by Dirk Struik. New York: International Publishers.

———. 1973b. *Grundrisse—Foundations of the Critique of Political Economy*. London: Penguin New Left Books.

———. 1973c. 'Wages, Price and Profit', in K. Marx and F. Engels, *Selected Works*, Vol. 2. Moscow: Progress Publishers.

———. 1975. *The Poverty of Philosophy—Answer to 'Philosophy of Poverty' by M. Proudhon*. Moscow: Progress Publishers.

———. 1977a. *Capital: A Critique of Political Economy*, Vol. 1. Moscow: Progress Publishers.

———. 1977b. *Capital: A Critique of Political Economy*, Vol. 3. Moscow: Progress Publishers.

Marx, Karl and **Frederick Engels**. 1967. 'The German Ideology: A Critique of the Most Recent German Philosophy as Represented by Feuerbach, B. Bauer and Stirner', in *Writings of the Young Marx on Philosophy and Society*, ed. and trans. by Loyd D. Easton and Kurt H. Guddat. New York: Anchor Books.

———. 1973. *Selected Works*, Vol. 2. Moscow: Progress Publishers.

Matthaei, Julie A. 1982. *An Economic History of Women in America—Women's Work, the Sexual Division of Labour and the Development of Capitalism*. New York: Schocken Books and Brighton: Harvester Press.

Mellon, Mary. 1992. *Breaking the Boundaries—Towards a Feminist Green Socialism*. London: Virago Press.

Mencher, Joan P. and **K. Saradamoni**. 1982. 'Muddy Feet, Dirty Hands—Rice Production and Female Agricultural Labour', *Economic and Political Weekly*, Vol. 17, No. 52, 25 December.

Merchant, Carolyn. 1980. *The Death of Nature—Women, Ecology and the Scientific Revolution*. New York: Harper and Row.

———. 1992. *Radical Ecology—The Search for a Livable World*. New York and London: Routledge and Kegan Paul.

Mies, Maria. 1973. *Indische Frauen Zwischen Patriarchat und Chancengleichheit—Rollenkonflikte Studierender und Berufstätiger Frauen* (Indian Women Between Patriarchy and Equal Opportunity). Meisenheim am Glan: Verlag Anton Hain.

———. 1980. 'Capitalist Development and Subsistence Reproduction: Rural Women in India', *Bulletin of Concerned Asian Scholars*, Vol. 12, No. 1: 2–14.

———. 1981. 'Dynamics of the Sexual Division of Labour and Capital Accumulation—Women Lacemakers of Narsapur', *Economic and Political Weekly*, March.

———. 1982. *The Lacemakers of Narsapur: Indian Housewives Produce for the World Market*. London: Zed Press.

———. 1986a. 'Indian Women in Subsistence and Agricultural Labour', *Women, Work and Development Series, No. 12*. Geneva: ILO.

———. 1986b. *Patriarchy and Accumulation on a World Scale—Women in the International Division of Labour*. London: Zed Press.

———. 1988. 'Capitalist Development and Subsistence Production: Rural Women in India', in Maria Mies et al. (eds), *Women: The Last Colony*. London: Zed Books.

Mies, Maria and **Kumari Jayawardena**. 1981. *Feminism in Europe—Liberal and Socialist Strategies, 1789–1919*. The Hague: Institute of Social Studies.

Mies, Maria and **Vandana Shiva**. 1993. *Ecofeminism*. Halifax: Fernwood Publications and London: Zed Books.

Mies, Maria, Veronika Bennholdt-Thomsen and **Claudia von Werlhof** (eds). 1988. *Women: The Last Colony*. London: Zed Books.

Ministry of Labour, Japan. 1989a. 'The Labour Conditions of Women, 1989 (Summary)', Tokyo, Foreign Press Centre, November.

Minsitry of Labour, Japan. 1989b. 'Analysis of the 1988 Labour Economy (Summary)', Tokyo, Foreign Press Centre, July.

Mitra, Debendra Bijoy. 1978. *The Cotton Weavers of Bengal: 1757–1833*. Calcutta: KLM Private Limited.

Mitter, Swasti. 1986. *Common Fate, Common Bond—Women in the Global Economy*. London; Pluto Press.

Mitter, Swasti and **Anneke van Luijken**. 1983. 'A Woman's Home is her Factory', in Wendy Chapkis and Cynthia Enloe (eds), *Of Common Cloth—Women in the Global Textile Industry*. Amsterdam: Transnational Institute.

Moghadam, Valentine M. 1992. 'Revolution, Islam and Women: Sexual Politics in Iran and Afghanistan', in Andrew Parker et al. (eds), *Nationalisms and Sexualities*. New York and London: Routledge.

Mohanty, Chandra Talpade. 1991. 'Under Western Eyes: Feminist Scholarship and Colonial Discourses', in C.T. Mohanty et al. (eds), *Third World Women and the Politics of Feminism*. Bloomington and Indianapolis: Indiana University Press.

Mukherjee, Ramkrishna. 1974. *The Rise and Fall of the East India Company*. New York and London: Monthly Review Press.

Nagaraj, R. 1984. 'Subcontracting in Indian Manufacturing Industries—Analysis, Evidence and Issues', *Economic and Political Weekly*, Vol. 19, Nos 31–33, August.

Nakano, Mami. 1995. 'Ten Years Under the Equal Employment Opportunity Law', *AMPO Japan–Asia Quarterly*, Vol. 25, No. 4 and Vol. 26, No. 1.

Nanda, Meera. 1991. 'Is Modern Science a Western, Patriarchal Myth? A Critique of the Populist Orthodoxy', *South Asia Bulletin*, Vol. 11, Nos 1 and 2.

Nayyar, Rohini. 1987. 'Female Participation in Rural Labour', *Economic and Political Weekly*, 19 December.

———. 1989. 'Rural Labour Markets and the Employment of Women in Punjab–Haryana', in A.V. Jose (ed.), *Limited Options—Women Workers in Rural India*. Geneva: ILO.

Nettle, Peter. 1969. *Rosa Luxemburg*. London: Oxford University Press.

Nichols, Theo (ed.). 1980. *Capital and Labour—A Marxist Primer*. Glasgow: Fontana Paperbacks.

Niggemann, Heinz. 1981. *Emanzipation zwischen Sozialismus und Feminismus* (Emancipation Between Socialism and Feminism). Wuppertal: Peter Hammer Verlag.

O'Brien, Mary. 1981. *The Politics of Reproduction*. London: Routledge and Kegan Paul.

Omvedt, Gail. 1983. 'Household Labour, Marxism and Patriarchy', *Weekly Frontier*, Vol. 50, Nos 43–45, June.

Operations Review Unit (OIV). 1993. *Flood Action Plan, Bangladesh—A Study of the Debate on Flood Control in Bangladesh*. The Hague: Netherlands' Ministry of Development Cooperation.

Pankhurst, Sylvia. 1977. *The Suffragette Movement—An Intimate Account of Persons and Ideals*. London: Virago.

Patnaik, Utsa. 1976. 'Class Differentiation Within the Peasantry: An Approach to the Analysis of Indian Agriculture', *Economic and Political Weekly*, Vol. 11, No. 39, 11 September.

Patrick, Hugh (ed.). 1976. *Japanese Industrialisation and its Social Consequences*. Berkeley: University of California Press.

Pearce, Fred. 1991. 'The Rivers that won't be Tamed', *New Scientist*, 13 April.

Petras, James. 1978. *Critical Perspectives on Imperialism and Social Class in the Third World*. New York: Monthly Review Press.

Phelan, Brian. 1986. *Made in Bangladesh? Women, Garments and the Multi-Fibre Arrangement*. London: Bangladesh International Action Group, Third World Publications.

Phillips, Anne and **Barbara Taylor**. 1978. 'Sex and Skill', in Feminist Review (ed.), *Waged Work—A Reader*. London: Virago Press.

Phizacklea, Annie (ed.). 1983. *One Way Ticket*. London: Routledge and Kegan Paul.

Plumwood, Val. 1992. 'Beyond the Dualistic Assumptions of Women, Men and Nature', *The Ecologist*, Vol. 22, No. 1, January–February.

Proceedings of the International Consultation on Micro-Chip Technology. 1986. *From Bonding Wires to Banding Women*. Quezon City: Centre for Women's Resources.

Proudhon, Pierre-Joseph. 1863. *Du Principe Fédératif et de la Nécessité de Reconstituer le Parti de la Revolution* (On the Federal Principle and the Necessity to Reconstitute the Party of the Revolution). Paris: Dentu.

———. 1865. *De la Capacité Politique des Classes Ouvrières* (On the Political Capacity of the Labouring Classes). Paris: Dentu.

———. 1875. *La Pornocracie ou les Femmes dans les Temps Modernes* (Pornocracy or Women in Modern Times). Paris: Lacroix et C.

———. 1888. *System of Economical Contradictions or the Philosophy of Misery*, Vol. 1, trans. by B.R. Tucker. Boston.

———. 1970. *Von der Anarchie zur Pornokratie* (From Anarchy to Pornocracy). Zürich: Die Arche.

———. n.d. *Qu'est-ce que la Propriété?* (What is Property?). First published in 1840 by Groupe Fresnes-Antony, Federation Anarchiste, Antony.

Pyne, Hnin Hnin. 1994. 'Reproductive Experiences and Needs of Thai Women: Where has Development Taken Us?', in Gita Sen and Rachel C. Snow (eds), *Power and Decision: The Social Control of Reproduction*. Boston: Harvard School of Public Health.

Quataert, Jean Helen. 1974. 'The German Socialist Women's Movement, 1890–1918: Issues, Internal Conflicts and the Main Personages.' Ph.D. Thesis, Los Angeles: University of California.

Rabaut, J. 1978. *Histoire des Feminismes Francais* (History of French Feminisms). Paris: Stock.

Raeburn, Antonia. 1973. *The Militant Suffragettes*. London: Michael Joseph Ltd.

Rahman, Ashabur. 1986. *Bangladesher Krishikathamo, Krishak Samaj O Unnayan* (The Agrarian Structure, Peasant Society and Development in Bangladesh). Dhaka: University Press Limited.

Rahman, Atiur. 1986. *Peasants and Classes: A Study in Differentiation in Bangladesh*. Dhaka: University Press Limited.

Rahman, Atiur and **Syed Azizul Hoque**. 1987. *Dhanik Goshtir Lutpater Kahini* (The Story of the Looting by the Wealthy Elite). Dhaka: Suchana.

Rahman, Md. Mahbubar and **Willem van Schendel**. 1994. 'Gender and Inheritance of Land: Living Law in Bangladesh'. Paper presented at the Workshop of the European Network of Bangladesh Studies, the Netherlands, August.

Rahman, Saira. 1994. 'Floating People Also have a Right to Live', *Holiday*, 11 February.

Raman, C.S. 1984. 'Development of Ancillaries', *Economic and Political Weekly*, Vol. 19, Nos 20 and 21, 19–26 May.

Rao, Sudha V. 1984. 'Rural Labour: A Case Study of a Karnataka Village', *Economic and Political Weekly*, Vol. 19, No. 18, 5 May.

Ravera, Camilla. 1978. *Breve Storia del Movimiento Femminile in Italia* (Short History of the Women's Movement in Italy). Rome: Editore Ruiniti.

Ray, Krishnendu. 1994. 'Crises, Crashes and Speculation—Hegemonic Cycles of the Capitalist World Economy and the International Financial System', *Economic and Political Weekly*, Vol. 29, No. 31, 30 July.

Ray, Suprakash. 1990. *Bharater Krishak Bidroh o Ganatantrik Sangram: Unabingsa Shatabdi* (Peasant Rebellions of India and the Democratic Struggle: The Nineteenth Century). Calcutta: Book World.

Reed, Evelyn. 1975. *Women's Evolution—From Matriarchal Clan to Patriarchal Family*. New York and Toronto: Pathfinder Press.

Reiter, Rayna R. (ed.). 1975. *Towards an Anthropology of Women*. New York: Monthly Review Press.

Resource Materials on Women's Labour in Japan. 1987. 'Equal Employment Opportunity Law After One Year', Centre for Asian Women Workers' Fellowship, *Newsletter No. 2*, September.

———. 1988. 'The Temporary Workers' Employment Act—Two Years After its Passage', Centre for Asian Women Workers' Fellowship, *Newsletter No. 3*, June.

———. 1989. 'Employers Seeking Part-time Workers', Centre for Asian Women Workers' Fellowship, *Newsletter No. 5*, November.

Ricardo, David. 1817. *The Principles of Political Economy and Taxation*. London: John Murray.

Richebächer, Sabine. 1982. *Uns Fehlt Nur Eine Kleinigkeit: Deutsche Proletarische Frauenbewegung, 1890–1914* (We Just Lack a Little: The German

Proletarian Women's Movement). Frankfurt am Main: Fischer Taschenbuch Verlag.

Risseeuw, Carla. 1980. *The Wrong End of the Rope: Women Coir Workers in Sri Lanka*. The Netherlands: University of Leiden.

———. 1991. *Gender Transformation, Power and Resistance Among Women in Sri Lanka*. New Delhi: Manohar Publications.

Rogers, Barbara. 1980. *The Domestication of Women—Discrimination in Developing Societies*. London and New York: Tavistock Publications.

Rogers, Peter, Peter Lydon and **David Seckler**. 1989. *Eastern Waters in the Ganges–Brahmaputra Basin*. Washington D.C.: US Agency for International Development, April.

Romatet, Emmanuel. 1983. 'Calcutta's Informal Sector—Theory and Reality', *Economic and Political Weekly*, Vol. 18, No. 50, 10 December.

Rosdolksy, Roman. 1977. *The Making of Marx's Capital*. London: Pluto Press.

Rosier, Mechteld. 1993. *Verborgen Verzet—Organisatie en Verzet door Werkneemsters in de Export Industrie: Hongkong, Malaysia en Sri Lanka* (Hidden Resistance: Organisation and Resistance by Female Employees in the Export Industry). Amsterdam: SOMO, Foundation for Research on Multinational Companies.

Rowbotham, Sheila. 1974. *Women, Resistance and Revolution*. Middlesex: Pelican.

Rowbotham, Sheila and **Swasti Mitter** (eds). 1994. *Dignity and Daily Bread—New Forms of Economic Organising Among Poor Women in the Third World and the First*. London and New York: Routledge.

Rubin, Isaak Illich. 1972. *Essays on Marx's Theory of Value*. Detroit: Black and Red.

Saffioti, Heleieth I.B. 1978. *Women in Class Society*. London and New York: Monthly Review Press.

Sahela, Begum and **Martin Greeley**. 1983. 'Women's Employment in Agriculture: Extracts from a Case Study', in 'Women in Bangladesh: Some Socio-Economic Issues', *Women for Women Series*, Seminar Papers, Vol. 1.

Salahuddin, Khaleda. 1986. *Impact of Technological Change in Agriculture on Rural Women of Bangladesh—Women and Technology*. Dhaka: Salahuddin Ahmed.

Samachar Reporter. 1991a. 'Breakthrough in the Garments' Sector: The Birth of the Oikho Parishad (Unity Council)', *Samachar*, newsbulletin of the Bangladesh People's Solidarity Centre, Amsterdam, March–April.

———. 1991b. 'Garment Workers Struggle Against the Beximco Company', *Samachar*, Amsterdam, June–July.

———. 1992. 'Women Garment Workers' Tough Struggle for Organisational Consolidation', *Samachar*, March–April.

Santen, J. van. 1968. *De Marxistische Accumulatie-Theorie*. Leiden: H.E. Stenfert Kroese.

Saradamoni, K. 1987. 'Labour, Land and Rice Production—Women's Involvement in Three States', *Economic and Political Weekly*, Vol. 22, No. 17, 25 April.

Sargent, Lydia (ed.). 1986. *The Unhappy Marriage Between Marxism and Feminism: A Debate on Class and Patriarchy*. London: Pluto Press.

Sau, Ranjit. 1978. *Unequal Exchange, Imperialism and Underdevelopment: An Essay on the Political Economy of World Capitalism*. Calcutta: Oxford University Press.

Saxonhouse, Gary R. 1976. 'Country Girls and Communication Among Competitors in the Japanese Cotton-spinning Industry', in Hugh Patrick (ed.), *Japanese Industrialisation and its Social Consequences*. Berkeley: University of California Press.

Seccombe, Wally. 1974. 'The Housewife and her Labour under Capitalism', *New Left Review*, No. 83, January–February.

———. 1975. 'Domestic Labour—A Reply to Critics', *New Left Review*, November–December.

Sen, Ilina. 1988. 'Class and Gender in Work Time Allocation', *Economic and Political Weekly*, 13 August.

Sen, Sunil. 1979. *Agrarian Relations in India (1793–1947)*. New Delhi: People's Publishing House.

Sharma, Hari. 1973. 'The Green Revolution in India: Prelude to a Red One?' in Kathleen Gough and Hari Sharma (eds), *Imperialism and Revolution in South Asia*. New York: Monthly Review Press.

Sharma, Ursula. 1983. *Women, Work and Property in North-west India*. London and New York: Tavistock Publications.

Shirokov, G.K. 1980. *Industrialisation of India*. New Delhi: People's Publishing House.

Shiozawa, Miyoko and **Michiko Hiroki**. 1988. *Discrimination Against Women Workers in Japan*. Tokyo: Asian Women Workers' Centre.

Shiva, Vandana. 1988. *Staying Alive—Women, Ecology and Survival in India*. New Delhi: Kali for Women and London: Zed Press.

———. 1991a. *The Violence of the Green Revolution—Third World Agriculture, Ecology and Politics*. Penang: Third World Network.

———. 1991b. 'Role of Modern Science in the Ecological Crisis', *Third World Resurgence*, No. 16, January.

———. 1992. 'The Seed and the Earth: Women, Ecology and Biotechnology', *The Ecologist*, Vol. 22, No. 1, January–February.

———. 1993. 'Women's Indigenous Knowledge and Biodiversity', in Maria Mies and Vandana Shiva, *Ecofeminism*. Halifax: Fernwood Publications and London: Zed Books.

Shiva, Vandana and **Radha Holla-Bhar**. 1993. 'Intellectual Piracy and the Neem Tree', *The Ecologist*, Vol. 23, No. 6, November–December.

Simmons, Pam. 1992. 'Women in Development: A Threat to Liberation', *The Ecologist*, Special Issue on Feminism, Nature and Development, Vol. 22, No. 1, January–February.

Singh, Manjit. 1991. *Labour Process in the Unorganized Industry—A Case Study of the Garment Industry*. New Delhi: Manohar Publications.

Sinha, Narendra K. 1956. *Economic History of Bengal: From Plassey to the Permanent Settlement*. Calcutta: Gossain and Company.

Slocum, Sally. 1975. 'Woman, the Gatherer: Male Bias in Anthropology', in Rayna R. Reiter (ed.), *Towards an Anthropology of Women*. New York: Monthly Review Press.

Sobhan, Rehman (ed.). 1991. *The Decade of Stagnation: The State of the Bangladesh Economy in the 1980s*. Dhaka: University Press Limited.

Sobhan, Salma. 1992. 'The Legal Rights of Women Workers'. Paper presented at the Seminar on Women Workers, Dhaka, October.

Steger, Manfred (ed.). 1996. *Selected Writings of Eduard Bernstein, 1900–1921*. New Jersey: Humanities Press.

Stites, R. 1977. *The Women's Liberation Movement in Russia: Feminism, Nihilism and Bolshevism, 1860–1930*. Princeton: Princeton University Press.

Storry, Richard. 1976. *A History of Modern Japan*. Middlesex: Penguin Books.

Sullerot, Evelyne. 1968. *Histoire et Sociologie du Travail Féminin* (History and Sociology of Female Labour). Paris: Gonthier.

———. 1979. *Geschiedenis en Sociologie van de Vrouwenabeid* (History and Sociology of Women's Labour). Nijmegen, the Netherlands: SUN.

Sultana, Hazera. 1989. 'The Violation of Garment Workers' Human Rights'. Statement presented at the Seminar on 'New Labour Relations—International Developments in the Garments' Industry and the Consequences for Women Workers', Dordrecht, the Netherlands, 19–21 June.

Sunderayya, P. 1972. *Telengana People's Struggle and its Lessons*. Calcutta: CPI (Marxist).

Sweezy, Paul. 1972. *Theorie der Kapitalistischen Entwicklung* (Theory of Capitalist Development). Frankfurt am Main: Edition Suhrkamp.

———. 1980. 'Japan in Perspective', *Monthly Review*, Vol. 31, No. 9, February: 1–14.

Tanaka, Kazuko. 1977. *A History of the Women's Movement in Modern Japan*. Japan, January.

Tax, Meredith. 1980. *The Rising of the Women—Feminist Solidarity and Class Conflict, 1880–1917*. New York: Monthly Review Press.

Taylor, Frederick W. 1964. *The Principles of Scientific Management*. New York: Harper and Brothers. First published in 1913.

Thönnessen, Werner. 1976. *The Emancipation of Women: The Rise and Decline of the Women's Movement in German Social Democracy, 1863–1933*. London: Pluto Press.

Transnationals Information Exchange (TIE). 1991. 'International Meeting on Toyotism in the Car Sector, Barcelona, 10–13 April. Amsterdam: TIE *Newsletter*.

Tristan, Flora. 1986. *Peregrinations of a Pariah*. London: Virago Press.

Ueno, Chizuko. 1987. 'The Position of Japanese Women Reconsidered', *Current Anthropology*, Vol. 28, No. 4, August–October.

Umar, Badruddin. 1978. *Chirasthayee Bandobaste Bangladesher Krishak* (The Peasants of Bangladesh in Permanent Settlement). Calcutta: Chirayat Prakashan.

———. 1986. *General Crisis of the Bourgeoisie in Bangladesh*. Dhaka: Papyrus Prakashanee.

Ummerkutty, A.N.P. 1991. *Science of the Oceans and Human Life*. New Delhi: National Book Trust.

Unni, Jeemol. 1990. 'Work Participation of Women in India', *Economic and Political Weekly*, Vol. 25, No. 10, 10 March.

van Vierssen, W. 1991. 'Ecology and the Bangladesh Disaster: On the Ecological Profile of Bangladesh and the Sustainable Use of its Natural Resources'. Lecture at the Bangladesh Seminar, Delft University, the Netherlands, September.

von Harder, Gudrun Martius. 1975. 'Women's Role in Rice Processing', *Women for Women Series*. Dhaka: University Press Ltd.

———. 1978. *Die Frau im Ländlichem Bangladesh—Empirische Studie in Vier Dorfern im Comilla Distrikt* (The Woman in Rural Bangladesh—Empirical Study in Four Villages in Comilla District). Saarbrucken: Verlag Breitenbach.

von Werlhof, Claudia. 1988. 'The Proletarian is Dead: Long Live the Housewife!' and 'Women's Work: The Blind Spot in the Critique of Political Economy', in Maria Mies et al. (eds), *Women: The Last Colony*. London: Zed Books.

Wahyana, Juliane. 1994. 'Women and Technological Change in Rural Industry—Tile-Making in Java', *Economic and Political Weekly*, 30 April.

Wallerstein, Immanuel. 1983. *Historisch Kapitalisme*. Weesp, the Netherlands: Uitgeverij Heureka.

West, Jackie. 1980. 'A Political Economy of the Family in Capitalism: Women, Reproduction and Labour', in Theo Nichols (ed.), *Capital and Labour—A Marxist Primer*. Glasgow: Fontana Paperbacks.

Westergaard, Kirsten. 1983a. *Pauperisation and Rural Women in Bangladesh—A Case Study*. Comilla, Bangladesh: Bangladesh Academy for Rural Development.

———. 1983b. 'Rural Pauperisation: Its Impact on the Economic Role and Status of Rural Women in Bangladesh', in 'Women in Bangladesh: Some Socio-Economic Issues', *Women for Women Series*, Seminar Papers, Vol. 1.

White, Sarah C. 1992. *Arguing with the Crocodile: Gender and Class in Bangladesh*. London: Zed Books and Dhaka: University Press.

Willcocks, William. 1988. *Ancient System of Irrigation in Bengal*. Delhi: B.R. Publishing Corporation.

Williams, C. Addams. 1966. *History of the Rivers in the Gangetic Delta: 1750–1918*. Calcutta: NEDECO/East Pakistan Inland Water Transport Authority.

Women for Dialog. 1988. 'Women Workers and the Garment Industry', *ISIS Bulletin*.

Women's Research Centre. 1984. 'Continual Displacement—Women Workers in The Cotton Textile Industry in Calcutta', *Manushi*, No. 23.

Woodcock, George. 1979. *Anarchism—A History of Libertarian Ideas and Movements*. Middlesex: Penguin Books.

Young, Iris. 1986. 'Beyond the Unhappy Marriage: A Critique of the Dual Systems Theory', in Lydia Sargent (ed.), *The Unhappy Marriage of Marxism and Feminism: A Debate on Class and Patriarchy*. London: Pluto Press.

Zetkin, Clara. 1958. *Zur Geschichte der Proletarischen Frauenbewegung Deutschlands* (On the History of the Proletarian Women's Movement of Germany). Berlin: Dietz Verlag.

———. 1979. '*Die Arbeiterinnen und Frauenfrage der Gegenwart*' (The Contemporary Question of Female Workers and the Women's Question), in Gisela Brinker-Gabler (ed.), *Frauenarbeit und Beruf*. Frankfurt am Main: Fischer.

Index